# Ontology and Economics

In the social sciences Tony Lawson has become a major figure of intellectual controversy on the back of juxtaposing two relatively simple and seemingly innocuous ideas. In two books and many papers he has argued first that success in science depends on finding and using methods, including modes of reasoning, appropriate to the nature of the phenomena being studied, and also that there are important differences between the nature of the objects of study of natural sciences and those of social science.

This original book brings together some of the world's leading critics of economics orthodoxy to debate Lawson's contribution to the economics literature. The debate centres on *ontology*, which means enquiry into the nature of what exists, and in this collection scholars such as Bruce Caldwell, John B. Davis and Geoffrey M. Hodgson present their thoughtful criticisms of Lawson's work while Lawson himself presents his reactions. Of course many social scientists disagree with him, but Lawson's arguments are so powerful that few economists now feel that his case can be ignored. Bringing Lawson head-to-head with eleven of his most capable critics, this is a book of intellectual drama. More than that, it is a collection of fine minds interacting with each other and being changed by the process.

This book is particularly useful for students and researchers concerned primarily with methodology and future development of economics. It is also relevant to the concerns of philosophers of science and to all social scientists interested in methodological issues.

**Edward Fullbrook** is the founder and editor of the *Real-World Economics Review* and a research fellow in the School of Economics at the University of the West of England.

# Routledge advances in heterodox economics
## Edited by Frederic S. Lee
*University of Missouri-Kansas City*

Over the past two decades, the intellectual agendas of heterodox economists have taken a decidedly pluralist turn. Leading thinkers have begun to move beyond the established paradigms of Austrian, feminist, Institutional-evolutionary, Marxian, Post Keynesian, radical, social and Sraffian economics – opening up new lines of analysis, criticism and dialogue among dissenting schools of thought. This cross-fertilization of ideas is creating a new generation of scholarship in which novel combinations of heterodox ideas are being brought to bear on important contemporary and historical problems.

*Routledge Advances in Heterodox Economics* aims to promote this new scholarship by publishing innovative books in heterodox economic theory, policy, philosophy, intellectual history, institutional history and pedagogy. Syntheses or critical engagement of two or more heterodox traditions are especially encouraged.

1   **Ontology and Economics**
    Tony Lawson and his critics
    *Edited by Edward Fullbrook*

This series was previously published by the University of Michigan Press and the following books are available (please contact UMP for more information):

**Economics in Real Time**
A theoretical reconstruction
*John McDermott*

**Liberating Economics**
Feminist perspectives on families,
work, and globalization
*Drucilla K. Barker and
Susan F. Feiner*

**Socialism After Hayek**
*Theodore A. Burczak*

**Future Directions for Heterodox Economics**
*Edited by John T. Harvey and
Robert F. Garnett, Jr.*

# Ontology and Economics

Tony Lawson and his critics

Edited by Edward Fullbrook

Routledge
Taylor & Francis Group

LONDON AND NEW YORK

First published 2009
by Routledge
2 Park Square, Milton Park, Abingdon, Oxon, OX14 4RN

Simultaneously published in the USA and Canada
by Routledge
270 Madison Ave, New York NY 10016

*Routledge is an imprint of the Taylor & Francis Group, an informa business*

Transferred to Digital Printing 2009

Typeset in Palatino by Wearset Ltd, Boldon, Tyne and Wear

*British Library Cataloguing in Publication Data*
A catalogue record for this book is available from the British
Library

*Library of Congress Cataloging in Publication Data*
Ontology and economics : Tony Lawson and his critics / edited by
Edward Fullbrook.
  p. cm.
Includes bibliographical references and index.
1. Economics–Methodology. 2. Ontology. I. Fullbrook, Edward.
HB131.O58 2009
330.01–dc22                                                    2008018362

ISBN10: 0-415-47613-5 (hbk)
ISBN10: 0-415-54649-4 (pbk)
ISBN10: 0-203-88877-4 (ebk)

ISBN13: 978-0-415-47613-3 (hbk)
ISBN13: 978-0-415-54649-2 (pbk)
ISBN13: 978-0-203-88877-3 (ebk)

# Contents

# Contributors

**Bruce Caldwell**, a leading authority on Austrian economics, is Professor of Economics at the University of North Carolina at Greensboro. His books include *Hayek's Challenge: An Intellectual Biography of F.A. Hayek*.

**Bjørn-Ivar Davidsen**, of Ostfold University College in Norway, is the author of *Arguing Critical Realism: The Case of Economics*. His areas of publication include economic methodology, history of economic thought and post-Keynesian economics.

**John Davis** is Professor of Economics at the University of Amsterdam and at Marquette University. He is editor of *The Journal of Economic Methodology* and the author of four economics books, his most recent being *Global Social Economy: Development, Work and Policy*.

**Paul Downward** teaches at Loughborough University and is the editor of *Applied Economics and the Critical Realist Critique*

**Edward Fullbrook**, of the University of the West of England, is the editor of *Real-World Economics Review* and of six economics books, including *Intersubjectivity in Economics*.

**Bernard Guerrien**, Professor of Economics at the Université Paris 1, is the author *La Théorie des Jeux, Dictionnaire d'Analyse Économique*, and *La Théorie Économique Néoclassique*.

**Geoffrey M. Hodgson**, Professor of Economics at the University of Hertfordshire, is editor of the *Journal of Institutional Economics* and the author of 12 books and 170 articles. His most recent books are *The Evolution of Economic Institutions* and *Economics in the Shadows of Darwin and Marx*.

**Tony Lawson**, Cambridge University, is the author of *Economics and Reality*, and *Reorienting Economics*.

**Bruce R. McFarling** lectures in economics at the University of Newcastle in Australia. His research interests are the economics of entrepreneurship, regional economic development, and input–output modelling.

**Andrew Mearman**, of the University of the West of England, is the author of *Teaching Heterodox Economics Concepts* and of numerous papers on economic methodology.

**David Ruccio** is Professor of Economics at the University of Notre Dame. His three most recent books are *Postmodern Moments in Modern Economics*; *Postmodernism, Economics, and Knowledge*; and *Postmodern Materialism and the Future of Marxist Theory*.

**Irene van Staveren** is Professor of Economics and Christian Ethics at Nijmegen University in the Netherlands. She is the author of over 50 papers on feminist economics and ethical issues in economics and the co-author of *Social Capital for Industrial Development*.

**Jack Vromen** is Associate Professor in Philosophy at Erasmus University Rotterdam. He is the author of many articles on economic methodology and of *Economic Evolution: An Enquiry into the Foundations of 'New Institutional Economics'*.

# Foreword

As a researcher, I cannot think of anything more gratifying than to have a group of respected scholars engage with one's own research output. I am enormously appreciative of the group of individuals that have taken the time to produce the critical assessments found in the following pages.

I am especially pleased in that whilst the analyses provided each picks out fundamental issues in my writing, collectively the commentaries span a wide range of its aspects.

As is usual in academic debate, each reviewer mostly concentrates on our differences; and so shall I. But I think it is worth recording at the outset that the scope of agreement between myself and each of the individual contributors appears substantial.

In fact, we will see that the common ground is actually somewhat larger than a few of the contributors at times appreciate. Where this has not been recognised, the reason, much of the time no doubt, is that I have been insufficiently clear. I thus welcome this opportunity to clarify relevant features of my various positions, although in the pages that follow I do further develop certain aspects of my arguments as well.

A process of clarification and development, of course, can take a good deal of space, whilst the expressing of a disagreement can be brief. Whereas the critics are mostly on the offensive, my role as respondent, and indeed defendant, means that I need to do most of the explaining, elaborating and justifying. For this reason, amongst others, my responses, tend to be rather longer than the original comments.

My rejoinders have been produced in a somewhat disjointed fashion, at different points over a period of roughly a year, with their writing being fitted into gaps between carrying through numerous other tasks. Perhaps because of this (and my poor memory) I found, on eventually looking over the whole manuscript, that I do sometimes cover similar ground in different responses; more so anyway than I had anticipated. In consequence, I have subsequently trimmed some of the repetition and used cross-referencing as a substitute. But I resisted eradicating all overlap, not least because I suspect different readers will be drawn to specific interchanges and not to others. It can be a nuisance to switch chapters (and topics) to follow an argument of interest. So, I have left each response as reasonably self-contained.

As always, my debts are huge and mostly impossible to pin down. I am sure that very many people who have interacted with me in an intellectual way over the last twenty years or more have made a difference to my thinking, and affected the beliefs I currently hold and the ideas expressed in the following pages. I am certainly aware of the enormous influence of those who have attended the Cambridge Realist Workshop since its inception in 1990, especially its most regular participants. And I am particularly grateful to the Cambridge Social Ontology Group. I must especially single out those of its members, namely Ismael Al-Amoudi, Vinca Bigo, Philip Faulkner, John Latsis, Clive Lawson, Nuno Martins, Nitya Mohan and Stephen Pratten, who, having read first drafts of my responses, communicated their impressions, comments and criticisms at an all-day seminar sometime in early October 2006. This group, or combinations of the individuals involved, also met with me at subsequent shorter meetings, and in this way and others, continued to supply criticisms on revised drafts. My gratitude to this collection of people is obviously enormous.

Finally, I owe a very special debt of gratitude to Edward Fullbrook who both invited the various contributors to submit their critical comments to the *post-autistic economics review* and conceived the idea of collecting these comments together, along with my responses, for publication in the current volume. I am enormously flattered and grateful that anyone, let alone such an important figure in the movement for a more relevant economics, should consider such a project to be of value. I can only hope that he feels that the result renders his efforts worthwhile.

Tony Lawson
January 2007

# Introduction

## Lawson's reorientation

*Edward Fullbrook*

Tony Lawson has become a major figure of intellectual controversy on the back of juxtaposing two relatively simple and seemingly innocuous ideas. In two books and over fifty papers he has argued:

1    that success in science depends on finding and using methods, including modes of reasoning, appropriate to the nature of the phenomena being studied, and
2    that there are important differences between the nature of the objects of study of natural sciences and those of social science.

Taken together, these two ideas lead to the conclusion that the methods found to be successful in natural sciences are generally not the ones that should be used in social science.

By relentlessly focusing on this pair of ideas, Lawson has in a short space of time changed one of economics' key conversations. His chapter, "A Realist Theory for Economics", published in Roger Backhouse's 1994 landmark collection *New Directions in Economics Methodology*, stands out like someone standing alone at a party. As recently as then the ideas of three thinkers, none of them economists, none social scientists and all of them dead, dominated economics' literature on methodology. The index of Backhouse's wonderful book powerfully illustrates this. It lists forty-seven pages that refer to Thomas Kuhn, sixty-nine to Karl Popper and seventy-three to Imre Lakatos. Twelve of the book's sixteen chapters (excluding Lawson's) refer to one or more of the three, and eight, as well as the back cover, to all three. Lawson does not refer to any of them. More significant, Lawson's key reference point is *ontology*, a word that, except in the Introduction when Backhouse is introducing his collection's odd man out, appears in none of the other chapters. Notably, when Lawson first uses "ontology" he feels it necessary, despite his highly specialized audience, to explain what the word means: "enquiry into the nature of *being*, of what exists, including the nature of the objects of study" (Lawson 1994, p. 257).

Thirteen years later and anyone in economics who knows anything about methodology knows what "ontology" means. They also have come to realize that if Lawson's basic conclusion were applied it would entail a programme of reform that would fundamentally change economics. A quick check with Google shows just how phenomenally successful Lawson has been at changing the conversation. Below are listed the number of web pages turned up for four trios of words (30 March 2007):

- Popper, economics, methodology: 300,000
- Kuhn, economics, methodology: 391,000
- Lakatos, economics, methodology: 82,300
- Lawson, economics, methodology: 264,000
- ontology, economics, methodology: 1,050,000.

To appreciate the significance of the huge debate begun by Lawson, we need to look at its historical background.

## Physics, economics and the philosophy of science

For those of you too young to remember, philosophy of science took off in a big way in the 1960s. Not for the first time, philosophy struggled to update its teachings to make them consistent with developments in science. Traditionally philosophers told the story, and the educated classes repeated it, that science, especially physics, progressed on the basis of the application of theories empirically proven true beyond question. But the first half of the twentieth century witnessed two "revolutions" in physics that made a mockery of that narrative. Physicists came to accept the theory of relativity and then quantum theory, both of which contradicted in fundamental ways Newton's theory, the most empirically confirmed theory in the history of science.

In an ideal world epistemologists would have jumped at this chance to develop new ideas. But even after the solar eclipse of 1919, which disproved Newton and confirmed Einstein, philosophers of science, under the banner of "logical positivism", persisted in telling the same old story. It was not until late 1934 that Popper published, in its original German, *The Logic of Scientific Discovery*, a book that ventured to rewrite epistemology in line with the no longer so recent events in physics. But two more decades passed before Popper and other innovators succeeded in forcing themselves past the gate keepers of the philosophical establishment. When resistance to the need for new ideas about how science succeeds and fails finally crumbled, a half-century of repressed questions shot to the surface. In consequence, the decades that followed rank among the most productive and interesting in modern philosophy.

Inevitably, economists joined the fun. So too did other social scientists, but for economists there was a special and virtually irresistible attraction, especially to the Popper–Kuhn–Lakatos triad. From the mid-nineteenth century onward economics has fancied itself as methodologically akin to physics. Therefore, almost inevitably economists saw the physics-related revolution in the philosophy of science as relevant to economics as well. Meanwhile the identification of economics with physics in the econo-mist's mind had became so strong that it almost completely obscured *the most fundamental difference* between the practice of physics (and indeed of all the natural sciences) and the practice of economics. Whereas physics invents and chooses its methods on the basis of the nature of the phe-nomena that it studies, economics does not. Let me explain.

## 1843 to today

John Stuart Mill not only turned economics primary concerns away from production and distribution to those of value, he also made the case that economics, and the social sciences in general, should ape the methodol-ogy of astronomy and physics. In *System of Logic* Mill appealed to Newton and in particular to a "law of nature" that

> is called, in dynamics, the principle of the Composition of Forces: and in imitation of that well-chosen expression, I shall give the name of the Composition of Causes to the principle which is exemplified in all cases in which the joint effect of several causes is identical with the sum of their separate effects.
>
> (1843, Book III, Ch. VI, sec. 1)

Mill then cautions that "This principle, however, by no means prevails in all departments of the field of nature" (1843, Book III, Ch. VI, sect. 1). But later in the book when considering the social sciences, without support-ing argument, Mill divinely declares: "In social phenomena the Compo-sition of Causes is the universal law" (1843, Book VI, Ch. VI, sect. 1). He has previously identified this linear relation between causes as what enables the application of the deductive method (Book III, Ch. XI, sect. 1). So in this a priori and pre-emptive way Mill declared that what he understood to be the method of Newtonian physics was the only proper one for economics.

Within a couple of decades major economists had got the message. Jevons and Walras certainly had when in the 1870s they set about invent-ing neoclassical economics. In the preface to his *Theory of Political Economy* (1871) Jevons wrote:

> But as all the physical sciences have their basis more or less obvi-ously in the general principles of mechanics, so all branches and divisions of economic science must be pervaded by certain general principles. It is to the investigation of such principles – to the tracing

out of *the mechanics of self-interest and utility*, that this essay has been devoted. The establishment of such a theory is a necessary preliminary to any definite drafting of the superstructure of the aggregate science.

(Jevons 1970, p. 50, emphasis added)

Walras began and proceeded in the same vain in his *Elements of Pure Economics* (1874–77). Alluding to the role of force and velocity in mechanics, he says: "Similarly ... this pure theory of economics is a science which resembles the physico-mathematical sciences in every respect" (Walras 1984, p. 71).

Walras does not have just any mathematics in mind, but rather that of classical mechanics. Like Mill, Walras, beyond some rhetorical flourishes, offers no argument in support of the presumed isomorphism between the mechanical and economic realms. What matters to Mill, Jevons and Walras is not the methodological fit but rather the method itself, *the method used in their day by physics*. Adopting this approach to methodology means that instead of being led by ontological enquiry, one defines a priori the ontology to fit the method. Nothing could be more against the procedures and mindset that have dominated the natural sciences from Copernicus on. In applying a system of analysis, mathematical or otherwise, to an empirical domain, the key question for the real scientist is always whether or not the structures described by the former are isomorphic to those found in the latter. For the scientist, although not for the mathematician, the mathematics is supposed to illuminate empirical reality rather than the other way around. This means that *ultimately* the choice of method, like the question of whether or not Mill's Composition of Causes pertains to a particular domain, is a question of ontology. In real science an ontology, however imperfect, decides the method, not the opposite. The birth of classical mechanics is a paragon case. Rather than pretend that the mechanical universe had properties isomorphic to an existing mathematics, Newton invented one, calculus, which did. Instead of bending his ontology to fit the mathematics, he created mathematics, a method, to fit his ontology. A similar sequence of events has characterized the development of twentieth century physics, especially the theory of general relativity. In the twentieth century the natural sciences, not just physics but also biology, underwent radical and more or less continuous ontological revision. The elementary entities and fundamental properties that populate the minds of physicists today are light years removed from those of Newton's time or even of Maxwell's.

The twentieth century, especially its second half, witnessed a gradual intensification of economics' obsession with dressing up in the methodological clothes of physics. Some economists, so carried away by their masquerade, even developed a taste for pretending that their achievements merited comparison with those of the great names of physics. The science historian Yves Gingras (2002) has described one such case:

> Paul Samuelson (1970 winner) wrote about his "Nobel coronation" – not his "Bank of Sweden Coronation" – and filled his talk with references to Einstein (4 times) Bohr (2 times) and eight other winners of the (real) physics Nobel prize (not to mention, of course, Newton) plus a few other names as if he were part of this family.

But some more recent winners of the Swedish prize have not, at least with hindsight, been so taken in. Milton Friedman (1999, p. 137) has acknowledged that "economics has become increasingly an arcane branch of mathematics rather than dealing with real economic problems", and similarly Ronald Coase (1999, p. 2) has written "Existing economics is a theoretical [meaning mathematical] system which floats in the air and which bears little relation to what happens in the real world." Method counts for virtually everything, substance for little or nothing, and disconnection from "real economic problems" and "the real world" is general in scope. In the typical research seminar, observes Bruce Caldwell in this volume, "No claims are ever defended with anything like the vigor with which one defends one's choice of econometric techniques" (p. 16).

## Ontologies

By unveiling the mainstream's ontology entailed by its methodology and by calling attention to economics' scientism, Lawson seeks to win the minds of the young and thereby bring about a reversal of the discipline's traditional order of priority between method and substance. Above all Lawson's project is one of persuading economists to do as physicists have always done: to take cognizance as best they can of the basic characteristics of their domain of inquiry and then proceed to develop and choose their methods accordingly.

Lawson builds his prescriptive analysis on the ontological platform of the social-philosophical school of thought called Critical Realism. This movement, a predominately Anglo-American affair, can through Continental eyes appear rather hackneyed. Lawson lists five key properties which "according to the philosophical ontological account" that underwrites his project, social phenomena possess (Reply to Davidsen, p. 71, this volume).

1   They are produced in *open systems*.
2   They possess *emergent* powers or properties.
3   They are *structured*.
4   They are *internally related*.
5   They are *processual*.

These core ontological ideas of Lawson's project include nothing that at the time of Critical Realism's inception in the 1970s was not already part of the woodwork of Continental philosophy and social theory. One example illustrates the case well. In Simone de Beauvoir's *The Second Sex* (1949), one of the last century's most influential books, the concept of gender and the ontological framework that supports it incorporate all five of the properties of social phenomena that Lawson embraces.

1   *open systems*:
    "humanity is something more that a mere species: it is a historical development" (Beauvior 1949, p. 725);
2   *emergent*:
    "Woman is not a completed reality, but rather a becoming" (p. 66);
    "One is not born, but rather becomes, a woman" (p. 295);
3   *structured*:
    "For us woman is defined as a human being in quest of values in a world of values, a world of which it is indispensable to know the economic and social structure. We shall study woman in existential perspective with due regard to her total situation" (p. 83);
4   *internally related*:
    "Otherness is a fundamental category of human thought" (p. 17). "The Other is posed as such by the One in defining himself as the One" (p. 18);
5   *processual*:
    "An existent *is* nothing other than what he does" (p. 287).

And of course above all Beauvoir was an existentialist so that, in Lawson's words, "there is no one-to-one mapping from social structure to individual pathways, experience or personal identities," (see Chapter 5, p. 65, this volume) and in Beauvoir's words,

> she acquires this consciousness under circumstance dependent upon the society of which she is a member.... But a life is a relation to the world, and the individual defines himself by making his own choices through the world about him
>
> (1949, pp. 80–1)[1]

Pointing out the historical pedigree of Lawson's core ontological ideas is not a criticism but, on the contrary, an endorsement. It is the unoriginality that so suits Critical Realism for the task of critiquing mainstream economics. The legitimacy and fecundity of the ontological ideas that it pushes are so well-tested and so widely embraced outside of economics that it makes an ideal replacement for the ontology implicitly assumed by mainstream formalist methods. To my knowledge no one of repute in economics has dared to come forward to argue, against Lawson, that the economy is a closed system, that it is not characterized by the property of emergence, that it is not structured, that in it internal relations do not play a pivotal role and that it does not consist of an interrelated series of unending processes. Only a fool would publicly take up these arguments. And most economists, but not all, are also too sensible to suggest that economics should not take cognizance of the fundamental properties of its object of enquiry. In consequence, defenders of the status quo when confronted with Lawson's ideas immediately find themselves in a tight corner. They don't have the option of frontally critiquing his ideas. They have to settle instead for a less attractive and less admirable approach. Easiest and in the short run probably strategically the wisest is just to ignore him. Another has been to hurl personal abuse at him, as in Herbert Gintis's amazon.com review of *Reorienting Economics*. Another and increasingly common tactic has been to misrepresent the current situation in economics. There can be a big payoff for this approach when addressing a non-economist public, including economics students, or when addressing oneself in bad faith. Out of the tens of thousands of papers published in mainstream economics journals over the past half century, one can easily find some, which having slipped past the gate keepers, embody one or more of the five properties. Wave these papers about vigorously enough and some people will be convinced that economics is already as Lawson would like it to be. Alternatively, one can misrepresent the formal properties of various methodologies, as when it is suggested that standard game theory describes an open system.

## Thirteen years on

Thirteen years on, Backhouse's collection belongs not just to another century but also to a different era. Although many economists, especially older ones, still entertain kissing-cousin fantasies about their relation to physicists, inhibitions have developed about acting them out in public. It is hard to imagine anyone accepting the Swedish prize today behaving as Samuelson did. Among methodologists the shift has been especially pronounced and quick. The majority may still in their heart of hearts prefer to view economic method through the physical science prism. But in the main they have, even if begrudgingly, taken on board the fact than any methodological commitment is also an ontological one. Questions concerning the fundamental nature of economic phenomena are not yet basic to the practice of economics, as the corresponding questions are in physics, but neither are they still treated as totally beneath attention. Today nearly all methodologists are either conversing with Lawson or heckling him from the edges of the room.

Many people, including all of the contributors to this collection (several in particular), have played a part in bringing about this shift, this *new* direction in economic methodology. But more than anyone, I believe, Tony Lawson deserves credit for the swing away from judging method in economics as an end in itself to judging it as a means to substantive knowledge and hence its ontological fit. It will be a long struggle to reverse the wrong turn that Mill made for economics in 1843. But Lawson's *Economics and Reality* in 1997 and *Reorienting Economics* in 2003 together with his many papers have provided the growing number of reformists in the profession with a formidable and expandable arsenal, and with the likes of which dissenters have not previously been armed.

## Lawson's critics

Over a period of eighteen months I commissioned for the *post-autistic economics review* the ten critical essays around which this volume is formed. I chose the critics partly on the basis of the particular approach I anticipated that they would take to Lawson's work and partly because in each case I held their critical powers in special regard. None of them disappointed me. Very briefly I will run through the arguments of the critics, whose chapters have been ordered alphabetically.

Bruce Caldwell declares his "substantial agreement with Lawson's fundamental complaint that the economics profession is dominated by a mainstream orthodoxy" (p. 13) is unhealthy because of its methodological approach. He also finds attractive Lawson's description of structured social reality. But unlike Lawson, Caldwell retains a strong faith in traditional "basic economic reasoning" as "a powerful tool" that enables us to understand the world, improve our decisions and order human behaviour (p. 16). He cautions us not to "worry about establishing causes" (p. 18) in lieu of using the tools we already have, and would like to see research into "why such reasoning works" (p. 18).

Bjørn-Ivar Davidsen argues that the social ontology upon which the Critical Realism project in economics bases itself lacks "epistemological credibility beyond a reasonable amount of doubt" (p. 48). Consequently, he sees it as "ill advised" to rely on Critical Realism in its present form as the basis for critiquing and reforming "scientific practices" in economics. Davidsen calls instead for a critical realist project that would develop "domain specific ontological theories" and then apply them to "scientific work directed toward analysis of substantive economic questions and issues" (p. 50). Critical Realism would then be judged by its success in offering improved accounts of old and new economic topics. If successful, the epistemological status of the critical realist ontology would be enhanced and acceptance from mainstream economics might follow.

John B. Davis believes that today heterodox economists have a choice between two strategies for reforming economics. They can hope for a "big scientific revolution" or they can gradually chip away at the mainstream core. Lawson's view of heterodoxy, says Davis, conceals this

choice. He sets about establishing its existence by inventing and applying a classification system to economics. This includes three principles
shared by heterodox economic approaches, and that "draw the dividing
line between orthodox and heterodox economics circa 1980" (p. 84), and
four ways by which an approach could become heterodox or vice versa.
Davis's argument also grows out of his recognition of promising new
research programmes in economics and their characteristics.

Paul Downward and Andrew Mearman, while generally backing
Lawson's analysis, argue that there needs to be more emphasis on practical methodology for guiding research projects informed by Critical
Realism. To this end, they advocate a principle that they call
*triangulation*, a "commitment in research design to investigation and
inference via multiple methods which are not placed in any a priori hierarchy" (p. 131). They argue that this approach makes operational
Lawson's principle of *retroduction*, promotes pluralism, cooperation with
other social sciences and leaves the door open to quantitative methods
that otherwise would be excluded. In this way they see triangulation as a
means for realizing Lawson's project of transforming economics.

Like Lawson, Bernard Guerrien was a mathematician before turning
to economics. Unlike Lawson, he identifies the type of social structure,
not the type of economic agent, implicitly assumed in the models of
modern economics as what makes them so irrelevant. When they assume
that households and firms are price-takers, they describe not a market
but a centralized economy. When they reduce the whole economy to the
choice of a "representative" agent, they are indulging in blatant nonsense. Guerrien argues that the real reason why intelligent people can
propose and endlessly study "such *stupid* models" is ideology and that
to overcome it ontological debates are no or little help.

Geoffrey M. Hodgson agrees with Lawson that modern economics'
malaise stems from "the victory of technique over substance", and its
dogmatic insistence on the use of formalism (p. 175). But he largely
rejects Lawson's critique of formalism and, more significantly, accuses
him of a dogmatism of his own. Hodgson makes the case that Lawson's
criterion of local closure for the use of mathematics together with his critical realist ontology, which rules out virtually all such closures, in effect
denies almost all possibility for legitimate use of mathematics in economics. Alternatively, Hodgson rejects strict local closure as a criterion
for the use of formal modelling, citing biology in support. He then
explores two types of situation in economics, heuristics and internal critiques, where applications of formalism, including "using closed models
to help understand an open reality", have proved useful.

Bruce R. McFarling makes the case that epistemology, not ontology,
should be given the "starring role" when it comes to reorienting economics. Ontological choices, he notes, ought to be founded on epistemology. His argument centres, however, on the mainstream mode of

explanation, which he identifies as the root cause "of why sixty years of determined empirical testing has left the mainstream project stalled" (p. 235). The failure stems from the method's unit of analysis, the problem solving isolated individual, which renders this approach "blind to important aspects of the economy" (p. 236). Researchers, wedded to the method, systematically ignore all those features of the economy incompatible with the standard unit of analysis. Degenerately, the method's failure perpetuates its use. Researchers, instead of reconsidering their methodology, reapply it but with a different selection of variables and parameters, hoping that at last success will come.

David F. Ruccio applauds Lawson's efforts to make economists self-conscious about the conceptual schemes and ontological presuppositions of contemporary economic discourse. But he objects to what he sees as Lawson's attempt to have the critical realist ontology adopted as "the singular reality appropriate for economic science" (p. 269), *the* conception of reality. Ruccio points to the existence of other ontologies, especially Marxism and postmodernism, which have proven useful, both in their own right and as critiques of mainstream economics. He elaborates on the contributions that have come through the application of these ontologies and which emanate from their particular characteristics. He concludes by withholding support for "the project of finding or producing a single ontology that will serve as the shared foundation of the various schools of thought that have come together in the post-autistic economics movement" (p. 272).

Irene van Staveren identifies Lawson as a strong supporter of the feminist cause in economics. Nonetheless, she levels three criticisms regarding feminism against him. In his encouraging feminists to study gender as an ontological category, she sees him as advancing a universalist and essentialist "claim about the nature of human beings, a claim against which the whole project of feminism is set up" (p. 299). Staveren then makes the case that Lawson's rejection of formalistic modelling can work against the aims of feminist economics. Feminists cannot afford to ignore either theoretical or empirical modelling, regardless of their ontological legitimacy, because they influence the way people think of society. She considers the example of modelling work on unpaid labour and the care economy, where the modeller is faced with the choice between constructing a model that permits changing gender relations and one that does not. Finally, she criticizes Lawson for failing to make the learning relations between Critical Realism and feminism run in both directions.

Jack Vromen takes strong exception to what he characterizes as Lawson's "presumption that adherence to a mathematical-deductivist style of modelling imposes a 'flat', non-layered empiricist ontology" (p. 325). He also argues, against Lawson, that mainstream economists believe both in underlying mechanisms, although different ones, and that a satisfactory economic theory should identify them. But unlike

Lawson, mainstream economists do not think that it is necessary to model them. Vromen explains why. He then sets out an argument against using ontology as "a final arbiter in assessing economic theories" (p. 328), especially the presumption that there "are many uncontested generalised observations about social reality" (p. 329). He concludes that ontological considerations should serve as "heuristic principles" for developing new economic theory.

As a year passed and these critical essays accumulated I came to fear their combined effect – that perhaps I was doing Lawson a disfavour. This fear grew when he declined to respond to any of his critics until the series was finished. Then a further silence followed, as he insisted upon writing all ten of his replies before revealing any of them.

Finally, his replies arrived on my desk. The week that followed, with its close back-to-back reading of the critiques and Lawson's replies, proved one of the most satisfying of my professional life. This is a collection of fine minds, stretching to near their limits, interacting with each other and being changed by the process. I was changed by reading it. I hope you will be too.

## Note

1 For more on Beauvoir's ontology see Edward Fullbrook and Kate Fullbrook, *A Critical Introduction*, Cambridge, UK: Polity Press, 1998, or Edward Fullbrook and Margaret A. Simons, "Simone de Beauvoir and Jean-Paul Sartre," in Karen J. Warren (ed.) *Gendering Western Philosophy: Pairs of Men and Women Philosophies from the 4th century B.C.E. to the Present*, New York: Rowman and Littlefield, 2008.

## References

Backhouse, Roger E. (ed.) (1994) *New Direction in Economics Methodology*. London: Routledge.

Beauvoir, de Simone (1949, 1972) *The Second Sex*, trans. H.M. Parshley. Harmondsworth, UK: Penguin.

Coase, Ronald (1999) "Interview with Ronald Coase", *Newsletter of the International Society for New Institutional Economics*, Vol. 2, No. 1 (spring).

Friedman, Milton (1999) "Conversation with Milton Friedman", in B. Snowdon and H. Vane (eds) *Conversations with Leading Economists: interpreting modern macroeconomics*. Cheltenham: Edward Elgar, pp. 124–44.

Gingras, Yves (2002) "Beautiful Mind, Ugly Deception: The Bank of Sweden Prize in Economics Science", *post-autistic economics review*, issue no. 17, 4 December. Online, available at: article 4. www.paecon.net/PAEReview/issue17/Gingras17.htm (accessed 10 June 2008).

Jevons, William Stanley (1871, 1970) *Theory of Political Economy*. Harmondsworth, UK: Pelican.

Lawson, Tony (1994) "A Realist Theory for Economics", in Roger E. Backhouse (ed.) *New Direction in Economics Methodology*. London: Routledge, pp. 257–85.

Lawson, Tony (1997) *Economics and Reality*. London, Routledge.

Lawson, Tony (2003) *Reorienting Economics*. London, Routledge.

Mill, John Stuart (1843, 1893) *A System of Logic*. London: Longmans, Green and Co.

Walras, Léon (1874–77, 1984, 2007) *Elements of Pure Economics: or the Theory of Social Wealth*, trans. William Jaffé. Philadelphia: Orion Editions.

# 1 Some comments on Lawson's *Reorienting Economics*

## Same facts, different conclusions

*Bruce Caldwell*

I welcome the opportunity to reflect on Tony Lawson's *Reorienting Economics* (2003). Lawson covers a considerable amount of ground in his book, so my comments will of necessity be selective.

I will begin by stating that, for what it is worth, I am in substantial agreement with Lawson's fundamental complaint that the economics profession is dominated by a mainstream orthodoxy which is "not in too healthy a condition" due to its insistence on following a specific methodological approach, one that is not well matched to the social reality it wishes to investigate (p. 3). I make similar complaints in the final chapter of my book on Hayek (Caldwell 2004), and indeed I quote liberally from Lawson's earlier book (Lawson 1997) in that chapter. In this regard I consider Lawson a colleague who shares a quest, that of fig-uring out why economics turned out the way it did in the twentieth century. This quest has historical, methodological, ideological, soci-ological, and even pedagogical dimensions, and we are but two of many who have contributed to it (a selective sample might include Mäki 1999, Mirowski 1989, 2002, Weintraub 2002, and selected articles in Colander and Brenner 1992).

As an aside, I will add that Lawson's broad-brushed description of structured social reality is quite attractive. For those who have read Hayek, it is also familiar: many of the things that Lawson identifies as features of social reality were similarly identified by the Austrian social theorist. For example, that "human social activity is intelligible" (p. 33), that we follow social rules (pp. 36–38), that human actions are "inten-tional human doings, meaning doings in the performance of which reasons have functioned causally, where reasons are beliefs grounded in the practical interests of life" (p. 47), that many actions are based on tacit knowledge (ibid.), that humans form plans that are forward-looking (pp. 50–51), and that all human agency takes place within given social struc-tures, but also produce changes in those structures (pp. 48–49), are all Hayekian themes.

That such claims appear in both Hayek and Lawson is perhaps not altogether surprising, for they are also recognizable in the writings of other heterodox economists, post Keynesians (at least of the Shacklian variety) for example. Lawson explicitly recognizes this in Chapter 7, where he suggests that different heterodox traditions share the broad-based description of social reality, and are to be distinguished from one another according to the different aspects of that reality upon which each chooses to focus (pp. 180–183). Given the richness of the complex reality before us, this too makes sense. It may also help to explain why (especially if one accepts the proposition that many issues that separate such groups are empirically undecidable, more on which in a moment) such groups inevitably persist. Some may agree with Lawson and me that pluralism makes good sense; the complex nature of social reality may also mean that it is inevitable.

In Chapter 4 Lawson recommends that economists reorient their discipline by resolving to seek causal explanations. He lays out an explanatory strategy for accomplishing this, which he breaks into three steps: identify event regularities, form causal hypotheses that can account for them, and then discriminate among the competing causal hypotheses that are consistent with the regularities (p. 81). Though he does not say so explicitly in his general formulation, it may be that Lawson is calling for more long run causal explanations here, or, put another way, for more economic history. Some of Lawson's examples (e.g., explanations of differential measured productivity growth rates, or of relative changes in primary versus produced goods prices over the last century) support this reading, as does Lawson's italicized statement at the end of the chapter that *"the explanatory process so facilitated is necessarily backward looking"* (p. 108).

If Lawson is advocating that economists do more economic history when he says that we should seek causal explanations, I have no quarrel, though as will be clear, I believe that there are other things that we can be doing as well. However, it may be that Lawson is calling for what might be termed *short run* causal explanations as well. In my opinion, seeking to produce valid *short run* causal explanations is an extremely ambitious goal, and in many instances an unreachable one. The complex nature of the open system that constitutes social reality, one that poses such problems for mainstream efforts at its analysis, will cause similar problems for any such program.

A homely example will illustrate the problem. I work in a largely empirical department of economics. Though the kind of research that I like to do is very different from theirs, I have come to admire and respect the carefulness with which my colleagues undertake their work. This is best revealed in departmental seminars, countless numbers of which I have attended (the high price of good departmental citizenship). Over the years certain features of a "typical" empirical seminar have emerged. A problem or puzzle is posed. Sometimes the problem arises from surprising relationships that have been discovered among the data (e.g., one colleague found that, during recessions, a number of variables associated with "better health" improved); other times it is an attempt to identify the impact of some policy change on some set of variables of interest (e.g., the impact of changes in the welfare laws on household and labor market variables of interest, or of the institution of charter schools on variables associated with educational outcomes). As the speaker goes through her presentation, typical questions arise. If the data set is a well-known and frequently used one, the speaker is asked about how she handled the equally well-known problems associated with it. If it is a new data set, there are questions about how the variables of interest were constructed, and whether their composition raises problems for the questions that the speaker seeks to answer. Usually they do. The peculiarities of the data dictate which subset of econometric methods should be used to correct for the problems. A good speaker knows the limitations of her data, and has chosen the subset of methods that hold the best chance of correcting for them. Speakers judged as ineffective are either unaware of problems or of the appropriate tools for correcting for them, or worse, both.

Sometimes the speaker draws policy conclusions from the study. This typically provokes animated discussion, for a number of reasons. First, the relations among the data are correlations. To move from there to policy conclusions, one must speculate about *causes*, and there are typically many plausible interpretations on offer. Next, all empirical economists recognize that adding new variables to an existing set of variables, or using new data sets that include different variables or which cover different time periods, or using different types of corrections, all typically yield different results, always in terms of the coefficients attached to various variables of interest, and sometimes in terms of their signs. The latter phenomenon is sufficiently ubiquitous that an economist who has studied them has given them a name: "emerging recalcitrant results." Robert Goldfarb draws the obvious inference about such findings:

> These emerging contrary results or "potential reversals" present a dilemma for the conscientious economist who is part of an empirical literature's audience. How is he or she to make believable inferences from such a literature, when results may have already been, or in the future be, challenged and even conceivably overturned?
>
> (1997, p. 222)

The implications are evidently quite profound if one wants to take the step towards making policy recommendations. As a result, the most successful seminar presenters (the most "scientific") are very careful about trying to discuss the policy implications of their papers. It is usually done only in the last five minutes, when the substance of the talk is over, sometimes with a bit of a smile or other body language to suggest that this is the speculative part, always using very careful language ("this study would seem to suggest…"). No claims are ever defended with anything like the vigor with which one defends one's choice of econometric techniques.

The main reason why making the jump from the empirical results of a study to policy conclusions is so difficult is that a given set of facts always give rise to multiple plausible interpretations as to why the facts are as we find them. In my estimation, precisely the same holds true when one seeks short run causal explanations. To restate this using Lawson's own framework, my point is that the third stage of his recommended strategy, that of formulating ways of discriminating among competing causal hypotheses, is in the short run extremely problematical. People are always able to reach different conclusions from the same set of facts.

The bedrock claim that underlies this pessimistic conclusion is that the complexity of social phenomena implies severe limitations on what we can expect of empirical work in economics. This does not mean that progress in the empirical domain is impossible. We now have better and more varied statistical methods, more powerful computers, and more detailed data, so that we can describe the economy at a point in time much better than we could even a generation ago. But even with all of these advances, the complexity of the phenomena we analyze means that forecasting will be difficult, it means that making the move from an econometric study to a policy conclusion will be difficult, and it means that discriminating among competing causal hypotheses, at least in the short run, will be difficult. These are not problems that will go away through time, once we have better tools. They are a permanent feature and are due to the nature of the open system that we study. This pessimistic conclusion is probably the most important implication that I drew from my study of Hayek's writings on the study of complex phenomena. My working subtitle for my book, and one I had wished now that I had retained, was "F.A. Hayek and the Limits of Social Science."

Does providing long run causal explanations exhaust the contributions that economists can make? No, there are other things that we can and should do. For example, economists have long contributed a method of analysis that helps all of us to make better sense of the world. I have discussed this contribution both in my book and on the pages of the *post-autistic economics review* under the not very well-defined label "basic economic reasoning" (Caldwell 2002, 2004, pp. 382–388). What constitutes basic economic reasoning is hard to describe (though I am tempted to say, like pornography, I know it when I see it), so instead of offering a definition I have provided a number of examples of what I have in mind in my article and book.

Basic economic reasoning uses simple tools, like production possibility curves or demand and supply curves, to facilitate understanding of real world events. Such diagrams almost "think for themselves." They embody common sense, even proverbial knowledge (e.g., the notion of opportunity cost suggests the adage, "you can't have your cake and eat it too"), knowledge that has survived and been passed down through time in various forms because it has proved useful.

Because they embody common sense, the diagrams themselves are not really even necessary. Last week I read in the paper that, due to the hurricanes that hit Florida in the summer and fall of 2004, Americans should expect that the prices of certain produce (oranges, grapefruit), of lumber and other products used in construction, and of certain types of insurance to rise, and that east coast resort beaches outside of Florida should experience more business. One could use a demand and supply diagram to show why we might expect such things to happen, one carefully hedged with *ceteris paribus* clauses, but one doesn't need to do all that, and they certainly did not do it in the newspaper. Nor does such reasoning depend on humans acting like the perfectly rational agents that are necessary for deriving such predictions in our formal models.

So what is the status of such knowledge? In a recent paper on Frank Knight and pragmatism, Wade Hands (2006) describes Knight's views about economic science. Knight's views are helpful here, because what he describes is very similar to what I have in mind when I talk about basic economic reasoning.

> For Knight ... even though economics is not a positivistic science, it *is* a type of science: an intentional or *common-sense* science based on the beliefs and desires of economic agents. Such economic science is essentially a formalization of age-old common sense, but it successfully provides both predictions and explanations of human behavior (though a different type of prediction than available in the natural sciences). Given the particular character of the objects in its domain – humans – this intentional common sense science is not only useful, it actually predicts better than the application of positivistic science to the human domain. As Knight says, "in this instance the position of common sense is better grounded in terms of the ultimate and inclusive facts of experience than is that of scientific logic".
>
> (p. 580; the quotation from Knight is from Knight 1935, p. 81)

Basic economic reasoning is a powerful tool, it helps us to make sense of the world, it allows us to make better decisions, and it makes human behavior more ordered. It is part and parcel of what makes human behavior intelligible, and predictable in certain domains, to the extent that it is at all. Seeking to explicate and to expand the domain of such reasoning is one of the most important contributions that economists can make.

Yet as Hands' passage makes clear, the status of such knowledge is ambiguous. It clearly does not meet the criteria of positivistic science. Nor, as far as I can see, does its use fit easily into the categories that Lawson provides.

But perhaps I am wrong. It may be that the phenomena that basic economic reasoning identifies are event regularities, or "demi-regs." So it may be that I am saying that we should not worry about establishing causes, but simply use these tools that have proven to be so useful in identifying event regularities in the past, even if we do not know precisely why they work. Alternatively, I also suggested in both my article and my book that exploring just why such reasoning works might also be a fruitful research endeavor: this may well be equivalent to Lawson's call for forming and discriminating among causal hypotheses. But such activity should not, in my view, obscure the fact that such reasoning is essential, and should be retained even if we are not sure (because we are unsure of the underlying causal mechanisms) why it works as well as it often does. In any event, I would welcome hearing Lawson's views on such matters.

In conclusion, though Lawson and I share much common ground in terms of our descriptions of what ails the economics profession, our "policy conclusions" as to the best way forward appear, at least, to be different. Given all that I have said above, the fact that we might reach different conclusions starting from the same set of facts is not surprising to me.

## References

Caldwell, Bruce. "In Defense of Basic Economic Reasoning," *post-autistic economics review*, no. 13 (May 2, 2002), article 4. Online, available at: www.btinternet.com/~pae_news/review/issue13.htm (accessed 12 June 2008).

——. *Hayek's Challenge: An Intellectual Biography of F.A. Hayek.* Chicago, IL: University of Chicago Press, 2004.

Colander, David and Brenner, Reuven (eds). *Educating Economists.* Ann Arbor, MI: University of Michigan Press, 1992.

Goldfarb, Robert. "Now You See It, Now You Don't: Emerging Contrary Results in Economics," *Journal of Economic Methodology* 4, no. 2 (December 1997), pp. 221–244.

Hands, Wade. "Frank Knight and Pragmatism," *European Journal of the History of Economic Thought* 13 (December 2006), pp. 571–605.

Knight, Frank. "Economic Psychology and the Value Problem," in Frank H. Knight (ed.) *The Ethics of Competition and Other Essays.* New York: Harper, 1935, pp. 76–103.

Lawson, Tony. *Economics and Reality.* London and New York: Routledge, 1997.

——. *Reorienting Economics.* London and New York: Routledge, 2003.

Mäki, Uskali. "Science as a Free Market: A Reflexivity Test in the Economics of Economics," *Perspectives on Science* 7, no. 4 (1999), pp. 486–509.

Mirowski, Philip. *More Heat Than Light: Economics as Social Physics, Physics as Nature's Economics.* Cambridge: Cambridge University Press, 1989.
——. *Machine Dreams: Economics Becomes a Cyborg Science.* Cambridge: Cambridge University Press, 2002.
Weintraub, Roy E. *How Economics Became a Mathematical Science.* Durham, NC: Duke University Press, 2002.

# 2 History, causal explanation and "basic economic reasoning"
## Reply to Caldwell

*Tony Lawson*

It is hugely desirable to be charitable in interpreting an opponent's arguments. Being so constitutes not only an expression of respect, but also a principle of good methodological practice. For revealing the limitations of a simplistic caricature of someone else's position rarely constitutes much of an advance in understanding.

I expect most commentators will agree with this. But I am aware of few who seek more to put such a principle into practice than Bruce Caldwell. Caldwell's commendable desire to be charitable to those whom he engages or studies, no doubt accounts for his balanced contributions to the history of economic thought in particular. His recent biography of Hayek (Caldwell, 2004) is an especially impressive and insightful work of this sort.

This avowedly fair-minded orientation is equally manifest in the continued patience Caldwell shows for the mainstream tradition. Although Caldwell himself contributes mostly to heterodoxy, economic methodology and the history of economic thought, he keeps abreast of mainstream developments and seeks to rescue as much as he can from heterodox or philosophical critique.

I do worry, though, that this may involve him in ultimately claiming more worth in the mainstream project than is tenable. This in itself is not an overly bad thing, unless this emphasis results in too little attention being paid to critically formulated alternatives. I wonder if this is not the case with his discussion of the approach he terms short run causal explanation. Caldwell, it seems to me, dismisses the possibility of success in this domain a bit too quickly. And I think he does so because he believes that the application of mainstream tools under the head of "basic economic reasoning" is a fitting substitute that succeeds in giving us a good deal of what we need. On this, I am not yet convinced.

## History

But let me start closer to the beginning of Caldwell's piece. After first surveying parts of *Reorienting Economics*, Caldwell asks whether I am advocating that economists do more economic history. My short answer is that not only am I advocating that they indeed do more history, I believe that, *qua* economists, they should almost *never not be doing history*. For all of reality is in time, and so has a historical dimension.

This applies equally to phenomena of the natural realm of course; it is even conceivable that gravity operates differently the further we are from any "big bang" (see e.g. Richard P. Feynman, 1988, p. 206). But if the speed of change of certain natural phenomena is sufficiently slow that, for most practical purposes that concern us, we can treat them as approximately constant, this is usually not the case regarding social developments. Social reality is that realm of phenomena that depends for its existence (at least in part) on us; it is constituted, and so is being continually reproduced and/or transformed, through variable human practice. Hence, most social phenomena are not only space–time grounded but also inherently more quickly transformed or more transient than most natural phenomena. So, for a discipline like economics, the temporal dimension of its objects is always likely to be fundamental to its analysis.

This does not mean, of course, that economics cannot, or should not, be theoretical. It merely follows that good social theory warrants the skilful combining of abstract and concrete history, and particularly of pure and applied explanatory endeavour. I know of no better illustration than Marx's theoretical, and yet just as obviously historical, analysis of the nature or mode of functioning of the specific human system that is capitalism.

Of course, social reality also stretches over space as well as time (or perhaps better over space–time). Hence, all social theory, including any serious economics, is inherently geographical as well as historical.

Clearly in setting out these assessments, I am taking the view that the nature of economics ought in some way to reflect the nature of its subject matter. That is, I am not wishing economics to be tied to some particular method in an a priori fashion, as is the practice of the current mainstream, but suggesting that its orientation be tailored, at least to some degree, to ontological insight.

Parenthetically, once we take this latter route of orienting processes of investigation to ontological insight, it is reasonable that (as is the case in the natural sciences) the social disciplines more widely be carved up according to any differences found in the *sorts* of structures, processes and principles being studied. However, if the social domain is as I describe in *Reorienting Economics* it is clear that economics, sociology, politics, anthropology and human geography, etc., deal not only with the same spatially temporally rooted reality, but also with the same sorts of structures and processes.

So in answering Caldwell's question I find myself (given the nature of my answer) setting off to address the more fundamental one: can we find a non-arbitrary basis for distinguishing economics from any of the other disciplines that study the social realm? And I have to conclude that I believe there is really only the basis for a single social science.

Such a contention does not undermine the need to retain divisions of labour, along the lines found in other sciences, such as physics, with its various sub-branches. On this conception, the division of labour adopted by the various sub-disciplines of social science like economics will be a matter largely of each sub-discipline's own history. In *Reorienting Economics*, I make the case for economics being traditionally the study of those social factors bearing on the material conditions of well-being (see Lawson, 2003, Chapter 6).

Here, though, I am straying increasingly far from the point. My simple answer to Caldwell is: yes, I believe actual economic analysis needs to become more historical. In fact, to be explanatorily successful, it can only be an intrinsically historical discipline; any ahistorical economics is likely to be an irrelevance. My reasons for this answer, though, lead me also to conclude that economics ought to be far more integrated with all the other branches of a single (geo-historical) social science.

## Long run and short run causal explanation

So far so good, in the sense that Caldwell and I seem to agree that economics needs more history. However, agreement is less clear when Caldwell writes:

> If Lawson is advocating that economists do more economic history when he says that we should seek causal explanations, I have no quarrel [...]. However, it may be that Lawson is calling for what might be termed *short run* causal explanations as well. In my opinion, seeking to produce valid *short run* causal explanations is an extremely ambitious goal, and in many instances an unreachable one. The complex nature of the open system that constitutes social reality, one that poses such problems for mainstream efforts at its analysis, will cause similar problems for any such program.

I must admit I am not completely sure of Caldwell's distinction between long run and short run causal explanation. Most likely long run causal explanations are distinguished from short run explanations simply in referring to causal processes that are relatively more enduring. But whatever the distinction, it should already be clear from the discussion above that I am of the view that all causal processes (long run, short run or whatever) operate in time and so warrant historical analysis.

I take it, though, that Caldwell's main point is that causal processes that are less enduring are more difficult to identify. I suspect this is sometimes so. But I am not yet convinced that an understanding of them is typically unattainable. Let me briefly explore Caldwell's reasons for his pessimistic conclusion.

## The problem of short run causal explanation

The most direct reason for Caldwell's pessimism is already given in the passage above: the complex nature of the open system that constitutes social reality. But this begs the question as to why, in the face of such a complex open system, similarly pessimistic conclusions are not reached about long run causal explanation. The key seems to lie in Caldwell's conception of economic history, but I am not sure he elaborates further.

Rather he focuses on the problems of short run explanation. And Caldwell offers to illustrate the nature of such problems with a homely example. In it, Caldwell describes, in admirably respectful terms, some of the practices of his colleagues in his own "largely empirical" economics department. The picture that emerges is of research that mostly comprises one or both of two stages: first empirical analysis and second the (more optional) drawing of policy prescriptions or other implications.

The carrying out of the first stage is described as typically thorough and competent, the second as cautious and speculative. Caldwell further informs us that in a typical seminar presentation, only a small amount of time (and sometimes no time) is allocated to the discussion of the implications of the analysis; and when it occurs it is always situated at the end. However, when it does take place, this part of the presentation usually generates the most animated response or debate.

The reason for this, Caldwell explains, is that to move from data correlations "to policy conclusions, one must speculate about *causes*, and there are typically many plausible interpretations on offer". In addition,

> all empirical economists recognize that adding new variables to an existing set of variables, or using new data sets that include different variables or which cover different time periods, or using different types of corrections, all typically yields different results, always in terms of the coefficients attached to various variables of interest, and sometimes in terms of their signs.

Furthermore, reasons Caldwell,

> The main reason why making the jump from the empirical results of a study to policy conclusions is so difficult is that a given set of facts always give rise to multiple plausible interpretations as to why the facts are as we find them. In my estimation, precisely the same holds true when one seeks short run causal explanations. To restate this using Lawson's own framework, my point is that the third stage of

his recommended strategy, that of formulating ways of discriminating among competing causal hypotheses, is in the short run
extremely problematical. People are always able to reach different
conclusions from the same set of facts.

I find Caldwell's observations on academic economic practice to be
familiar and convincing. But the first question that pulls on my mind
(but apparently not on Caldwell's) is what use is *any* of this? If policy
discussions based on such studies warrant being animated and critical,
do not discussions of the empirical econometric work warrant the same?
   Specifically, what is the value of the correlations reported? As Caldwell in effect notes, they do not reflect (the triggering and effects of) isolated causes (unlike the event regularities produced in controlled
experimental conditions), and they vary according to who is using the
data set (i.e. they are sensitive to variables included in the model, etc.). Is
it not the case that just about all such reported correlations are essentially
spurious; the result of repeatedly manipulating/transforming the data
until something presentable is concocted? Indeed, it is no secret that
reported econometric results are usually the outcome of very many
(sometimes thousands of) econometric estimation exercises being carried
out (thereby of course contravening the stipulations of classical statistical
theory), with only those that conform most to prior expectations being
reported. Furthermore, even the "correlations" that are eventually
reported typically "break down" once new/additional data is obtained.
   Some econometricians do suppose that their own results "this time"
will not break down and can at least be used for purposes of forecasting,
even if, as Caldwell argues, the causal forces giving rise to actual outcomes cannot be identified. But in an open system of multiple countervailing causes, it seems an especially heroic act of faith to believe that
closures (systems supporting event regularities), facilitating successful
forecasting, will nevertheless occur very often. And nor is there any
evidence that they do.
   In any case, this latter orientation or act of faith is clearly not Caldwell's.
For in the paragraph following the two passages just noted, after observing that economists "now have better and more varied statistical methods,
more powerful computers, and more detailed data", Caldwell adds:

> But even with all of these advances, the complexity of the phenom-
> ena we analyse means that forecasting will be difficult, it means that
> making the move from an econometric study to a policy conclusion
> will be difficult, and it means that discriminating among competing
> causal hypotheses, at least in the short run, will be difficult. These
> are not problems that will go away through time, once we have
> better tools. They are a permanent feature and are due to the nature
> of the open system that we study.

But if empirical econometric analysis of the sort in question fails to facilitate either causal explanatory insight, or successful forecasting, or the derivation of policy implications, what is the point of it? Ultimately, it is possible that Caldwell is no more optimistic than am I about the usefulness of any part of the whole practice. But if so he does not convey his pessimism. Rather he provides passages like the following that seem mostly to encourage an impression that the econometric analysis itself (the choice and application of econometric technique[s] given a body of data, etc.) is somehow more defensible (certainly more vigorously defended) than attempts to make use of the analysis:

> the most successful seminar presenters (the most "scientific") are very careful about trying to discuss the policy implications of their papers. [...] No claims are ever defended with anything like the vigour with which one defends one's choice of econometric techniques.

The point of my running through all this is to clarify (my understanding of) Caldwell's assessment of the nature of the problems of short run explanation. In the light of the foregoing, it seems that by short run causal explanation Caldwell effectively means identifying causes behind the outcomes expressed, or correlations produced, in the rather limited sets of time-series data that econometricians mostly use. And, in observing that econometricians cannot easily identify the causes at work, Caldwell concludes that I cannot do so either, for similar reasons.

But I am not so sure about this; I am rather optimistic that it *is* very often possible to uncover causal mechanisms, whether short run or otherwise.

Of course, I do not want to suggest that there is some foolproof method that allows insights that are not open to question or progressive development. Even in the face of the most successful of natural scientific theories, natural scientists are able to come up with competing hypotheses that provide a real challenge. Thus, despite even the spectacular explanatory power of Newton's theory of gravitation, Einstein was able to produce an alternative that equally accounted for the existing "data". The production of a theory that performs at least as well as that currently most widely accepted, however, is not in itself inherently problematic, but rather an opportunity for advance.

The point, of course, is that the theories of Einstein and of Newton yield different (including conflicting) implications for certain types or spheres of phenomena.[1] As a result, scientists have been able to assess which hypothesis is the more explanatorily powerful by collecting new observations in domains revealed to be relevant for comparative evaluation. No hypothesis, however explanatorily powerful, can be wholly treated as the last word. But where new competing hypotheses are formulated, their nature will determine the sorts of further observations that can be used to discriminate, and scientists set out to obtain them.

I believe this way of proceeding is relevant and feasible with respect to natural and social realms alike, and to long run and short run explanation equally. I suspect Caldwell accepts that it is feasible for long run causal explanation of social phenomena, which he interprets as the task of economic history. But for some reason he views such an approach as unavailable or inappropriate for short run explanatory endeavour.

Why? It seems to me that it is precisely because he still cedes too big a role to the methods and conventions of modern econometrics. Anyway, let me indicate how I believe it is frequently possible to discriminate even between short run causal hypotheses of social phenomena.

## Contrast explanation

No doubt, there are various ways of identifying short run causal factors. Here I want to describe one such, a dialectical approach that can be termed *contrast explanation* (or the *method of explaining critical contrasts*). It turns on explaining differences in outcomes[2] considered surprising, noteworthy, inconsistent, disturbing or in some other way interesting from the standpoint of current understandings; that is, differences in outcomes that, prior to their occurrence, we had good reason to expect to be the same. Let me quickly elaborate a case of this.

The problem of identifying the nature of a causal mechanism in an open system, as Caldwell indicates, is that there is always so much going on. That is why certain natural scientists seek experimentally to insulate certain mechanisms of interest from countervailing or interfering causes: in order empirically to identify them.

Typically, we cannot insulate social phenomena. However, it is often the case we can determine regions of time–space, those that I refer to as *contrast spaces* (see e.g. Lawson, 2003, Chapter 4), in which we expect a set of outcomes to be reasonably similar because of a shared (recent) causal history. Now if in such a contrast space a subset of outcomes turns out to be systematically different from the rest, we have reason both to suppose that a single (set of) causal feature(s) may be responsible, and also anticipate that we can isolate it.

In such a situation, contrast explanation is feasible. It turns on asking not the question "why x?" but the question, "why x rather than y?" in conditions where we had reason to expect "y".

Clearly, this method may prove relevant in any context, not just in the social realm. In the mid-1980s in the UK, cows started behaving in ways inconsistent with control of their bodily movements. By comparing these cows with others who acted in ways taken for centuries to be "normal", the causal factor making the difference (the "prion") was isolated. We act in this contrastive fashion when we find our car/bike/computer is not functioning just as we expect it to (i.e. as it did yesterday and the day before, etc.), or if we hear an unusual and unexpected sound in the adjacent room, or, on waking say, discover unexpected symptoms of disorder in ourselves (abnormal temperature, sore throat, pains or rashes, etc.), and so forth.[3]

I believe that this sort of explanatory endeavour, turning on surprising contrasts, has significant relevance to the study of social phenomena.

In describing this approach above as dialectal, I have in mind a process whereby advance in knowledge is triggered by the recognition of a contradiction or tension or problem within the existing level of understanding, the resolution of which takes us to a new higher level of understanding (whereupon the explanatory process can start all over again).

In contrast explanation as described above, the puzzle or contradiction takes the form of a surprising contrast, itself presupposing a level of prior understanding, and its resolution taking us to a better more powerful, new understanding.

I elaborate more about this mode of explanation elsewhere in this volume (for example in my replies to McFarling and Ruccio) as well as in Chapter 4 of *Reorienting Economics*. There are various complex issues that might be discussed.[4] But rather than elaborate further at an abstract level here, I suspect that the most useful thing I can do at this stage is to provide some illustrations; I do so using examples drawn from (or anyway of relevance to) economics.

## Long run and short run contrasts

In his comment, Caldwell actually refers to examples of contrast explanation (though without naming it as such) that I provide in *Reorienting Economics*. As it happens these can be considered illustrations of long run causal explanations. For example, I look at the fact that *over about a 100-year period* prior to about 1980, measured UK productivity growth was, on a fairly systematic basis, significantly below the corresponding rates of numerous otherwise reasonably similar Western industrial countries, an observation or demi-reg that many found surprising. And I suggested an explanation (turning on the UK's relatively undisturbed experience of highly localised collective bargaining).

But if long run contrasts of this sort seem especially surprising or otherwise interesting, short run examples abound. In such cases we are concerned not with surprising contrasts that endure over long periods, but with short blips or structural breaks or some such that may be unanticipated. I believe such eventualities occur all the time. My hesitation here lies only in deciding what sort of examples to use as illustration: those familiar or those unfamiliar to the academic economist? Let me give one of each, starting with the perhaps less standard or familiar. Of course, I cannot provide full-blown explanatory accounts here. I hope, though, that the explanatory sketches provided might be sufficient to raise a doubt that Caldwell's pessimism is premature.

## Tea...

On 4 July 1990, demand for energy in the UK, especially England, suddenly (over a matter of seconds) soared significantly, apparently by about 2,800 megawatts. It was as if the majority of households decided to run their electrical appliances at the same time. The contrast between energy demand at this moment and that during the rest of the day, or between the increased demand and that experienced at the same time on a typical day was obviously quite sharp.

Now all knowledge production is situated. And the historical record suggests that, for a British observer, the obvious hypothesis to entertain in pursuit of the explanation was that the British public were making very many cups of tea. Apparently, the UK public consumes about 165 million cups of tea a day, a seemingly uniquely British phenomenon. Even so, 2,800 megawatts is equivalent to more than a million kettles being switched on, providing enough hot water for three million cups of tea.

In any case, one question that certain observers were moved to ask is whether some event, prior to the surge in demand, so absorbed the population that tea brewing was delayed until it was over (or interrupted). Alternatively, was there an event of a nature such that its very conclusion actually stimulated an unusually heavy demand for this calming beverage?

Clearly one very pertinent question (if we follow this line of thinking at all) is what sort of event, if any, could affect the whole (or a significant fraction) of the nation simultaneously?

Presumably, something celestial could, like a total eclipse of the sun. But nothing obvious along these lines is recorded for that day. Alternatively, the explanation could be something occurring on the radio or the TV (or both). (Advertising breaks are less frequent on UK television than seemingly in most other countries, and on two of the main five channels do not occur at all.)

It turns out that just prior to this surge in demand much of the population was absorbed in watching England play West Germany in the semi-final of the 1990 FIFA (football) World Cup, a game that culminated in a penalty shoot-out (which England lost). It was immediately following the conclusion of this "shoot-out" that demand soared by 2,800 megawatts. The nation, having delayed venturing off to the kitchen, at this point, or so we can speculate, sought its solace in a multitude of cups of tea (or something similar).

The suggested explanation of the noted surge in energy demand may seem doubtful to some, especially to non-UK based economists, who might be inclined to look for other causal factors in play on 4 July 1990. But if such a competing hypothesis is formulated it will clearly be easy enough to discriminate between it and the one here described. For example, it is surely possible to seek out other important football games involving England that do not coincide with the posited alternative cause being in play, and vice versa. It seems likely that one explanation will do better in terms of relative explanatory power (with respect to the contrast of a surge in energy demand over the "norm").

As it happens a surge in energy demand associated with international sports events, and in particular England World Cup football games, is now observed to be, if not uniform, reasonably common. So much is this so that the term "TV pick-up" has been coined to capture the phenomenon. Moreover, so sure are the relevant authorities that this is indeed a causal factor that is triggered on relevant occasions that significant resources are allocated to anticipating the likely effects. I could go on.[5] But the point is that the short run causal hypothesis in question is now widely accepted because of its empirical adequacy.

I actually think this example can serve as an exemplar of short run causal explanation in economics quite widely. However, I expect many economists prefer a more respectable, or anyway familiar, example, one that figures on the pages of economic journals. So let me briefly sketch one.

### ...and lemons

The example I want briefly to discuss is provided by George Akerlof in his (1970) "The Market for 'Lemons': Quality Uncertainty and the Market Mechanism". Clearly if Akerlof's study is to be interpreted as an example of contrast explanation there must be a surprising or puzzling phenomenon to explain, one that at least suggests that an explanatory enquiry is called for. Akerlof puts the phenomenon he intends to address as follows:

> From time to time one hears either mention of or surprise at the large price difference between new cars and those which have just left the showroom. The usual lunch table justification for this phenomenon is the pure joy of owning a "new" car. We offer a different explanation.
>
> (p. 489)

Here, then, to reconstruct Akerlof's analysis in my own terms, we do have a surprising or interesting contrast. The subject matter is the selling prices of cars recently out of the showrooms, and the contrast addressed is that these prices are significantly below those of new cars rather than close to or equal to these prices.

Notice that the objective is not to explain a set of prices. This would require a knowledge of too many factors, a significant proportion of which are likely to be highly contingent and transient as well as unobservable. The stated contrast is regarded as interesting because the new cars and those that have recently left the showroom appear, on the face of it, to be reasonably similar, leading to the expectation that their prices too would not be especially far apart. Yet this proves not to be the case.

In endeavouring to explain the contrast in question, the large and surprising discrepancy between the prices, Akerlof, in effect, seeks to identify a causal mechanism adversely affecting the price of used cars that does not affect the price of new ones.

The term "lemon" that appears in the title of Akerlof's paper is US slang for a commodity that is regarded as substandard or inferior compared to the average standard of those available at the going price. In many markets, the products sold are found to be of variable quality; and this is likely as true of the car market as any other.

Akerlof's proposed explanation of the noted contrast is, in the first instance, a mechanism resulting in a tendency for the proportion of lemons amongst cars being re-traded to be significantly higher than amongst those yet to be sold.

Significant here is the assessment that once a newly acquired car has been driven for even a short period, its owner will posses a unique knowledge of whether or not he or she has acquired a lemon.

Simply put, Akerlof reasons that if, or where, the price of used cars stays at, or close to, the price of new ones, there will be a tendency for the worse than average cars, or "lemons", to be put up for sale. It is the dissatisfied customers that are most likely to off-load their cars. Thus, there will a tendency for the relatively new cars that reappear in the used market to be sub-standard. Realising (or anyway anticipating) this, would-be-buyers, who unlike the sellers cannot detect the quality of cars put on the market, are unlikely to be prepared to pay anything like the full cost (of a new car) for a used car. In consequence, the prices of used cars will tend to fall significantly below those of new cars.

So, the basic mechanism is one that is hardly a novel discovery. The causal process we are seeking comprises the self-interested interactions of different groups of individuals, and specifically those with a clear interest in off-loading/trading known-to-be substandard goods if they can get their money back, and those with an equally clear interest in avoiding purchasing likely-to-be substandard goods at a price for which they can buy the same item from a retailer. The latter group, of course, can expect that the proportion of "lemons" amongst new cars obtained from a retailer is significantly lower than amongst those cars available from second-hand sellers.

This retrodicted mechanism can be considered to be operating in the car market to reduce the resale price of newly purchased cars only under certain conditions of course. These are the following:

1   cars, including new ones, are of variable quality;
2   a knowledge of which cars are better or worse cannot be determined from their appearance;
3   by purchasing a car the owner acquires knowledge of the quality of that car not shared by others (and in particular whether it is above or below that assumed to be the roughly known average quality of a car of a given make and model);
4   there is a basic lack of trust between buyers and sellers.

I take it that this example is familiar to economists and I do not need to develop it further. Clearly, the hypothesised mechanism is not restricted to cars. And Akerlof, indeed, successfully demonstrates the empirical adequacy of the causal hypothesis in question in accounting for a wide range of phenomena (reduced demand for "regarded as inferior" goods from developing countries, patterns of lending to borrowers of varying abilities to repay, lack of insurance markets for the elderly, etc. – see Lawson, 2006). If an alternative hypothesis is advanced, it will need to explain a good deal if it is to dislodge Akerlof's account of the surprising contrast he addresses.

I could give numerous other examples. But I hope I have at least provoked Caldwell into considering further whether it is not after all feasible that short run causal explanation is possible. As far as I can see the process is as feasible as it is for longer run causal explanation.

The point, though, is that the explanatory process I am endeavouring to describe and defend is an enterprise quite different from the econometric studies that Caldwell discusses. In the latter, structural breaks, blips, outliers and "noise" etc., are viewed as nuisances hampering the process of producing stable correlations. I believe these "nuisances" are no such thing but rather opportunities for (dialectical) advance, marking locations where causal mechanisms (short run, long run or whatever) can be uncovered. Indeed, I would say that it is the insistence on everywhere seeking stable correlations that is the nuisance hampering the process of social understanding.

## Basic economic reasoning

If Caldwell is pessimistic about uncovering short run causal mechanisms (a pessimism, as I say, that I believe is unjustified), he does not suggest that we just give up on economics at this point. Rather he suggests that, to go further, we fall back on something he calls "basic economic reasoning". As I understand him, Caldwell is suggesting that this amounts to manipulating economists' supply and demand curves, and other familiar tools, and thereby generating insight.

I certainly fully sympathise with Caldwell's emphasis on giving what he terms traditional wisdom greater reign. But I do think that Caldwell's optimism about the usefulness of the basic tools he mentions is misplaced. Personally, I find the use of demand and supply curves, or, more generally, the functional relations employed by economists (of which supply and demand curves are particular instances) can all too easily get in the way of clear thinking about the sort of world in which we live.

In saying this, I do not of course deny that causal factors affecting the demand for, or supply of, a commodity will bear on its price and vice versa. This indeed is traditional wisdom. Rather I am thinking of all the additional assumptions required to transform these insights into functional representations. Thus, it has to be supposed that the response of certain (presumed to be) measurable phenomena to changes in "measurable" others is fixed and typically unaffected by context. It is also necessary to suppose that all the (non-constant and/or non-orthogonal) influences on the phenomenon of primary focus are known and fixed whatever the context, that the various influences on it do not interact organically but can just be added up, and so on. This certainly, is not how I find social reality to be.

However, Caldwell bypasses all such considerations in suggesting that the manipulation of certain models or curves, etc., just is helpful. That is, he does not spend time analysing the sorts of conditions that need to prevail in order that we might *expect* such methods to be useful; he just asserts that in fact they are useful (acknowledging however that it would be useful to know why). As such, Caldwell proposes that the tools in question constitute a non-dispensable substitute for (short run) causal analysis. And he ends his proposal by emphasising that he "would welcome hearing Lawson's views on such matters".

As it happens my views on such matters are almost the opposite of those of Caldwell. Not only do I think that short run causal mechanisms can very often be identified, but I also believe that the sorts of basic tools to which Caldwell refers are not only mostly *un*helpful, but also carry any insight they do, just when, and precisely because, some (set of) short run causal mechanism(s) has already been identified. Let me briefly elaborate.

If I understand Caldwell correctly, when he writes that certain basic tools work or are useful, he is suggesting that constructions like supply and demand curves, etc., are somehow relevant to understanding.[6] Now Caldwell admits that such constructions express quite unrealistic counterfactual scenarios. The question that presents itself to my mind is just how could such counterfactual reasoning be relevant to understanding?

## Counterfactuals and insight

It seems to me that the answer to this question is that counterfactual reasoning can be relevant when both (1) a causal mechanism has been
found to operate in some location, and (2) we have reason to think it will
continue to operate in the same fashion in some alternative (counterfactual) scenario. For this we need the notions of tendencies and transfactuality. Tendencies are forces or mechanisms in play and having their
effects *whatever the actual outcome*, i.e. transfactually (on all this see
Lawson, 1997, especially Chapters 4 and 9, and also my response to
Geoffrey Hodgson in this volume).

Gravity provides an example. Gravitational forces or tendencies
operate on the cup currently in my hand as I sit in my study; it is not the
case that they do so only when the cup is isolated in an experimental
vacuum (currently a counterfactual scenario) or, say, located in a further
counterfactual situation where all countervailing forces are some how
fixed and/or well behaved. Gravity operates on the cup as a transfactual
tendency, i.e. whatever the context and location and whatever the countervailing conditions. And this knowledge of gravity allows us to build
bridges and successfully launch rockets in open systems, and so forth.

The point is that it is this prior knowledge of gravitational tendencies
that licenses any counterfactual claim to the effect that gravity would
continue to operate on this cup even if I take it from my study into the
garden (or anywhere else). That is, the causal claim *precedes and justifies*
(where it does) any counterfactual claim. Without the causal insight any
counterfactual claim seems groundless.

And this analysis of transfactual tendencies carries over to (purely)
social phenomena too. I have discussed this at length elsewhere (especially in Lawson, 1997; and also in my response to Hodgson the current
volume). At this point, I will develop the framework no further but
instead pull out certain points of relevance for understanding the sort of
"basic economic reasoning" that Caldwell encourages us to consider.

Given Caldwell's central contention that his basic economic reasoning
can be called upon in the absence of (and as a substitute for) short run
causal analysis, the first and perhaps most fundamental point to stress
here is that it is the diagrams (demand and supply curves or whatever)
that must be manipulated somehow to express *prior knowledge of causal
mechanisms, not the other way round*. It is the causal analysis that provides
insight, and only this that can give validity to any *ensuing* counterfactual
claim. Without short run causal analysis Caldwell's preferred basic economic reasoning could not legitimately proceed.

Second, although prior causal analysis may licence the subjunctive
conditional expressed by a counterfactual scenario that is the formal
model, we know that because social reality is open, almost all the counterfactual conditions assumed by economists to get the standard supply

and demand analyses etc., going, are not at all real possibilities. As a result, any insights expressed by a prior understanding of some causal tendency will, through adopting the standard supply and demand framework or some such, be embedded within, and likely thereby distorted or obscured by, a set of known-to-be fictitious assumptions. Only if economists are extremely subtle in their analysis and prepared over and again to emphasise appropriate qualifications, is such distortion likely to be (at least in some part) avoided.[7]

Third, even if such an exercise is carried through in a subtle and cautious manner, it is in any case unnecessary. For all the insight available is already expressed in our prior knowledge of the relevant causal tendency.

Interestingly enough, not only does Caldwell not provide an example of basic economic reasoning that contradicts what I am saying, the particular example of economic reasoning that he does mention seems actually to support my assessment. Specifically, and despite suggesting that short run causal factors cannot be identified Caldwell writes:

> Last week I read in the paper that, due to the hurricanes that hit Florida in the summer and fall of 2004, Americans should expect that the prices of certain produce (oranges, grapefruit), of lumber and other products used in construction, and of certain types of insurance to rise, and that east coast resort beaches outside of Florida should experience more business. One could use a demand and supply diagram to show why we might expect such things to happen, one carefully hedged with *ceteris paribus* clauses, but one doesn't need to do all that, and they certainly did not do it in the newspaper. Nor does such reasoning depend on humans acting like the perfectly rational agents that are necessary for deriving such predictions in our formal models.

The hurricanes hitting Florida constitute precisely a short run causal factor expected to impact the prices of oranges, grapefruit and lumber, etc. It is a causal factor identified by Caldwell and the newspaper in question, and it is identified prior to (or independently of) any demand and supply diagram. Even if such a diagram, heavily qualified and manipulated with subtlety, could be used to say something of relevance, it remains the case, as Caldwell himself observes, that "one doesn't need to do all that". In fact, from what we are told we can really only anticipate (the workings of a set of mechanisms resulting in) a *tendency* for the prices of oranges and grapefruit and so forth to rise, a transfactual force (or set of forces) pushing the prices of such items upwards. What actually happens to the prices of oranges, etc., will depend on everything else that goes on.[8]

Fourth, the prior statement of a causal tendency ultimately underpinning any counterfactual reasoning actually contains more information than is typically captured by the latter (supply and demand curves etc.). For whilst the counterfactual exercise may capture what would happen in some specific non-actual (and in social analysis typically impossible) scenario, a tendency is an expression of a force in play and having its effects whatever the accompanying conditions and whatever the actual outcome. Not only is any legitimate counterfactual unnecessary, it is but one particular case of the scenarios about which the causal tendency underpinning it provides insight.

So, in sum, I remain cautious about the merits of the approach that Caldwell designates "basic economic reasoning". Where short run causal mechanisms of relevance cannot be identified, it seems to me that the sort of analysis that Caldwell favours could not actually be operative. So basic economic reasoning of this sort is not a meaningful substitute for causal analysis. But even where some significant short run causes bearing on some phenomenon of interest are uncovered, the forms of basic economic reasoning in question do not seem attractive. For where, or if, reference to prior causal insight seems to allow the manipulation of supply and demand curves, etc., in a manner that sustains some relevance, this focus will likely still fail to carry the full force of an analysis couched in terms of tendencies. It also seems likely very often to mislead.

To emphasise all this is not to contend that economists have nothing to say, of course. But I suggest that closer examination of actual practices reveals that the modelling methodologies do little in fact to help the knowledge process along. My own view is they mostly get in the way.

## Applied explanation

Let me express my differences with Caldwell in a slightly different way. If, as I am suggesting, we often can gain knowledge of causal processes after all, the question arises as to what purposes this knowledge can serve. One answer is that it can facilitate policy formulation and practical action. Another is that it facilitates applied analysis or explanation. By applied explanation, I mean not the uncovering of new causal processes, but the using of causal knowledge already acquired to explain particular events after they have occurred; it involves investigating how already understood mechanisms conspired jointly to bring about some (possibly unique) outcome of interest. Scientists everywhere, even when knowledgeable of the causal mechanisms in play, are far more adept at accounting for something after it has happened (why something went wrong, or why something worked out in a manner other than was expected), than they are at predicting or controlling events in advance (think of meteorology).

The openness of the open social system is such that, in social science, even this kind of applied explanatory work will typically be highly partial, requiring something like the contrastive explanatory approach described above. Indeed the example of explaining the prices of "lemons" that I earlier discussed is arguably a case of this sort. The explanation advanced does not really identify new mechanisms but theorises how previously known mechanisms come together to account for the contrastive phenomenon that, prior to reflection, was surprising. Schelling's (1969) account of racial segregation (discussed in my reply to Hodgson in this volume) may be a further example (in contrast, Marx's theory of value produced to explain various contrasts of interest to him[9] is an example of *pure* explanatory endeavour).

Now I mention all this because it seems to me that Caldwell's "basic economic reasoning" seems to be primarily addressed to questions of *applied* analysis or explanation. That is, Caldwell is attempting to comprehend specific outcomes or events in terms of *already existing* (widely accepted) views or understandings. Thus, Caldwell writes:

> Basic economic reasoning uses simple tools, like production possibility curves or demand and supply curves, to facilitate understanding of real world events. Such diagrams almost "think for themselves." They embody common sense, even proverbial knowledge (e.g., the notion of opportunity cost suggests the adage, "you can't have your cake and eat it too"), knowledge that has survived and been passed down through time in various forms because it has proved useful.
>
> Because they embody common sense, the diagrams themselves are not really even necessary.

My contention, as set out in the discussion above, then, is that this applied analysis is feasible only if relevant causal factors are already known and forms the basis on which any "understanding of real world events" is achieved. In other words, I think the real difference between us here is that whereas the "common sense" and "proverbial knowledge" to which Caldwell refers are considered by him to be alternatives to causal knowledge, I am arguing that (appropriately expressed) they are much the same thing as, or at least highly inclusive of (insights presupposing), causal knowledge. Thus, when Caldwell concludes that "the diagrams themselves are not really even necessary" just because "they embody common sense", my arguments (laid out above) lead me to add that because these diagrams further include much that is typically contrary to this "common sense", they are not only unnecessary but typically misleading and often best avoided.

## Final comments

As Caldwell emphasises, on very many of the matters that tax economic methodologists, he and I are in broad agreement. However, I think he does succeed in identifying an important point of divergence. Caldwell believes that in the face of our inability to do (what he terms) short run causal analysis we must continue using the functional relations or simple curves (e.g. supply and demand diagrams) that are the stock in trade of the mainstream tradition. I have argued, to the contrary, that such methods, which in themselves do not take us forward, can only be utilised meaningfully (if at all) where short run (and other forms of) causal analysis has already been carried through, no matter how informally. Such causal analysis, I maintain, usually hinges upon (if again informally and in an unacknowledged fashion) dialectical processes such as the method of contrast explanation. As such, I suspect that the most fundamental task facing economic methodologists concerned with causal explanation, or anyway a very significant challenge, is to elaborate more fully such processes of dialectical reasoning and to facilitate their being more widely recognised and applied.

## Notes

1  From the perspective of Einstein's (1905) Special Theory of Relativity, Newton's Three Laws of Motion are only approximately correct, breaking down when velocities approach that of light. From the perspective of Einstein's General Theory of Relativity (1915), Newton's Law of Gravitation breaks down in the presence of very strong gravitational fields.
2  All outcomes are interpreted and so theoretical. But I include in outcomes here competing theories of the same outcome by different research groups and so forth.
3  Actually, the controlled experimental situation is ultimately a special case of contrast explanation. The controlled experiment is distinctive just because the background conditions are, where feasible, held more or less constant. In such a set-up, whatever happens after the isolated mechanism is triggered can, with reason, be attributed to this mechanism. This is the relevant contrast here: between what goes on before and after mechanism's triggering.

   However, these laboratory experimental conditions (if vital to the production of an event regularity, correlating triggering conditions and unimpeded effects) are not strictly essential for identifying the way of acting of a causal mechanism. In principle all the background conditions can be allowed to change. So long as there is a control group experiencing all the same changing conditions except the one in which we are interested, and if any observed systematic differences coincide with the allocation of the selectively applied causal factor of interest, we can with reason attribute the former to the latter.
4  For example, social phenomena are usually pre-interpreted and contested, and they often present difficulties of interpretation of a sort, or to a degree, that may not typically be experienced in the natural sciences. In particular, the line between theory and evidence, though always contentious, seems potentially even more so in the social realm. In consequence, it will often seem clearer in social analysis, that a *prior* understanding utilised in contrast explanation and any a posteriori assessment (or empirical observation) that appears to contradict it, are both interpretations and so fallible and potentially open to revision.

The interpreted or theoretical nature of competing claims will not always remain implicit, of course. Indeed, the critical contrasts may be precisely provided by competing theories of a given situation or phenomenon. Such a clash of theoretical assessments is the situation found in the study of gender that I discuss in my response to Davidsen below. However, despite the interpreted and potentially contested nature of all social theorising including "observation", it is very often not impossible, or even especially difficult, to determine a reasoned resolution of a surprising set of (interpreted) outcomes. This, I contend, is so even in the complex case of getting at short run causes.

5   In fact, as I write these lines we are approaching the 2006 FIFA World Cup tournament to be held in Germany. And we have arrived at a stage where the relevant body is making contingency plans to cover the now expected surges. This body, the National Grid, manages the UK's large and complex energy delivery networks, owning, operating and developing the high-voltage electricity transmission network in England and Wales and Great Britain's principal natural gas transportation system.

As it happens, the National Grid even has a web page dedicated to the 2006 World Cup (www.nationalgrid.com/uk/Media+Centre/worldcup/). Here it states:

> At the sound of the half-time whistle and the end of every big match, we gear up for a massive surge in electricity demand as millions of people turn on their kettles for a cuppa, switch on the lights or reach for a cold drink from the fridge.
>
> For a short but dramatic period this almost instant increase – known as a "TV pick-up" – can be as high as 10% of existing demand. The popularity of a comparatively small number of channels, combined with the country's legendary tea-drinking habits and a marked preference for the electric kettle rather than stove-top varieties make TV pick-ups a uniquely British phenomenon.

They add:

> In the run up to the 2006 World Cup, our demand forecasters have been collating a wealth of information to give them as accurate a picture of demand as possible. In addition to looking at previous World Cups, the team also has to consider a range of other factors. For example, what is the time of the broadcast? Will it get dark during the match, causing people to switch on the lights at the end of the game? Does the end of the match coincide with the end of a film on another channel?
>
> Changing viewing habits over the years may also have an impact on demand during this tournament, with the increasing popularity of watching major sporting events in pubs and at large screen venues, together with an ever-rising number of television channels on offer.

I suspect their forecasts will not be overly accurate, but they are making contingencies to cover different eventualities (and even promoting campaigns to influence the tea-brewing behaviour of the football watching population).

6   It seems clear from Caldwell's wider statements that this is his meaning in claiming that the basic tools are useful. It might be thought, however, that he instead means (when he says that these methods have been "useful in identifying event regularities in the past") that econometricians have managed to use available data sets to obtain good fits. This too, though, where it is the case, is neither difficult to explain nor worth shouting about. Most econometricians concern themselves with time series analyses, and most times series reveal a combination of trends and cycles. It is not too difficult to run very

many (thousands) of regressions and pick out a set of "parameter estimates" that give a good fit in the sense of relating the trends and cycles in one data set (the dependent "variable") to forced combinations of numerous other (transformed) data sets (or independent variables), about which some story can be told. As indeed I have already observed, rarely do the reported results hold up when new data points are obtained. More to the point, how do we know when the story that can be told is a good one? How do economists know which parameter estimates from the huge variety typically obtainable are sensible? I suggest that the answer is that economists can determine this only through prior (if often implicit and unacknowledged) short run (or long run) causal analysis. It is the latter that contributes any insight.

7  If a causal mechanism is identified it may be feasible to make limited claims of the following sort. If there are no offsetting factors, and if this is independent of that, and if we can assume a closed system for the bits on which we focus (or a functional relation connecting prices and quantities), etc., etc., then we are justified in manipulating the curves to indicate that variables will behave as demonstrated.

8  It is not inconceivable that harvests elsewhere, either inside or outside the US, are more bountiful than normal. If the former then the increased supply will likely give rise to mechanisms countering the tendency for prices of oranges to rise. If the increased supply arises outside the US, the strength of any countervailing tendencies will depend on transport costs, etc. So, the net result and actual outcome all depends on context, including developments in international trade.

9  Not least the seemingly surprising observation that exchange values are apparently not accidental and merely relatively but rather stable and uniform (suggesting the existence of a third feature common [and intrinsic] to all commodities which effectively serves as a measure and basis of their relative worth in terms of exchange values).

# References

Akerlof, George A. (1970) "The Market for 'Lemons': Quality Uncertainty and the Market Mechanism", *Quarterly Journal of Economics*, 84(3), pp. 488–500.

Caldwell, Bruce (2004) *Hayek's Challenge: An Intellectual Biography of F.A. Hayek*, Chicago, IL: University of Chicago Press.

Feynman, Richard P. (1988) "Superstrings", in P.C.W. Davies and J. Brown (eds), *Superstrings: A Theory of Everything*, Cambridge: Cambridge University Press, 192–210.

Lawson, Tony (1997) *Economics and Reality*, London and New York: Routledge.

Lawson, Tony (2003) *Reorienting Economics*, London and New York: Routledge.

Lawson, Tony (2006) "Applied Economics, Contrast Explanation and Asymmetric Information", Mimeo: Cambridge.

Schelling, Thomas C. (1969) "Models of Segregation", *American Economic Review*, 59(2), pp. 488–93.

# 3 Critical realism in economics

## A different view

*Bjørn-Ivar Davidsen*

## Introduction

Among the new perspectives introduced to the discipline of economics over the last few decades, critical realism, for various reasons, stands out as one of the most challenging. Two seminal books by Tony Lawson, *Economics and Reality* and *Reorienting Economics*, have played a pivotal role in the developments so far, setting the agenda for the unfolding of a critical realist project within economics. Lawson and his associates downplay endeavours aimed at developing critical realist-inspired analyses of substantive economic phenomena and issues. Rather, they choose to restrict the scope of the project to philosophical underlabouring for various scientific practices within the discipline. The overall goal of these endeavours seems to be to reorient the whole discipline of economics towards increased attention to ontological questions in general, and especially to the ontological theories embodied in the critical realist position.

It is my purpose here to question this strategy of developing a critical realist project within economics. I will argue that the attempts made to establish dialogues with various existing mainstream and heterodox positions by way of critical endeavours and invitations to ontological unification and co-development have been less than successful so far and that the prospects of any future success are equally slim. One of the main reasons for this is the fact that critical realists tend to give the ontological theories central to their project too much status and credibility. The properties of critical realist ontological theories do not render them apt as arbiters in critical endeavours or as some sort of unifying or common ontological basis for various heterodox schools of thought. In fact, I will argue that critical realist ontological theories are primarily, and perhaps only, suited for the one purpose that critical realists within economics seem to eschew – for establishing a basis for the development of critical realist-inspired analyses of substantive economic questions and issues.

To indicate what I have in mind I will offer some suggestions as to how tenable critical realist-informed economic theorising and substantive analyses can be developed from the philosophical stances and the general ontological theories of critical realism. In this critical realist-inspired approach to economics, ontological theorising is embedded in, or made part of, the overall scientific endeavours. According to this view then, critical realism can, and should, define itself as one among a range of other approaches to economic enquiries in a true pluralist fashion rather than as some common philosophical underpinning of already existing schools of thought. At the end of the day, assessments of such a critical realist approach to economics would be due to its adherents' ability to shed light on old as well as new problems and issues pertaining to the realm of economics.

## Situating critical realism and the role of ontology

Critical realism is a fairly new project within the discipline of economics. As with any newcomer to a well-established academic tradition it has taken the proponents of the project some time to find its place and role. We do now, however, see a pattern emerging. To most external observers, whether sympathetic or hostile to the project, critical realism was at first noted for its far-reaching critique of mainstream economics. The purpose of these critical endeavours seemed to reject most of what goes for mainstream economics as part of a strategy advocating critical realist approaches to economic analyses. With time, however, it has become increasingly clear that Lawson and his close associates rather aspire at generating dialogues with various schools of thought within the discipline – mainstream as well as heterodox.

The critical realist attempt at establishing a dialogue with mainstream economics is mainly based on critical assessments of the latter. At a general level the critique points to a mismatch between the mathematical-deductive methods allegedly adhered to by mainstream economists and the properties of social reality as seen by critical realists. According to critical realism social reality is an open and evolving system comprising intentional individual agents and emerging, layered social structures. The social structures of society, it is argued, enable and restrict individual actions, while at the same time being reproduced and potentially transformed by such agency. Mainstream economics is considered unable to capture this reality due to its adherence to a deductive mode of explanation in which event regularities of the form 'whenever event x then event y' are claimed to play a crucial role. Moreover, reinforcing these allegations, it is stated that mainstream economics is confined to analyses of issues pertaining to 'closed systems', defined as systems in which event regularities occur or obtain.[1] The implication of the critical realist critique then, amounts to urging mainstream economists to re-tailor their analytical tools to fit the basic features of social reality, as viewed by adherents of critical realism.

As opposed to the mainstream position within economics, critical realists do find that they have a lot in common with several schools of thought within the heterodox tradition. Initially, adherents of the critical realist programme approached heterodox economics through studies of the works of a number of outstanding representatives of such positions, like Commons, Hayek, Kaldor, Keynes, Marshall and Marx. It has been argued that these, and other, highly respected contributors to various heterodox traditions actually incorporated important aspects of critical realist thinking in their work, albeit spelled out in a different vocabulary.[2] These insights have recently been further developed, and the critical realist dialogue with heterodox economics now turns on the argument that, as a number of schools of thought within this tradition allegedly share basic ontological understandings with the critical realist position, they would benefit from redefining themselves under a common critical realist ontological banner. Critical realism would then be considered a position providing a common ontological basis for schools of thought whose identity would flow not from different ontologies but rather from the aspects of a common ontology upon which they choose to focus. The heterodox positions in question would, in other words, be rendered distinct according to a division of labour within a collective framework predicated upon critical realist ontology.[3]

A strategy for future development along these lines would contribute, it is argued, to increased awareness of commonalities as well as to distinguishing features accruing to positions within the heterodox tradition. More specifically, a unification and 'linked co-development' based upon an acceptance of, or subscription to, critical realist ontology would allegedly provide: 'philosophical resources that can help heterodox economists to make explicit, clarify and systematise their insights into the nature of socio-economic being and its implications for appropriate methodology for economics' (Lewis 2004: 2). Possible virtues of such critical realist underlabouring are illustrated when Lawson (2003a) intervenes philosophically in a number of heterodox positions with critical realist ontology as a reference point. In the analyses, overlaps with critical realist ontology are indicated and deficiencies and weaknesses of embedded ontological presuppositions are noted, according to the critical realist perspective.

As critical realists apparently have had a lot to say about the academic practices of others, it is no wonder that they have been asked how they themselves would go about analysing substantive economic issues or developing economic theories. Lawson reports of such queries and provides at the same time an answer:

> Probably the 'request' I come across most frequently in the context of
> discussing critical realism is for examples of 'critical realist substan-

tive theory' meaning *the* critical realist account of some highly concrete phenomena. In my view there can be no such thing.

(1999: 14, italics in original)

The arguments Lawson offers for this stance towards critical realist economic theorising and critical realist analyses of substantive economic
issues are once again ontological. Lawson draws attention to the fact that
critical realist ontology depicts social reality as 'open, structured,
dynamic, and in part holistic'. Consequently, critical realist ontology, so
the argument goes, can sustain a range of theories and explanations. Theories and explanations supported by this ontology may even stand out as
competing scientific accounts of the same phenomenon, and they may
have to be considered explanations more or less in continuous change
and transition. Accordingly, it is stated that 'at no stage can a substantive
theory be said to qualify as *the* critical realist one' (Lawson 2003a: 178,
italics in original).

Now, these arguments may seem somewhat bewildering. First of all, I
do question why critical realists are requested to come up with *the* critical economic realist theory or *the* critical realist account of any economic
phenomena. We are all well aware of the fact that critical realism is a
budding project within the discipline of economics. Accordingly, no one
expects critical realists to come up at this stage with *the* critical realist
account of any issue, theoretical or practical. If such a thing were ever to
occur it would, of course, take a considerable amount of time to be
worked out. Moreover, most of us would, on grounds that Lawson
rightly points out, not expect *the* critical realist account of anything to be
possible or even something to be strived for – just as we do not ask for
*the* post Keynesian, *the* institutionalist etc. account or theory of concrete
economic issues or phenomena.

A request, however, that is fair and one in fact that I myself have
heard raised by many taking interest in the perspectives brought to the
fore by critical realism, is for *examples* of critical realist studies of substantial economic issues and phenomena. What is asked for, in other words,
are illustrating analyses indicating what difference it would make if economic theorising and analyses of concrete economic phenomena started
out from, or at least explicitly incorporated, serious ontological reflection
pertaining to the issues and questions at hand. Critical realists do,
however, seem to refrain from going into such matters. The arguments
brought up against the possibilities of providing *the* critical realist
account or theory of substantive economic phenomena tend to be considered a good reason for not attempting to provide *any* critical realist
account of them.[4]

The aspirations of the current critical realist project within economics
then tend to be directed towards establishing a pluralistic discourse at
the level of economic theory and methodology based upon a critical

realist monist understanding of social reality. A barrier is more or less erected between philosophical deliberations on the one hand and theoretical and empirical work on the other, with critical realists thriving on the philosophical side of the fence. The activities undertaken, or aimed at, are often referred to as 'philosophical underlabouring' for scientific practice within the field of economics.

A critical realist project within economics thus conceived, however, has so far experienced limited success. As several commentators have argued, the critique levelled against mainstream economics is ineffective due to descriptions and characterisations of the latter.[5] Leaving these important matters aside for now, I would like to draw attention to the ontological aspects of the critical realist critique. The critique states, it will be remembered, that there is a mismatch between the mathematical-deductive methods of mainstream economics and the properties of social ontology as claimed by critical realists. What would be required then, for such a critique actually to be paid attention to by mainstream economists?

For one thing, mainstream economists would have to be concerned about questions ontological. They would, in other words, have to be seriously concerned with the question of whether their models and theories actually capture some systematic ontological account of social reality. Being somewhat reluctant about characterising all of mainstream economics in sweeping and general terms, I find it quite safe to submit that mainstream economists tend to favour different criteria for evaluating their theories and models. In the mainstream scheme of things criteria pertaining to formal consistency, elegance, simplicity, tractability and more generally 'what works', seem to be held in high esteem. If some sort of methodological position were to be ascribed to at least much of current mainstream economics, I do find 'pragmatism' in some broad sense the best candidate. In any case, critical realist appeals to criteria of evaluation pertaining to questions of ontology seems to be a far cry from what occupies the minds of most mainstream economists.

And even if we, at least for the sake of the argument, envisage mainstream economists in the near future persuaded to consider how questions of ontology might impinge upon their work, we all know that there are several theories out there offering competing accounts of basic questions pertaining to 'existence' and 'being'. Are there, then, any reasons why the ontological theories of critical realism would occupy some sort of privileged position in this race? This is a most important question that needs to be convincingly answered in the affirmative if the critical realist critique of mainstream economics is to encompass any prospects of success in the future.

Turning to the critical realist solicitations with heterodox positions, the question of identity needs to be addressed. Will the identity of the respective heterodox schools of thought, some of them long established, be preserved if they were to join up with other positions in a linked co-development based upon critical realist ontology? If the prospects for identity retainment are considered slim, how would this fact affect adherents of the respective programmes and positions? In my view, possible dissenting and opposing attitudes stemming from such considerations should not be underestimated. Evidence so far seems to corroborate such scepticism. With the exception of the post-Keynesian school of thought, most positions approached by the critical realist solicitation seem to respond with different degrees of reluctance and polite distancing.[6]

As relevant as the fear of and opposition to possible identity debasements may be, reluctant responses to the critical realist position may also be due to considerations of a different and perhaps more fundamental character. It might be the case that critical realists tend to overstate the scope of ontological overlaps amongst heterodox positions within economics and between such positions and the critical realist view of social reality. And to the extent that the suggested unification and co-development were to require adjustments of implicit or explicit ontological presuppositions pertaining to different heterodox positions in order to bring them in line with critical realist ontology, the question arises as to how such an implied privileged position for the latter is, or can be, justified. In my view, this is an essential question that needs to be addressed also when considering the future prospects of the critical realist invitation to the heterodox schools of thought.

To take stock, it seems that proponents of the critical realist position within economics aim at establishing critical realism as a philosophical project engaging itself in critical and constructive dialogues with various schools of thought within the discipline. Questions of ontology play a pivotal role in the endeavours. The critique launched against the practices of mainstream economists is predicated on a critical realist social ontology. Mainstream economists are criticised for an adherence to modes of explanation that allegedly cannot capture social reality as spelled out in the critical realist account of the social realm. Moreover, in arguing the case for moves towards unification and co-development of heterodox positions, the critical realist ontology is presented as the gathering point for such activities. And when critical realists explain why they tend to downplay, or abstain from, substantive economic theorising and analyses of concrete economic issues, the arguments are couched in terms of properties pertaining to social reality as seen by critical realists. A heavy burden is consequently laid on the shoulders of critical realist ontology. The prospects of any future success of the chosen strategy of situating critical realism within economics is crucially dependent upon the status or credibility that can be ascribed to the critical realist ontological account of social reality.

## Assessing critical realist ontological theories

The argument set forth in the critical realist account of social reality makes the claim that society must be understood as made up by intentional actors as well as social structures with emergent powers that enable and facilitate, but also restrict and direct, individual action. Social structures are conceived as pre-existing individual actions, and are thus irreducible to them. However, by employing social structures in planning and performing individual action, the agents contribute to reproducing and transforming these structures. The account offered then represents an elaboration of the agency-structure problem in which the links between actions and structures are carefully argued. In this critical realist account social reality is, moreover, claimed to be an open system in a broad sense of this term

In what sense, one might ask, will such an account pertaining to the level of ontology differ from scientific theories of social reality or some delimited aspects of it? The distinction is mainly due to differences in the degree of specificity. An ontological account of social reality is kept at a rather abstract level, while in social science we are more specific about the elements of our analyses and relations between them. The point at which an account of social reality ceases to be ontological and becomes scientific may be difficult to pin down in exact terms. It should be quite clear, however, from the context when ontological matters and when scientific ones are addressed.

At a sufficiently general level there is in principle no difference between ontological accounts of social reality and scientific accounts pertaining to aspects of this reality. They are all *theories* about the social world in the sense of being hunches, conjectures or hypotheses about social phenomena, albeit at different levels of specificity. The critical realist account of social reality as sketched above should accordingly be considered an ontological *theory* of the social realm. And as with any theory, the credibility or authority accruing to it will depend upon epistemological considerations; that is, upon what arguments are provided in support of it. It should be noted here that when drawing attention to questions epistemological in assessing ontological as well as scientific theories, I do refer to epistemology in a broad sense meaning all arguments – empirical, rational or otherwise – that is, or could be, offered in order to substantiate a theory.

Roy Bhaskar, the philosopher to whom the critical realist project within economics owes much by way of inspiration and initial conception, warns against what he terms 'the epistemic fallacy'. According to Bhaskar Western philosophy has for centuries been under the spell of this fallacy implying that questions of being (ontology) have been reduced to questions of knowing (epistemology).[7] However, Bhaskar's urge to avoid this fallacy should not be understood as implying that questions of ontology can be entirely separated from questions of epistemology. As soon as we move on from basic ontological stances, like the critical realist stance pertaining to a reality that exists independently of our investigations of it, to make more substantive claims about this reality, we enter into the world of theories. In Bhaskar's terminology the independently existing reality belongs to the 'intransitive' dimension of knowledge production while theories, including ontological theories and other knowledge material, belong to the 'transitive' dimension. Knowledge is, in other words, considered a social product liable to critique, change and transition. The ontological account of social reality pertaining to critical realism in economics then is a theory in the transitive realm of knowledge production whose credibility or authority is not automatically assured in any way. It has to be argued and defended, and the defence should be made subject to critical assessments.[8]

Like Bhaskar, Lawson sets out to derive and substantiate a social ontology by way of transcendental deduction (or inference), a method that complies well with the retroductive form of argument held high in regard by critical realists.[9] In Bhaskar (1989a) this method is employed to derive what is termed a 'transformational model of social activity'. Lawson, then, spells out the same argument but in more detail, while at the same time adjusting and adapting it more specifically to major concerns of the economics discipline.[10]

In general, a transcendental argument takes some generalised features of experience (the premises) and infers conditions for these features to be the case (the conclusion). The status or credibility of a transcendental argument depends, therefore, in part upon the premises from which the argument proceeds. To what extent are the premises employed really generalised and uncontested observations? Moreover, the status of a transcendental argument will rest on the deductions made from the premises to their underlying conditions. If it is claimed that these conditions are *necessary* for the features of experience to be possible, deductions made can leave no room for doubt. The full epistemological burden of the argument will rest upon the initial premises and the subsequent deductive inferences made. If the claim made, however, is relaxed from necessary conditions to *plausible explanations* that will render the premises intelligible, the epistemological burden of the argument will be somewhat different. In such cases, the transcendental deductions will only aim at rendering acceptable and likely explanations of the initial observations. There may, in other words, be other possible explanations. Additional support for the conclusion offered may then be sought in sources outside the transcendental argument itself, such as specific empirical examples, illustrations and so on that bear on the questions at hand. Invoking additional backing of this kind, however, makes us leave the realm of 'pure' philosophising and enter the realm of combined philosophical and scientific enterprise.

While transcendental arguments, under ideal conditions, might be relied upon to produce conclusions of high credibility, the prospects for such attainment when applied to social material are rather unpromising. Within the social sphere it is hard to find uncontested generalised observations of relevant features. And even if sufficiently interesting and uncontested generalised features were to be obtained, deductions made from them are quite unlikely to support claims to *necessary* underlying conditions for the premises to be the case. Due to the complexity of social reality one will, more often than not, have to settle for the more modest claim of plausible explanations in deductions or inferences of this kind. In general then, transcendental arguments within the social realm can hardly be relied upon to provide decisive arguments for the existence of any phenomena of interest, and hence for supplying a 'pure' philosophical or rationalistic support of any social ontology.

All of this is regularly spelled out by Lawson and his associates. In *Reorienting Economics*, for example, Lawson states quite explicitly that: 'Any results achieved by way of transcendental reasoning are clearly conditional. They are contingent upon the human practices selected as premises and our conceptions of them, as well as upon the adequacy of the transcendental arguments employed' (2003a: 34). As a consequence, Lawson repeatedly reminds us that the critical realist ontological theory introduced to the discipline of economics is contingent and fallible, liable to change and even replacement. Equally cautious statements are to be found throughout Lawson's impressively prolific publications, and they are echoed in the contributions of other members of the inner circle of the critical realist project.

Turning to the critical realist practices, however, a somewhat different picture emerges. First of all, Lawson does not refrain from claiming conclusions to the effect of 'necessary' conditions for the premises invoked when elaborating his transcendental deductions (e.g. Lawson 2003a: 36, 37, 39). Moreover, the ambitious strategy of situating critical realism as a philosophical underlabourer for a wide range of scientific practices within the discipline of economics, if anything, suggests confidence in the ontological theory of critical realism beyond any reasonable amount of doubt. The only way to reconcile the cautious pronouncements made regarding transcendental arguments and the observed practice of critical realists must be to understand their position as one of considering the critical realist ontological theory of the social realm to be fallible but nevertheless by far the best account of social reality available to us at the present. More specifically, they seem to be convinced that this theory outperforms competing candidates by a margin large enough to submit it as a cornerstone in a project of philosophical underlabouring for the whole discipline of economics.[11]

Other commentators upon the critical realist project within economics, however, do not share this favourable evaluation. In the literature pertaining to and commenting upon the development of the critical realist project in economics, there are examples of outright repudiations, or else severe critical appraisals, of the ontological theory invoked.[12] And even among commentators sympathetic to the project, a cautious line is advocated on grounds epistemological. Dow finds it timely, on reasons paralleling those set forth above, to remind critical realists that 'different ontologies are possible', and to suggest that, apart from a common conception of an open-system ontology, heterodox positions within economics entertain 'different conceptions of reality' (Dow 2004: 308, 310). And when Vromen considers the transcendental arguments offered in defence of critical realist ontology, he finds Lawson's exposition of it 'far from transparent', starting from generalised observations that 'appear to be somewhat arbitrary', followed by deductions that 'are rarely if ever carried out (or presented) in any detail' (Vromen, Chapter 19, this volume). A more penetrating study is reported in Guala (2002). Based upon a reconstruction of the transcendental inference offered by Lawson (1997b: 30–31) in support of claims made for the existence of social structures, Guala convincingly argues that the claims made are not, and probably cannot be, supported by the suggested method of 'pure' philosophical, or transcendental, reasoning.

From all this we should not draw the conclusion that there is necessarily something wrong or defective accruing to the ontological theory of critical realism. What is at stake here is the question of what status or degree of credibility we can reasonably ascribe to this theory, and the implications of such evaluations for the future development of a critical realist project within economics. In my view, the ontological theory of critical realism seems intuitively sensible and of potential interest for scientific work within the realm of economics. I do also accept that the transcendental arguments offered in favour of it, in spite of their deficiencies, lend some support to the theory, a support that is further strengthened by invoked practical examples and illustrations. However, and crucially, advocates of the critical realist project within economics have so far failed to produce anything like a decisive or broadly accepted set of arguments in support of their theory. The critical realist theory of social ontology remains in the sphere of hunches, guesses and hypotheses. In my assessment, Vromen has made the most adequate characterisation of the critical realist ontological theory when he considers it a 'conjectural revisionary ontology'; conjectural in the sense that it represents 'a first guess about how social reality in fact is constituted' and revisionary in the sense that 'it is different from the ontological views that mainstream economists entertain' (Chapter 19, this volume).

To sum up then, the transcendental arguments offered in support of the ontological theory at the heart of the critical realist project within economics do not provide this theory with an epistemological credibility beyond any reasonable amount of doubt. The critical realist account of social reality can only be ascribed status as a 'conjectural revisionary ontology'. As a consequence, the current endeavours to situate critical realism as a project of philosophical underlabouring for scientific practices within the discipline of economics appear ill advised. Such endeavours are not likely to be successful due to the fact that they are based upon an unfounded trust in the universality of the critical realist account of basic features of social reality. The critical realist critique of the practices of mainstream economists is not likely to have any effect if mainstream economists cannot be persuaded by the arguments supporting the critical realist ontology. Moreover, invites to a heterodox unified co-development are also in the future likely to be met with reluctance and polite rejections for basically the same reasons. Such a pessimistic assessment of the current strategy of situating critical realism within economics does not, however, imply anything like a general debasement of critical realist projects within the discipline. What is called for is a strategy of developing a project in which the epistemological status of critical realist social ontology is taken seriously into account.

## Towards a critical realist-inspired economics

The epistemological status of critical realist ontological theory implies that it cannot be ascribed any privileged position in scientific work within the discipline of economics. The critical realist theory of social reality may, however, be considered a constructive and helpful first step in processes of economic theorising and analyses. If critical realism is to make any difference to economics, it will have to be by demonstrating positive virtues of introducing explicit ontological reflection to scientific work directed towards analyses of substantive economic questions and issues.

Against this background it is my purpose here, *pace* Lawson, to make some initial steps towards elaborating a critical realist approach to economics in which systematic ontological reflection is an indispensable and integrated part of the scientific process. Before addressing this matter in some detail, let me make clear the philosophical stances underpinning this position. Two basic philosophical stances are taken. First of all, philosophical realism is adhered to in the sense that the world, social and natural, is assumed to exist independently of our investigations of it. Second, an anti-foundational stance on epistemology is endorsed. Knowledge of the world is in principle considered possible, but we do not have direct access to it by way of observation or by any other means. An epistemological relativism is consequently adopted. These philosophical stances separate the position argued here from various forms of positivism on the one hand and social constructivist idealism on the other.

By adopting the philosophical stance that the world exists independently of our investigations of it, no substantial claims are made about this reality. The critical realist ontological theory of the social realm, however, moves on from this general philosophical stance elaborating an account of social reality in which social structures are claimed to have real existence as emergent properties irreducible to individuals or individual actions. Social reality is, in other words, claimed to consist not only in intentional actors but also in social structures enabling, facilitating as well as restricting and directing individual agency, while being reproduced and possibly transformed by the latter. The critical realist-inspired approach to economics argued here proceeds on the view that this theory, even if fallible and due to possible change or even replacement, at the outset is considered the best account of social reality currently available as a point of departure for theory developments and more concrete empirical work.

The main tenets of the critical realist social ontology thus perceived come with some helpful guidelines for scientific activities aimed at illuminating substantive economic issues. For economic theories and more practical work to be in accordance with the basic properties of the socio-economic world they should incorporate relevant interactions between economic agents and enabling and restricting social structures. Processes by which social structures are reproduced and transformed by individual action should also be paid due attention, highlighting the geographical and historical specificity of social structures and their emergent powers. Accommodating economic theorising and economic analyses to these guidelines would contribute to establishing critical realist approaches to economics as a position distinguished from much of current work within the field. The noted guidelines are, however, kept at a rather general level and further concretisation may be called for.

Drawing to some extent upon Cruickshank (2003) I will suggest that the development of 'domain-specific' ontological theories may meet such requirements for further specification in a critical realist scheme of scientific activity. Domain-specific ontological theories may be established by invoking the method of immanent critique and knowledge transformation. The general idea of this method is the conception that nothing is created out of nothing. Knowledge-like material, like hypotheses and theories, for example, has some form of origin. Most of the time they are developed by processes in which pre-existing material of the same category is transformed and elaborated upon.

In order to develop domain-specific ontological theories within the realm of economics, existing theories and explanations pertaining to substantive economic issues and phenomena may be subjected to immanent critiques probing into the question of whether the theories at hand offer adequate and consistent accounts of the reality they purport to explain. To the extent that they do not, ideas and hunches as to how to provide a more satisfactory account will readily ensue. The next step in the process then is actually to work out an alternative account overcoming and transcending identified deficiencies and shortcomings.[13] In a critical realist approach to economics, these undertakings will naturally be guided by the precepts flowing from the general critical realist account of social reality.

Starting out with different economic theories and explanations of issues like consumer choice, employment, inflation and so on, the suggested method can be invoked in order to develop critical realist domain-specific ontological theories pertaining to the issue at hand. The resulting ontological theories will be 'domain-specific' in the sense that they relate to a particular research area within economics rather than to the entire socio-economic world, and they will be 'critical realist' in the sense that they are elaborated according to critical realist accounts of social reality. Domain-specific ontological theories developed in this way will furnish more specific guidelines for activities directed towards conducting critical realist analyses of substantial economics issues and phenomena. They will supply precepts for more specific critical realist-informed economic theorising and for empirical work within the domain in question.

A critical realist approach to economics developed along these lines comes with some notable advantages. Being elaborated in accordance with the general critical realist theory of social reality, the resulting analyses will incorporate an awareness of the interplay between economic agents and social structures, including processes of reproduction and transformation of such structures. Moreover, by being based upon domain-specific ontological theories developed from immanent critiques of pre-existing economic theories and explanations pertaining to relevant economic issues and phenomena, emerging critical realist-inspired economic theories and analyses will be kept in close contact with prevailing discourses within the respective research areas. In the process of elaborating a critical realist analysis of this kind, perceived shortcomings of existing theories and explanations will be rendered clear and the reasons for submitting an alternative thoroughly argued. The suggested process would consequently contribute to promoting understanding and communication between different positions or schools of thought within the field of economics in a true pluralist fashion.

It should be noted, moreover, that even if general and domain-specific ontological theories were envisaged as providing guidelines for the development of economic theories and analyses, and thus influence the direction and focus of scientific work within this critical realist scheme, they would not determine work at the scientific level. Rather, the proposed ontological theories may ground alternative economic theories or analyses. Systematic ontological reflection thus would not render scientific activities directed towards developing more concrete theories or models superfluous. It would, however, provide a more secure and relevant foundation for this kind of activity.

To sum up, the process of developing a critical realist approach to economics suggested above should be seen as a gradual and integrated one. The process starts out with general ontological theorising enquiring into basic questions of being and existence within the social realm as explicated by the critical realist 'transformational model of social activity', elaborated by Lawson and others. This general account of social reality is accepted as a point of departure in the process. It is important to note, and remember, however, that this account is only considered a contingent and fallible theory of social reality. The next step in the suggested critical realist-inspired approach is aimed at increasing the level of specificity of precepts flowing from the ontological reflection undertaken. By invoking the method of immanent critique of pre-existing theories and explanations combined with endeavours to offer an alternative to overcome noted deficiencies and shortcomings, domain-specific ontological theories may be developed in the light of precepts flowing from the general social ontological theory of critical realism. Domain-specific ontological theories then, if successfully elaborated at a required level of specificity, would yield more detailed precepts for the development of critical realist-inspired economic theories and empirical analyses pertaining to concrete or substantive economic issues and topics.

The critical realist approach to economics suggested here obviously takes a clear stance on the assumptions debate, which has haunted the discipline of economics at least since Friedman's influential methodology article dating back to the 1950s (Friedman 1953). The suggested framework indicates clearly that invoked assumptions are considered of crucial importance in critical realist approaches to economics, and systematic ontological reflection is set forth as the preferred way of introducing and elaborating upon fundamental presumptions in economic theorising and applied analyses. General and domain-specific ontological theories invoked in the process of developing critical realist-inspired economic analyses are not, however, introduced as dogmatic or metaphysical assertions about being or existence. Rather, they are carefully argued contingent and fallible theories liable to change and even replacement in the face of decisive critical assessments or the procurement of better alternatives. If scientific analyses stemming from, or based upon, the ontological theories invoked do not stand up to systematic epistemological scrutiny, this fact may reflect back upon any element in the suggested scheme. The problem may lie at the level of scientific activity, but it may just as well be located at the level of ontology. Insufficient epistemological support pertaining to critical realist analysis of some substantial economic issue may thus induce changes and revisions in the domain-specific ontological theories of the scheme in question. Changes or adjustments in the general ontological theory may moreover be initiated by considerations made at the level of domain-specific ontological theories, or as the result of other information. The suggested critical realist approach to economics then would be one in which ontological, or more generally philosophical, and scientific endeavours are considered mutually interrelated activities.

## Concluding remarks

The main claims of critical realism are ontological. Questions of situating and developing a critical realist position within economics, therefore, turn crucially on the epistemological status of the ontological claims made. According to the arguments set forth above I do not find the ontological claims of critical realism sufficiently substantiated to warrant the current endeavours aimed at situating critical realism as a project of philosophical underlabouring for various positions or schools of thought within the discipline of economics. These endeavours have been less than successful so far, and the prospects of any future improvement in this state of affairs are at best quite uncertain.

Taking on board the fact that the critical realist account of social reality is a contingent and fallible theory, however, does not entail anything like a general dismissal of critical realist projects in economics. But it does indicate something different from the current endeavours of grand scale philosophical underlabouring. Above I have argued for a critical realist approach to substantive economic theorising and empirical analyses developed from the general social ontological theory of critical realism. By invoking domain-specific ontological theories developed from immanent critiques of pre-existing theories and explanations pertaining to particular research topics, precepts will flow for the elaboration of critical realist-inspired economic theories and analyses pertaining to the issues at hand. The distinguishing character of this critical realist approach then, is its recourse to explicit integration of systematic ontological reflection and more traditional scientific endeavours.

The criteria of success for a critical realist project thus conceived would shift from the current dependency upon general acceptance of critical realist ontological theories to evaluations of its proponent's abilities to shed light on substantive economic issues. Moreover, the nature of the dialogue with well-established positions or schools of thought within the discipline would change dramatically. The current uncompromising critique of mainstream economics and the ontological solicitations with various heterodox positions would be substituted for critical realist endeavours to come up with improved accounts of and solutions to new and old economic problems and issues. To the extent that the suggested line of development were attended to, the envisaged critical realist project would situate itself as yet another position of economics alongside already existing schools of thought with the purpose of advancing its own line of inquiry, while respecting and communicating with competing and complementary positions in accordance with true pluralist virtues.

# Notes

1 Statements to these effects are prolific throughout the critical realist literature; for example Lawson (1994a: 259–262, 1997b: 17–20, 2003a: 4–8); Fleetwood (2003: 28–31) and Lewis (2003: 183–186).

2 Representative studies of this kind are to be found in Fleetwood (1995, 1996); Lawson, C. (1994, 1996); Lawson, T. (1989, 1994b, 1994c, 1997a, 2003b); Peacock (1993) and Pratten (1993, 1998).

3 This strategy is quite explicitly stated for example in Lawson (2003a: xxiii, xxiv, 165–168) and Lewis (2004: 1, 2, 13–18).

4 Some moves towards critical realist approaches to empirical studies in economics are initiated in a number of contributions in Downward (ed.) (2003). It remains to be seen if these initiatives will amount to anything like a 'reorienting of (critical realism) in economics', paraphrasing Nielsen (2004).

5 The problem of distorted characterisation stems mainly from the invoked definition of 'deductivism', in which event regularities are claimed an essential element. This is not the way the term 'deductivism' is generally understood in the literature of philosophy, and it is certainly not the way deductive arguments are treated within mainstream economics. In the analytical scheme typically endorsed by mainstream economists, axioms and basic postulates may, of course, refer to underlying causal mechanisms, rendering observable phenomena explained by several, potentially reinforcing or countervailing, forces and mechanisms. Problems pertaining to the critical realist characterisations of mainstream economics are commented upon in Hands (1999, 2001); Walters and Young (2001, 2003); Reiss (2004); Hodgson (this volume) and Davidsen (2005).

6 The positive reception of critical realism among post Keynesians is noted in a number of contributions to the *Journal of Post Keynesian Economics*, Fall 1999. See also Dunn (2004).

7 See for example Bhaskar (1978: 16, 36–42), (1989b: 13, 38–39).

8 Dow (2004: 308) seems to indicate that there is 'a grey area between ontology and epistemology'. According to my arguments here, I am somewhat reluctant to accept this point made by Dow.

9 A retroductive argument is one in which we move 'from a conception of some phenomenon of interest to a conception of some totally different type of thing, mechanism, structure or condition that, at least in part, is responsible for the given phenomenon' (Lawson 1997b: 24).

10 Lawson's transcendental argumentation to this effect is spelled out quite explicitly for example in Lawson (1997b: 30–32, 2003a: 35–40).

11 Bhaskar, being keenly aware of the possible weaknesses pertaining to transcendental arguments, invokes the method of immanent critique of competing positions in order to strengthen the arguments for his own favoured account of social as well as natural reality. In the case of natural reality, Bhaskar's deductive argument is supported by an immanent critique of empirical realism, and in the case of social reality he invokes immanent critiques of voluntarism, collectivism and the 'dialectic' approach of Berger and Luckman in order to substantiate the propositions embedded in Bhaskar's 'transformational model of social activity'. Against this background, it is surprising that critical realists within economics only occasionally, and then rather sketchily, explore this method for strengthening their ontological arguments.

12 See for example Hausman (1998), Parsons (1999), Boylan and O'Gorman (1995, 1999).

13 Bhaskar employs this method in his endeavours to work out and substantiate

ontological theories of both the natural and the social realm. See Note 11 above.

## References

Bhaskar, R. (1978) *A Realist Theory of Science*, Hemel Hempstead: Harvester Wheatsheaf.
Bhaskar, R. (1989a) *The Possibility of Naturalism*, 2nd edn., Hemel Hempstead: Harvester Wheatsheaf.
Bhaskar, R. (1989b) *Reclaiming Reality*, London: Verso.
Boylan, T.A. and O'Gorman, P.F. (1995) *Beyond Rhetoric and Realism in Economics: Towards a Reformulation of Economic Methodology*, London: Routledge.
Boylan, T.A. and O'Gorman, P.F. (1999) 'Critical realism and economics: a causal holist critique', in S. Fleetwood (ed.). *Critical Realism in Economics: Development and Debate*, London: Routledge: 137–150.
Cruickshank, J. (2003) *Realism and Sociology*, London: Routledge.
Davidsen, B-I. (2005) 'Arguing critical realism – the case of economics', *Journal of Critical Realism*, 4 (2): 291–314.
Dow, S.C. (2004) 'Reorienting economics; some epistemological issues, Round-table: Tony Lawson's reorienting economics', *Journal of Economic Methodology*, 11 (3): 307–312.
Downward, P. (ed.) (2003) *Applied Economics and the Critical Realist Critique*, London: Routledge.
Dunn, S.P. (2004) 'Transforming post Keynesian economics: critical realism and the post Keynesian project', in P. Lewis (ed.). *Transforming Economics: Perspectives in the Critical Realist Project*, London: Routledge: 33–54.
Fleetwood, S. (1995) *Hayek's Political Economy: The Socio-Economics of Order*, London: Routledge.
Fleetwood, S. (1996) 'Order without equilibrium: a critical realist interpretation of Hayek's notion of spontaneous order', *Cambridge Journal of Economics*, 20 (6): 729–747.
Fleetwood, S. (2003) 'Conceptualizing unemployment in a period of atypical employment: a critical realist approach', in P. Downward (ed.). *Applied Economics and the Critical Realist Critique*, London: Routledge: 27–50.
Friedman, M. (1953) 'The methodology of positive economics', in M. Friedman (ed.). *Essays in Positive Economics*, Chicago, IL: University of Chicago Press: 3–43.
Guala, F. (2002) 'Talking about the "transcendental" argument', Paper prepared for the INEM Conference in Stirling, September 2002.
Hands, W.D. (1999) 'Empirical realism as meta-method: Tony Lawson on neo-classical economics', in S. Fleetwood (ed.). *Critical Realism in Economics: Development and Debate*, London: Routledge: 169–185.
Hands, W.D. (2001) *Reflections without Rules: Economic Methodology and Contemporary Science Theory*, Cambridge: Cambridge University Press.
Hausman, D.M. (1998) 'Problems with realism in economics', *Economics and Philosophy*, 14 (2): 185–213.
Lawson, C. (1994) 'The transformation model of social activity and economic activity: a reinterpretation of the work of J.R. Commons', *Review of Political Economy*, 6 (2): 445–464.

Lawson, C. (1996) 'Holism and collectivism in the work of J.R. Commons', *Journal of Economic Issues*, 30 (4): 967–984.

Lawson, T. (1989) 'Abstraction, tendencies and stylised facts: a realist approach to economic analysis', *Cambridge Journal of Economics*, 13 (1): 59–78.

Lawson, T. (1994a) 'A realist theory for economics', in R.E. Backhouse (ed.). *New Directions in Economic Methodology*, London: Routledge: 257–285.

Lawson, T. (1994b) 'Realism and Hayek: a case of continuing transformation', in M. Colonna, H. Hageman and O.F. Hamouda (eds). *Capitalism, Socialism and Knowledge: The Economics of F. A. Hayek, vol II*, Aldershot: Edward Elgar: 131–159.

Lawson, T. (1994c) 'The nature of post Keynesian economics and its links to other traditions', *Journal of Post Keynesian Economics*, 16 (4): 503–538.

Lawson, T. (1997a) 'Development in Hayek's social theorising', in S. Frowen (ed.). *Hayek, The Economist and Social Philosopher: A Critical Retrospect*, Basingstoke and London: Macmillan Press: 125–148.

Lawson, T. (1997b) *Economics and Reality*, London: Routledge.

Lawson, T. (1999) 'Critical issues in economics as realist social theory', in S. Fleetwood (ed.). *Critical Realism in Economics: Development and Debate*, London: Routledge: 209–257.

Lawson, T. (2003a) *Reorienting Economics*, London and New York: Routledge.

Lawson, T. (2003b) 'Keynes's realist orientation', in J. Runde and S. Mizuhara (eds). *The Philosophy of Keynes's Economics: Probability, Uncertainty and Convention*, London: Routledge: 159–169.

Lewis, P. (2003) 'Naturalism and economics', in J. Cruickshank (ed.), *Critical Realism: The Difference that it Makes*, London: Routledge.

Lewis, P. (2004) 'Transforming economics? On heterodox economics and the ontological turn in economic methodology', in P. Lewis (ed.). *Transforming Economics: Perspectives on the Critical Realist Project*, Routledge: 1–32.

Nielsen, P. (2004) 'Reorienting (critical realism in) economics?', *Journal of Critical Realism*, 4 (2): 370–377.

Parsons, S.D. (1999) 'Why the "transcendental" in transcendental realism?', in S. Fleetwood (ed.). *Critical Realism in Economics: Development and Debate*, London: Routledge: 151–168.

Peacock, M. (1993) 'Hayek, realism and spontaneous order', *Journal for the Theory of Social Behaviour*, 23 (3): 249–264.

Pratten, S. (1993) 'Structure, agency and Marx' analysis of the labour process', *Review of Political Economy*, 5 (4): 403–426.

Pratten, S. (1998) 'Marshall on tendencies, equilibrium and the statical method', *History of Political Economy*, 30 (1): 121–163.

Reiss, J. (2004) 'Critical realism and the mainstream, Roundtable: Tony Lawson's Reorienting Economics', *Journal of Economic Methodology*, 11 (3): 321–327.

Walters, B. and Young, D. (2001) 'Critical realism as a basis for economic methodology: a critique', *Review of Political Economy*, 13 (2): 483–501.

Walters, B. and Young, D. (2003) 'Critical realism, methodology and applied economics', in P. Downward (ed.). *Applied Economics and the Critical Realist Critique*, London: Routledge: 51–65.

# 4 Underlabouring for substantive theorising
## Reply to Davidsen

*Tony Lawson*

Numerous individuals and groups are working to bring about an economics that is more explanatorily powerful than the approach that currently dominates the modern academy. There is no unique way of going about this, of course. As Bjørn-Ivar Davidsen notes my own strategy has been to pursue a project often depicted as philosophical or Lockean underlabouring.[1] This involves seeking to clear the ground of obstacles that stand in the way of progress rather than substituting an alternative set of substantive theories.

My specific orientation to such ground clearing or philosophical underlabouring has been primarily ontological. By ontology, I mean the *study* of both the nature and structure of a domain of reality as well as the sorts of worldviews presupposed by accepted methods and theories. I take the emphasis on ontology to be vital at this point not least because it is easily shown that the ontological presuppositions of the mainstream project of modern economics do not fit with our best understanding of the nature of social reality.

Davidsen is unhappy with my using ontology in this underlabouring fashion, appearing to suggest that the ontological conception that I defined is insufficiently grounded for the (underlabouring) uses to which I put it. At one point, indeed, Davidsen expresses the view that the conception I support "remains in the sphere of hunches, guesses and hypotheses".

Davidsen contrasts this underlabouring project with his own proposed programme of seeking constructively to guide substantively oriented social research. Although the specific ontological conception I defend is key to both sets of endeavour, Davidsen seems to think that his preferred, seemingly more empirically/substantively oriented, programme has legitimacy while the more generalised underlabouring activity he attributes to me does not. Indeed, Davidsen even concludes that, in order to stick within the bounds of what is legitimate, the project to which I have contributed should reconstitute "itself as one among a range of other approaches to economic enquiries in a true pluralist fashion rather than as some common philosophical underpinning of already existing schools of thought".

In my response, I hope to demonstrate that the ontological conception I defend, and so the underlabouring uses to which I put it, are rather more justified than Davidsen allows, whilst Davidsen's suggested alternative is actually not very different from ongoing strands of the underlabouring activity of my own that he seeks to criticise. Further, and not unrelated, I shall argue that the legitimacy and usefulness of at least some of the applications Davidsen proposes for the ontological conception in question equally presuppose/require of the latter that it already has some achieved grounding (of the sort that Davidsen seems to imply is lacking).

## Grounding the ontological conception in question

Davidsen's central critical contention is that the ontological theory I defend is not sufficiently grounded for the uses I make of it. Indeed, as I say, he seems to suppose, at one point at least, that the ontological conception I advance has moved little beyond the status of hunch or mere conjecture. Before examining why Davidsen so concludes let me give my own assessment of these matters.

In fact, I believe to the contrary that the ontological conception in question has received grounding in many ways. One such is through resolving explanatory puzzles that emerge in substantive contributions. This is a practice that Davidsen seems to recommend but, at some point at least, suggests that contributors like myself avoid. Indeed, he suggests that what is lacking are illustrations of how the conception I defend can constructively aid substantive work. So let me start with this issue.

It is important, first, to examine how it is even possible to use a philosophical conception to throw light on substantive issues *and in that way receive grounding as an explanatorily powerful conception*. The difficulty I have in mind here is that, because the move from ontological conception to substantive theorising typically requires numerous additional empirical claims, very often a number of competing successful, as well as unsuccessful, theories of some phenomenon of interest can each be shown to be consistent with the ontological conception drawn upon. The question, then, is how can any result (whether successful or not) at the substantive level affect our confidence in the ontological conception guiding our substantive derivations?

Before answering this question, I might very briefly note that it is because an ontological conception does not map uniquely on to any given substantive theory, that I have often stressed that it is unhelpful to refer to substantive claims in terms of any ontological conception it presupposes. The particular philosophical position I defend is often systematised as critical realism. And specifically I am suggesting that it is unhelpful to *identify* specific substantive theories as critical realist, even if their construction has been guided by that theory. Davidsen seems to criticise me for taking this position. But it is important to see that I do so for the reasons given, namely because each of competing conceptions may be constructed using the insights of that philosophical position. I do not adopt this stance, as Davidsen seems to suggest, as a way of avoiding giving illustrations of how the results of critical realism might provide insight at the substantive level (a matter to which I shall shortly turn).

Actually, I resist identifying substantive theories as critical realist not only because it is, for the reason given, seemingly inappropriate, but also because it can so easily cause unnecessary problems. This follows just because (no matter how often I and others repeat cautionary remarks emphasising the contrary) the use of the critical realist label encourages some opponents of critical realism to think that *if* they are successful in critiquing some more substantive project that draws on its insights they somehow thereby inevitably undermine or damage the underpinning philosophical theory of critical realism itself. Contributions not even labelled critical realist, but advanced as illustrations, are sometimes found to be treated in this fashion; so calling substantive theories critical realist can only make things worse.[2] It must be admitted that mistakes of this sort are easy enough to redress. But this does take time, it gets in the way of debate of a more productive nature and newcomers to a literature can easily be misled.

Still the question or puzzle I raised earlier remains. If numerous competing substantive claims can be shown to be consistent with the philosophical conception I defend, so that the explanatory successes or failings of any one substantive theory has no bearing on the groundedness or otherwise of the philosophical conception in question, how can support for the latter be achieved at the substantive level at all? Indeed how can the philosophical conception have much of an impact, or a role of any kind, at this level?

## Generalised puzzles and philosophical alternatives

My answer is that a philosophical project, and specifically an ontological one like critical realism, carries bite at a substantive level where problems or tensions of a *general* nature are involved; especially where it can be shown that the problems or tensions arise in large part because a competing philosophical theory is being drawn upon and can be resolved by way of replacing that philosophical conception by critical realism. In such cases, it is the *general* nature of the (substantive) problems that allow inferences at the level of philosophical ontology. And when the conception in question is revealed to have superior explanatory power, it is so with respect to competing philosophical theories.

Now it may surprise Davidsen if I point out that I believe that an example of increasing the explanatory groundedness of critical realism is provided by my use of it to explain, and to point to a way of transcending, various generalised tensions, problems and failures of modern main-stream economics. The essence of the latter project, let us recall, is an insistence that mathematical-deductivist methods be everywhere employed. The event regularities presupposed by these methods in turn rest on an implicit ontology of isolated atoms. Although I do not want to rehearse the argument here (it is hopefully unnecessary given it has often been repeated – but see for example *Reorienting Economics*, chapter 1), it has been easy enough to show that if the ontological conception systematised as critical realism is correct, the generalised failings and tensions of the mainstream project are much as we would expect them to be.

Moreover critical realism can explain not only the generalised experience of explanatory and predictive failure on the part of formalistic modellers in contemporary economics, but also the generalised pre-ponderance of fictitious assumptions that are to be found in economic theorising (entities such as people, firms or whatever, everywhere forced to conform to conceptions of isolated atoms), the various theory/practice inconsistencies that characterise that project (see especially *Economics and Reality*, chapter 1) as well as the limited successes that have emerged (mathematical-deductivist methods applied to a localised sphere of reality where behaviour approximates that of isolated atoms – again see *Reorienting Economics*, chapter 1).

So, in the manner noted critical realism not only underlabours for modern economics (by making sense of its failings and peculiarities as well as indicating the likely orientation of a more successful economics) but also is simultaneously shown thereby to receive grounding as an explanatory claim (adding, I shall argue below, to claims to its ground-edness already achieved by more direct means). Though certain commentators interpret this analysis as merely a critique of the main-stream (which of course it also is), it is better viewed as an endeavour to resolve (or shed light) on problems of modern economics in order that the whole discipline can make progress.

I should stress that there is no paradox in the claim that the ontologi-cal conception I defend is grounded in terms of observations of the ten-sions it explains and serves to resolve. In science, indeed, it is widely understood that hypotheses are supported by the very observations they are designed to explain. Moreover, it is not just that the observations support the hypotheses that account for them; it is just because, and when, a hypothesis explains them that they support it. The same is no less true with regard to ontological hypotheses explaining the (observa-tions of) generalised tensions and paradoxes that characterise certain social practices (that presuppose an unsustainable alternative [ontologi-cal] conception). So underlabouring can itself produce increased ground-ing for the ontological conception I defend.

I might also note that if accounting for the various tensions and fail-ings of the mainstream adds to the groundedness of critical realism, the latter is further enhanced by its ability to make sense of the continuing heterodox opposition to the mainstream, despite the latter's frequent shifts in fads and fashions (and also despite Davidsen's reservation of my using it in this way). For this sustained opposition can be explained in terms of a reasonably widely shared heterodox opposition to the implicit (closed and atomistic) ontology of the mainstream, and an (perhaps sometimes equally implicit) acceptance of (something like) the critical realist alternative. We can understand, too, the separate heterodox emphases on, and indeed frequent *identification with*, issues that are inconsistent with, and indeed standing opposed to, this mainstream ontology. Here I am thinking of categories like openness (especially post Keynesianism with its emphasis on uncertainty), process (especially old institutionalism with its emphasis on evolution), relationality (especially feminist economics, with its emphasis on care, gender and discrimination, etc.), and so forth. Furthermore, in this way, we can also understand these emphases as signalling divisions of labour in one overall project, explaining perhaps the large overlap of (and regular communication between) the participants at the separate heterodox events (a matter that is discussed in the current volume in my response to John Davis).

So, I think that the very analysis of the heterodox situation that Davidsen thinks is one step too far for the ontological conception I defend, is itself one that actually adds further reason to accept the explanatory adequacy of this conception.[3] Of course, Davidsen questions my call for further programmes of linked or co-development amongst the separate heterodox traditions. But this follows because the conception I defend seems to contribute to explaining the situation of contemporary economics, and so because, and just as, that conception is found to receive (further) grounding of a sort that (further) legitimises its role in underlabouring.

Let me now move to a quite different illustration of the explanatory power of the ontological conception I defend. It has proven to be fairly easy, I believe, to demonstrate the explanatory adequacy of critical realism where, as with mainstream economics, deductivism or some associated position is the competing underpinning philosophical theory. But I believe that the relative explanatory power of critical realism is not too difficult to demonstrate either where hermeneutic foundationalism (see Lawson, 1997, Chapter 10) or postmodernism or some such (see Lawson, 2007) are the alternatives.

An example, of the way in which the ontological conception I defend achieves grounding in being shown to be explanatorily superior to postmodernism, is provided by a consideration of the way this ontological conception allows us to resolve problems and tensions thrown up in the discussion of the nature of gender. Because the example I have in mind is perhaps less known (than the critique of the mainstream), I will elaborate it here at greater length. Any reader who prefers to get on with the logic of the argument can easily skip past the next part of the chapter (or conversely anyone who wants more detail might consult Lawson, 2007).

## Theorising gender

In the late 1970s and early 1980s, feminists began increasingly to emphasise the partiality of all knowledge, and to criticise the tendency of (typically white, middle-class male) scientists to presume their views to be uninfluenced by local biases, personal histories and values. The dominant message of these feminists was that a fuller vision of reality could be uncovered by drawing attention to gendered locations, that a theorising of gender was a useful way of uncovering previously hidden aspects of the social process (see, for example, Nancy Chodorow, 1978 and Evelyn Fox Keller, 1985). These gender theorists argued that concepts commonly used to evaluate behaviour (such as calculative rationality in economics) do not express universal values or ideals, but male ones in particular.

Although insightful, by the late 1980s this early feminist contribution was being challenged by other feminists for making the same sorts of ("essentialist") mistakes that it itself criticised. Specifically, the earlier (typically white, middle-class) feminists were charged with treating their own particular experience of gender differences as universal; they were criticised for taking "the experience of white middle-class women to be representative of, indeed normative for, the experience of all women" (Elizabeth Spelman, 1990, p. 1x). In so doing, these early feminists were accused of marginalising differences of race, ethnocentricity, culture, age and so forth; women of colour, lesbians and others found their history and culture ignored in the ongoing discussions relating to gender.

As a result of this criticism there emerged an epistemological position often referred to as gender scepticism, characterised precisely by its "scepticism about the use of gender as an analytic category" (Susan Bordo, 1993, p. 135). Gender sceptics argue that an individual's gender experience is so affected by that individual's experience of class, race or culture, etc., that it is meaningless to consider gender at all as a useful category. For, once we are attentive to differences of class, ethnic origin, sexual orientation and so on, the notion of gender disintegrates into fragments unusable for systematic theory. According to this assessment it is impossible to separate facts about gender from those about race, class, ethnic origin and so on (Spelman, 1990, pp. 135–136).

In short, early feminist (and other) gender theorists were criticised for assuming cross-cultural stability of facts about gender, and a separability of the parts of a person's achieved identity.

If the intent of this criticism was to be corrective, it was soon to be pushed to destructive extremes. Specifically, some "postmodernists" came to argue that, because of differences of ethnic origin, sexual orientation, culture and so forth, not only is each individual's experience unique but no category can legitimately be treated as stable or separable. The fact of differential historical experiences means that each "woman" differs from every other and it is impossible or meaningless to talk of the "authentic woman" and so to unify different individuals under the signifier "woman". There is no woman's (or of course man's) experience, situation or point of view. As a result, it is difficult to make sense of feminist projects of collective emancipation. For who is to be emancipated, and from whom? The sort of perspective in question leads to a view of a world containing only differences, an individualist perspective in which it is impossible to make much sense of any system or collectivity, whether oppressive or otherwise.

This postmodernist critique of (interpretations of) early gender theorising contains much insight and can indeed be read in part as a corrective of the excesses or errors of naive essentialist positions. However, the critique itself is ultimately not satisfactory in that it loses the central insight of the earlier feminist contribution entirely. For according to the logic of this critique there is no basis for systematic forces of societal discrimination. Yet it cannot really be denied that there are systematic forms of domination in society as we experience it, and in particular that (individuals classified as) biological females are very often dominated or oppressed by (those classified as) males, and in ways that have little if anything to do with sexual as opposed to social differences.

Put differently, the postmodernist critique, in highlighting the problems of essentialism, loses the insight for which gender analysis was originally formulated, namely the discrimination of individuals classified as "women" in ways that have little direct relation to biological constitution or actual capacities. If it is widely recognised that there are many types of differences between members of society, specifically between those classified as men and women, we need to attend to ways of disentangling rather than neglecting the types that there are.

Such considerations suggest that what is needed is a conception of gender that can sustain both (1) the (widely recognised) feature of our world that gender is an objective category that (currently) marks the site of domination of one (gendered) group by another, as well as (2) the insights underpinning the noted criticisms of early gender theorising, specifically the fragmented experiences of us all and the difficulties of partialling out the gendered aspects of our experiences.

What is needed is a conception that can sustain the insight that we all are different, that our experiences and identities are historically, geographically and culturally, etc., variable and indeed unique, as well as the deep intuition that there is a need for, and legitimacy to, as well indeed as a basis for, collective organisation and struggle.

The ontological conception I defend, I believe, can precisely explain the simultaneous existence of both the sorts of differences to which postmodernists point, as well as an objective basis to systematic discrimination. That is, it can simultaneously make sense of the insights of both gender theorists and gender sceptics.

The key to combining both sets of insights lies in recognising ontological distinctions between social structure, human agency and practice. These distinctions allow that individuals can indeed have unique, including fragmented, experiences and social identities, and yet be conditioned (and facilitated) by relatively enduring, if always space–time specific, social structures, including internally related positions, and associated rights and practices, that allow the systematic subjugation or oppression of some by others.

For if the continually reproduced and transformed social structures, comprising networks of internally related positions and associated rights and obligations, provide the sites, the objective bases, for forms of discrimination, it warrants emphasis that there is no one-to-one mapping from social structure to individual pathways, experience or personal identities.

Furthermore, each individual occupies many positions simultaneously, and life is a unique path of entering and exiting positions. So the perspective sustained is quite consistent with the insight of multiple or fragmented experiences.

Of course, the fact of systematic discrimination presupposes there is nevertheless a way or sense in which some individuals, whatever their experiences, are nevertheless marked as similar (and different from some others). The markers can be age, skin colour, language, accent and a host of other (actual or perceived) human qualities.

Gender, I suggest, is bound up with one such system of identification and differentiation, one that (as it happens in seemingly all societies so far) serves to privilege some over others (as I say, the conception of gender that I go on to elaborate is found in Lawson, 2007).

Of course, all this is rather quick and schematic. But it ought to be sufficient to indicate that, in managing to accommodate and account for empirical generalities that most commentators believe are valid, yet which many have also presented as being mutually oppositional and contradictory, critical realism extends the groundedness of its claims to explanatory power at precisely the point of underlabouring for the relevant branch of social theory.

My claim, then, is that there are various ways the conception I defend does shed light at the level of substantive puzzles and tensions, and in doing so gains, in each case, in explanatory groundedness. If all such cases are considered together, I think the conception is seen to be grounded indeed.

## Transcendental reasoning

Davidsen largely overlooks this aspect of my output, and so its contribution to providing support for the philosophical conception to which I hold. But even if we leave such explanatory interventions aside, it seems to me that the conception I defend in any case receives adequate grounding more directly, from the use of transcendental arguments.

Indeed, in the longish chapter 2 of *Reorienting Economics* I provide a good deal of direct grounding for the conception in question by way of carrying out transcendental deductions. The latter are actually rather similar to the explanatory exercises sketched above. The difference is mainly that, for the transcendental arguments, I have sought initiating premises that describe generalities that appear likely to be relatively non-contentious, whereas in resolving explanatory questions of the sort described above I start from context specific puzzles and principles as are thrown up in substantive analyses.

After all, some commentators will no doubt dispute (or anyway refuse to acknowledge) the observation that the mainstream project continually fails by its own criteria (even though this observation is regularly repeated by leading proponents of that project). And, I doubt that disagreement or puzzles concerning the theorising of gender and discrimination constitute a starting point that will appeal to the intuitions or interests of all contributors to methodological debate in modern economics.

Certainly, I anticipate that there will be more agreement about the generalised (if, on reflection, often still somewhat puzzling) features of experience that, in *Reorienting Economics*, I use to initiate the transcendental deductions. These include the observations that despite the complexity of social reality much of social life is routinised (presupposing social structure in the form of social rules), that different sorts of people follow different practices, with their practices often oriented to those of other groups (presupposing internal relations connecting positions with rules attached), that social structure and agency each depend on and influence (but neither create or wholly determine) the other (presupposing that structure and agency are reproduced through practice), and so on.

As I say, I have devoted a good deal of space to defending the ontological conception in question in *Reorienting Economics*, starting with such seemingly (relatively) non-contentious generalised features of experience, and demonstrating that the conception in question can explain them. In this way, I suggest the ontological conception achieves a reasonable grounding.

So, I am interested to examine Davidsen's reasons for rejecting my claims that the conception I defend is grounded. Above I indicate something of this conception's explanatory power with respect to substantive puzzles. In *Reorienting Economics*, as I say, I take myself to have grounded the conception by way of transcendental arguments. Why then does Davidsen demur? Davidsen does not seem to pay very much attention to the sorts of explanatory contributions referred to above, but does reference the transcendental arguments of *Reorienting Economics* and elsewhere. Why then does he suppose that these in particular fail?

## Davidsen's resistance

In fact, Davidsen does not address my arguments for grounding the ontological conception in question at all. Rather the only problem he really points to is that there are others who do not accept the validity of my case.

Davidsen first notes that the ontological conception I defend is acknowledged as being fallible, and he infers (as indeed I have often made clear) that given the use that I have made of it, I myself must take it to be the most explanatorily grounded conception available. Davidsen suggests, though, that some others seem not to share this evaluation:

> Assessments made by commentators upon the critical realist project within economics, however, do not bolster this favourable evaluation. In the literature pertaining to and commenting upon the development of the critical realist project in economics, there are examples of outright repudiations, or else severe critical appraisals, of the ontological theory invoked.

I suspect Davidsen would agree that, if the aim is to justify some position, it is not good enough merely to claim the support of some "authority". For example it would not constitute a defence of my position to list some of those who are convinced by it. But it is equally insufficiently undermining of a position to indicate instances of lack of support. I have to say that most doubters of the sort to whom Davidsen makes reference seem merely assertive in their scepticism. As a result, we are mostly faced with little more than declarations of dissent.

The critic that Davidsen supposes "has made the most adequate characterisation" of the ontological theory I defend is Jack Vromen. As the Vromen paper in question is included in the current volume, and is followed by my response to his criticisms, I shall not repeat the latter here, except to say I do not find a telling case.

## The real basis of Davidsen's concern?

But to seek to expand, or even clarify further the nature of, the defence of my position at this stage would likely be beside the point anyway. For, as I say, Davidsen seems to think that what counts most in legitimising the application of the theory is not the latter's revealed explanatory power or adequacy (as indicated by the calibre or extent of argumentation or evidence in its favour), but its status in terms of what others think of it. In fact, a close reading of Davidsen reveals, here and there, that his evaluation of the conception I defend is not actually that different from my own. Thus, he writes:

> From all this we should not draw the conclusion that there is necessarily something wrong or defective accruing to the ontological theory of critical realism. What is at stake here is the question of what status or credibility we can reasonably ascribe to this theory, and the implications of such evaluations for the future development of a critical realist project within economics. In my view, the ontological theory of critical realism seems intuitively sensible and of potential interest for scientific work within the realm of economics. I do also accept that the transcendental arguments offered in favour of it, in spite of their deficiencies, lend some support to the theory, a support that is further strengthened by invoked practical examples and illustrations. However, and crucially, advocates of the critical realist project within economics have so far failed to produce anything like a decisive or broadly accepted set of arguments.

Except for the unexplained reference to certain "deficiencies" and the asserted lack of "a decisive" set of arguments at the end, this passage could be summarised by saying that Davidsen is convinced by the arguments for the ontological conception in question but notes "crucially" that others are not.

When is an argument decisive? Davidsen does not say. Nor, to repeat, does he identify any deficiencies. But everything else he does add in his chapter seems to elaborate the claim of there being a "lack of broad acceptance" of the conception in question.

In fact, this may even be Davidsen's real concern with my defence of the ontological conception in question: that the problem is not whether the argument is correct, but that in making it I have failed to be sufficiently persuasive.

Let me concentrate on this a little further just to convey how important the idea of generalised acceptance is to Davidsen's evaluation of whether or not the ontological conception should be considered sufficiently justified for purposes of underlabouring.

Two features that Davidsen draws out from his reading of *Reorienting Economics* are first that I seek to engage the mainstream, and second that I argue that the heterodox groups are best conceived as divisions of labour in one overall project, and that there are likely gains to be had here from linked or co-development. Fundamental to this unification, I argue, is a common set of ontological presuppositions.

Davidsen's criticism is not that I am wrong in my argumentation in all this, but that I fail to solicit any meaningful response from the mainstream, or to gain much positive assent for my arguments from the heterodox traditions. Actually, Davidsen qualifies the latter assertion in considering the response of some branches of heterodoxy. However, he imagines that I expected more, and offers an explanation of my failure and presumed disappointment.[4] Davidsen's suggested explanation relates to the mainstream and heterodox responses separately. So, let me consider each in turn.

## The mainstream and ontology

Davidsen first considers how the conception I defend bears on the mainstream project. His main point here is that mainstream economists will ignore my critique just because they are not concerned with ontological issues. Rather they have their own alternative more "pragmatic" criteria such as "formal consistency, elegance, simplicity, tractability, and more generally 'what works'".

I certainly agree that mainstream economists prioritise criteria such as formal consistency, elegance, simplicity and tractability (although I am not sure they have a category of "what works" that is additional to, or makes reference to something other than, these sorts of attributes). I also agree that mainstream economists, by and large, are not concerned in any explicit way with ontological issues. Indeed, I suspect most have little idea that there exist (ontological) limits to the explanatory usefulness of the mathematical-deductivist methods they insist upon.

If this is so, then I further agree that we may find it rather difficult to make significant headway through ontological discussion with committed members of the mainstream. But what follows? Not that the account I defend is thereby erroneous. In any case, there certainly is an audience at the level of PhD students currently undergoing mainstream training. Here I experience openness and engagement regularly. A few even totally transform the direction of their research. I regard these few cases as sufficient in themselves to justify the emphasis I (and numerous others) have been taking.

Davidsen continues by posing the following question: even should "mainstream economists in [the] near future [be] persuaded to consider how questions of ontology might impinge upon their work" are there any reasons to suppose that the ontological conception that I defend would be the one accepted?

There can be no guarantee that the conception I defend would, in such circumstances, be accepted. But a first question to ask is why does that matter? Currently the mainstream is unreflective about ontology. If this changed, if the goal of getting an explanatorily powerful ontological conception really mattered to the people involved and indeed was prioritised, I suspect that (mathematical-deductivist) methods carrying the current presuppositions of closure and isolated atoms would not be retained for long. Equally, if an ontology-sensitive (significant) body of thinkers found reason to accept an alternative conception to my own, there would presumably be good reason for this.

Moreover, were an alternative conception to be widely defended we could hopefully evaluate which is the more explanatorily powerful of the two, or perhaps advance dialectically to a third conception incorporating the insights of both. Naive though I know it seems to some in this postmodern age, I am not nearly as wedded to any existing conception as I am to the search for truth. My assessment, however, is that it is the search for truth that is unfortunately the primary casualty in the current mainstream's efforts to control everything that happens in the economics academy.

Still this is all rather speculative. Whatever an ontologically informed mainstream might do, I see no reason in such speculations to lose faith in what seems to me the most grounded ontological conception available so far, or in the sorts of uses I have made of it.

## Heterodoxy and ontology

Next Davidsen turns to explain (what he interprets as) the heterodox reluctance to accept the ontological conception I defend as a basis for uniting the various separate heterodox traditions. As already noted, in *Reorienting Economics* and elsewhere, I argue that the heterodox groups are best conceived as divisions of labour in one overall ontologically oriented project, and that there are likely gains from linked development here. As I say, Davidsen does acknowledge that this argument and assessment has been taken up in some quarters, but he is keen to explain why (his assessment of) the degree to which it has been accepted is less than (apparently he) expected.

His explanation is effectively that prominent heterodox figures will be threatened by the thought of linking with other traditions, with the process likely bringing a loss of identity (and thereby, Davidsen might have added, a loss of academic status or power). Davidsen expresses his explanation as follows:

> [In respect to the question of] solicitations with heterodox positions the question of identity needs to be addressed. Will the identity of the respective heterodox schools of thought, some of them well established since ages, be preserved if they were to join up with other positions in a linked co-development based upon critical realist ontology? If the prospects for identity retainment are considered dim, how would this fact affect adherents of the respective programmes and positions? In my view, possible dissenting and opposing attitudes stemming from such considerations should not be underestimated.

Some individuals closely associated with specific heterodox traditions clearly do resist aspects of analyses such as my own for dubious reasons (whether or not good reasons for doing so exist). Notably, some resist unification where they anticipate an undermining of the exclusivity of their position. This is what Davidsen is getting at.

But the feature that Davidsen is pointing to here is not a set of flaws in, or lack of grounding for, my argument (whether or not my argument holds) but an aspect of human psychology, and the fact that the academy involves a good deal of power play, just like any other institution. I am sure he is right to do so. But who knows how things will pan out? We all adopt different strategies. The point, though, is that there is nothing in all this to undermine the ontological conception I defend, or the uses to which it has been put.[5]

In short, Davidsen worries that the ontological conception in question does not command from others the degree of support I would like. But even if this were true, it has little to do with the justification of the conception I defend (any more than the support of mainstream economists for the notion that their mathematical-deductivist approach is scientifically grounded means that it is so grounded). As a result, I see no reason to curtail activities of the underlabouring sort that I, along with various others, have undertaken.

## Scientific ontology

Davidsen, we have seen, is resistant to underlabouring activity of the sort I pursue, just because he worries that the philosophical ontology drawn upon in this is not (considered to be) grounded. I have indicated that such worries are unjustified. I want now to suggest that Davidsen's proposed alternative project is actually similar to a strand of my own research, and that, if so, in the end it can itself be seen to rest for its efficacy precisely on the requirement that the ontological conception under discussion is indeed grounded. For at one point Davidsen writes of the desirability of producing "critical realist domain-specific ontological theories". He does not expand overly upon this conception, but it seems similar to a project that I and some others are pursuing under the heading of *scientific ontology*.[6] If it is the same thing, then, as I say, for it to be used to guide substantive research (in the manner Davidsen seems to suggest) the groundedness of critical realism must first be accepted. Let me briefly elaborate, indicating first what I mean by scientific ontology.

Most of the ontological discussion in my published writings has concerned *philosophical ontology*, the study of the properties of phenomena of a domain of reality. According to the philosophical ontological account I defend, social phenomena bear the properties of being produced in open systems, possessing emergent powers or properties, being structured, internally related, processual and so forth.

*Scientific ontology*, in contrast, is concerned with studying the nature, including properties, of particular entities or categories of a specific domain regarded at a point in time as significant (for example, money, markets, firms, social rules, gender, race or class).

With scientific ontology (as is the case with philosophical ontology), there is no unique way of proceeding. However, given my current assessment of the relative groundedness of the philosophical ontology systematised as critical realism, one obvious procedure has been to render the conceptions of money, markets, technology, etc., consistent with it (see Lawson, 2004).

Even so, such a strategy is insufficient to characterise fully any particular entity of category. An additional step has been the (empirically controlled) transformation of pre-existing, seriously sustained, conceptions of the categories of interest, by way of immanent critiques, determinate negations and dialectical sublations or syntheses, as seems appropriate in the relevant context. My own most recent contributions to scientific ontology include, for example, accounts of gender (Lawson, 2007), institutions (2006) and social evolution (2003, chapter 5).[7]

As I say, scientific ontology appears to be the sort of research that Davidsen is advocating, especially when he talks of developing "domain-specific ontological theories" that:

> will furnish more specific guidelines for activities directed towards conducting critical realist analyses of substantial economics issues and phenomena. They will supply precepts for more specific critical realist-informed economic theorising and for empirical work within the domain in question.

For reasons already given, I remain resistant to the idea of talking of specifically "critical realist analyses of substantial economics issues" and such like (though the phrase "critical realist-informed" is certainly appropriate). And I recognise that, at times, Davidsen implies that his own goal is substantive (or scientific or "more concrete") theorising (as opposed to "domain-specific ontological theories"). However, he mostly emphasises the seeking of domain-specific ontological theories, and, significantly, he seems explicit that he expects this latter ontological project to stop short of providing (substantive) scientific theories; or at least he is clear that such a project "would not determine work at the scientific level":

> It should be noted, moreover, that even if general and domain-specific ontological theories were envisaged as providing guidelines for the development of economic theories and analyses, and thus influence the direction and focus of scientific work within this critical realist scheme, they would not determine work at the scientific level.

Rather, the proposed ontological theories may ground alternative economic theories or analyses. Systematic ontological reflection thus would not render scientific activities directed towards developing more concrete theories or models superfluous. It would, however, provide a more secure and relevant foundation for this kind of activity.

Clearly, if Davidsen is not proposing exercises in scientific ontology he is, much of the time at least, suggesting something similar.

## The status of scientific ontology

If Davidsen is proposing to guide substantive theorising by way of "domain-specific ontology" (where I am supposing that the latter is something like scientific ontology), the obvious question to be asked is: in virtue of what is he able to assert (as in the previous passage extracted) that "the proposed ontological theories may ground altern- ative economic theories or analyses"? And in virtue of what is he able to conclude that: "Systematic ontological reflection" […] [would] provide a more secure and relevant foundation for this kind of activity"?

I suggest Davidsen has no basis to make such claims unless he is after all implicitly accepting that the philosophical ontology being drawn upon in all this, namely critical realism, is more securely grounded than he is letting on.

Critical realism is a theory about the nature or properties of social phenomena. As such, it can, as Davidsen supposes, be brought to bear on the elaboration of social scientific *categories*, that is, brought to the service of scientific ontology. It can influence the selection between definitions of such categories to the extent that only one of a few of the competing con- ceptions are consistent with it. Or, where none sit easily with critical realism, perhaps a dialectical resolution of competing categories is feas- ible to arrive at new conceptions consistent with critical realism. The fun- damental point in all this, though, is that it seems worthwhile embarking on this path of rendering some conception consistent with the ontology of critical realism only if critical realism is first considered to be grounded. Otherwise why bother? It is the (achieved) prior support for this philosophical ontology that renders worthwhile the employment of the latter in elaborating specific scientific categories like profits, money, markets, gender and so forth.

Of course, even if critical realism is recognised as being sufficiently grounded, the question remains as to how these scientific ontological contributions, if so derived, can themselves be of help. The most promis- ing answer (perhaps ironically for Davidsen given his reluctance to promote it) is as a form of philosophical underlabouring. Matters here are not straightforward though; for it is not yet transparent that scientific ontology can itself be interpreted as something that can legitimately provide further guidance. If it can be, the case for this has yet to be made.

## Scientific ontology as underlabouring

I think scientific ontology can serve as a form of underlabouring in two ways or senses: in a weaker sense and in a stronger one. First, any conception elaborated (say of money, the market, gender, etc.) can be offered for illustrative purposes only: to illustrate how the insights of a particular preferred philosophical ontological conception might be used to transform existing accounts of the categories in question. Or, more strongly, a conception achieved may be defended as the seeming most grounded or otherwise sustainable account of the relevant specific category (market, money, institution, etc.), and in effect offered up to others pursuing more substantive questions of cause and effect, or whatever, but who are not concerned to elaborate relevant categories themselves.

The application of scientific ontology in either manner can be interpreted as philosophical underlabouring (though not warranting being identified as critical realist or as being necessarily associated with any other supporting philosophical ontology [even if presupposing it and having been constructed through drawing on its insights] because alternative accounts of the social category elaborated might also have been derived consistent with the same philosophical ontology). Of course, to underlabour in the second (stronger) sense is simultaneously to underlabour in the first (weaker) sense. For even if specific conceptions derived are rejected by any reader, the process of derivation may prove instructive none-the-less.[8]

In some cases of scientific ontological research, a grounding for the ontological conception drawn upon can be achieved by way of first resolving tensions or problems in the literature relating to the socio-scientific category being elaborated (as in my own research on gender discussed above).[9] However, this way of achieving grounding "on the job", as it were, will not always be possible. Where it seems infeasible, the researcher may start out by seeking merely to develop conceptions of, say, institutions, social rules, technology, etc., consistent with critical realism (or whatever the preferred philosophical conception). And this seems to me to be precisely the sort of contribution that Davidsen himself is proposing. But it is a reasonable way to proceed only if it is thought that the ontological conception utilised is already grounded. Thus, it seems to me, Davidsen, certainly no less than I in my own underlabouring activities, needs to know that the philosophical ontological conception he favours is justified in advance of some of the uses to which he wishes it put.

In any case, it should be clear that Davidsen's proposed project, so interpreted, is not something I wish to avoid; indeed I am involved in something at least very similar (even if I am more circumspect about referring to the more substantive aspects as critical realist). And to the point, it is clear that our seemingly shared goal of elaborating social categories through drawing upon philosophical ontological insights (as well as the making use of these derived categories to guide more substantive economics), presupposes the prior grounding of this philosophical ontological conception (no less than do the other uses to which this conception has been put). Fortunately, grounding for the ontological conception drawn upon seems, in the end, to be well established after all; so herein, there lies no problem for Davidsen's preferred programme.

## Final comments

Despite Davidsen's belief that he and I adopt quite different orientations, and despite, too, my reasonably lengthy reply, I must emphasise, finally, that I concur with much of Davidsen's analysis and interpretation of my position; many other commentaries on my work are not nearly so coherent with my own understanding of it.

Only at a few critical points do we diverge, and then perhaps unnecessarily. *Prima facie*, the most fundamental difference between us stems from disagreement as to the extent to which the ontological conception we both draw upon is grounded. Davidsen implies that it receives insufficient grounding for the uses I make of it, and consequently urges a somewhat more cautious orientation. But he does not really make a case for doubting that the conception in question is grounded and some of his comments suggest that he actually accepts its validity. Rather, on close examination, Davidsen's main concern appears to be that various others do not accept the conception as their own. I am not sure the wider reception of the ontological arguments in question is precisely as Davidsen presents it. But even if it is, this is not yet a reason for treating the ontological conception in question as though it is mere conjecture (any more than widespread support would by itself demonstrate that it is well grounded).

Davidsen also seems to think that I do not seek in any way to support substantive work. I hope I have demonstrated sufficiently that this is not so. If Davidsen believes that individual substantive success would help ground the ontological conception I defend, I believe he is mistaken. Otherwise, our ideas of what can be achieved in this direction seem similar.

In any case, Davidsen makes many good points. Despite his fears, it is the case that an ontological conception that is fallible, and perhaps not accepted by everyone, can yet be grounded. Moreover, his proposed alternative programme seems to require that the ontological conception on which it draws is itself much more than mere conjecture. Perhaps this realisation, along with a recognition that the ontological conception in question is after all relatively grounded, will induce Davidsen into considering whether (instead of my narrowing the range of underlabouring activities in which I engage) he himself might perhaps broaden his own important proposals for working for a more relevant discipline of economics.

## Notes

1   The interpretation of philosophy as an underlabourer for science originates with John Locke. It is found, albeit almost as an aside, in the "Epistle to the Reader" of his *An Essay Concerning Human Understanding*, where Locke writes:

> The commonwealth of learning is not at this time without master-builders, whose mighty designs, in advancing the sciences, will leave lasting monuments to the admiration of posterity; but everyone must not hope to be a *Boyle* or a *Sydenham*; and in an age that produces such masters as the great *Huygenius* and the incomparable Mr. *Newton*, with some others of that strain, it is ambition enough to be employed as the under-labourer in clearing the ground a little, and removing some of the rubbish that lies in the way to knowledge.
>
> (Locke, 1985 [1690])

This assessment does indeed express my own conception of the role and possibilities of philosophy. As the extract reproduced makes clear, underlabouring for science is not the same as doing science. Rather philosophy, on this conception, is about clearing obstacles to science, about clarifying possibilities and limits and the like. Thus, as Davidsen intimates, I do draw the line of my philosophical contribution somewhere short of actually doing substantive science (see especially, Lawson, 2005).

2   Let me belabour the point somewhat, because it is important, and the misunderstandings to which I point do arise too easily. An example of the sort of would-be criticism that I have in mind is provided by Geoffrey Hodgson (2004). In *Economics and Reality* (1997), I illustrate explanatory work that is consistent with the approach I defend, in the context of examining the nature of the relative industrial decline of the British economy over the century or so up until the 1980s. Hodgson is a good example to focus on here because he has clearly spent a good deal of time on my contributions and is cautious enough not to claim too much in making his criticisms. Thus, he notes that I label the relevant chapter "Illustrations", which I do precisely to make sure no one could interpret me as claiming more for the examples provided. Hodgson even reproduces the following passage from this chapter:

> Substantive explanations, then, even when serving illustrative purposes, ought not be tagged "critical realist". Nor, incidentally, should they be interpreted as constituting evidence by which the critical realist explanatory framework is itself to be assessed [...] In short, the examples and discussion which follow merely provide [...] an indication that explanatory endeavours consistent with critical realism are feasible in the social realm.
>
> (Lawson, 1997, p. 326)

And Hodgson also notes various other remarks I make in an effort to warn the reader that the focus of the chapter is merely illustrative and partial, and that the example provided in no way follows necessarily from the critical realist perspective I defend.

Despite all this Hodgson seems to think he can criticise critical realism by focusing on the illustration already mentioned. He even entitles his piece "Some claims made for Critical Realism" (rather than say "Some Illustrations of…"), and in his abstract represents himself as raising "important questions concerning the claims made for critical realism on behalf of its adherents".

How does he proceed? He makes but one "argument" against me. It is that explanations of relative industrial decline in Britain that compete with (or anyway differ from) the one I use as an illustration, are not only feasible but may also be consistent with critical realism.

But this is no argument against me or critical realism at all. I have always accepted and indeed emphasised that this is so, as have others; even theories shown to be explanatorily the most grounded are likely in due course to be superseded by theories that are more grounded still. All may be consistent with critical realism.

Hodgson sums up the relevant section of his paper as follows:

> The contentious claim is that the workplace organization thesis is somehow an "illustration" here of critical realism. But the point here is that critical realism could just as well be illustrated by other explanations, including some that Lawson chooses to ignore or reject. My argument here is not that the chosen theory is right or wrong, but that after some suitably critical realist tests, critical realism is consistent with a variety of rival explanations of the British decline, and gives us inadequate guidance to choose one "illustration" over another. As a result, Lawson's notion of an "illustration" of critical realism itself becomes severely weakened.

I imagine the weakness of the logic here is evident to all. According to Hodgson: I choose one example to illustrate. I could have chosen others. Therefore my example is not an illustration after all, or its power of illustrating is somehow "severely weakened". On this sort of reasoning, I doubt anything could ever be used for purposes of illustration.

Hodgson further writes: "In fact, critical realism gives us no reason to exclude or belittle alternative explanations." Quite so. It is substantive work that gives us reasons to do this, not a philosophical theory (even if the substantive work is informed by critical realism). Critical realism will never show that some substantive theories are more empirically grounded than others, nor lead us to any one specific explanation; as I say substantive theorising does.

My point in taking this detour, to repeat, is that if a someone like Hodgson, despite noting some of my numerous qualifications, can base a whole article on such a mistake, we can imagine the mayhem that is likely if substantive theories are labelled critical realist just because they are constructed by social theorists informed by critical realism.

3 Perhaps a related example I might mention here (and hope to develop on a future occasion) is that critical realism, more than any other project of which I am aware, can make sense of (i.e. explain) the repeated, but typically untheorised, call for, and continuing activity of, interdisciplinary research. Although vocal support for the latter is often found, rarely is the case for it made. Critical realism, though, straightforwardly grounds the case for inter- (and cross-, and multi- and post-) disciplinary research. For according to the ontological conception in question social reality is open meaning that phenomena are the result of a multiplicity of varying mechanisms. And these mechanisms will be of varying types and so the objects of study of different disciplines (or sub-disciplines). How the different mechanisms combine in producing outcomes will always depend on context. We can think of an incapacitating illness with

a patient suffering not only the direct consequences of some affliction but (additional) physical, psychological, financial, social, ethical and other problems or difficulties, as a result of complications, worry, being unable to carry on working, not wanting to impose caring responsibilities on others and so on. Understanding the patient's situation will clearly necessitate interdisciplinary attention. But then so will the attempt to provide more than a very partial understanding of any real world phenomenon. From the perspective of critical realism it is easy to understand the continuing attention to interdisciplinary research, at least by individual researchers, despite the lack of encouragement and opportunities in most academic departments, and indeed seemingly reduced promotion prospects for those that undertake it.

4   My own reaction is that, whilst I perhaps expected little from established mainstream practitioners (as opposed to graduate students), and have indeed witnessed not much more than I expected, I am hugely inspired by the positive reactions of many contributors to the various heterodox traditions. For example, I personally find very gratifying the invitations I receive to talk about these matters at international meetings of the different heterodox groups (both in Europe and elsewhere), and even to teach on the topic in question at summer schools and the like. (As I pen these lines, in fact, I am about to leave for Mexico to give invited lectures at a summer school on Gender and Macro Economics in a session entitled "the links between feminist economics and other heterodox traditions".)

5   Davidsen does voice some further concerns, like wondering how, if some heterodox groups did not share the ontological conception I defend, I would justify their giving up their own conception and accepting that which I put forward.

My answer is that such action would be justified only if it could be shown that the ontological conception I defend were more explanatorily powerful than their preferred alternative. Indeed, to the extent that strands of heterodoxy have adopted alternative meta-theories, my strategy has indeed been to argue the advantages of the conception I defend (see part III of *Reorienting Economics*).

But of course, I think this is mostly a counterfactual consideration, just because I do believe, and think I have shown, that most strands of heterodox economics do indeed hold (albeit implicitly) to the ontological conception in question.

I do not here want to run through the arguments for this contention again. But a point I do want to stress is that the case for linked development of heterodox research is not an a priori suggestion, but an a posteriori assessment of the actual prevailing situation of modern economics. And nor even is it an a posteriori assessment after the fact of constructing a specific ontological theory. The ontological conception I defend has at least three types of grounding for me. One is the philosophical defence provided in *Reorienting Economics* and elsewhere. A second is the resonance that it has with understandings I have held to be the case for as long as I can remember. But a third is that it is a conception that I have found to be presupposed in the most compelling parts of heterodox thinking over a long period of engaging with heterodox traditions.

Indeed, Davidsen will remember that he and I used to meet fairly regularly at heterodox events going way back, events that regularly threw up questions like "What are we doing?"; "Are we coherent?"; "What connects this heterodox group to that one?"; and so forth. My various claims for ontology in this context express my own answers to such questions. The mere fact that my answers in part emerged in this way, because of endless engagements with heterodox contributors, does not make them right, of course. But what I am hoping to convey is that they have emerged organically. I have not been involved with deriving a philosophical theory and then wilfully distorting the heterodox perspectives to make them fit (that is, I have not pursued a project of "top down philosophising" as some call it). Rather my ontological assessment, as an explicit perspective, has emerged in part because of, *and through*, my long engagement with the heterodox traditions.

I repeat that I may well of course be wrong in all I argue. But to establish this Davidsen needs to provide more than a loose airing of possibilities, presented on occasion as if the associations or recommendations I make are perhaps little more than displays of speculative optimism. In any case, there is nothing yet of substance here to challenge the conception I defend or the uses I have made of it.

6   Several years ago, various associates and I instigated the Cambridge Social Ontology Group (CSOG), a research group concerned with exploring all questions of social ontology, without presupposing in advance (though equally without precluding the possibility) that one set of results or ontological conception will be found to do better in explanatory terms than competing conceptions.

This group is concerned not only with *philosophical ontology*, with exploring the properties, if any, of all social objects, but also with studying the nature of specific social phenomena or entities. This latter research, which we designate *scientific ontology*, seems to be the sort that Davidsen is advocating.

7   Examples of scientific ontology pursued within CSOG more widely include studies of money (Geoffrey Ingham, 1996, 2004); conventions (John Latsis, 2005, 2006, 2007); the region (Clive Lawson, 1999, 2003); transactions (Stephen Pratten, 1997); social order (Steven Fleetwood, 1995, 1996); collective learning (Clive Lawson, 2000); tendencies, (Stephen Pratten, 1998; Tony Lawson, 1989, 1997, 1998); households (Kanchana Ruwanpura, 2002, 2007); consciousness (Philip Faulkner, 2002); probabilities (Jochen Runde, 1996, 1998, 2001; Tony Lawson, 1988); trust (Tony Lawson, 2000); technology (Clive Lawson 2006, 2007) and metaphor (Paul Lewis, 1996).

8   It is the former less definite activity of providing weaker guidance that is so far included in CSOG's remit. I say "included" because, in principle, this is an open-ended research or discussion group that identifies itself by the sorts of (ontological) questions it pursues rather than by any specific theory accepted (such as critical realism).

Having said that, most members, as I say, are persuaded by much of critical realism. So in practice we largely investigate the nature of specific social entities accepting that they conform to the properties (openness, structure, process, internal relationality and so forth) defended in critical realism.

For whom does CSOG underlabour in this suggestive-only fashion? Currently just for the individual members of the very same group, for it is the latter that have drawn on the philosophical ontological insights developed and utilised them in further more categorical work. Specifically, as noted above, individual members have themselves set out and defended various scientific-ontological categories.

In putting these latter contributions in the public domain, individual members of CSOG, *qua individuals*, are, I suppose, underlabouring in the stronger (as well as of course the weaker) sense. Perhaps in the future CSOG will also be doing the stronger form of scientific-ontological underlabouring as a group.

9   I repeat, though, it is only after the ontological conception I defend is shown to have explanatory power (relative to alternative philosophical conceptions)

with respect to generalised features (puzzles or tensions) of the relevant domain, that I use it to suggest a conception of gender consistent with it. And even if I eventually do advance a (scientific-ontological) conception of gender that I believe is empirically grounded, and as sustainable as any competing conception of which I am aware, and so is offered up not only as a viable conception, but also (more weakly) as an illustration of how the ontology I defend might be applied, I see good reason to avoid designating it critical realist and to emphasise that alternative conceptions consistent with this philosophical theory are likely feasible.

# References

Bordo, Susan (1993) "Feminism, Post Modernism and Gender Scepticism", in *Unbearable Weight: Feminism, Western Culture, and the Body*, Regents of the University of California; reprinted in Anne C. Herrmann and Abigail Stewart (eds), (1994), *Theorizing Feminism: Parallel Trends in the Humanities and Social Sciences*, Boulder, San Francisco and Oxford: Westview Press, 458–481.

Chodorow, Nancy (1978) *The Reproduction of Mothering: Psychoanalysis and the Sociology of Gender*, Berkley, CA: University of California Press.

Faulkner, Philip (2002) "Some Problems with the Conception of the Human Subject in Critical Realism", *Cambridge Journal of Economics*, 26(6), pp. 739–751.

Fleetwood, Stephen (1995) *Hayek's Political Economy: The Socio Economics of Order*, London: Routledge.

Fleetwood, Stephen (1996) "Order without Equilibrium: A Critical Realist Interpretation of Hayek's Notion of Spontaneous Order", *Cambridge Journal of Economics*, 20(6), pp. 729–747.

Hodgson, Geoffrey (2004) "Some Claims Made for Critical Realism in Economics: Two Case Studies", *Journal of Economic Methodology*, 11(1), March, pp. 71–91.

Ingham, Geoffrey (1996) "Money is a Social Relation", *Review of Social Economy*, LIV, Winter, pp. 507–530. Reprinted in Fleetwood, S. (ed.), (1999), *Critical Realism in Economics: Development and Debate*, London: Routledge, pp. 103–124.

Ingham, Geoffrey (2004) *The Nature of Money*, Cambridge: Polity Press.

Keller, Evelyn Fox (1985) *Reflections on Gender and Science*, New Haven, CT: Yale University Press.

Latsis, John S. (2005) "Is there Redemption for Conventions?", *Cambridge Journal of Economics*, 29(5), pp. 707–727.

Latsis, John S. (2006) "Convention and Intersubjectivity: New Developments in French Economics", *Journal for the Theory of Social Behaviour*, 36(3), pp. 255–277.

Latsis, John S. (2007) "Conventions and Exemplars: An Alternative Conceptual Framework", *EconomiX Working Papers*.

Lawson, Clive (1999) "Towards a Competence Theory of the Region", *Cambridge Journal of Economics*, 23(2), pp. 151–166.

Lawson, Clive (2000) "Collective Learning and Epistemologically Significant Moments", in David Keeble and Frank Wilkinson (eds), *High-Technology Clusters Networking and Collective Learning in Europe*, Aldershot: Ashgate, pp. 182–198.

Lawson, Clive (2003) "Technical Consultancies and Regional Competencies", in Charles Dannreuther and Wilfred Dolfsma (eds), *Globalisation, Social Capital and Inequality*, Cheltenham: Edward Elgar.

Lawson, Clive (2006) "Technology, Technological Determinism and the Transformational Model of Technical Activity", in Clive Lawson, John Latsis and Nuno Martins (eds), (2006), *Contributions to Social Ontology*, London and New York: Routledge, pp. 32–49.

Lawson, Clive (2007) "Technology", in M. Hartwig (ed.), *A Dictionary of Critical Realism*, London: Routledge.

Lawson, Tony (1988) "Probability and Uncertainty in Economic Analysis", *Journal of Post Keynesian Economics*, 11(1), pp. 38–65.

Lawson, Tony (1989) "Abstraction, Tendencies and Stylised Facts: A Realist Approach to Economic Analysis", *Cambridge Journal of Economics*, 13(1), March, pp. 59–78. Reprinted in Tony Lawson, Gabriel Palma and John Sender (eds), (1989), *Kaldor's Political Economy*, London and San Diego: Academic Press. Also reprinted in Paul Ekins and Manfred Max-Neef (eds), (1992), *Real-Life Economics: Understanding Wealth Creation*, London: Routledge, pp. 21–37.

Lawson, Tony (1997) *Economics and Reality*, London: Routledge.

Lawson, Tony (1998) "Tendencies", in J. Davis, W. Hands and U. Mäki (eds), *The Edward Elgar Companion to Economic Methodology*, Cheltenham: Edward Elgar, pp. 493–498.

Lawson, Tony (2000) "Evaluating Trust, Competition and Cooperation", in Yuichi Shionoya and Kiichiro Yagi (eds), *Competition, Trust and Cooperation – A Comparative Study*, New York, Berlin and Tokyo: Springer Verlag, pp. 42–76.

Lawson, Tony (2003) *Reorienting Economics*, London and New York: Routledge.

Lawson, Tony (2004) "A Conception of Ontology", Mimeo: Cambridge.

Lawson, Tony (2005) "Philosophical Under-labouring in the Context of Modern Economics: On Aiming at Truth and Usefulness in the Meanest of Ways", in John Davis, Alain Marciano and Jochen Runde (eds), *The Elgar Companion to Economics and Philosophy*, Aldershot: Edward Elgar, pp. 322–330.

Lawson, Tony (2006) "The Nature of Institutionalist Economics", *Evolutionary and Institutional Economics Review*, 2(1), pp. 7–20.

Lawson, Tony (2007) "Gender and Social change", in Jude Brown (ed.), *The Future of Gender*, Cambridge: Cambridge University Press, pp. 136–162.

Lewis, Paul (1996) "Metaphor and Critical Realism", *Review of Social Economy*, LIV(4), pp. 487–506. Reprinted in Stephen Fleetwood (ed.), (1999), *Critical Realism in Economics: Development and Debate*, London: Routledge, pp. 38–102.

Locke, John (1985 [1690]) "An Essay Concerning Human Understanding", *An Abridgment Selected and Edited by Yolton, J.*, London and Melbourne: Dent.

Pratten, Stephen (1997) "The Nature of Transaction Cost Economics", *Journal of Economic Issues*, 31(3), pp. 781–803.

Pratten, Stephen (1998) "Marshall on Tendencies, Equilibrium and the Statical Method", *History of Political Economy*, 30(1), pp. 121–162.

Runde, Jochen (1996) "On Popper, Probabilities and Propensities", *Review of Social Economy*, 54, pp. 465–485. Reprinted in Stephen Fleetwood (ed.), (1999), *Critical Realism in Economics: Development and Debate*, London: Routledge: pp. 63–82.

Runde, Jochen (1998) "Probability, Uncertainty and Long-Term Expectations", in Philip O'Hara (ed.), *Encyclopedia of Political Economy*, London: Routledge, pp. 1189–1192.

Runde, Jochen (2001) "Chances and Choices: Notes on Probability and Belief in Economic Theory", in Uskali Mäki (ed.), (2001), *The Economic Worldview*,

Cambridge: Cambridge University Press: 132–153. Revised and extended version of a paper that originally appeared in *The Monist* 78, (1995), pp. 132–153.

Ruwanpura, Kanchana N. (2002) Social Transformations in East Sri Lanka: A Feminist Economic Reading of Female Headship, Ethnicity, Gender Relations and Political Economy, PhD, Cambridge.

Ruwanpura, Kanchana N. (2007) "Shifting Theories: Partial Perspectives on the Household", *Cambridge Journal of Economics*, 31(4), pp. 525–538.

Spelman, Elizabeth V. (1990) *Inessential Woman: Problems of Exclusion in Feminist Thought*, London: Women's Press.

# 5 The nature of heterodox economics

*John B. Davis*

Tony Lawson's critique of mainstream economics is that it is everywhere formalistic and deductive, that this leads it to a closed systems approach based on identifying social event regularities, and that this is an inappropriate strategy for dealing with the subject matter with which economics is concerned (Lawson, 1997, 2003). Heterodox economics is then distinguished by its rejection of all this and by its commitment to an ontological analysis that takes social reality to be intrinsically dynamic or processual, interconnected and organic, structured, exhibits emergence, and includes value and meaning and is polyvalent (Lawson, 2006, pp. 495–496). Broadly, I agree with these conclusions. My concern is that they may be truer of economics *circa* 1980, and neither fully capture the state of economics since then, nor provide us with a sufficient understanding of the current direction of development of economics. I have previously argued that in the last two decades the economics research frontier has undergone significant transformation associated with the emergence of a collection of new research strategies, most of which criticize traditional neoclassical assumptions and originate in other sciences (Davis, 2006c; also cf. Colander *et al.*, 2004). Here, however, my goal is to discuss heterodox economics, or more specifically, the changing nature of heterodox economics and its changing relation to orthodox economics. I will argue a view I believe is largely contrary to Lawson's, namely, that: (i) heterodox economics is more heterogeneous than he and many others believe and moreover heterogeneous in ways generally not recognized by many who see themselves as heterodox, (ii) the reference of the term "heterodox economics" is quite different from what most economists, heterodox and orthodox, believe it to be, and (iii) understanding this heterogeneity is important for understanding the direction of development of current economics.[1]

## The heterogeneity of heterodox economics

Lawson and I agree that heterodox economics is a dynamic, changing phenomenon. He thus asks whether there exists a (set of) trait(s) or causal condition(s), etc., that these [different heterodox approaches] hold in common.... For if there is a set of characteristics by virtue of which any tradition qualifies as heterodox ... it is presumably included among the features, if any, that the often very differently oriented traditions share.

(Lawson, 2006, p. 484)

I argued at the 2003 Kansas City ICAPE conference (Davis, 2006a) that what most people identify as heterodox economic approaches (excluding neo-Austrian economics and related research programs) shared three specific commitments *circa* 1980:

1   rejection of the atomistic individual conception in favor of a socially embedded individual conception,
2   emphasis on time as an irreversible historical process,
3   reasoning in terms of mutual influences between individuals and social structures.

These three commitments also differentiate or draw the dividing line between orthodox or neoclassical economics and heterodox economics *circa* 1980. But neither this snapshot point-in-time contrast and identification of standard heterodox commitments, nor Lawson's focus on heterodoxy's shared commonalities, tells us very much about the dynamics of change in economics, particularly as concerns the changing relationship between what counts as orthodox and heterodox economics not just recently but also across the long history of economics. To understand these dynamics, I believe it is necessary to develop a more complex, structural analysis of heterodoxy and its relation to orthodoxy that, as in point (2) above, emphasizes the historical development of economics and changing nature of this division.[2] This structural analysis takes *research approaches* as its main units of investigation, and then examines four different ways in which both orthodox and heterodox research approaches *originate* as orthodox and heterodox respectively, and two ways in which heterodox approaches *orient* toward economics as a whole. This makes it possible to classify different research approaches as different types of dynamic phenomena that are distinguished according to their different *sources* and *directions* of development, and then go on to talk about the nature of economics as a whole in terms of how these different approaches interact. Here the analysis is applied to postwar economics, but the history of economics offers many other examples of episodes of transition regarding what counts as orthodox and heterodox that can be analyzed using this framework.[3]

Regarding how orthodox and heterodox approaches originate, the four cases set out here are formulated from the heterodox perspective in terms of how particular approaches *become* heterodox, though the framework also describes how other approaches become orthodox. In Davis and Sent (2006) these four cases are termed *origin stories*. Thus, heterodoxy arises because of:

1   failure to become orthodox following a period of pluralism,
2   loss of the status of orthodox when a new orthodoxy emerges,
3   failure to redirect orthodoxy from outside orthodoxy,
4   failure to redirect orthodoxy from inside orthodoxy.

I suggest that institutionalism might be taken as an example of (1), post Keynesianism is an example of (2), Marxism and radical political economy are examples of (3), and social economics and feminism are examples of (4).[4] Orthodoxy's origin stories, in contrast, are stories of success rather than failure. Thus the reverse of case (1), becoming orthodox following a period of pluralism, might be taken to be the story of neoclassicism's origins in the contest with institutionalism during the period of interwar pluralism (cf. Morgan and Rutherford, 1998), case (2), the successful substitution of one orthodoxy for another, might take the rise of postwar formalist neoclassicism and rejection of prewar psychologism as an example, case (3), the successful redirection of orthodoxy from outside orthodoxy, might take the rise of game theory as an example, and case (4), the successful redirection of orthodoxy from inside orthodoxy, might take the ordinalist defeat of cardinalism as an example.

Whether the interpretation of these examples is correct, of course, is subject to debate by historians of economics. Nonetheless, the history of economics seems to tell us that there are different types of origin stories for different research approaches in economics, and thus that what most people take to be heterodox economics exhibits considerably more heterogeneity when seen from this dynamic perspective than appears to be the case when point-in-time comparisons between different approaches are made.

But my argument regarding the nature of the heterogeneity of heterodox economics also addresses different heterodox approaches' *orientation* toward economics as a whole. Using a simple structural distinction between orthodox and heterodox as one between core and periphery, I suggest that heterodox approaches orient either inward or outward, that is, toward the orthodox core of the field or away from it toward the periphery of the field, where we find the field's boundaries and points of contact with other sciences.[5] Orientation toward the field's core is associated with challenging the core's own principles from the vantage point of those *same* principles. An example might be feminists' efforts in the 1980s to introduce the sexual division of labor into Gary Becker's models of the household. Orientation toward the field's periphery is a matter of placing emphasis on principles closer to other sciences beyond the field's boundaries, principles moreover that appear at any given point in time to be clearly not part of the field's core. An example might be post Keynesianism with its emphasis on uncertainty and path-dependency. Again, the examples may be debated, so that the emphasis here rests rather on differentiating heterodox approaches according to their main orientations (allowing that any approach involves a combination of inward and outward orientations).

Heterodox economics is heterogeneous, then, because different approaches differ in the ways that they combine different origin stories and different orientations. Their origin stories and orientations, that is, distinguish their different dynamics, and accordingly serve to place their point-in-time shared commitments in historical context as temporary and transient states of affairs. This is not to say that the shared commitments of different heterodox economics approaches and differences with orthodoxy *circa* 1980 are insignificant. But it does suggest that they may not identify the ways in which critique and change in economics influence the relationship between what counts as orthodox and heterodox, since on the analysis here shared commitments do not drive work within the different heterodox approaches. Indeed the implication of this treatment of heterodoxy is that often temporary structural alignments between different heterodox approaches associated with perhaps accidental shared pathways are the more likely source of change in the relationship between orthodoxy and heterodoxy. How, then, does this all apply to economics post 1980?

## Heterodox economics post 1980

I take 1980 or thereabouts to be significant for economics in that a number of new research programs began in various ways to be recognized in the mainstream. These include game theory, behavioral economics, experimental economics, evolutionary economics, neuroeconomics, and complexity economics. Other new approaches and combinations of these have emerged in their wake. With the possible exception of game theory, however, none of these new approaches has yet come to be regarded as orthodox. Orthodoxy typically requires moving from being purely a research program to being a well-established teaching program, where changes in teaching work their way from top downward through the social hierarchy of universities and top programs. Neoclassicism, of course, still dominates economics teaching (though this dominance has become more uneven as courses in experimental economics and non-linear simulation techniques are added to more and more department curricula).

But if these new research programs in economics are not orthodox, what are they? I have argued (Davis, forthcoming) that these new research programs taken as a group – though not individually – accept in varying degrees all three of the commitments of heterodox economics listed above. As these three commitments in my view and that of many others also constitute the dividing line between orthodoxy and heterodoxy *circa* 1980, these new research programs taken as a group must thus be by definition heterodox. Of course, this conclusion is not one that those who traditionally regard themselves as heterodox are in many cases inclined to accept. I believe there are two grounds for this, one that is reasonable and one that I think is not.

The reasonable grounds concern the nature of the attachment that the new research programs exhibit to the three principles of heterodoxy. Though they appear as a group to accept all three principles, no single program, it can be argued, ought to be regarded as heterodox unless it accepts all three.[6] This is a fair response if the standards of heterodox economics *circa* 1980 are to be thought good for all time. But if we accept that what counts as orthodox and heterodox is historically changing, then, as reasonable as this response may seem to many today, it seems we should also be open to the reconstitution of what counts as heterodox. Indeed, *prima facie* the new research programs in economics are heterodox in virtue of their origins *outside* of economics in other sciences. It would be a mistake, I think, to claim that the understanding of science in other fields is essentially the same as it is in economics, since why otherwise are there different sciences? Thus the emergence of the new research programs in economics presumably imports new science principles into economics. Examples include behavioral and neuroscience foundations for choice, graph-based network analysis, experimental techniques, and non-linear, non-equilibrium simulation methods. Identifying these developments as heterodox is not to say, of course, that they represent those heterodox principles most valued by those individuals who currently self-identify themselves as heterodox. Nor is it to say that these are all necessarily valuable principles for economics. The main point, as emphasized in Davis (2006c), is that what has come into economics from other sciences cannot be orthodox, at least at the outset.

The argument, on the other hand, I believe to be unreasonable for questioning the status of the new research programs as heterodox is a sociological one. Individuals in the new research programs seem to have two social characteristics. First, they frequently occupy stronger professional locations than those traditionally known as heterodox. Second, they do not consistently hold left-of-center political orientations, as do those traditionally known as heterodox (excepting neo-Austrians). Thus the inference is that they must be mainstream rather than heterodox. While as a traditional heterodox economist, I am sympathetic to both of these complaints vis-à-vis the mainstream, it seems to me that they confuse concerns with openness in the profession and progressive politics with what is involved in characterizing the difference between orthodoxy and heterodoxy in the subject matter of economics. No doubt the two issues are not completely separate, but nonetheless they also do not clearly line up when we are trying to understand the dynamics of economics as a field. The effect, moreover, of thinking sociological factors define heterodoxy is to reinforce continually the idea that there is but one single and unchanging definition of heterodoxy – *circa* 1980. Such a conviction in my view not only misses the dynamic relationship between heterodoxy and economics. It may also be argued to be anti-pluralist if it underlies an unwillingness to consider what else might not be orthodox in economics, if not traditionally heterodox.

What is the significance of these conclusions, then, for thinking about heterodoxy and the future development of economics?

## Contingencies in the future of economics

The argument above is that heterodox economics post 1980 is a complex structure, being composed of two broadly different kinds of heterodox work, each internally differentiated with a number of research programs having different historical origins and orientations: the traditional left heterodoxy familiar to most and the "new heterodoxy" resulting from other science imports. This complex structure, perhaps not surprisingly, is one in which there is relatively little cross-communication *across* the two types of heterodoxy, whereas there is considerable cross-communication across research programs *within* each of these two heterodoxies. I think there are a number of reasons for this, one being – and one not to be underestimated – the social effects of the opprobrium cast upon heterodoxy per se in fields with strong orthodox–heterodox divides, where economics is one of the worst offenders.[7] At the same time, it is still odd on the surface that there is little cross-communication between these two broad groupings, since both share a number of critiques of mainstream neoclassicism, and accordingly I want to suggest a reason for this lack of broader communication in terms of the origins and orientations analysis above, which has implications for prospective heterodox strategies vis-à-vis orthodoxy.

On the origins side, all of the new research programs in economics – the "new heterodoxy" – exhibit origin story (3); that is, as research programs *inside* economics drawing on principles originally developed *outside* economics, they are all still unsuccessful attempts to redirect economics orthodoxy from outside orthodoxy. On the orientations side, all of these new research programs in economics display an inward orientation; that is, they largely aim to change the principles reigning in orthodoxy, and do not aim to substitute new ones altogether (ironic though this may seem with their outside economics origins).[8]

By comparison, it seems to me that perhaps the only traditional heterodox research program that shares this particular combined origin and orientation is neo-Ricardian economics. Ricardian thinking has been heterodox and in the periphery of economics since marginalism supplanted classical economics. It only became an actual heterodox movement, however, after the failed attempt to redirect orthodoxy associated with the Cambridge capital controversies inspired by Sraffa's work. Also, neo-Ricardianism retains an inward orientation in that its conceptual elaboration is aimed at redeveloping and revising the framework and categories of general equilibrium theory, which are part of the orthodox core.

Of the remaining traditional heterodox research programs, the few that share periphery origin stories are all oriented toward the periphery of economics. Traditional forms of Marxism plus newer approaches such as the Re-thinking Marxism school of course want to see change in economics, but they are not interested in engagement with orthodoxy, addressing it only in critique to set off entirely different frameworks that favor closer connections with what goes on outside of the boundaries of economics. Other traditional heterodox approaches that have different origin stories are all also outward oriented. It is not revision and adjustment of the core that drives them, but its wholesale abandonment. Feminism may be an exception, since with many of its representatives having had neoclassical beginnings – thus origin story (4) – revision and adjustment of the core is still entertained by some, though this seems to have become a minority and declining position.[9]

Thus the state of affairs in economics as a whole is that orthodoxy has come into question – here I agree with Lawson – but that the two heterodox groupings both interested in changing the field have almost entirely different views about how this should happen, and accordingly have little to say to each other. Which is the correct scenario then? Most of traditional heterodoxy has clearly bet on a big scientific revolution; the new heterodoxy is rather intent on chipping away at the core on a gradualist schedule. Either scenario could be correct, but I imagine that if even most traditional heterodox economists had to make a prediction about the nature of possible future change, they would be skeptical about there being a revolution within any future they can foresee.

If this is true, then traditional heterodox economists have two choices. They can maintain their outward orientation, so that if change occurs in economics it will likely be on the terms determined by behavioral economists, experimentalists, and others in the new approaches. The risk here is that these movements may become more conservative as their success at influencing the core improves. Alternatively they can reverse their orientation, and turn to trying to shift what exists in the core, looking for allies in the "new heterodoxy" along the way, so as to improve the chances of successful change for both.[10,11]

Lawson's view of heterodoxy, in my view, does not allow this choice to emerge. As a point-in-time, shared characteristics conception, it misses the heterogeneity and dynamics of heterodoxy, both traditional and new. Moreover, by asserting, "there is a set of characteristics by virtue of which any tradition qualifies as heterodox" (Lawson, 2006, p. 484), and by associating these shared characteristics with the rejection of the core of economics, he counsels an outward orientation. And with the recommendation of an outward orientation, he bets on the unlikely big scientific revolution, so that, should traditional heterodox economists in any great number accept his advice, the chances of gradual change in economics being more conservative are increased.

Note that if change does occur in economics in a gradual way, this does not rule out that it ends up being far reaching. One way to see this is to take further stock of the nature of the new research programs. Thus if one characterizes the new research programs in economics as primarily synchronic (behavioral, experimental, game theory, etc.) or diachronic (evolutionary, complexity, etc.) in nature, the possible differential success of these programs in any process of change in economics paints out two basic kinds of redevelopment pathways for the future, one more conservative and one more transformative. The reason for this has to do with the differential attachment of the new research programs to the three commitments above that draw the dividing line between orthodox and heterodox economics *circa* 1980. Basically, diachronic programs go deeper in the changes they seek to bring to the core by including principles (2) and (3), whereas the more synchronic programs principally aim at principle (1). The moral in all this, then, seems to be that the alliances between traditional heterodoxy and "new heterodoxy" likely to have the greatest impact on economics lie along the axis of principles (2) and (3). In my view, however, success in changing orthodoxy along these lines also implies change in principle (1), though success in changing orthodoxy solely in terms of principle (1) may well leave the other principles unchanged, and would probably imply a very modest departure from the atomistic individual conception.

I conclude with a brief comment about ICAPE, the International Confederation of Associations for Pluralism in Economics. Though most traditional heterodox economists know what the acronym means, it is not clear what they take pluralism to mean. For many it seems to mean an open stance toward the different heterodox research programs associated with ICAPE that seeks to promote a unity within difference. This stance seems to me to be shortsighted and anti-pluralist in important respects. But I agree with Lawson that the vitality of traditional heterodox economics "is alive and flourishing" (Lawson, 2006, p. 483). And just as new "traditional" heterodox research programs have emerged since 1980 (for example, feminism, the Re-thinking Marxism school, new evolutionary currents, SABE, and others), it seems we should expect this dynamic process to continue in the future, hopefully to make ICAPE an increasingly pluralist organization in strategy as well as membership.

## Notes

1 A fuller statement of many of the arguments here can be found in Davis (2006b).
2 In Davis (2006b) I argue that a division between orthodox and heterodox is characteristic of some fields – economics being one of them – but that others employ weaker divisions between standard and unconventional.
3 For example, two other important periods of transition are late nineteenth century British political economy and interwar US economics.
4 For further discussion, see Davis and Sent (2006).
5 Heterodox approaches can also change their orientation over time. I also assume orthodoxy only orients toward the core of the field, and does its best to ignore if not suppress heterodoxy (see Davis, 2006b).
6 In fact some versions of complexity economics can be argued to accept all three principles.
7 Though much the same can be said of the system of social exclusion practiced in political science.
8 This point requires more argument than can be given here, and essentially involves a case-by-case examination of the new research programs.
9 Part of the ambiguity here concerns many feminists' attachment to Sen's capabilities framework, which was an inward oriented strategy outside the core at the outset – and a case (4) heterodox origin story – but may be evolving toward an outward oriented one.
10 There are heterodox economists who have come to this conclusion, for example, followers of SABE (Society for the Advancement of Behavioral Economics), which has links to traditional social economics, and a number of proponents of evolutionary economics, which has links to institutional economics.
11 My own research strategy, accordingly, has been to take a principal core concern – individualism – and seek to push it from atomism to social embeddedness or a relational conception, thus an inward orientation aimed at changing the core, rather than to argue for holism, an outward orientation aimed at introducing a new principle into the core. I should add that my own personal taste is for a more outward orientation and greater dialogue with other fields, and that I identify with traditional heterodoxy for this reason. But as a matter of practical strategy I recommend an inward orientation.

## References

Colander, D., Holt, R., and Rosser, J. (2004) 'The changing face of mainstream economics," *Review of Political Economy*, Vol. 16, No. 4: 485–499.
Davis, J. (2006a) "Heterodox economics, the fragmentation of the mainstream, and embedded individual analysis," in R. Garnett and J. Harvey, eds., *Future Directions in Heterodox Economics*, Ann Arbor, MI: University of Michigan Press: 53–72.
Davis, J. (2006b) "The Turn in and Return of Orthodoxy in Recent Economics," paper presented at the annual History of Economics Society meetings, Grinnell, Iowa, USA.
Davis, J. (2006c) "The Turn in Economics: Neoclassical Dominance to Mainstream Pluralism?" *Journal of Institutional Economics*, Vol. 2, No. 1: 1–20.
Davis, J. (forthcoming) "Competing Conceptions of the Individual in Recent Economics," in H. Kincaid and D. Ross, eds., *Oxford Handbook of Philosophy and Economics*, Oxford: Oxford University Press.

Davis, J. and Sent, E-M. (2006) "Heterodoxy's Strategic Pluralism," paper presented at the annual European History of Economics Society meetings, Porto, Portugal.

Lawson, T. (1997) *Economics and Reality*, London: Routledge.

Lawson, T. (2003) *Reorienting Economics*, London: Routledge.

Lawson, T. (2006) "The Nature of Heterodox Economics," *Cambridge Journal of Economics*, Vol. 30, No. 4: 483–505.

Morgan, M. and Rutherford, M. (eds.) (1998) *From Interwar Pluralism to Postwar Neoclassicism*, Durham, NC: Duke University Press.

# 6 Heterodox economics and pluralism
## Reply to Davis

*Tony Lawson*

Recent years have seen the emergence of numerous activities in economics identified first and foremost as heterodox.[1] In the modern academy, it seems, heterodox economics is alive and flourishing. But what (sort of thing) is it?

John Davis and I are both concerned to understand the nature of the contemporary heterodoxy in economics. We are so, I believe, not because either of us is especially fond of taxonomy, certainly not for its own sake. Nor, I believe, do either of us wish to reify or fix the project. There is no reason at all to suppose that heterodox economics, any less than any other social phenomenon, is other than intrinsically dynamic and indeed ultimately transient. However, things in process can still be known, if only as historical (and geographical and cultural) products. And there are always likely to be gains to critical self-reflection upon the nature of that with which we are dealing or involved at any point in time. For my own part at least, I also think a critically self-aware heterodoxy is of vital strategic importance at this moment, given the degree of dominance and exclusionary orientation of the contemporary mainstream.

If, Davis and I, then, seek, for whatever reason, to gain insight into the nature of the contemporary economic heterodoxy, our assessments of what it is are seemingly not the same, with Davis using his present contribution to set out an alternative to the conception I elaborate in *Reorienting Economics*. In the main part of my response, I indicate why I prefer to stick with my conception in the face of Davis' arguments for an alternative.

Discussions of the nature of heterodox economics are not overly common in the economics literature, but those that do emerge seem increasingly to be linked to discussions of pluralism, or being pluralistic, in economics. At the end of his piece, Davis hints that there may be problems with my own professed pluralistic orientation stemming from my very conception of the nature of heterodoxy. One or two other commentators have been more explicit in expressing concerns of this sort. I thus treat this current chapter as an opportunity not only to clarify my conception of the nature of heterodoxy but also to indicate why I believe the expressed concerns (that my position may carry undesirably anti-pluralistic features) are in the end mistaken.[2]

I start by briefly summarising my account of the nature of contemporary economic heterodoxy before turning to assess why Davis rejects it for some alternative. I deal with the topic of pluralism (or being pluralistic) in due course.

## A conception of contemporary heterodoxy in economics

I take it to be analytic to the notion of heterodoxy that it involves the rejection of some doctrine held to be true by a prevailing orthodoxy. That is simply what it means to be heterodox. And it is clear that the self-identifying heterodox traditions in modern economics not only all ardently oppose the mainstream output currently, but also have done so persistently over a lengthy period of time, even through changes in the mainstream forms. Thus, it seems reasonable to conclude that the heterodox opposition stands against some feature that is enduring and central to the modern mainstream; certainly it is opposed to something common to, or presupposed by, all its contributions.

In order to distinguish the modern economic heterodoxy *qua* heterodoxy I thus start by identifying the (set of) feature(s) of the modern orthodoxy or mainstream that is common to all its contributions. The assessment I defend in *Reorienting Economics* and elsewhere is the following. The project that has dominated the discipline of economics for the last forty years or so is one that, although highly heterogeneous in detail, and fluid in revising its manifest form, is united and stable in, *but only in*, adhering to the following single doctrine or edict. This is an insistence that mathematical methods be more or less always employed in the study of economic phenomena. This insistence often runs over to claiming that any contribution that does not take the form of a mathematical model is not proper economics (see Lawson, 2003a, chapter 1).

This is not to say that there is not an elite within the mainstream who feel their privileged positions allow them sometimes to set out some less-than-overly formalistic pieces, especially in presidential addresses and such like. But it is only in virtue of their previous, and other, formalistic contributions that such deviations are rendered legitimate. Such individuals may even introduce their favourite non-mathematical associates into the mainstream scene. But whilst the latter chosen few are few indeed, they are not really part of the mainstream as such, and are seemingly mostly included/tolerated only because of their associations with powerful others who are. Even here, though, the mathematical contributions of their patrons (or matrons) constitute the essential condition.

If an oppositional stance to the noted orthodox doctrine (that formalism is normally compulsory) is the nominal essence of the current heterodoxy, what is its real essence, the explanation of this opposition?

It is the recognition (albeit one that is often no more than implicit) that the universal application of the sorts of mathematical methods that mainstream economists formulate presupposes an untenable account of social reality as everywhere composed of systems of isolated atoms. In *Reorienting Economics* I argue that underpinning this heterodox oppositional stance is an implicit (and sometimes more explicit) commitment to the alternative sort of social ontology I defend in that book, namely of emergence, structure, process, internal relationality and so forth.

So in short, if the only common and so distinguishing feature of the current mainstream is its continuing insistence upon forms of mathematical-deductivist reasoning, the real essence of the heterodox opposition (*qua* heterodox opposition) is an accepted (but rarely explicitly acknowledged) ontological conception. It is a conception that is at odds with the implicit (closed-system and atomistic) ontology of mainstream deductivist reasoning, and so ultimately accounting for the heterodox oppositional stance.

Notice, though, that I do *not* distinguish the individual heterodox traditions from each other according to ontological commitments; indeed I suggest that ontological presuppositions are something they broadly hold in common. Nor, incidentally, do I believe it is possible for the separate traditions to be identified or distinguished according to their own results or methodologies principles and such like. Rather my assessment is that old institutionalism, post Keynesianism, feminist economics, Austrianism, Marxian economics, etc., are each best conceived in terms of *questions and issues traditionally addressed* within their own programme.

Thus old institutionalism, I argue, is a project concerned first and foremost with questions of stability and change in economics. Hence, its traditional and ongoing concerns are especially with technology (perceived as an important source of change), habits and institutions (seen as important sources of stability), evolutionary science and so forth (see *Reorienting Economics* Chapter 8, and also Lawson, 2002, 2003b). I return to this issue of characterising the different heterodox traditions below.

With this heterodox emphasis on questions and interests rather than answers, there is scope both for different members of any given heterodox tradition to produce competing conceptions, as well as for the best-substantiated contributions to be continually improved upon. So, the conception I defend is quite consistent with the sort of (shifting) variety of contributions we find within any heterodox tradition.

Notice, too, that I do not suggest that heterodox contributors do not, or should not, experiment with mathematical-deductivist techniques and the like. Social conditions may occasionally arise that are locally of a sort presupposed by methods of formalistic modelling. If I characterise the mainstream in terms of its usual *insistence* that (for a contribution to count as economics) various sorts of mathematical-deductivist methods be everywhere and always employed, I conceive heterodoxy as an (implicitly) ontologically motivated rejection of *the universalising and dogmatic aspects of this stance*, not as a refusal ever to experiment with formalistic methods, or to employ them where conditions indicate their relevance.

The mainstream itself is pluralistic within its constituting constraint, of course. Despite the best advice of those economists associated with the Bourbaki school, it is impossible to pursue a mathematical economics purely in the abstract. There has to be content, and this is found to be highly variable. Indeed, both the substantive programmes pursued by the mainstream, and the sorts of mathematical-deductivist methods employed (along with their interpretation) are highly variable (Lawson, 2005b). There are those who argue that *within* orthodoxy there exists a dominant and relatively enduring (though by no means fixed) "neoclassical core" or some such. But assessments of what this entails vary quite significantly (see for example, Ben Fine 2006, Geoffrey Hodgson 2006, Christian Arnsperger and Yanis Varoufakis 2006, or Edward Fullbrook, 2005). For the purposes at hand, I do not need to consider these matters further at this point, though they do eventually bear on some of the contentions made by Davis. So, I return to this topic as necessary below.

Similarly, I will have more to say on this overall conception of the broad structure of modern economic projects or groupings when I turn, in due course, to consider the issue of pluralism. But for now, this outline is sufficient to allow a contrast to be made with the alternative conception of economic heterodoxy that Davis is seeking to promote.

## Davis' alternative conception

How does Davis' assessment differ? After summarising my conclusions concerning the respective natures of mainstream and heterodox economics, Davis writes:

> Broadly, I agree with these conclusions. My concern is that they may be truer of economics *circa* 1980, and neither fully capture the state of economics since then, nor provide us with a sufficient understanding of the current direction of development of economics.

Now on the face of things this is an unpromising response, certainly a surprising one. For since 1980 the mainstream has become increasingly formalistic in orientation, not less so, certainly in my neck of the woods, but seemingly in most other places too. The mainstream output is still basically deductivist in nature presupposing the same closed and atomistic scenarios. In consequence, if the formalistic emphasis, given the nature of social reality, was inappropriate around 1980 it remains at least as inappropriate today. And any heterodox tradition worthy of being so identified presumably continues to recognise the inappropriate nature of mainstream formalistic contributions. Thus, if the heterodox opposition around 1980 was motivated, if implicitly, by the acceptance of an onto-logical orientation that was significantly different from, opposed to, and indeed far more sustainable than, the presuppositions of these formalis-tic methods, I see little obvious reason for heterodox economists to reori-ent the nature of their opposition since that time.

So how or why does Davis argue that things have changed? He has little to say about the mainstream project per se. His main concern is instead with "the changing nature of heterodox economics and its chang-ing relation to orthodox economics". Specifically he writes:

> "I will argue a view I believe is largely contrary to Lawson's, namely, that: (i) heterodox economics is more heterogeneous than [Lawson] and many others believe and moreover heterogeneous in ways generally not recognized by many who see themselves as het-erodox, (ii) the reference of the term "heterodox economics" is quite different from what most economists, heterodox and orthodox, believe it to be, and (iii) understanding this heterogeneity is import-ant for understanding the direction of development of current economics.

Let me consider each contention in turn.

## The heterogeneity of heterodox economics

Now whether or not heterodox economics is more heterogeneous than I and many others believe, and in unrecognised ways, this constitutes a challenge to my conception of the nature of heterodoxy only if the latter conception is somehow found to be at odds with, or unable to sustain, the forms of heterogeneity that Davis has in mind. Our conception of apples may remain stable despite the introduction/discovery of new varieties or heterogeneity in terms of size, shape, colour, texture and so forth.

So what sort of heterogeneity does Davis have in mind? Davis focuses on features to which he refers as the "origins" of these projects, on the processes that certain projects pass through (or have passed through) in becoming heterodox (or orthodox). Specifically, he distinguishes those that fail to become orthodox following a period of pluralism; those that lose the status of orthodox when a new orthodoxy emerges; those that fail to redirect orthodoxy from outside orthodoxy; and others that fail to redirect orthodoxy from inside orthodoxy.

Davis recognises that his interpretation of specific heterodox strands from this perspective is contentious, but adds:

> Nonetheless, the history of economics seems to tell us that there are different types of origin stories for different research approaches in

economics, and thus that what most people take to be heterodox economics exhibits considerably more heterogeneity when seen from
this dynamic perspective than appears to be the case when point-in-
time comparisons between different approaches are made.

Now contra Davis' suggestion, I have no problem with any of this. I
cannot see, though, how it bears on the issue before us. If I am right that
the only coherent way to identify the mainstream is according to its
insistence on a particular form of method, and that modern heterodoxy
is appropriately distinguished by its ontological grounds for opposing
this insistence, it is not obvious that the origins of forms of either mainstream method or heterodox opposition have any necessary bearing (any
more than our conception of apples is necessarily threatened by recognising that competing varieties may originate in different countries or
regions). Certainly Davis gives no reason to conclude to the contrary.

Instead of explaining why he supposes the traits he observes somehow
undermine the conceptions of the nature of the current heterodoxy that I
defend (a conception that Davis seemingly accepts as characterising the
situation *circa* 1980) Davis proceeds by distinguishing a further form of difference or heterogeneity within the heterodoxy, one that he interprets as a
matter of "orientation". This relates to whether heterodox criticism of the
mainstream or "core" is internal/immanent or external. Or, as Davis
prefers, it relates to whether the approaches are "inward" or "outward" in
orientation, or oriented towards or away from the "orthodox core".

The former orientation is that of engaging the mainstream by "challenging the core's own principles from the vantage point of those *same*
principles". If this seems clear enough (though as I argue in response to
Geoffrey Hodgson later in this volume, I believe it unlikely to be successful), the outward orientation, for Davis, seems to involve drawing on
principles found in different disciplines:

> Orientation towards the field's periphery is a matter of placing
> emphasis on principles closer to other sciences beyond the field's
> boundaries, principles moreover that appear at any given point in
> time to be clearly not part of the field's core.

Again I feel bound to say "so what?" I cannot see how these considerations, certainly in the form presented so far, bear on the issue before us.
Moreover, some heterodox groups clearly lean both ways, with some of
their members emphasising internal critiques, others looking away from
the core and some doing both.

Davis summarises his position as follows:

> Heterodox economics is heterogeneous, then, because different
> approaches differ in the ways that they combine different origin

stories and different orientations. Their origin stories and orientations, that is, distinguish their different dynamics, and accordingly
serve to place their point-in-time shared commitments in historical
context as temporary and transient states of affairs.

Now no one is denying that most things in this universe, and not least
social phenomena, including the various traditions in economics, are
transient. Everything becomes and begoes in time, and often in complex
ways. And the heterodox traditions are clearly heterogeneous in numerous ways, including their origins and intellectual strategies or orientations. But it is not yet clear that differences in origins or even of
orientations *of the sort* that concerns Davis, bear significantly on the issue
of the relative transience/persistence of "shared commitments" at this
point in time.

My assessment, as I say, is that the feature that unites the various
contemporary heterodox projects *qua* heterodox projects is recognition
that the mainstream mathematical-deductivist emphasis presupposes
an ontology that is at odds with (or at best a very special case of) our
most sustainable account of the nature of social reality. If this is so,
then so long as an insistence on such formalism remains orthodox doctrine, and to this point support for this doctrine is certainly proving
resilient, the heterodox traditions have a rationale for actively uniting
through any differences, including differences in origins and debating
strategies. Though Davis' comments on certain forms of heterogeneity
are interesting, they do not yet give any reason for rejecting the conceptions I have been defending, nor provide a sustainable basis for some
alternative.

## Heterodoxy is not what we think it is

In the second part of his chapter Davis observes that after around 1980 a
number of new research programs begin to emerge: "These include
game theory, behavioral economics, experimental economics, evolutionary economics, neuroeconomics, and complexity economics. Other new
approaches and combinations of these have emerged in their wake."
Davis' primary goal in this part of the chapter seems to be to establish
that these new programmes must be regarded as heterodox. Now this is
something on which we do disagree quite significantly and as this
appears to contain the heart of Davis argument, I will spend some time
on it. I start by very briefly sketching my own interpretation of the status
of the "new programmes" before examining whether Davis gives any
compelling reason to reject it.

My own assessment is that it is an error to suppose that any new
method or programme of the sort in question (whether or not it figures
on Davis' list) is inherently either mainstream or heterodox (any more

than, say, mathematics is). Notice that the sorts of programmes on Davis' list are not constituted in terms of substantive (economic) results or questions (whether about how the individual or economy or society works). Rather they are essentially methodological programmes concerned with ways of doing economics, including ways of incorporating "observations" or results from other (experimental, animal studies, neuroscience, etc.) disciplines.

The feature that makes the difference in terms of whether any "programme" becomes in practice associated with the orthodoxy or heterodoxy is how it is used. I have already argued that what distinguishes the mainstream is its *insistence* on formalism. But, as already noted, I do not suggest that heterodox economists should not experiment with formalistic methods. The mainstream abuses formalism by repeatedly using it in situations in which it is inappropriate to do so, failing to seek to understand its scope and limitations. But use of formalism is not in and of itself essentially mainstream. And nor need be any new method or any (aspects of) the new methodological programmes. As I say, it all depends on how things are done.

Of course, the form that any new programme does take (or the manner in which it is presented) is likely to influence its reception in the academic institutions of modern economics. Specifically, if a programme is not (or cannot easily be) formulated mathematically, the existing mainstream is unlikely to be receptive at all (though there can be no guarantee that each particular approach will be accepted anyway). But then again a formalistic programme may in principle be ignored by the mainstream, and yet used by heterodox economists, albeit typically only under conditions in which it seems *prima facie* appropriate; or for purposes of trial and error experimentation. As I say, much depends on how things are done.

Davis' position or interpretation, though, is rather different. According to him, as I say, these new programmes are simply to be characterised as heterodox. Let me trace through his reasoning as to why.

Davis starts out by suggesting that with "the possible exception of game theory [...] none of these new approaches has yet come to be regarded as orthodox". The nearest that Davis comes to saying what he means by orthodox at this stage is via the following passage:

> Orthodoxy typically requires moving from being purely a research program to being a well-established teaching program, where changes in teaching work their way from top downward through the social hierarchy of universities and top programs. Neoclassicism, of course, still dominates economics teaching (though this dominance has become more uneven as courses in experimental economics and non-linear simulation techniques are added to more and more department curricula).

This sort of process, if it is indeed more than a contingent feature of how a new (feature of) orthodoxy may be established, seems to be precisely what Davis (even in the parenthesis of the noted passage) is arguing is happening with regard to the "new programmes".

However, believing himself to have established with the above remarks that "these new research programs in economics are not orthodox", Davis asks: "what are they?" Suggesting that they accept in varying degrees all three of the commitments of "heterodox economics" that, Davis supposes, "constitute the dividing line between orthodoxy and heterodoxy *circa* 1980", Davis concludes that "these new research programs taken as a group must thus be by definition heterodox".

## Davis' (initial) conception of heterodoxy

What precisely are these three commitments that constitute the dividing line between orthodoxy and heterodoxy *circa* 1980? In the opening paragraph of his chapter Davis writes:

> Tony Lawson's critique of mainstream economics is that it is everywhere formalistic and deductive, that this leads it to a closed systems approach based on identifying social event regularities, and that this is an inappropriate strategy for dealing with the subject matter with which economics is concerned (Lawson, 1997, 2003a). Heterodox economics is then distinguished by its rejection of all this and by its commitment to an ontological analysis that takes social reality to be intrinsically dynamic or processual, interconnected and organic, structured, exhibits emergence, and includes value and meaning and is polyvalent (Lawson, 2006a, pp. 495–6). Broadly, I agree with these conclusions.

However, on the next page he sets out his own conception of "what most people identify as heterodox economic approaches". Here he lists the "three commitments of heterodoxy" to which he refers in the passage noted above (where he questions what these new research programmes are). According to Davis, the "shared three specific commitments *circa* 1980" are:

(1) rejection of the atomistic individual conception in favor of a socially embedded individual conception,
(2) emphasis on time as an irreversible historical process,
(3) reasoning in terms of mutual influences between individuals and social structures.

Despite Davis' declaration of broad agreement with my own position, it is not clear that these commitments, as formulated, express precisely the same ontology as I defend. In fact, I worry that, as formulated, they may be too vague to do the job.

For example, the idea of an individual being embedded, expressed in commitment (1), is not inherently inconsistent with it being an atomistic individual. To embed is firmly to enclose; there is no connotation of the entity in question being continually transformed or re-constituted associated with the notion of embeddedness. When we employ the metaphor of an atomistic individual I presume we do not mean a small one, nor even a randomly moving one, but (like, for example, Keynes, 1973, pp. 276, 277) an entity that has its "own separate, independent, and invariable effect" whatever the context. In modern engineering, for example, the category of *embedded system* tends to refer to a special-purpose system in which a computer is completely encapsulated by the device it controls and (unlike general-purpose computers) performs but one (or a few) pre-defined tasks only.

The point is that human beings are not so much socially embedded as in large part socially constituted; human beings are social beings. From birth (and perhaps earlier) onwards, our personal identities are moulded in relation to others as well as to existing socio-cultural structures. Eventually we also take on various positional or social identities, with all such identities determined in relation to others and continually reproduced/transformed through practice.

Nor, turning to commitment (3), is it just that there are "mutual influences between individuals and social structures". This is too weak or contingent a claim. Rather each is in part constituted in relation to the other. Teachers presuppose students (and vice versa) as well as the connecting relationships between the two, relations to the educational authorities, to funding agencies and so forth.

The notion of time irreversible historical processes, expressed in commitment (2), is fine if by this category we really mean "processes" and "historical" and indeed real time. Everything that happens in the social world is reproduced and/or transformed through human (transformative) practices, practices that are situated in space–time, in geography and history, and constitute an open-ended continuous process of becoming.

I am not merely suggesting that my reworking of Davis' three heterodox commitments is the more sustainable interpretation of the ontology in question. I believe, too, that it is the conception implicit in heterodox thinking. We find it (whether implicit or explicit) in thinkers like Marx, Veblen, Keynes and Hayek around whom heterodoxy was organised in the 1980s (see Lawson, 2003a, Part III). But, more to the point, an acceptance of this ontology explains heterodoxy's loud and persistent opposition to the mainstream. For it is only some such ontology (or Davis' commitments interpreted in some such fashion), that resists being expressed as the presuppositions of the sorts of mathematical-deductivist methods that mainstream economists continually wield.

Remember there is no heterodox opposition to the use of mathematical methods in natural science even where (as in super-string theory) such methods dominate; an opposition exists in economics just because of a conviction that the sorts of mathematical-deductivist methods continually employed are not especially appropriate to social analysis.

Now it may well be that, in setting out his three principles or "commitments of heterodoxy", Davis intends precisely the interpretation that I have just elaborated, where both human beings and structure are repeatedly reproduced/transformed through practice. I suspect he does intend this understanding. If not, then I think he is mischaracterising the traditional heterodox opposition. But if Davis does indeed intend my interpretation/elaboration of these "commitments" then I think there are problems with his assessments of recent developments. Let me briefly elaborate.

## The nature of the new programmes

The "new research programs" Davis mentions as emerging post 1980, let me recall, "include game theory, behavioral economics, experimental economics, evolutionary economics, neuroeconomics, and complexity economics". According to Davis these programmes must be heterodox just because they *collectively* (but only collectively, not individually) adhere to Davis' three commitments of heterodox economics listed above:

> these new research programs taken as a group – though not individually – accept in varying degrees all three of the commitments of heterodox economics listed above. As these three commitments in my view and that of many others also constitute the dividing line between orthodoxy and heterodoxy *circa* 1980, these new research programs taken as a group must thus be by definition heterodox.

I do confess to finding this criterion, as expressed, not only unconvincing, but also rather puzzling. It seems to allow that we can render any individual programme heterodox just by virtue of grouping it with others that collectively span the three Davis commitments. If so, we could, of course, add in the mainstream itself and thereby render it heterodox.

We might suppose that we can rule out the latter incongruous possibility by stipulating that for a new programme to qualify as heterodox in the (collectivist) manner suggested, it must satisfy at least one of Davis' three commitments. Perhaps this indeed is what Davis has in mind. But as a criterion this too is hardly satisfactory. For, consider a programme thought to satisfy a (proper) subset of Davis' three heterodox commitments. It seems to follow that the claims to heterodoxy of any such programme depends on how it is grouped with others, and in particular on its being lined up with a package of programmes that collectively satisfies the commitment(s) it does not itself satisfy. Whether or not the programme in question is included in such a package (one that thereby spans the three Davis commitments) is something that can seemingly be changed at will, thus rendering the (heterodox/orthodox) status of any such programme largely arbitrary, certainly open to manipulation (and of course any two contributors can reach opposed conclusions just by selecting the members of their package of programmes differently).

Davis does anticipate the objection (from "those who traditionally regard themselves as heterodox") that, because no single one of the new programmes exhibits all of the "three principles of heterodoxy" (they only do so as a group), then no single programme ought to be regarded as heterodox. But without examining the nature of this objection, and I suspect without appreciating the tensions or apparent incoherencies that arise, Davis dismisses the objection for reasons I come to below.

Before looking at Davis' response to that anticipated objection, however, it is not without interest to question whether the programmes listed by Davis, *in the form in which they are in fact entering the discipline*, do, even collectively, meet his revised criterion of heterodoxy. And I must admit that it is not clear to me that (individually or collectively) these "new programmes" inevitably meet *any* of the three commitments (let alone all of them) *in practice*. At least this is so if we are to interpret the latter commitments according to the ontological sketch (or elaboration of Davis' commitments) that I have given in the preceding part of the chapter.

Consider complexity theory, which Davis suggests in a footnote is the most promising candidate for meeting all three of his "heterodox commitments". As this has entered economics, this is basically a form of non-linear modelling. As such it is nothing more than an additional form of mathematical-deductivist method. Its implicit ontology is still one of closed systems of isolated atoms. Perhaps complexity theory will be thought to be at least consistent with Davis' second "heterodox principle" of "time as an irreversible historical process". Certainly the path mapped out in any simulation will be irreversible. But there is no history, no time and no real process. There is merely a one-way relationship. If we consider the functional relationship $y = x^2$, then we find that for any given value of $x$ we can determine a unique value of $y$, but we cannot take the reverse path, a given value of $y$ does not lead us "back" to a unique $x$. Complexity economics, as it stands, is merely a complex version of such a functional relationship. As I say, the ontology is clearly still one of isolated atoms. All that has changed is the degree of complexity of the system formulations.

I recognise that the concept of complexity (like "equilibrium" and some other system concepts, see Lawson, 2005a, 2005b, 2007) can be interpreted in a multitude of ways (see especially Perona, 2004). But the interpretation I am giving here is fairly characteristic, not a peculiar deviation advanced merely by, say, a few members of the mainstream. Consider an enthusiastic defence of complexity economics found in a recent edition of (the hardly mainstream) *post-autistic economics review*. Here we are told that in complexity economics the "dynamics of a complex system are best described by non-linear as opposed to linear relationships, but as yet it is not possible to accurately model the former. The closest one can come are simulations based on cellular automata" (Smith, 2004).

I am also not sure how game theory, a further programme on Davis' list, as it figures in modern economics, even begins to qualify according to Davis' heterodox commitments. As far as I can see it is a formal modelling approach focusing on typically isolated worlds of optimising atoms "making" decisions in contexts where the anticipated decisions of other optimising atoms are considered. No societal constitution of individuals, and no real time or history.

Behavioural economics is a programme that claims to combine psychology and economics in investigating what happens in markets where people display (what economists seem to perceive as) "non-rational" motivations or behaviours (such as fairness, envy, present-bias and so forth).[3] So conceived, the programme need not be formalistic at all. However, as it is being taken up in economics it seems still to be mostly a deductivist modelling endeavour, thus presupposing the usual systems of isolated atoms. In most cases, indeed, atomistic agents continue to maximise a preference relation over some space of consequences where any solution typically involves standard equilibrium concepts.

Neuroeconomics is a form of analysis that makes use of data on brain processes to suggest new underpinnings for economic theories concerned with issues like how much people save, why there are strikes, why the stock market fluctuates, the nature of consumer confidence and its effect on the economy, and so forth. As such, it too need not be tied to formalistic modelling. Moreover, there does indeed seem to be a (relatively non-formalistic) strand of neuroeconomics, mostly content with reporting (albeit typically rather uncritically) the research findings of neuroscience and suggesting how these findings might be tied to "non-rational" motivations. But it seems to me that the increasingly more dominant strand is a further form of mathematical-deductivist modelling closely allied to behavioural economic modelling. Thus whilst behavioural economics concerned with formalistic modelling has previously relied heavily (if again rather uncritically) on the findings of experiments and animal behaviour studies, this second strand of neuroeconomics seems to be developing largely as a version of this form of behavioural economics that seeks also to draw (uncritically yet once more) on the reported findings of neuroscience.[4]

I could go on. But my concern is surely clear. If we interpret Davis' three heterodox commitments in a manner that actually fits with the ontological conception I defend (to which Davis signals agreement), and if we examine the form in which the new programmes are mostly being taken up, it is not even clear that these new programmes (collectively or otherwise) conform in practice to *any* of Davis' commitments, let alone all of them.

I emphasise, that from my own perspective none of this matters anyway (at least for the question of deciding how the new programmes are best to be classified). For on my own interpretation, the feature that characterises heterodoxy *qua* heterodoxy is opposition to the mainstream insistence that only formalism be used. From this perspective, as I say, the new programmes are not inherently heterodox or mainstream; it all depends on how they are used.

## A new criterion of heterodoxy?

As we have seen, though, Davis demurs, insisting that the new programmes, seemingly whatever their form or mode of application, are necessarily a part of the contemporary heterodoxy, just because *collectively* they adhere to Davis' three commitments. As I say, I am not sure that even the latter is actually so. However, at this point I want to turn, as promised, to Davis' response to the objection he anticipates, namely that some heterodox economists might resist characterising the new programmes as heterodox just because any single programme on its own might not meet all of three of Davis, "heterodox commitments".

What is Davis' response? It is to suggest that this criticism is "fair" only "if the standards of heterodox economics *circa* 1980 are to be thought good for all time". He continues suggesting that "if we accept that what counts as orthodox and heterodox is historically changing, then ... it seems we should also be open to the reconstitution of what counts as heterodox".

Well yes, we can accept that everything is changing, so clearly it would be wrong to reify what counts as heterodox. So let us be open to the possibility that what counts as heterodox will shift. By similar reasoning, we should be, and are, open to the idea that what counts as being human, copper, organic, a tree or an apple may shift. But still we need an argument or something to persuade us that the defining criteria for any of these, including what counts as orthodox or heterodox, has shifted. Instead, all we really get from Davis is the statement that because everything is historically changing "we should also be open to the reconstitution of what counts as heterodox".

It seems to me that, at this stage of his discussion at least, instead of seeking somehow to ground his case, Davis' argument for interpreting the new programmes as heterodox has become rather self-serving: *Here is a criterion of what currently counts as heterodox. Here are some new programmes. They do not fit our criterion for counting something as heterodox. To infer thereby that they are not heterodox is only a fair criticism if we stick to our criterion of what it is to count as heterodox. Everything changes eventually, so let us change our criterion of what is to count as heterodox, and in such a manner as to admit the new programmes into the heterodox.*

In short, Davis seems not to provide any good reason for adopting his revised criterion for heterodoxy; but rather is driven more by an interest in finding a criterion that, if accepted, will allow heterodoxy to accommodate the new programmes. Moreover, it is not obvious that his revised formulation is especially coherent (the status of an individual programme depends on the package of others in which it is included) or even that, appropriately interpreted, any of these three commitments (let alone all of them) are satisfied by the new programmes in the form they are being taken up. In consequence, to this point at least, I do not really find compelling reason to abandon our seemingly previously shared (Davis' *circa* 1980) conception of heterodoxy.

## A second new criterion of heterodoxy?

Instead of moving to provide the missing argument for his case that, because collectively satisfying the three commitments, "these new research programs taken as a group must thus be by definition heterodox", Davis seems next to confuse matters further by suggesting the existence of a yet additional new criterion of heterodoxy, one that again is said to render the new programmes heterodox. For Davis next writes:

> Indeed, *prima facie* the new research programs in economics are heterodox in virtue of their origins *outside* of economics in other sciences. It would be a mistake, I think, to claim that the understanding of science in other fields is the same essentially as it is in economics, since why otherwise are there different sciences? Thus the emergence of the new research programs in economics presumably imports new science principles into economics. Examples include behavioral and neuroscience foundations for choice, graph-based network analysis, experimental techniques, and non-linear, non-equilibrium simulation methods. Identifying these developments as heterodox is not to say, of course, that they represent those heterodox principles most valued by those individuals who currently self-identify themselves as heterodox. Nor is it to say that these are all necessarily valuable principles for economics. The main point, as emphasized in Davis (2006), is that what has come into economics from other sciences cannot be orthodox, at least at the outset.

It is feasible that Davis is maintaining here his first transformed criterion of heterodoxy (namely that the programs in question collectively satisfy his identified heterodox commitments), and arguing that because the "new programmes" originate outside economics they must (collectively) qualify. But if, as we have seen, it is not clear that *in practice* these new programmes Davis lists collectively do satisfy his three commitments, it is even less obvious that *any* set of new programmes must do so merely in virtue of originating outside economics.

So Davis, as I say, is seemingly presupposing here some second new criterion of orthodoxy. It is one that can presumably make sense of both the contention of the first sentence of the noted passage, namely that a program originating outside economics must be heterodox, and also the contention of the last sentence, namely that "what has come into economics from other sciences cannot be orthodox, at least at the outset". Why should these contentions be accepted? Is originating outside economics a criterion of heterodoxy in itself? As I say, here Davis seems to be returning to his earlier focus on origins and orientation.

Davis seeks to motivate his latest contentions by suggesting that it is a "mistake ... to claim that the understanding of science in other fields is essentially the same as it is in economics, since why otherwise are there different sciences?" Actually this does not follow. The fact of different fields of science does not mean that we must understand science differently in the various fields, only that the different fields treat different sorts of materials (possessing different sorts of properties), and are likely do so using different methods (see *Economics and Reality*, chapters 1–4).

But even overlooking this, if approaches originating outside of economics could not be immediately regarded as orthodox because they are different, we are left wondering why, by this reason alone, they should they be regarded as necessarily heterodox. Davis seems to regard this as self-evident. So here we seem to uncover Davis' second implicit new criterion of heterodoxy, namely: openness to, or encompassing of, anything that the orthodoxy does not (yet) do.

If this is indeed Davis' revised criterion of heterodoxy, it, too, seems an unhelpful way to proceed. For, to adopt such a criterion is to trivialise the heterodox traditions, to reduce them to little more than a concern for difference for the sake of difference alone. In contrast, any heterodoxy worthy of the name, like the traditional heterodox traditions in economics, takes a principled and reasoned stance for opposing some specific orthodox doctrine and indeed for putting something else in its place.

Heterodoxy, I repeat, simply means opposed to orthodox doctrine. As far as I know there is no orthodox doctrine to the effect that "new programmes in economics should all originate within the discipline", or that "programmes new to economics cannot be (immediately) accepted". And if we can define heterodoxy without reference to it being opposed to orthodox doctrine, why not according to any arbitrary criterion?

The traditional heterodox opposition in economics has arisen, and is sustained, in response to the failings and inappropriateness of the formalistic emphasis in economics. That is, there already is a huge self-identifying heterodoxy, opposing the mainstream defining doctrine, including post Keynesians, Old Institutionalism, Austrians, Marxian economists, feminist economists and so forth. Many of these were pushed into being heterodox only in virtue of the rise to dominance of a project that takes as its central doctrine an insistence that mathematical methods be everywhere used. A criterion for heterodoxy of merely being different to the mainstream would significantly blunt the heterodox oppositional message (and of course if the relevant criterion of heterodoxy is just "originating outside economics", this would seem to exclude these traditional projects from heterodoxy entirely).

Or to view the same tension from a different perspective, suppose furthermore that a group of mainstream economists were to devise, or import, some new methods of a mathematical-deductivist nature, and integrate them into a research programme. Let us suppose too that the existing heterodox projects saw little reason to incorporate such methods, viewing them as not especially appropriate to social analysis. On his second new criterion, Davis would still have to accept these methods, or the project by mainstream economists incorporating them, as heterodox, at least initially; which does seem rather unhelpful, not to mention counter-intuitive.

Davis' response is to distinguish the "new heterodoxy" and the "old heterodoxy", with the former designating the new programmes and the latter the traditional projects. But I think as it stands this response merely signals the incoherence of Davis' position rather than resolves it (though I think there may be a resolution to this problem, a matter I return to shortly).

I might also note, somewhat parenthetically, that Davis' conception, if accepted, would not only serve to water down the heterodox opposition to the mainstream, it would also serve to distract attention from what is wrong in economics. The insistence that mathematical methods should be everywhere used is not only mainstream doctrine; it is the cause of the discipline's continuing ills (see *Reorienting Economics*, chapter 1). As I say, in other disciplines where there is an exclusive reliance on formalism, there is no heterodox opposition, and there is none just because the formalism is perceived to be doing the job. I repeat that the traditional heterodox opposition in economics is precisely a constructive response to the failings and inappropriateness of the formalistic emphasis in economics.

We can see, looking back over the passage by Davis extracted above (at the start of this part of the chapter), that Davis himself seems to recognise some of this:

> Identifying these [new] developments as heterodox is not to say, of
> course, that they represent those heterodox principles most valued

by those individuals who currently self-identify themselves as heterodox. Nor is it to say that these are all necessarily valuable principles for economics.

So the new programmes may not be of value, as currently formulated they appear not to fit with the orientation of the existing heterodoxy, and, in the manner by which they are constituted as heterodox, they are not opposed to any particular orthodox doctrine. I thus remain as cautious about embracing this second new criterion of heterodoxy as I am in adopting Davis' previous one.

## Developments within the mainstream

To this point, I have merely indicated problems that arise from Davis' attempts to devise criteria that render the new programmes heterodox. If we add to these difficulties the claims of David Colander, Richard Holt and J. Barkley Rosser Jr (2004) that new programmes of the sort Davis considers are in any case being taken up by the mainstream (and not just entering economics as formalistic systems) then the picture Davis gives seems troublesome indeed. For, focusing explicitly on the mainstream, Colander *et al.* report how evolutionary game theory is redefining the manner in which (notions of) institutions are integrated into mainstream analysis; how ecological economics is redefining the manner in which rationality is treated; how econometric work dealing with the limitations of classical statistics is defining the manner in which economists think of empirical proof; how complexity theory is providing a new way to conceptualise equilibrium states; how computer simulations offer a new approach to analysis; how experimental economics is changing the way economists think about empirical work, and so on.

Unsurprisingly, although the authors in question focus on the changing features of the mainstream, they find that the latter's insistence on mathematical-deductive modelling prevails in all cases; the essential feature of the recent and current mainstream remains intact: "modern mainstream economics is open to new approaches, as long as they are done with a careful understanding of the strengths of the recent orthodox approach and with a modelling methodology acceptable to the mainstream" (Colander *et al.*, 2004, p. 492). Perceiving an "elite" within the mainstream that determines which new ideas are acceptable Colander *et al.* also write: "Our view is that the current elite are relatively open minded when it comes to new ideas, but quite closed minded when it comes to alternative methodologies. If it isn't modelled, it isn't economics, no matter how insightful" (p. 492).

So where does Davis' desire to render the new programmes heterodox leave us? It seems that we acquire two new and not wholly compatible conceptions of heterodoxy. Neither seems to be well motivated or justified or especially successful in facilitating the desired outcome; and both create their own problems of coherence. Moreover, if the first conception (being heterodox in virtue of accepting at least one of Davis' early assessments of heterodox commitments and/or in virtue of being part of a package that covers them all) seems especially arbitrary, the second criterion (of including anything orthodoxy does not cover) seems unhelpfully dismissive of the traditional heterodox critical opposition, being not even connected to the explicit opposition to some specific orthodox doctrine.

Central, to such problems as are created is Davis' conviction that it is necessary to interpret the new programmes as necessarily mainstream or heterodox independently of how they are applied; and in particular his desire to see them as necessarily heterodox. If instead we accept that methodological approaches (and to repeat the new programmes are indeed primarily methodological in orientation) are not inherently heterodox or mainstream, then problems of the noted sort do not arise. The mainstream just is constituted by its insistence that formalism is compulsory; the heterodoxy is a principled resistance to this doctrine. The principle behind this resistance is that social reality is of such a nature that the presuppositions of formalistic method cannot have universal relevance. Where or when local conditions render formalistic methods relevant is always a matter of trial and error experimentation or empirical investigation; not something for prior dogmatic assertion.

It is conceivable that in seeking to claim the new programmes for heterodoxy Davis is primarily motivated by a concern not to abandon them entirely to the orthodoxy. If this is so, then the conception I am defending not only avoids all the tensions that Davis' alternatives introduce, but manages to meet Davis' motivating concern anyway; for it follows from the framework I am defending that these programmes, as any others, need not be confined to orthodox or heterodox take up. What matters, as I say, is the manner in which they are applied.

In any case, whatever may be Davis' motivation for seeking to revise his criterion of heterodoxy, I see no compelling reason in any of this to abandon or even transform my own conception in favour of Davis' revised formulation. To the contrary, given the noted ease with which the original conception can avoid the sorts of tensions and potential incoherencies introduced by Davis' proposed transformations, my commitment to it is probably strengthened.

## The future of economics

Davis opens his third and final part of this chapter noting there is little communication between the (traditional) heterodox groups and the new programmes (which as I say he refers to as a "new heterodoxy" to distinguish it from the former traditional or "old heterodoxy"), whilst acknowledging that there is considerable cross-communication *within* the separate groups (for example between post Keynesians and Old Institutionalists, etc.).

If the new programmes, at least in the manner they are mostly taken up, are being rendered largely formalistic in nature, *irrespective* of whether this is the route to insight, then this should not surprise us.

This is not to say that the new methods will not (and I certainly do not suggest that they should not) also be explored by (some) heterodox economists. Nor is it to suggest that there should not be any inter-group communication; exploration and engagement is always desirable, where feasible, whatever the groups involved. But to the extent that the "new programmes", as introduced, are essentially based on forms of mathematical-deductive reasoning, they will carry the atomistic presuppositions that, when advanced as universal claims, the heterodoxy continues to reject.

So, to the extent that proponents of the new programmes seek to apply the latter without regard to conditions of relevance, and this does seem to be happening, engagement may be limited.

Indeed, all things considered, it is likely that the new programmes will enter the discipline mostly through a revision in (or perhaps more likely through additions to) the concrete (formalistic) practices of the current mainstream, not by transforming its (formalistic) nature; a conjecture that, as we have seen, is assessed by Colander *et al.* (2004) as already being carried through. Behavioural economics is an obvious example of this.

From the perspective of Davis' analysis, however, this lack of cross-communication between the traditional heterodoxy and the new programmes is viewed as "odd" and in need of an explanation. The reason Davis finds this odd is that "both share a number of critiques of mainstream neoclassicism".

Here, as in several other places in Davis' commentary, we come across an expressed association between mainstream economics and neoclassicism. I confess that I have never considered the latter to be a useful nor an appropriate label. I assume that by using it here, Davis is referring to one form of formalised system, perhaps one especially associated with the introduction of marginalism in economics. It is possible that Davis understands it as Ben Fine (2006) does, "as the technical apparatus established [...] from the marginalist revolution onwards [...] [fundamentally involving] the use of utility functions and production functions, with accompanying assumptions to allow the theory to proceed". Or perhaps it is understood as the triptych of rationality, equilibrium and (something like) perfect knowledge (see for example Hodgson, 2006). Or perhaps instead it is understood as a formalism turning on the triptych of methodological individualism (explanations always couched in terms of individuals), methodological instrumentalism (preference driven behaviour) and methodological equilibration (equilibrium as an organising concept), as argued by Christian Arnsperger and Yanis Varoufakis (2006). For a more complex overview, see Fullbrook (2005).

Whichever the interpretation, we can see that Davis' surprise at the lack of communication between the groups appears to stem from his supposing that my opponent's opponent must be like me, that any two approaches that oppose "neoclassicism", must be of similar nature. This clearly need not follow.

## Orthodoxy's heterodoxy?

Still, to the extent that Davis is correct in characterising the "new pro- grammes" as rejecting a set of doctrines that are accepted by a majority of mainstream economists, albeit whilst nevertheless refusing to chal- lenge the mainstreams' most basic and universal doctrine, there may yet be coherence in thinking of the new programmes (even if only applied in a formalistic manner, and by mainstream practitioners) as a form of het- erodoxy, *albeit as a heterodoxy within the mainstream.* After all heterodoxies are often acknowledged within various religions, as for example in the Roman Catholic Church, designating (typically relatively small) groups whose members do not accept all the doctrines but retain sufficient faith in the most fundamental doctrine(s) to avoid heresy (or we might say to avoid a more fundamental heterodoxy). So, to the extent that proponents of the new programmes accept the doctrine that formalism be compul- sory in economics, but stand in some way opposed to certain specific for- malisms practiced by a majority (or perhaps even a dominating large minority), the pursuit of these programmes might be referred to as a "mathematical economics heterodoxy", or as a heterodoxy within the mathematical-deductivist church, or some such.

For this strategy to be sustainable it is beholden on Davis to establish that something called neoclassicism continues to be a majority or domin- ant project within the mainstream, and that the new programmes both are accepted by (some) mainstream economists and also are ranged against any neoclassical (or other) core. I am not actually convinced this is the case. But, if Davis can establish something like this, then, as I say, such an interpretation of a "heterodoxy within" carries some coherence. And it may capture some of Davis' thinking. In any case, I shall not refer to any "mathematical economics heterodoxy" in what follows, but leave it to Davis or others to ground further the case for interpreting matters in this way.

The relevant point in all this, though, is that whilst it is quite feasible that certain proponents of the new programmes do indeed advance a critique of one form of mathematical-deductive reasoning in order (and by way of seeking) to replace it with a different form of such formalis- tic reasoning (one that still retains the atomistic ontology of the methods it seeks to challenge), the (traditional) heterodoxy challenges the mainstream as a whole, and does so in order (and by way of seeking) to achieve a space for methods that presuppose a more realistic social ontology.

Davis' explanation of the lack of cross-communication between the two groupings supports this interpretation, although I am not sure he fully appreciates the significance of what he writes. Basically, he points to differences of "origins" and more especially "orientations" of the two groupings. He writes:

> the new research programs in economics – the "new heterodoxy" ... drawing on principles originally developed *outside* economics ... display an inward orientation; that is, they largely aim to change the principles reigning in orthodoxy, and do not aim to substitute new ones altogether.

In contrast the majority of traditional heterodox programmes, whatever their perceived origin are what Davis describes as outward oriented, meaning not wanting to adjust the mainstream core, but to do things entirely differently:

> [Focusing on the majority of the] traditional heterodox research programs, the few that share periphery origin stories are all oriented toward the periphery of economics ... Other traditional heterodox approaches that have different origin stories are all also outward oriented. It is not revision and adjustment of the core that drives them, but its wholesale abandonment.

And Davis sums up the resulting situation as follows:

> Thus the state of affairs in economics as a whole is that orthodoxy has come into question – here I agree with Lawson – but that the two heterodox groupings both interested in changing the field have almost entirely different views about how this should happen, and accordingly have little to say to each other.

As I say, the obvious inference to draw here is that the two groups have little to say to each other just because, in practice, they are committed to projects that are not only entirely different but perhaps fundamentally oppositional. The one, the traditional heterodoxy, is concerned to break away from the *insistence* on formalism in order to produce a more realistic or relevant economics; the other, *in the form that it is actually taking*, appears to be more concerned with introducing new formalistic programmes. Given the mathematical emphasis of the mainstream, the former group truly is heterodox in rejecting the formalistic emphasis, the latter group is not; in effect the latter group (in practice if not in principle) is a set of potential mainstream (or even mainstream core) activities in waiting.

## The way forward

Instead of treating his explanation (of the limited communication across the two groups) as a further reason to abandon his revised (two pronged) conception of the heterodoxy (or at least to see one as a heterodoxy within the formalist camp), Davis responds by asking a quite different question: "Which is the correct scenario?" By this, he means which is the best way to transform the mainstream. Is it by adopting the orientation of the new programmes or by following the path of the traditional heterodoxy?

Davis presents this option as a choice between "chipping away at the core on a gradualist schedule" or "betting on a big scientific revolution". I believe this presentation is misleading, on two accounts.

First, new forms of formalism that still carry all the existing problems of the old are not a solution to anything. If "chipping away at the core" is motivated simply by a desire to replace one form of largely irrelevant formalism with another, then it is not obvious that a great deal of progress is involved. Game theory has largely replaced general equilibrium theory in academic faculties like my own, but I do not see how this can be interpreted as a move forward, as a transformation worth having worked for. However, if "chipping away" is motivated by a desire to undermine the formalistic emphasis per se then, whilst no one wishes to discourage any move that might improve matters, it is difficult to see *how* introducing new formalisms is expected to help.

Second, a comparison between "chipping" and "betting" makes the former seem active, and the latter passive (or even irresponsibly speculative or indulgent). Heterodox economists and others, who underlabour for a more relevant economics, are just as concerned to work to transform the situation (though perhaps a real difference, over and above strategic ones, lies in the visions of the sort of outcome that is worth working for).

Davis, in any case, persists with his notion of a choice, and presents it as one facing the traditional heterodoxy:

> traditional heterodox economists have two choices. They can maintain their outward orientation, so that if change occurs in economics it will likely be on the terms determined by behavioural economists, experimentalists, and others in the new approaches. The risk here is that these movements may become more conservative as their success at influencing the core improves. Alternatively they can reverse their orientation, and turn to trying to shift what exists in the core, looking for allies in the "new heterodoxy" along the way, so as to improve the chances of successful change for both.

This statement begs various questions. What does it mean to say the new programmes are likely to become more "conservative" as they influence the core? Why are the new programmes likely to become more "conservative" as/if they influence the core? Is there any reason to suppose that if the traditional heterodoxy oriented itself more towards the core it could thereby achieve changes worth having?

I presume that by "more conservative", Davis means something like becoming more sympathetic to, and having minimal or reduced impact on, the current mainstream insistence that formalism be everywhere used.[5] If so, Davis is surely correct that it is only through adopting such an inward orientation that proponents of the new programmes will be accepted by the mainstream. But this is the case whatever the orientation of the traditional heterodoxy. Putting forward a formalistic programme is the only basis on which the current mainstream has been found to accept change. Furthermore, the traditional heterodoxy is, by its nature, opposed to the insistence that formalism be everywhere involved. The only way it could thus orientate itself to the mainstream in the manner Davis suggests is to drop this opposition, and relinquish its generalist heterodox status. But then it is unclear why any changes subsequently wrought by such a transformed project, should any occur, would be any less "conservative" than any brought about by the new approaches acting alone.

## Pluralism: some concerns

Davis finishes his piece by indicating his support for pluralism in economics. Although he does not actually say it, the reader could certainly interpret him as suggesting that my own position, whether wittingly or otherwise, is somehow less pluralistic in orientation than Davis' position, and perhaps even inconsistent with pluralism.

Thus, before mentioning pluralism, but after suggesting that the (traditional) heterodoxy has the choice of adopting either an outward orientation or an inward one, Davis offers the opinion that "Lawson's view of heterodoxy ... does not allow this choice to emerge".

Davis further adds that I council an outward orientation anyway: "Moreover, by asserting, 'there is a set of characteristics by virtue of which any tradition qualifies as heterodox' (Lawson, 2006a, p. 484), and by associating these shared characteristics with the rejection of the core of economics, [Lawson] counsels an outward orientation." And in his final paragraph Davis asserts:

> For many [an expression of pluralism] seems to mean an open stance toward the different heterodox research programs associated with ICAPE [the International Confederation for Pluralism in Economics] that seeks to promote a unity within difference. This stance seems to me to be shortsighted and anti-pluralist in important respects.

Davis ends by hoping that "ICAPE will become an increasingly pluralist organization in strategy as well as membership". Davis does not actually associate me explicitly with the "many" to whom he refers in the above passage, but I am, as he notes, concerned with promoting "unity within difference".

Whether or not Davis is indeed suggesting that my position is somehow less pluralist than is reasonable, I will treat this as an opportunity to allay the fears of others who wonder more explicitly whether such is not the case.

An example is provided by Robert Garnett (2006), the current ICAPE Secretary and Conference Organiser. In an important and wide-ranging (and I believe overall a very fair) contribution, Garnett does actually first express the view that "To date, the most rigorous justifications for [...] heterodox pluralism have been offered by 'open-systems realists'", a grouping in which he explicitly places myself (see also Garnett, 2005). But later in his piece, he sounds a note of caution. Criticising those heterodox "paradigmist economists" who seek to replace a mainstream paradigm with their own hopefully superior one, Garnett worries that my own approach carries residual traces of such a vision:

> Even the open system pluralisms of [...] Lawson carry residual traces of this paradigmist vision, insisting that heterodox economics define itself as the Other of orthodox economics. This is Cold War paradigmism in a different guise but still the same oppositional project, with the same truncated pluralism: offering intellectual openness and respect to persons and arguments within our own paradigm communities but not to outsiders. To define heterodox economics in this way is to warrant the charge that heterodox economics has no positive identity, that it defines itself only in terms of what it is not, rather than in terms of what it is. (Colander *et al.*, 2004, p. 491). This keeps us in the reactive position of "permitting the mainstream to set the heterodox agenda for heterodox economics ... to define its structure and content" (King, 2004). It also demonstrates that our professed commitments to pluralism are fundamentally ill-conceived, insincere, or both.
>
> (2006, pp. 531–2)

Somewhat more trenchant in his criticism is Jeroen Van Bouwel (2005). After distinguishing five different motivations for declaring oneself a pluralist (the ontological, the cognitive limitations, the historical and geographical, the pragmatic and the strategic motivations) Van Bouwel worries about the motivation for my support for pluralism:

> Lawson's quest for heterodox economics is not so much focusing on elaborating compatibility and complementarity with *mainstream* (or

neo-classical) economics, but rather creating his own alternative, that would be the new (monist) standard.

If we call Lawson's contribution pluralist, as he does, we can distinguish two different forms or conceptions of pluralism. Firstly, Lawson's work is pluralist in the sense that it provides us with an alternative to the mainstream, and as such we have more than one alternative (hence we have plurality). Secondly, we can understand pluralism as engaging in a conversation, as exchanging ideas, and not merely developing different isolated (and essentially monist) alternatives.

Lawson's account does not defend this second kind of pluralism. He does not develop a form of pluralism that shows how the different schools or alternatives can be used for different occasions. He rejects the *mainstream* completely, without considering possible positive contributions. He does not elaborate a form of pluralism that might show the complementarity of the schools or make us understand the origin of the differences between and the plurality of schools.

(2005, article 3)

And in his conclusion Van Bouwel adds:

I claim that a *really* pluralistic approach should engage in a conversation, in spelling out compatibilities and complementarities between the mainstream and the heterodox approaches (both sides should be engaged). The pluralism of Lawson risks leading us to an isolated diversity, to a lack of exchange of ideas.

(ibid.)

## A pluralistic orientation maintained

I take it that by pluralism is meant something like the affirmation, acceptance and encouragement of diversity. Clearly, such a notion itself has a plurality of meanings or inflections, of which two in particular are worth distinguishing.

One such is the notion of pluralism as description, as a claim about the way (some domain of) reality is.

Accepting this notion, then, for example, *ontological pluralism*, on one conception, designates the claim that multiple non-overlapping worlds exist (see Bruce Erlich, 1986, p. 527). A second notion of *ontological pluralism* has it that our *one* reality contains an (at least synchronically) irreducible multiplicity of constituents.[6]

To believe that at the base of everything is one substance, say energy, or vibrations, is to be a monist rather than pluralist in some metaphysical sense. Many eastern religions support a monistic rather than a pluralistic philosophy. It seems to me that either of the two conceptions of ontological pluralism just described may (or may not) be consistent with such a monistic metaphysics.

Clearly, this is not the place to attempt to elaborate an account of all the various kinds of descriptive pluralisms imaginable, and to indicate where I might stand with respect to them. I mention the foregoing merely to indicate the complexities of the topic, and ambiguities of any personal declaration to be a pluralist.

A second inflection on the term pluralism interprets it as a (normative) orientation, one of inclusiveness, of supporting and encouraging the acceptance of all interested parties, whatever their differences, within some process. The latter could be a society, or an academic conversation, a sports club or whatever.

It is possible that because this second notion expresses an orientation rather than a state of affairs it is best captured by the adjective pluralistic. In any case, the two conceptions appear distinct. For it seems to me that no matter how pluralistic an individual might be in the second sense, they could still be led to the view that some domain of reality is, as a matter of fact, monistic in nature.

In any case, it is this second inflection of pluralism, or "being pluralistic", that seems most relevant here. For each of the commentaries just discussed seems to be motivated by the worry that, by virtue of my conceiving heterodoxy in oppositional terms, my position is necessarily insufficiently pluralistic in the sense of somehow excluding, or showing insufficient respect or tolerance for, or engagement with (the views of) certain others in the academic conversation.

It is this particular set of worries, then, and specifically a concern that I am advancing a conception in which heterodoxy is somehow discouraged from engaging others, is necessarily oriented to replacing the mainstream with an undesirably monolithic paradigm, and/or is encouraging of isolationism, that I seek to allay in what follows. For I am indeed convinced that a pluralistic orientation in the sense in question is desirable, not least because it seems essential both to human flourishing in general and knowledge advance in particular. But I also believe that such an orientation is quite consistent with the position I am defending. Let me briefly elaborate.

## A positive orientation for heterodoxy

Actually, before addressing these specific concerns, there is a further worry, expressed in the middle of the quoted passage by Garnett, which really has little to do with pluralism, or being pluralistic. Here, drawing on the fears of Colander *et al.* (2004) and King (2004), Garnett suggests that to conceive heterodox economics in oppositional terms is to "warrant the charge" that "heterodox economics has no positive identity". Rather "it defines itself only in terms of what it is not, rather than in terms of what it is". As a result, the mainstream sets the agenda for heterodox economics.

If the situation were as Garnett describes, that is if heterodoxy had no positive identity (and this does at one point appear to be Davis' conception – but it is not mine), this, it seems to me, would be a weakness of heterodoxy, a consequence of a supposed non-pluralistic orientation, rather than a further example of it.

In any case, and considering things first in general terms, it does not follow for any heterodoxy characterised by its rejection of specific orthodox doctrine(s), that it must thereby be a purely reactive programme, lacking identity and defining itself purely in terms of the orthodoxy. It does mean that heterodoxy can be *identified as heterodox* in virtue of the opposition (its nominal essence). But if the opposition is to a specific set of doctrines, rather than opposition for opposition's sake, there will typically be a determinate cause, or set of causes, of this opposition rooted in the nature of the opposed doctrines(s), revealing something more fundamental about the heterodoxy *qua* heterodoxy (its real essence).

And over and above any rejection of specific orthodox doctrine, including the reasons for this rejection, any heterodoxy or heterodoxies can be as complex and heterogeneous as you like. As projects in their own right, each separate heterodox grouping can have its own identity, set its own agenda and be continually evolving. Moreover, this can be so even if, throughout this variety and evolution, a rejection of fundamental orthodox doctrine is sustained. Indeed, this is precisely my conception of the situation of modern heterodox economics.

As I say, only if it were the case that any opposition to orthodox doctrine was caused solely by a desire to be oppositional for opposition's sake irrespective of doctrine would it follow that heterodoxy is purely reactive. I repeat that if this does, at moments, seem to be Davis' conception of the heterodoxy of modern economics, it is certainly not mine. Rather, on my understanding, contemporary economic heterodoxy possesses deep-seated and valid reasons for its enduring and widespread opposition to specific orthodox doctrine. If the relevant orthodox doctrine were to be abandoned, this would be reason for the traditional heterodoxy to abandon the heterodox ascription, not for its seeking some other doctrine to oppose, nor for its abandoning the constructive endeavour by virtue of which each division of this heterodoxy constitutes one particular heterodox group rather than another.

I turn, then, to the concerns that more clearly bear upon the issue of whether the conception I defend is consistent with being sufficiently pluralistic.

# Engagement

First, just because heterodox traditions are constituted as heterodox traditions through their rejection of some orthodox doctrine, it does not follow that engagement with orthodox practitioners is thereby rendered necessarily infeasible or undesirable. Nor need communication be other than open and respectful. The possibilities for exchange will depend on context and the nature of the differences. But this will be so however heterodoxy is constituted. I myself have never wished to discourage respectful engagement with others.

Being more concrete, it is clear that a rejection of the defining doctrine of contemporary orthodoxy does not involve a rejection of all endeavours to explore the usefulness of formalistic methods. Heterodoxy *qua* heterodoxy, as I conceive it, involves a necessary opposition *not* to the use of formalism but only to *the dogmatic insistence that only these sorts of methods be used, irrespective of their ability to illuminate*. I do not see how a pluralist can accept this insistence, this orthodox doctrine, in the circumstances. Indeed in rejecting this one enduring orthodox doctrine, heterodoxy *qua* heterodoxy is inherently pluralistic in its very constitutive orientation (whether or not specific heterodox contributions remain pluralistic in all other respects). If, however, individuals within or outside the traditional heterodox groups wish to explore new formalisms, or methods of any kind, who is going to object?

To date, formalistic methods that presuppose an atomistic ontology have met with very little success, and from the perspective of the ontological framework I defend, this is none too surprising. But even if the ontology I defend is roughly right, there may yet be pockets of social reality that provide the appropriate conditions for successes with formalistic modelling, as I regularly acknowledge. In addition, of course, I recognise that the ontological conception I defend may yet turn out to be significantly mistaken in various ways; all knowledge claims are fallible. So no one wants to inhibit any serious methodological experimentation, whether involving formal techniques or otherwise. All that is being rejected by heterodoxy is the orthodox constraint on a pluralistic approach to economics analysis. This takes on a special significance just because the mainstream is constituted through this constraint. But if that is the nature of the beast, we just have to accept that opposing the mainstream (rejecting its constitutive doctrine) is a pro-, not an anti-, pluralistic stance.

It warrants emphasis, though, that any desire to engage does not mean heterodox economists must resort to constructing formalistic models (although of course there is no reason not to try that route if there is thought to be some promise of success). In particular, meta-theoretical discussion is at least as valid, where feasible. This can take the form of engagement via publications. Other forms depend on context.

I well understand the problems. As Richard Lipsey reminds us, if anyone presents an economics seminar without formulating a mathematical model it is not unknown for the mainstream economists "to turn off and figuratively, if not literally, to walk out" (Lipsey, 2001, p. 184).

But not all mainstream contributors are like this, especially the more thoughtful ones, despite appearances. While I was originally formulating my critique of the mainstream, Frank Hahn was head of the Cambridge economics faculty in which I am located. Hahn's commitment to the mainstream is clear enough from his retirement speech to the Royal Economic Society, where he famously gave advice to students to "avoid discussions of 'mathematics in economics' like the plague" (Hahn 1992a, see also Hahn, 1992b), adding that we should "give no thought to methodology". Elsewhere, as I have often observed, Hahn writes of any suggestion that the emphasis on mathematics may be a problem that this is "a view surely not worth discussing" (Hahn, 1985, p. 18). But appearances or rhetoric can mislead. This set of beliefs did not prevent Hahn himself, on various occasions, accepting invitations to talk at the Cambridge Realist Workshop that I coordinate.[7] In that forum, a genuine exchange of ideas took place on the sorts of issues here in contention, with large audiences of mostly PhD students listening (and indeed joining) in. I mention this just to reinforce the idea that possibilities for engagement depend very much on people and context. In particular, there should be no presumption that we should always hide our real critique, or perpetuate approaches we actually think are very unlikely to reveal insight, just in order to be able to engage.

## Paradigmism

Second, it also does not follow that, just because heterodoxy is characterised by its rejection of some orthodox doctrine, heterodox conceptions need be monolithic, monist, paradigmist or whatever. In principle, such heterodox projects can be as small, partial, open, multifaceted, fragmented, transitory, and inclusive as you like. Having said that I see nothing inherently anti-pluralistic about specific individuals exploring the possibility of creating a successful substantive paradigm of any sort.

Perhaps, though, it will be said that I am being less than pluralistic in supporting one specific social ontological conception above others. I hope it is clear that the conception I defend is consistent with many modes of explanation and forms of substantive theorising (see, for example, my response to Bjørn-Ivar Davidsen in this volume). Indeed, I would describe my position as one that is, if ontologically bold, then epistemologically and substantively very cautious. But still some might worry that my defence of a specific ontology, and my resting my arguments for inter-, or across-, group collaboration upon it, constitutes an undesirably anti-pluralistic stance in itself.

I do not think it does though. No one is saying that alternative ontological conceptions are not possible. Clearly they are. And to the extent that competing conceptions are produced, the point, once more, is to do whatever it takes to encourage all parties to engage constructively. But if one ontological conception can be shown to be better grounded than available alternatives, is that not a reason for drawing on it? Would anyone counsel a different approach in any other walk of life? Yes, let us leave options open. Let us also (repeatedly) try out alternatives, where appropriate. Certainly, let us include everyone in the conversation, whether it is oriented to the nature of ontology, substantive work, the nature of pluralism or being pluralistic, or whatever, and seek to do so with respect for, and encouragement of, each other. But *if*, when the time comes to act, we need to make use of an ontological conception, and there is one such conception (whatever the focus) that seems to be significantly more appropriate than others, not least because it is found to be far more explanatorily grounded, then it seems reasonable (for at least those that believe in it) to make use of the latter. This applies to our theories of the nature(s) of pluralism(s), of how we ought to be pluralistic, as well as to everything else.

## Differences in economic traditions as divisions of labour

Third, there is nothing inherently isolationist about the heterodox stance I set out. Van Bouwel complains that I do not "develop a form of pluralism that shows how the different schools or alternatives can be used for different occasions", that I do "not elaborate a form of pluralism that might show the complementarity of the schools or make us understand the origin of the differences between and the plurality of schools". I have actually had much to say on this not only in *Reorienting Economics* (Lawson, 2003a), but also in Lawson (2004, 2006a). Let me briefly outline my position.

The basic thesis I advance concerning the (traditional) heterodox projects is that they are best conceived as divisions of labour in one overall project. Remember I do not think the heterodox projects can be distinguished by the answers given (within any given tradition these are far too variable, both at any point in time and over time). Rather I argue that the individual heterodox traditions, like, I think, research endeavour in almost all other disciplines, are identifiable more by the sorts of questions asked (see Lawson, 2003a, 2006a). It is with this understanding of heterodoxy in mind that we can view the separate traditions as divisions of labour.

Central to this interpretation is the ontological conception that I defend, a conception that I also believe these heterodox traditions mostly implicitly presuppose. This conception has many facets. Social phenomena are, for example, viewed as bearing emergent powers, being structured, open, processual, highly internally related, comprising value, carrying meaning and so forth. The various heterodox traditions I believe are best viewed as exploring, if implicitly, specific aspects of this ontology (whilst maintaining a commitment to the whole).

Post Keynesians, for example, make fundamental uncertainty a central category. This clearly presupposes an ontology of openness as many post Keynesians have in recent years come increasingly to acknowledge. Such a focus has involved examining the implications of uncertainty or openness for the development of certain sorts of institutions, including money, for processes of decision making, and so forth. At the level of policy, the concern may well include the analysis of contingencies that recognise the fact of pervasive uncertainty, given the openness of social reality in the present and to the future, etc. For those influenced by Keynes, especially, a likely focus is how these matters give rise to collective or macro outcomes, and how they in turn impact back on individual acts and pressures for structural transformation, etc. (see Lawson, 1994, 2003a, chapter 7).

By similar reasoning, and as already noted earlier in this chapter, I believe that it is best to distinguish (old) Institutionalism, following Veblen especially, as concerned with the processual nature of social reality, and so as focusing especially on those forces working for stability and on others working for change. This orientation has taken the manifest form of a traditional concern with evolutionary issues, and with studying those aspects of social life that are most enduring, such as institutions and habits, along with those most inducing of continuous change, such as technology (see Lawson, 2002, 2003a (chapter 8), 2003b, 2006b).

Feminist economics, I believe, is best distinguished in terms of a focus on social relationality. Relations of care are of course a central issue. But relationality in itself seems central to most feminist concerns. Very often feminist economists have identified their own project as one that first of all concerns itself with women as subjects (which may include, for example, giving attention to differences among women, as well as between genders) and takes a particular orientation or focus, namely on the position of women (and other marginalised groups) within society and the economy. In practice this project includes an attention to the social causes at work in the oppression of, or in discrimination against, women (and others), the opportunities for progressive transformation or emancipation, questions of (relations of) power and strategy, and so forth.

Austrians may perhaps be best identified in some part according to their emphasis on the role of inter-subjective meaning in social life (see Lawson, 1997, chapter 10), and so on.

I suggest, then, that at least some heterodox traditions are most easily viewed as primarily (though not exclusively) concerned with different aspects of the properties of social phenomena (openness, processuality, internal relationality) uncovered through philosophical ontology.

Other traditions, though, seem to be more interested in elaborating the nature of specific social categories, and in particular how the features uncovered through philosophical ontology (openness, relationality, process, etc.) coalesce in certain social items of interest within that particular tradition. An obvious example is Marxian economics, a project primarily concerned to understand the nature of the relational totality in motion that is capitalism. But we also find a significant Austrian interest in the nature of "the market process" and entrepreneurship in particular. And as already noted there is significant post Keynesian interest in the nature of money, institutionalist interest in institutions and technology, feminist interest in care and so forth.

How does the current mainstream join the party? Clearly its *insistence* that mathematical-deductivist methods be more or less always and everywhere used and by all of us, is ill-fitted to this pluralistic picture. Of course, the argument can be heard, but there can be no compulsion for anyone to follow. But those who experiment with formalistic methods, without insisting that others always and everywhere do so, certainly have a place. Formalistic endeavour will likely be most fruitful where social conditions most approximate the atomistic ontology that such endeavour presupposes. In *Reorienting Economics* (Chapter 1), I sketch the sorts of scenarios under which the emergence of such conditions appears most feasible and wherein, indeed, some successes seem occasionally to have been achieved.

I hope it is clear, then, that there is a place for more or less all types of research practice on the conception I defend; I am not at all advancing a vision of (or seeking to encourage) isolated practices.[8] To the contrary, according to the conception I am advancing it is actually vital that the various divisions perpetually keep in touch with each other's contributions and developments. For all are working on aspects of the same whole, and each tradition requires some understanding of the whole (and so of each other's contributions) in order to carry out its own division of labour competently (an issue I consider further in my response to David Ruccio in the current volume).

In short, the very fact that (or my defending the contention that) heterodoxy is identified through its opposition to a specific orthodox doctrine does not in or of itself undermine the possibility of maintaining pluralistic orientations of the sort that most seem to concern Davis, Garnett, Van Bouwel and others.[9] In fact, the realising of such pluralistic orientations, I hope it is clear, is also something that I, like very many others, continue to support.

## Conclusion

Davis' chapter along with other papers he has recently produced provide a valuable assessment of ongoing developments in the modern economics; in these papers we find many insights into the dynamics, including various transient aspects, of much that is going on. In this work Davis is raising fundamental questions and providing stimulating answers.

Clearly, though, I am yet to be convinced of all of Davis' conclusions. In his current piece, Davis advances a picture of heterodoxy in the context of modern economics (that challenges my own interpretation). In truth, though, his revised notion of heterodoxy is either arbitrary, or not consistently oriented to any accepted doctrine of the existing orthodoxy. Moreover, the result of following Davis' lead, however interpreted, is seemingly two different forms of heterodoxy (the old and the new) that appear to have little in common with each other, with each grouping, as Davis notes, being rather cautious about the other's contributions. Furthermore, Davis does not really give us any good reason for taking his path.

Having said that, there is a point at which Davis suggests that the "new programmes", like the traditional heterodoxy, oppose (what Davis labels) neoclassical economics. Davis does not seem to characterise the new programmes by this opposition. But it is an opposition, nevertheless, one focused on a doctrine accepted by at least a significant portion of the modern mainstream (albeit not the mainstreams' most basic and universal tenet: that mathematical-deductivist methods should be employed). As such, if the designation heterodoxy is really so important for the new programmes, it may be the case that, given the mathematical form they are taking in practice, there is coherence to thinking of them as coming to constitute a heterodoxy within the mainstream, perhaps being designated a "mathematical economics heterodoxy" for clarity.

In the end, though, the primary concern here, Davis would probably agree, is not with characterising either the mainstream or heterodoxy per se. I think we both start with an assessment that all is not well with modern economics, and are both first and foremost concerned that something is done to repair the situation.

From there on in, though, our paths seem to diverge. We may even differ in our assessments of the nature of the problem. For my part, as I have often repeated, I am opposed to the mainstream insistence that only mathematical-deductivist methods be used. Not only is this an undesirably anti-pluralist stance but also, in my assessment, it accounts for the continuing poor intellectual state of modern economics (see especially Lawson, 2003a, Chapter 1). Perhaps, though, this orthodox insistence bothers Davis less. It may be that Davis' primary worry is more with the sort of formalism that prevails, and that Davis is opposed in particular to the sort of formalism to which he refers as neoclassicism. Certainly, this would explain our different emphases and strategies.

But whatever Davis' assessment of the primary nature of the problem, if the accepted goal is ultimately to introduce new forms of formalism into the mainstream, then Davis' preferred strategy of "looking inwards" is surely the superior. If, though, the goal is a more genuinely pluralistic economics, one that does not support an unreasoned insistence on mathematics only and everywhere, and this of course is my own preference, then Davis' strategy, I believe, is almost as surely the inferior.

## Notes

1 For example 1999 witnessed the formation of the UK based Association for Heterodox Economics (AHE), an organisation that now sponsors an annual conference, and has run numerous postgraduate training workshops and more. In October 2002 the University of Missouri at Kansas City hosted a conference on "The history of heterodox economics in the 20th century". December 2002 saw the inaugural conference of the Australian Society of Heterodox Economists (SHE) at the University of New South Wales. Six months later, in June 2003, back at the University of Missouri at Kansas City, ICAPE (the International Confederation of Associations for Pluralism in Economics) celebrated its ten-year birthday with its "first world conference on the future of heterodox economics". The July 2004 edition of the *Review of Radical Political Economics* comprised a special issue on the History of Radical Heterodox Economics. The University of Utah sports a Heterodox Economics Student Association (HESA). And on the Internet it is possible to find a large number of sites dedicated to promoting specifically "heterodox economics". As I write, for example, it is possible to find at www.orgs.bucknell.edu/ afee/hetecon.htm (accessed August 2006) a "heterodox economics web" listing: heterodox economics associations; heterodox economics journals (scholarly); heterodox publications (news, commentary and analysis); heterodox teaching resources; heterodox discussion groups and so on.

2 In doing so I am also responding to Edward Fullbrook's editorial request to "discuss pluralism somewhere in the book".

3 In essence the typical paper starts with some description of phenomenon uncritically accepted from research in psychology, or frequently even studies of animal behaviour.

4 For a useful critical overview of these developments see Ariel Rubinstein, 2006.

5 Thus I assume Davis does not mean politically conservative. Davis explicitly rejects the idea that we should relate distinctions in the sorts of economic programmes pursued (and in particular any differentiations as to whether they are orthodox or heterodox) to political differentiations/allegiances.

6 Typically, it is also held that each constituent or entity can be known only fallibly and partially, in various ways, under various competing descriptions, with all ways of knowing reflecting the situatedness and specific capacities of the "knower", etc.

7 For a listing of programmes for the last ten years or so, including several presentations by Hahn, go to: www.econ.cam.ac.uk/seminars/realist/ previous_workshops.htm (accessed August 2006).

8 This indeed is something I have endeavoured to emphasise over and again. Thus, for example, in Lawson 2006a I wrote:

> I should finally perhaps emphasise (though it is hopefully apparent throughout) that, although I am arguing that each heterodox tradition be distinguished according to a traditional set of concerns and emphases (rather than answers or methodological principles), I do not want to

suggest that each somehow works with isolated components of society or economy. The object or subject matter of social theory/science, no less than economics, is an interrelated whole (in process). To focus competently on specific aspects requires an understanding of the totality (just as the investigation of any specific aspect of the human body presupposes some prior understanding of its functioning within the whole). There is no part of the social realm that does not have an economic aspect (although social reality does not reduce to its economic aspects). And, similarly, there is no part of social life that cannot be viewed under the aspect of its degree of openness, or its processuality/fixity, or the nature of its social relationality, etc. In other words, on the conception laid out each of the various heterodox traditions is viewed as approaching the same totality but with a distinguishing set of concerns, emphases, motivating interests and (so) questions. And, ideally, each will be achieving results that warrant synthesising with the findings of others (again see Lawson, 2003a, especially part III).

9   This is not, of course, to imply that things couldn't be improved (for an argument that heterodoxy could be more pluralistic see Randall Holcombe, 2006).

## References

Arnsperger, Christian and Yanis Varoufakis (2006) "What is Neoclassical Economics?" *post-autistic economics review*, Issue 38, July, pp. 2–13.

Colander, D., R. Holt and J. Rosser (2004) "The Changing Face of Mainstream Economics", *Review of Political Economy*, 16(4), pp. 485–99.

Davis, J. (2006) "The Turn in Economics: Neoclassical Dominance to Mainstream Pluralism?" *Journal of Institutional Economics*, 2(1), pp. 1–20.

Erlich, Bruce (1986) "Amphibolies: On the Critical Self-Contradictions of 'Pluralism'", *Critical Inquiry*, 12(3), spring, pp. 521–49.

Fine, Ben (2006), "Critical Realism and Heterodoxy", mimeo: SOAS.

Fullbrook, Edward (2005) "The RAND Portcullis and PAE", *Post-autistic economics review*, Issue 32, 5 July, article 5.

Garnett, Robert F. (2005) "Wither Heterodoxy?", *Post-autistic economics review*, issue 34, article 1, pp. 2–21.

Garnett, Robert F. (2006) "Paradigms and Pluralism in Heterodox Economics", *Review of Political Economy*, 18(4), October, pp. 521–46.

Hahn, Frank H. (1985) "In Praise of Economic Theory", the *1984 Jevons Memorial Fund Lecture*, London: University College.

Hahn, Frank H. (1992a) "Reflections", *Royal Economics Society Newsletter*, 77.

Hahn, Frank H. (1992b) "Answer to Backhouse: Yes", *Royal Economic Society Newsletter*, 78, p. 5.

Hodgson, Geoffrey (2006) "An Institutional and Evolutionary Perspective on Health Economics", Mimeo: University of Hertfordshire. Paper presented at the *Cambridge Realist Workshop*, 20 November.

Holcombe, Randall G. (2006) "Pluralism Versus Heterodoxy in Economics and the Social Sciences", Mimeo: Florida State University. Paper presented at the Annual Meetings of the Association for Heterodox Economics, in London, July.

Keynes, John M. (1973) *The Collected Writings of John Maynard Keynes, Vol. XIV, The General Theory and After: Part II Defence and Development*, London: Macmillan for the Royal Economic Society.

King, John E. (2004) "A Defence of King's Argument(s) for Pluralism", *post-autistic economics review*, Issue 25, article 3, May.

Lawson, Tony (1994) "The Nature of Post Keynesianism and its Links to other Traditions", *Journal of Post Keynesian Economics*, 16: 503–38. Reprinted in D.L. Prychitko (ed.), (1996), *Why Economists Disagree: An Introduction To The Contemporary Schools of Thought*, New York: State University of New York Press, pp. 115–54.

Lawson, Tony (1997) *Economics and Reality*, London and New York: Routledge.

Lawson, Tony (2002) "Should Economics Be an Evolutionary Science? Veblen's Concern and Philosophical Legacy", The 2002 Clarence Ayres Memorial Lecture, *Journal of Economic Issues*, XXXVI(2), pp. 279–91.

Lawson, Tony (2003a) *Reorienting Economics*, London and New York: Routledge.

Lawson, Tony (2003b) "Institutionalism: On the Need to Firm up Notions of Social Structure and the Human Subject", *Journal of Economic Issues*, XXXVII(1), pp. 175–201.

Lawson, Tony (2004) "On Heterodox Economics, Themata and the Use of Mathematics in Economics", *Journal of Economic Methodology*, 11(3), September, pp. 329–40.

Lawson, Tony (2005a) "The (Confused) State of Equilibrium Analysis in Modern Economics: an (Ontological) Explanation", *Journal for Post Keynesian Economics*, 27(3), spring, pp. 423–44.

Lawson, Tony (2005b) "Reorienting History (of Economics)", *Journal for Post Keynesian Economics*, 27(3), spring, pp. 455–71.

Lawson, Tony (2006a) "The Nature of Heterodox Economics", *Cambridge Journal of Economics*, 30(4), July, pp. 483–507.

Lawson, Tony (2006b) "The Nature of Institutionalist Economics", *Evolutionary and Institutional Economics Review*, 2(1), pp. 7–20.

Lawson, Tony (2007) "Tensions in Modern Economics. The case of Equilibrium Analysis", in Valeria Mosini (ed.), *Equilibrium in Economics: Scope and Limits*, London and New York: Routledge, pp. 133–49.

Lipsey, Richard G. (2001) "Successes and Failures in the Transformation of Economics", *Journal of Economic Methodology*, 8(2), June, pp. 169–202.

Perona, Eugenia (2004) "The Confused State of Complexity in Economics: An Ontological Explanation", Facultad de Ciencias Económicas, Universidad Nacional de Córdoba, Argentina.

Rubinstein, Ariel (2006) "Discussion of 'Behavioral Economics'", in Richard Blundell, Whitney K. Newey and Torsten Persson (eds), *Advances in Economics and Econometrics: Theory and Applications, Ninth World Congress* (Econometric Society Monographs), Cambridge: Cambridge University Press.

Smith, Lewis L. (2004) "Complexity Economics and Alan Greenspan", *post-autistic economics review*, 26, article 2, 2 August.

Van Bouwel, Jeroen (2005) "Towards a Framework for Pluralism in Economics", *post-autistic economics review*, 31, article 3, 16 May.

# 7 Reorienting economics through triangulation of methods

*Paul Downward and Andrew Mearman*

## Introduction

Tony Lawson's widely acclaimed book *Economics and Reality* (1997) provided a systematic ontological critique of mainstream economic analysis. The critique focused upon the inappropriateness of the 'deductivist method' of neoclassical economics, which implicitly assumes a closed-system ontology, and the open-system nature of reality. Deductivism is an approach that invokes covering laws of explanation, whether or not these are derived from formally deductive or inductive premises. This method in turn assumes a *closed-system ontology*, in which strict regularities of the type 'if event X, then event Y' will occur. For Lawson, the emphasis on mathematical modelling and econometric testing are evidence of this closed-system approach. Further, the use of econometric testing, so defined, is an example of *empirical realism* – reflecting a belief in a flat ontology comprising only observations of events.

While essentially a critique, *Economics and Reality* also advocated *retroduction* – the movement in thought from a phenomenon of interest to the mechanism(s) that (at least in part) caused it – as the appropriate logic of inference for an open system. The reasons are broadly twofold. First, cause cannot be associated with the constant conjunction of events in a non-experimental open system, but rather the emergence of events out of causal mechanisms that draw upon human agency and structures. Using this method to gain an understanding of events, the researcher then needs to establish the mechanisms that gave rise to them. Second, our empirical observation of actual events and the mechanisms that produce them will be related *transfactually*; i.e. the causal mechanisms exist and may operate irrespective of the observed events. Consequently our understanding of them will be fallible, a fact that follows not only from the complex co-determination of events, but also because of the hermeneutic issues associated with interpreting and communicating our understanding of causes.

For Lawson, retroduction is likely to be achieved most successfully through *contrast explanation*, a method based on the premise that research should be directed towards explaining 'surprising' breakdowns in patterns of events, because here changes in causal mechanisms may be more apparent. Contrast explanation thus shares the same structure as experimental reasoning but, of course, reflects an open-system context in which causal mechanisms are not isolated and stable.

One criticism of *Economics and Reality* is that its practical guidance to economists remains limited, beyond informing them what they ought *not* do. *Reorienting Economics* (2003) also emphasises the ontological critique of mainstream method, although in cautious terms. However, there is an expanded account of 'contrast explanation' and a discussion of the merits of borrowing biological metaphors in producing social explanation. Lawson demonstrates that heterodoxy's appeal to evolutionary biological metaphors as opposed to mathematical systems has promise, but should be tempered by concern with the ontological relevance of mathematics to social systems. Lawson then focuses upon a discussion of the broad, often implicit, ontological similarities between heterodox approaches to economics and Critical Realism. As such they offer possibilities for redefining economics in a much more pluralistic way.

We believe that there is a need for practical guidance in conducting research projects informed by Critical Realism, and in this chapter we argue, drawing upon ongoing work, for the adoption of *triangulation* as a principle of research design. Triangulation is commitment in research design to investigation and inference via multiple methods that are not placed in any a priori hierarchy. We argue that triangulation allows retroduction to be made operational, facilitates pluralism – rather than rejecting outright entire methods – and allows economics to be reorientated towards other social sciences, as Lawson recommends (Downward and Mearman, 2004a, 2004b, 2007). Thus, triangulation can be an important step towards fulfilling Lawson's project.

## Triangulation

In social research in its broadest sense, and moving away from the spatial origins of the metaphor, triangulation implies combining together more than one set of insights in an investigation. Denzin (1970) offers a taxonomy of triangulation: (1) data triangulation – the combination of different data types; (2) investigator triangulation – the combination of insights from different investigators; (3) theoretical triangulation – the combination of different theoretical perspectives; and (4) methodological triangulation – the combination of different methods. Denzin further distinguishes between *within-method* triangulation, i.e. combining different cases of the same method; and *between-method* triangulation, i.e. combining studies of different methodologies. Clearly, between-method triangulation is more radical, because it could involve, for example, an econometric methodology in combination with an ethnographic method.

We have argued elsewhere that Critical Realism can create a philosophical basis for triangulation.

Triangulation is common in other applied social sciences (see below) but not in economics. There is some use of triangulation by professional (including government) economists, such as those at the Bank of England, but its use by academic economists is rarer; and when used it tends to be for pragmatic reasons. A common reason for combination of data types is that the main source of data is incomplete. For example, the Bank of England uses survey and anecdotal evidence from its Agents as the most up to date picture of economic conditions. This compensates for the inevitable lag in official quantitative data. Economists cite epistemological reasons for triangulation, such as the fallibility of knowledge, relatively rarely.

In the literature of social science research methods there is discussion of the basis for triangulation. It is common to *reject* triangulation for ontological reasons. *Positivist* social scientists (or those influenced by positivism) tend to hold that methods should only be used that conform to positivist principles, such as objectivity, observability and precision. All of these principles are met by quantitative data. For *interpretivists*, the opposite position is taken. Interpretivism includes hermeneutic concerns that social phenomena are intrinsically meaningful; that meanings must be understood; and that the interpretation of an object or event is affected by its context. Moreover, for the above reasons, meanings cannot be measured, counted or understood. Unsurprisingly, interpretivist approaches tend to focus on the limitations of quantitative analysis in the social arena. Silverman (1993) offers a typical example of the interpretivist approach. Silverman argues that quantitative methods retain a positivist perspective in which data collectors basically follow established protocols and data providers simply reveal aspects required of the protocol as 'objective' entities. In contrast, qualitative methods are 'interactionist' and reflect the interviewer creating the interview context and the interviewee engaging in a dialectic with the definition of the situation, so that the research reflects social relationships that are inherently subjective and not objective. On this basis Silverman rejects quantitative methods as inappropriate to social research.

It remains the case that the justification for triangulation in social science tends to emphasise pragmatism. This is clearly unsatisfactory for a Critical Realist, whose concern is for ontological consistency between method and material. This chapter argues that such consistency can be established because triangulation is essential to retroduction. The argument proceeds by considering alternative research methods.

## Triangulation rather than rejection of methods

Lawson (1997) spends considerable time critically examining the use of econometrics in an open-system reality, in which event regularities are unlikely to occur. It is easy to form the impression from Lawson's work that econometrics is being rejected as inappropriate practice. Lawson (1999) clarifies this position, arguing that econometrics is perfectly permissible providing that it is used in closed systems; however, given that these are held to be unlikely to occur, econometrics is likely to have extremely limited use. Downward and Mearman (2002) examine such Critical-Realist objections and find them unsustainable. If methods are to be rejected because they impose some degree of closure on an open reality, then in fact, all methods so far proposed must also be rejected. Any method that supposes that an entity remains fixed for long enough for it to be identified as an object of study imposes closure on an open reality. Thus quantitative analysis involves closure, because the act of quantification involves the assumption of qualitative invariance across subjects. Likewise, *if* qualitative investigation is concerned with collating insights and offering stylised interpretations and narratives, this assumes qualitative invariance – or, in Critical-Realist terminology, *intrinsic closure*. Contrast explanation is thus challenged because, first, it tends to involve quantitative contrasts; second, because it makes assumptions about what are surprising, abnormal or significant instances, which in turn presupposes a notion of a normal deviation from a trend or fixed pattern, and finally because qualitative endeavours to explain the contrasts are not fundamentally distinct in terms of maintaining a degree of closure. However, this is not necessarily problematic per se. As Mearman (2007) notes, a Critical-Realist *abstraction* necessarily involves a focus on what is real and essential to the temporary exclusion of other factors, regarded as transient or insignificant. Moreover, by abstracting from other factors, one *assumes that those factors are behaving in particular, consistent ways.*

Therefore, we argue that for practising economists, Lawson's arguments are potentially too destructive, leaving no techniques available for concrete analysis. In contrast, as reality comprises parts that have different degrees of openness, these should be explored by methods that also exhibit different degrees of openness: for example, statistical inference requires more closure than statistical estimation.

The above discussion can be viewed as reflecting (an aspect of) the fallibilism of all knowledge claims. More generally, fallibilism of theory tends to have two geneses: ontological and epistemological. Epistemologically, humans have limited computational capacity to deal with the world, even one of a simple structure, particularly when faced with multiple meanings and incommensurability. Thus, no one theory is likely to be able to capture adequately these aspects. Furthermore, if the object of enquiry (and by extension, the world) is highly complex, it is extremely difficult for any theory to capture its aspects adequately. This concern applies when the social world is held to comprise open systems, in which, for example, the future is open, because current agency affects future structures in unpredictable ways. Even for a super computer, society is complex and unpredictable. In this light, no one model should be relied upon to give an accurate picture of the object of enquiry.[1] Rather, methodological triangulation requires that in any act of inference to causal claims about an object of enquiry, two (or more) methods with different degrees of openness, are combined. Simultaneously, triangulation provides the researcher with a means of inference that addresses the concern over open systems and avoids the rejection of methods. Thus, triangulation offers a way out of the practical impasse found in *Reorienting Economics* and in *Economics and Reality*.

## Triangulation and retroduction

As we have argued elsewhere, a Critical-Realist position can provide an ontological justification for triangulation; and triangulation is a necessary element of the logic of retroduction and hence is crucial for operationalising Critical Realism (Downward and Mearman, 2002, 2007).

A central element of the Critical-Realist programme is that every paradigm (and its associated methods and theories), has an underlying ontology. Thus, the link between a method or theory and its ontology cannot be avoided (Danermark *et al.*, 2002: 152–3). How far do other philosophical positions meet this criterion? Above it was argued that both positivist and interpretivist approaches make a strong pre-commitment to a particular ontology that explicitly rules out the need for (methodological) triangulation. Specifically, positivism and interpretivism both reject methods that do not meet their ontologies. Consequently, one might imagine that both meet the Critical-Realist criterion. Nevertheless, Critical Realists criticise both perspectives because each has empirical realist foundations: the empirical is the basis for, and in fact constitutes, reality. For example, positivism embraces an inductive view of explanation to which value-free or observation of objective reality is crucial. Furthermore, either informally or formally, through statements of initial conditions and assumptions, deduced consequences or predictions are assessed empirically. Additionally, as noted earlier, for Critical Realists, there is a factor common to deduction *and* induction and which characterises their essential logic: explanations are presented in the form of 'covering laws', which commits an *epistemic fallacy*, i.e. to conflate what is experienced with what exists. The conception or knowledge of phenomena manifest in the theorist's ideas and arguments is treated as logically equivalent to the phenomena under review. In this sense, knowledge is presented as being effectively complete. This is either in a literal or positivist sense in which theories directly represent an external world, or in the 'idealist' or interactionist sense that the world is merely the proposed collection of ideas, whether these are deductive constructs or subjectively specific concepts.

Thus, from the Critical-Realist perspective, both quantitative and qualitative analysis (either based on phenomenology or on hermeneutics) commit an epistemic fallacy; that is, they conflate the subject and object of analysis through the invocation of covering laws. Therefore, the traditional quantitative/qualitative choice can be viewed as unnecessary and, moreover, reflects fallacious thinking from a Critical-Realist perspective. This argument opens up the possibility of triangulation.

Critical Realists also espouse an ontology of depth realism, which has two prongs: realism and depth. Realism holds that the nature of the object drives the process of research. Depth implies that specific types of methods are necessary for (social) scientific investigation. Critical Realism implies that, because the objects of social science are inherently complex and have many important aspects that belong in various categories, it is not possible to capture some of the broader aspects of the objects with narrow methods (for instance counting the frequency of the entity). Furthermore, because, according to Critical Realists, agency is absolutely crucial, so people's motives cannot be ignored; and because reasons are causes, it is essential to explore these different concepts in analysis. Moreover, because reasons are causes, Critical Realists reject the traditional equation of, on the one hand, qualitative equals exploratory or descriptive; and on the other, quantitative equals explanatory methods (Danermark *et al.*, 2002: 163). Indeed, Critical Realists share with pragmatists the view that to associate qualitative methods with hermeneutics (or whoever) and quantitative analysis with positivism (or whoever) is limiting – instead they are looking to transcend the dichotomy. Also, research is governed by the need to get to the bottom of a question – i.e. to uncover generative mechanisms – and whichever are the best methods to use should be used (Danermark *et al.*, 2002: 162–4). However, unlike pragmatism, realism has an ontological grounding to that position.

The connection between the ontology and the method – added to the belief that reality is stratified – can be argued to lead some Critical Realists to abandon the strict dual of quantitative/qualitative in favour of one in terms of intensive versus extensive research design (Sayer, 1992: Ch. 9; Danermark *et al.*, 2002: Ch. 6). The former design is what is typically thought of as a characteristic of social science. Research explores the contextual relations surrounding a particular unit of analysis (i.e. qualitative research). This is as opposed to the latter research design that emphasises the formal relations of similarity between units of analysis, that is, it produces taxonomic descriptions of variables (i.e. quantitative research).

However, this seems to reinstate the old dual despite the two types of method being treated as complementary empirical procedures with complimentary strengths and weaknesses. Thus it is typically argued that the causal insights from extensive research will be less. Moreover, one is reminded that the validity of the (qualitative) analysis of cases does not rely upon broad quantitative evidence. In this sense the traditional view put forward for triangulation as validating qualitative insights is not necessarily applicable.

The focus on intensive/extensive research designs in combination seems necessary because of the nature of reality. A number of authors (for example, Olsen, 2003) have talked in terms of a *zoom-lens* approach, in which the investigator necessarily zooms in to focus on critical detail of a case (intensive research) but, for various reasons (including the often necessary relations between an object and other objects), the investigator must then zoom out, to get a wider sense of the object's context. Yet, the ontological basis for making such claims seems unclear.

In a number of papers we address these issues and argue that combining methods is *central* to retroductive activity. The following discussion briefly restates these arguments.

One of the consequences of the above discussion is that 'quantitative' and 'qualitative' approaches are not a dual: they overlap to a degree in underlying logic and can also refer to the same objects of analysis. They can share, or be conditioned upon, the same ontological perspective and are not of necessity wedded to particular, and different, ontological presumptions. Rather, the choice of method is not paradigmatic or one of ontology, because that ontology is shared by the methods, but simply reflects the specifics of the question being asked. If the questions probe different features of a phenomenon then different methods might be needed. It remains that they focus on the *same* phenomenon.

Two conclusions follow from this discussion. The first is that different research methods can be logically employed in a triangulating strategy to reveal different features of the *same* reality without the presumption of being exhaustive. The second is that the Critical-Realist perspective renders a need for the triangulation to have an explicitly ontological dimension to capture related but different layers of this reality. Figure 1, adapted from Downward (2003: 298) illustrates potential options.

In the first column are the two opposing positions identified in the Critical-Realist literature; Critical Realism and empirical realism. The latter is, of course, the empirical counterpart to deduction, induction and the hypothetico-deductivist model of explanation. The next column describes the focus of analysis framed within these alternative philosophical positions, which are, respectively, real causes and empirical events. In the case of empirical realism, relationships between events are purported to reveal causes in the covering law sense as indicated by the horizontal broken line linked to, say, typical statistical testing methods.

In contrast, Critical Realism maintains that investigating causes involves moving below the level of events through retroduction. The third column thus reveals that corresponding to what is typically identified as 'qualitative' research methods, the context-laden meaning of con-

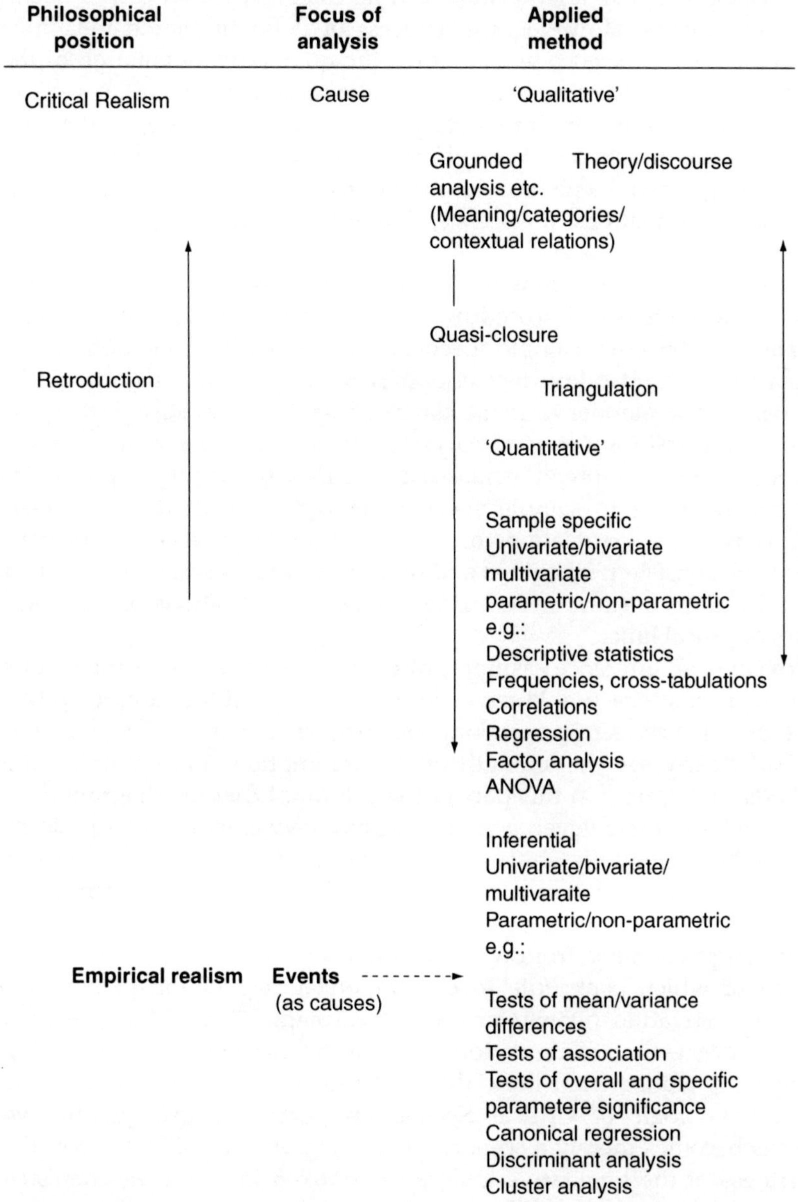

| Philosophical position | Focus of analysis | Applied method |
|---|---|---|
| Critical Realism | Cause | 'Qualitative' |

Grounded        Theory/discourse
analysis etc.
(Meaning/categories/
contextual relations)

Quasi-closure

Triangulation

'Quantitative'

Sample specific
Univariate/bivariate
multivariate
parametric/non-parametric
e.g.:
Descriptive statistics
Frequencies, cross-tabulations
Correlations
Regression
Factor analysis
ANOVA

Inferential
Univariate/bivariate/
multivaraite
Parametric/non-parametric
e.g.:

**Empirical realism**    **Events** -------→
(as causes)

Tests of mean/variance
differences
Tests of association
Tests of overall and specific
parametere significance
Canonical regression
Discriminant analysis
Cluster analysis

Retroduction

*Figure 1* Applied Critical Realism.

cepts, categories and relationships can be established and causal narratives constructed. However, this process of defining shared meanings and categories in essence breaks down the qualitative orientation of the research and, of necessity, begins to invoke aspects of closure in seeking a degree of generality and purporting to refer to the same object of analysis. Hence the direction of 'quasi closure' indicated in the column. Thus, categorising phenomena implies assuming invariant (or a degree of invariance in) qualities. In essence, defining a variable requires at least intrinsic closure.

Increasing the degree to which closure is invoked thus begins to 'legitimise' various statistical procedures. These can refer to one, two or many variables but be either sample specific or inferential in orientation, which means that a probability distribution is referred to in a parametric or non-parametric manner to make claims about the generality of the purported relationships between variables. It is, of course, clear that the degree of closure assumed increases as one moves *down* the column. For example referring to sample specific descriptive methods of analysis such as averages, correlations or regression implies that values of variables have consistent meanings and that these variables can be combined in a relatively constant or enduring manner as indications of, say, outcomes of causal links.

Probabilistic inference assumes, much more strongly, that the results carry over, in a measurable sense, to contexts beyond the sample. In this sense one is increasingly invoking the *extrinsic condition of closure*, and one can clearly see the strength of the assumptions underpinning the methods that appear in this part of the column. What the diagram does reveal, in entirety however, is that in general, movements towards statistical methods naturally shifts attention towards 'events' as opposed to 'causes', which are in essence qualitative. On this basis one can argue that rather than revealing covering laws, in contrast statistical methods can reveal phenomena from which causal research can begin and combinations of which contribute to our understanding of the phenomena under investigation (Downward and Mearman, 2004c). Thus the final column reveals that triangulation between the methods – that is linking the insights gained from these different research methods captures the retroductive logic of Critical Realism. Importantly, any quantitative analysis becomes merely a scenario whose legitimacy will rest upon the robustness of the qualitative invariance invoked in causal mechanisms and, of course, the lack of influence of countervailing causes. The discovery and robustness of such causal claims, along with their implications, will of necessity always be open to revision. In this respect, probabilistic inferences are also conditional upon and should be assessed in connection with analysis of the nature of the object under investigation.

## Conclusions

This chapter has argued that Lawson's *Reorienting Economics* still leaves significant lacunae in its implications for what economists, if they take Lawson seriously, are to do in their concrete research. Moreover, we interpret Lawson's new contribution as reinforcing his previous ones on the proper role of econometrics and other 'traditional' methods in economics: that such methods should not be used unless in highly specific narrow circumstances. It has been argued that a commitment in one's research design to methodological triangulation, i.e. inference via the combination of methods (informed by different and perhaps competing philosophies), can contribute several significant benefits: (1) the rejection of methods apparently implied by Lawson is avoided; (2) the self-defeating implication of (1), namely, that all empirical analysis is invalid in open systems, is also avoided; (3) triangulation is consistent with depth realism; and (4) triangulation is essential to the operationalisation of the Critical-Realist logic of retroduction.

Moreover, triangulation allows economics to be reoriented towards the social sciences, as Lawson recommends in *Reorienting Economics*. In other social sciences, and implied by Denzin's taxonomy, triangulation is much more widespread. For example, Danermark *et al.* (2002: 152) claim that within the sociological community the view is widely supported that there is no universal method and that there is a need for multimethodological approaches. Thus, in the applied social sciences, triangulation is common in nursing, health and education, and tourism (see, for example, Downward and Mearman, forthcoming). Yet in economics, 'scientific status' is sought, where scientific status is thought to mean systematic explanation, shaped by empirical evidence, and arrived at via a narrow set of methods. Hence, economics is typically perceived to be closer to the 'hard' sciences than other social sciences because of the axiomatisation of the discipline (Hausman, 1998). Economics stands alone from other branches of social enquiry and, indeed, disciplines.

Thus, triangulation raises interesting questions concerning the nature of social science. If one mixes methods of research and, in so doing, attempts to bring specific disciplinary tools to the analysis then such a 'multidisciplinary' approach will entail the ontological clashes discussed earlier because, by construction the different disciplines embrace different methods and, as a result, different ontologies as expressed by traditional philosophy of science. In contrast, to 'unite' social science, what is required is an attempt to transcend the separate disciplines to produce an 'interdisciplinary approach'. Social science, so defined, *naturally* involves triangulation, because the methods *qua* disciplinary boundaries are removed. It is argued in this chapter that Critical Realism provides the methodological apparatus within which such a view of social science can be constructed. Aspects of the subject matter of the disciplines, if not the currently expressed nature of the disciplines, thus become branches or fields of the same domain of investigation brought together by triangulation.

## Note

1 Bhaskar (1978: 43) supports fallibilism as concomitant with realism. However, he (1978: 197–9) rejects fallibilism as an overarching concept, because it can be confused with judgemental relativism, i.e. the notion that all beliefs or theories have equal merit. Bhaskar prefers his concept of epistemic relativism, which allows for theories to be incorrect, but more correct than other theories. However, Sayer (2000: 20) notes that in open systems, there is always the possibility of 'misattributions of causality'; i.e. fallibilism. Danermark *et al.* (2002: 152–3) caution that investigators must be very careful when making inferences. They also refuse to rule out a priori any type of methods; however, this might reflect more strongly their position that any methods must be informed by the nature of the object under study. Furthermore, though, Critical Realists argue that agents' responses are corrigible, which means that replies to question-naires, etc. cannot be taken completely at face value. Thus, the investigator's evaluation of a subject's responses is an important element in research; and given the corrigibility of responses, other data types or methods should be utilised. More generally, data might also be fallible, perhaps because it is incomplete or its collection was difficult.

## References

Bhaskar, R. (1978). *A Realist Theory of Science*, London: Verso.

Danermark, B., Ekstrom, M., Jakobsen, L. and Karlsson, J. Ch. (2002). *Explaining Society: Critical Realism in the Social Sciences*, London: Routledge.

Denzin, N.K. (1970). *The Research Act in Sociology*, Chicago, IL: Aldine.

Downward, P. (2003). 'Conclusion', in P. Downward (ed.) *Applied Economics and the Critical Realist Critique*, London: Routledge.

Downward, P. and Mearman, A. (2002). 'Critical Realism and Econometrics: A Constructive Dialogue with Post Keynesian Economics', *Metroeconomica*, 53 (4): 391–415.

—— (2004a). 'Triangulation and Economic Methodology', paper presented at the conference of the International Network of Economic Methodology, Amsterdam, August.

—— (2004b). 'Triangulation and Economics: Reorienting Economics into Social Science', paper presented to the Cambridge Realist Workshop.

—— (2004c). 'Presenting "Demi-regularities" of Pricing Behavior: the Need for Triangulation,' in M. Forstater and L.R. Wray (eds). *Contemporary Post Keynesian Analysis: A Compendium of Contributions to the Seventh International Post Keynesian Workshop*, New York: Elgar: 285–98.

—— (2007). 'Retroduction as Mixed-Methods Triangulation: Reorienting Economics in Social Science', *Cambridge Journal of Economics*, 31 (1): 77–99.

Hausman, D. (1998). 'Economics, Philosophy of', in E. Craig (ed.). *Routledge Encyclopaedia of Philosophy*, Routledge: London.

Lawson, T. (1997). *Economics and Reality*, London: Routledge.

—— (1999). 'Connections and Distinctions: Post-Keynesianism and Critical Realism', *Journal of Post Keynesian Economics*, 22 (1): 3–14.

—— (2003). *Reorienting Economics*, London: Routledge.

Mearman, A. (2006). 'Critical Realism in Economics and Open-Systems Ontology: A Critique', *Review of Social Economy*, 64 (1): 47–75.

Olsen, W. (2003). 'Triangulation, Time and the Social Objects of Econometrics', in P. Downward (ed.). *Applied Economics and the Critical Realist Critique*, London: Routledge: 153–69.

Sayer, A. (1992). *Method in Social Science: A Realist Approach*, London: Routledge.

—— (2000). *Realism and Social Science*, London: Sage.

Silverman, D. (1993) *Interpreting Qualitative Data: Methods for Analysing Talk, Text and Interaction*, Sage: London.

# 8 Triangulation and social research
## Reply to Downward and Mearman

*Tony Lawson*

In both *Economics and Reality* and *Reorienting Economics*, I fail to provide sufficient practical guidance for the conducting of research projects informed by the perspective I defend. This is the central contention of Paul Downward and Andrew Mearman. These reviewers seek in their chapter to provide the extra guidance they believe is required. And in their view, it is best achieved by encouraging economists and others to adopt *triangulation* as a principle of research design.

In the course of the following response, I indicate why I am not sure that introducing the notion of triangulation actually makes much difference. Although I am broadly sympathetic to the basic approach of these contributors, and indeed we seem to concur on rather a lot, I find issues to disagree with in some of the details of their argument.

## Triangulation

As a preamble, however, let me first make some observations on Downward and Mearman's preferred method of triangulation in order to see how, in my view, it might provide the practical guidance my contributions so far lack.

What first is meant by the category? The term triangulation, in the context of analysis, takes its meaning from specific techniques associated with activities such as surveying and navigation. Essentially triangulation denotes the technique whereby the coordinates of an unknown position are established given the latter's observed bearings from two further known positions. For example, an observer on a ship sailing in a straight line from A to B and noting the angle of the lighthouse C from this path at both points A and B, as well as the distance AB, will be able to determine the approximate distance of the lighthouse. For example $BC = (\text{Sin } \alpha) \times (AB)/(\text{Sin } [\beta - \alpha])$. Of course the absolute position of the lighthouse can be determined only if the absolute positions A and B are known. Otherwise, only its position relative to the other points can be approximately determined.[1]

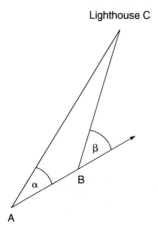

*Figure 2* Nautical triangulation.

## Social research

Now in the social sciences triangulation has come to mean something more like using several alternative approaches, methods or sets of data, in the investigation of a research question in order either to enhance confidence in the ensuing findings, or to render the results more comprehensive. Thus for Downward and Mearman: "Triangulation is commitment in research design to investigation and inference via multiple methods which are not placed in any a priori hierarchy." Or more simply: "triangulation implies combining together more than one set of insights in an investigation". Drawing on Denzin they write:

> Denzin (1970) offers a taxonomy of triangulation: (1) data triangulation – the combination of different data types; (2) investigator triangulation – the combination of insights from different investigators; (3) theoretical triangulation – the combination of different theoretical perspectives; and (4) methodological triangulation – the combination of different methods. Denzin further distinguishes between *within-method* triangulation, i.e. combining different cases of the same method; and *between-method* triangulation, i.e. combining studies of different methodologies.

Notice, then, that this social-scientific notion is quite different in spirit to the original nautical practice. In the latter case illustrated above, two bearings of the lighthouse are taken (forming the triangle) *because one alone is insufficient to locate its distance or position*. In other words, the second bearing is taken not to see if it agrees with the first, but because *both are required if either is to contribute* to identifying a third position, that of the lighthouse.

Now as far as I can see, when the category of triangulation is employed in social analysis, social theorists do not typically seek to carry over this feature of the nautical navigational situation. Instead the term is used to indicate that different methods or data sets, etc., are being used in combination mostly because either:

1   any one research contribution provides insights that taken alone are regarded as overly partial,[2] or
2   any one research contribution is used as a check on the results of one or more others.[3]

### Relevance of triangulation

It seems to me that stated at this level of generality the approach is useful, so long as:

3   there is no reason to suppose either (a) that any methodological approach or data set etc., utilised is inappropriate in some way, or (b) that the different parts or processes being combined are (used in ways that are) mutually inconsistent.

Even if condition (3) is met, the calling of the approach in question "triangulation" often seems a bit forced, or at least it does so where the point of the triangle in the nautical/navigational approach does not carry over. I guess in such cases the analogy concerns the idea of coming to locate or understand better some pre-existing object, through focusing in on it in different ways.

Now let me immediately address a criticism that some constructivists and others make of triangulation, but which I believe is not a problem at all. This is to suppose that because social reality is constructed it cannot be uncovered (in the sense that the position of a lighthouse can be).

This is not a problem just because it does not follow that, with social objects depending on us, they cannot also constitute objects of knowledge, even where the various processes of learning about something leads us to transform it. At one extreme, certain objects require minimal maintenance. A lighthouse itself (which after all is a social construction) perhaps falls into this category. Other items, such as language systems are being continually reproduced and in part transformed. But clearly this does not put their comprehension beyond us. And even momentary events can be uncovered or our conceptions of them revised. An obvious example is an incident in a football game covered by a multitude of cameras from different "angles". Perhaps this sort of example is indeed a good exemplar of the process of "triangulation" meaning viewed from different perspectives (a more extensive discussion of some of these issues is contained in my reply to Ruccio in this volume).

So, do I have any problems with the idea of triangulation in research? Not unless justifications (1) or (2) above are misinterpreted or unless condition (3) is not satisfied.

Notice that justification (1) does not assert that two or more research contributions must (or will always) provide more information than one. If, for example, the situation is inescapably open, it is not obvious that supplementing a method of analysis that allows for this with a second one that presupposes that a closed system obtains (i.e. that a system containing event regularities holds) will generate any new insight; indeed it seems mostly likely to confuse matters.

And justification (2) does not assert that where two research contributions (broadly) agree the results *must* be true, though, so long as condition (3) is thought to be satisfied we will likely have grounds for greater confidence in our findings.

What if condition (3) holds but the results of different exercises are contradictory? Then we are in the dialectical situation of contrast explanation that I discuss elsewhere in this book as well as in Chapter 4 of *Reorienting Economics*. I return to this topic below.

So, what can triangulation add to the perspective I have set out in *Reorienting Economics*? In truth, I am not sure, and I turn to examine what Downward and Mearman have to say below. There is no doubt that the perspective I defend supports a plurality of methods being employed *in combination*. For example, the detection of surprising contrasts will involve a different set of practices than does the retroduction of possible causes. And assessing the explanatory power of competing causal hypotheses will require a different set of methods again. If this reliance at different stages on different methods or procedures is triangulation then I have no problem with it. Indeed, I clearly already triangulate, as I suspect we all do. But I am not sure that we need the label, or (as I say) that the term triangulation is especially appropriate, or that using it takes us any further forward.

Still I do not either find it objectionable. So let me move on, and turn to the specifics of the case presented by Downward and Mearman to see if there is much about which we seriously disagree.

## Agreement

There are indeed issues on which we disagree. But before turning to them, let me emphasise points of agreement. Actually, we seem to agree on the broad thrust of the argument advanced by Downward and Mearman; it is over some of the details that we seem to differ.

As noted, for Downward and Mearman "triangulation implies combining together more than one set of insights in an investigation".

Now if I understand these contributors well, they are arguing that the conception that I defend both grounds, and needs, triangulation (so interpreted) in a way that competing conceptions do not.

Pragmatism is recognised as giving a role to triangulation. However, Downward and Mearman suggest that in pragmatism, method and its object need not match, and they seem to think it should.

By contrast, positivism and interpretivism, according to Downward and Mearman, do match method to material, but, given the narrow (if opposed) conceptions of method in each tradition, these traditions later provide limited scope for what Downward and Mearman refer to as methodological triangulation. Essentially Downward and Mearman view positivism as concerned with methods for dealing only with quantitative data, whilst interpretivism, including hermeneuticism, is viewed as concerned with methods for dealing with material only of a qualitative nature. However, Downward and Mearman seem to reason that both positivism and interpretivism are flawed, not least for resting on an impoverished empiricist ontology.

According to Downward and Mearman the project to which I have contributed advances a different ontology involving depth. This ontology, along with the "realist" principle that "the nature of the object must drive research", is said to support readily the view that different sorts of methods be used in combination. Downward and Mearman recognise that the conception I defend leads us to "reject the traditional equation of, on the one hand, qualitative equals exploratory or descriptive; and on the other, quantitative equals explanatory methods". Rather specific given phenomena are recognised as comprising both qualitative and quantitative aspects.

They write that a consequence of all this is that:

> "quantitative" and "qualitative" approaches are not a dual: they overlap to a degree in underlying logic and can also refer to the same objects of analysis. They can share, or be conditioned upon, the same ontological perspective and are not, of necessity wedded to particular, and different, ontological presumptions. Rather, the choice of method is not paradigmatic or one of ontology, because that ontology is shared by the methods, but simply reflects the specifics of the question being asked. If the questions probe different features of a phenomenon then different methods might be needed. It remains that they focus on the *same* phenomenon.

The result is that "different research methods can be logically employed in a triangulating strategy to reveal different features of the *same* reality" and that triangulation can entail combining different methods to "capture related, but different layers of this reality".

Now I find this part of the discussion easy to accept, even if I remain unsure that the term triangulation adds much. According to the conception I defend (but not so clearly according to some competing conceptions) social reality comprises different sorts of phenomena as well as phenomena consisting of different sorts of features (some of which may indeed be quantitative and others qualitative [or perhaps better measurable and immeasurable]). These differences, plus the need, usually, to move from the known to the unknown, and to compare, contrast and test, etc., frequently require a plethora of different sorts of methods to be used in combination. If this is the gist of the argument being advanced then I agree with it.

## Disagreement

Where I am less clear is the basis on which Downward and Mearman infer that their analysis provides the "practical guidance in conducting research projects informed by" the conception I defend; this is a guidance that they find lacking in both *Economics and Reality* and in *Reorienting Economics*.

Central to their claim that their approach does provide this missing guidance, seems to be an assessment that my own analysis of explanatory method is both "too destructive" of some methods and "untenable" in relation to others. It may be that, to the extent that triangulation avoids these aspects, it contributes more to going forward. So, let me explore these issues now. For these are indeed matters which, on detail at least, we do seem to disagree.

In their chapter under the heading "Triangulation rather than a rejection of methods" Downward and Mearman describe me as "arguing that econometrics is perfectly permissible providing that it is used in closed systems". They continue suggesting that I hold that these closures are "unlikely to occur", with the result that "econometrics is likely to have extremely limited use". They dismiss such a conclusion as "potentially too destructive, leaving no techniques available for concrete analysis". They also view it as "unsustainable" just because whatever the approach that I myself advocate I must "impose some degree of closure on an open reality". It is thus inappropriate to criticise others who do the same.

Let me respond very briefly. Now I acknowledge that the first part of their statement of my position is broadly correct (though I would not use terms like "permissible"). I do think that methods that presuppose conditions $X$ are mostly limited in their usefulness to conditions $X$. The conditions that I have found to be relevant to standard forms of econometrics, but which seem rarely to occur, are specific forms of closure, namely closures of causal connection (where one event lies in the causal history of another to which it is supposedly correlated).

It is something of a leap, though, to describe my position in this way and then to dismiss it as "potentially too destructive, leaving no techniques available for concrete analysis", even if I do hold that sorts of closure in question rarely emerge.

First, it presupposes that all methods require the sorts of closures described. I will presently suggest that this is not the case. But even if it were the case, it would not be my position that would be destructive of concrete analysis, but reality itself (and given that social reality has turned out to be amenable to successful analysis there must be a flaw in the argument somewhere).

Second, I do not in any case hold that the sorts of closure presupposed by econometrics can never occur, or even have never occurred. To the contrary, I discuss seemingly successful econometric exercises in chapter 1 of *Reorienting Economics* and in my response to Hodgson in this volume. I do reject the dogmatic insistence that we use only these methods, especially when we have reason to doubt they have much relevance to social analysis. But reason can be wrong, so let experimentation have free rein.

More to the point, if the method of contrast explanation that I often defend does in certain cases presuppose closures, these closures tend to be of a very different sort to those (closures of causal connection) presupposed by standard methods of econometrics and other forms of economic modelling. Let me briefly elaborate.

## Forms of closure

Closures of concomitance of relevance to contrast explanation take the form of "what happens here happens there" (see *Reorienting Economics*, chapter 4). They are typically to be found in those contrast spaces where outcomes share a relatively similar causal history. Thus, my computer took roughly the same time to start up today as yesterday. The degree of wear on one front tyre of my car is the roughly the same as on the other. Or the price increases for postage stamps experienced in Oxford are the same as those experienced in Cambridge. Because it is not unusual for similar items to share similar recent causal histories, these sorts of regularities are frequently found to hold for limited regions of time and space.

If closures of concomitance are reasonably widespread, this contrasts rather starkly with our experience of closures of causal sequence, that is systems supporting regularities of the form "whenever event $x$ then event $y$", where event $x$ can be said to be the causal history of $y$. In the social realm, these are found to be relatively rare occurrences indeed. The reason for this, no doubt, is the ever-changing combination of causes that give rise to actual outcomes. That is, if event $x$ (triggering causal mechanism $X$) is (given all the related causal factors in operation) followed by event $y$ this time round, it is unlikely to be so next time round (no matter how stable may be causal mechanism $X$ over time and space) just because many of the accompanying causes will likely be different.

Thus my planting a specific crop in a given field this year and next year is likely to produce two different average yields because of the shifting mix of additional causal factors. This is so even if, in any given year, the yield throughout the field (a contrast space if closures of concomitance are our concern) is fairly uniform, and even if the working of any specific causal mechanism (frost, rainfall, sunlight, insects) stays the same over time. Similarly, every occasion I cycle to work, or give the same seminar, the total outcome is different. Of course, events like increasing incomes, interest rates, spending on new technology and so forth produce widely varying outcomes when they occur at different times or more generally in different contexts.

Notice, too, that although an exercise in contrast explanation may make use of (expected) closures, albeit not closures of causal connection, but closures of concomitance, the explanatory project typically gets going only where such closures break down, that is where things turn out to be not as expected. Indeed, the goal is to explain precisely the unexpected. Closures of concomitance are very relevant here, more so than closures of causal connection, just because they are found (and expected) to hold significantly more often than the latter (so that their breaking down is surprising).

So I believe Downward and Mearman are wrong to suppose that my position is "unsustainable". I do not hold that all closures are rare; I hold only that (non-spurious) closures of the causal connection sort, typically presupposed my standard methods of econometrics and other forms of mathematical-economic modelling, are rare. Specifically, in advocating contrast explanation, I do not contradict myself by denying features that I sometimes presuppose in my own approach. The distinction between the different forms of closure here is significant.

## Terminology: open and closed systems

A second difference concerns our terminology. We use the same central categories but in somewhat different ways. And I fear that the usage of Downward and Mearman may often prove to be misleading. Let me briefly elaborate once more

As realists, Downward and Mearman seem more than happy to distinguish objects (of analysis) from any analysis of those objects. But they do, on occasion, seem to encourage a conflation of the properties of the two. These though are typically not the same, and using identical terminology for both sets of features risks confusing matters at best.

Now I have consistently reserved the term closed system or closure for a system in which an event regularity occurs. That is, it is a system that supports regularities of the form "whenever event $x$ then event $y$". Several features of such a conception are worth drawing out.

First, a closed system is thus a feature of reality open to analysis; it is an object of analysis. In my view, it is unhelpful at best, and usually misleading, to also refer to methods used to analyse closed systems as closed etc. On my conception of closure, it is not even clear what closed or open methods or methods exhibiting openness, etc., could mean; their usage, it seems to me is simply a category mistake.[4]

Second, a closed system supports one particular configuration of events from a potential infinity of possibilities (or perhaps two if in addition we choose to refer to stochastic near equivalents as [stochastic] closures). If we refer to systems containing any of the multitude of alternative event configurations as open, it clearly does not follow that an open system supports only situations of random flux. For example, open systems may support various forms of demi-regularities (see Lawson, 2003, chapter 4), that is rough and ready patterns taking various forms. Recognising this, we might find reason to refer to various systems as being in different states of openness. But it is misleading, I believe, to talk of degrees of openness, as though there is a linear progression of patterns from deterministic closures to systems supporting a totally chaotic flux. I believe there is no insightful way to construct a linear ordering of event patterns.

Now if indeed it is a mistake to conflate the properties of objects (of analysis) with the properties of the tools of their analysis, and a yet further mistake to talk of degrees of openness for the system being analysed, it seems to me that Downward and Mearman succeed in combing both. For this is the only way in which I can understand (though I do not know what they might mean by) their talk of degrees of openness exhibited by research methods. They write:

> Therefore, we argue that for practising economists, Lawson's arguments are potentially too destructive, leaving no techniques available for concrete analysis. In contrast, as reality comprises parts that have different degrees of openness, these should be explored by methods that also exhibit different degrees of openness: for example, statistical inference requires more closure than statistical estimation.

I have already indicated that the first sentence is erroneous. If however, these authors mean states rather than degrees of openness, and that the methods in question can be said to presuppose (rather than exhibit) different states of openness, then their statement does not stand "in contrast" to anything I say at all.

A further feature of the conception of a closed system I maintain is that the closure does not refer to the event regularity per se, but the system supporting it. And such a closed system is open to further analysis. In my own work, I have identified certain conditions that guarantee such a system. As such, these can with reason be labelled closure conditions. In particular, I have identified the intrinsic and extrinsic closure conditions. The former condition is that any mechanism be intrinsically stable (or if different mechanisms of the same type are employed, that each possesses the same fixed intrinsic structure) with the result that it produces given (predictable) responses to being triggered. The extrinsic closure condition is that any mechanism of interest be insulated from the effects of countervailing or reinforcing others.

Now it seems to me that to accept the terminology of closures for systems that support event regularities, and simultaneously to refer to any conditions that guarantee closures also as closures (as opposed to conditions for closure or some such) can only encourage (more) confusion. But again, this seems to be a terminological practice accepted by Downward and Mearman. In fact, they appear further to use the terms closure or closed to cover both any endurability of an object as well as any commonality/homogeneity revealed across objects (both being properties that are essential if the intrinsic closure condition is to be satisfied). For they also write:

> If methods are to be rejected because they impose some degree of closure on an open reality, then in fact, all methods so far proposed must also be rejected. Any method that supposes that an entity remains fixed for long enough for it to be identified as an object of study imposes closure on an open reality. Thus quantitative analysis involves closure, because the act of quantification involves the assumption of qualitative invariance across subjects. Likewise, *if* qualitative investigation is concerned with collating insights and offering stylised interpretations and narratives, this assumes qualitative invariance – or, in Critical-Realist terminology, *intrinsic closure*.

Now I just think that using terms like closures to cover so many different aspects, conditions or scenarios makes it difficult to compare and contrast arguments, and increases the likelihood of mistakes and confusions.

Actually I think there is confusion in the above passage. For the first sentence refers to (the Downward and Mearman interpretation of) my own argument suggesting that methods that presuppose a closure are unlikely to be successful in addressing an open reality.[5] But I am consistently using the term closure only to mean a system in which an event regularity occurs. And this is quite different from the usage they adopt in the rest of the passage.

But perhaps this mixing up of meanings is clearest in the discussion Downward and Mearman provide to explain their Figure 1. For although the third column of this figure is headed "applied method" and presented as though there is a linear progression – from the open or qualitative to the closed – in terms of method, the discussion of the figure frequently treats these properties as features of social reality to be analysed rather than the method. Thus, we find assessments like "the degree to which closure is invoked thus begins to "legitimise" various statistical procedures" or some such. For reasons given, I believe talking in terms of degrees of openness is mistaken. Here, though, I merely point out that those features that our authors are seeking to systematise are not always those that the heading ("applied method") would lead us to expect.

Perhaps some readers will react to all this by thinking that in the end the onus is on me to explain why I use the terms open and closed systems in the manner I do. Specifically, why do I use closure to express a system in which an event regularity occurs? The answer is simply that systems in which event regularities occur have for long been treated by many, and most especially by mainstream economists, as (erroneously in my view) fundamental to social theorising. Too often, the uncovering of such systems (or of the event regularities per se) has been accepted uncritically as the central goal of science. I needed a term for such a system, to identify it as a particular phenomenon, in order critically to examine its nature and conditions of possibility. For reasons given in *Reorienting Economics* (and see also Vinca Bigo, 2006) the terminology of open and closed systems was adopted. But if a different terminology had been used, the focus would have been the same. My interest has not been with the historical, or other disciplinary interpretations/usages or varying connotations of these terms, but with those aspects of reality to which I wished to refer (when using them). Thus, I can easily abandon my use of these terms if need be and replace them by others (though of course I recognise no such need, and see many reasons to persist in my terminology). My point here, though, is that however we wish to continue, it can be very misleading to use the same category to express very different features of very different things, not least in the context of the same analysis.

## Temporal continuity and commonality

Parenthetically, a further difference between us is that Downward and Mearman seem to view social reality as far less stable across time or different objects than do I. They seem to accept that everything is in flux and essentially unique so that to apply more or less any method is to involve a researcher in some kind of distortion.

I say this because I can only suppose that when Downward and Mearman argue that any "method which supposes that an entity remains fixed for long enough for it to be identified as an object of study imposes closure on an open reality", they are saying that the entity identification assumes a degree of stability or continuity that is not realistic.

My own view, to the contrary, is that social objects and structures and even events frequently exhibit sufficient stability or continuity as to allow their identification. Yes, there are problems of interpretation. But I think, for example, that institutions, technologies or the text by Downward and Mearman to which I am currently responding, are amongst the numerous forms of social phenomena that are sufficiently enduring for us to identify them (albeit, of course, that we each do so in our own situated, practically conditioned and fallible ways). Even momentary events can be identified and examined if "observed" by various parties. As already noted, an event on a football pitch captured by a multitude of cameras as well as spectators is an obvious example.

And when these authors suggest that "quantitative analysis involves closure, because the act of quantification involves the assumption of qualitative invariance across subjects", I think they again want to suggest that the latter is unrealistic. In this, in my view, they are (in using terminology like stylised and narratives) once more being overly pessimistic (certainly more so than myself) about the extent to which a degree of commonality can be found. Of course, no two objects or aspects are ever precisely identical, but in essential features, they can be sufficiently similar as to possess the same properties, including capacities, etc.

Thus, human beings do share numerous capacities (for example to enter social being, or, more specifically, to acquire language competency) and liabilities (e.g. are all subject to the forces of gravity; and each can be made to bleed). And within any culture, we experience similar position-related (transfactual) social forces (e.g. tax laws) including psychological ones; social structures are everywhere dependent on human practices, and so on.

As a result, similarly situated individuals do partake in similar experiences. In the UK, the rubbish is collected on the same day for all residents of any given street; if my rubbish is not collected because of a strike nor is that of my neighbours. If my local taxes go up, so do my neighbours'. These sorts of event regularities are everywhere to be found (not imposed). They arise because similar subjects are subject to similar conditions.

So, I find social reality to be more stable than do Downward and Mearman, both over time (for some specific structures) and over space (for some objects of the same type). And because I perceive there to be such stability, it is not too surprising to me at least that we regularly observe various closures of concomitance, that is situations in which regularities occur of the form "what happened here happened there". These occur precisely because similar are subject to similar (albeit constantly changing) social forces (the striking dustmen failing to collect the rubbish throughout the street).

What this all amounts to is the following. Like Downward and Mearman I find the world to be an open, dynamic and complicated place. But I also find it to be differentiated in the sense that there are areas in which we find greater endurability, continuity or commonality than others. And importantly we know something about the nature of this differentiation. Social structures are typically more stable than the events they in part condition. And regularities connecting events sharing a similar causal history are far more widespread than are regularities relating outcomes standing in a causal sequence. As a result, I think we are able to have greater confidence in (and indeed we do achieve greater successes with) methods that presuppose closures of concomitance than those that presuppose closure closures of causal connection.

Why do Downward and Mearman downplay such commonality and stability as is actually found? I am not sure. But perhaps their doing so explains their giving a greater emphasis to econometrics and related techniques than I think is fruitful. For if all methods can be said to be inappropriate to their objects, then it seems wrong to pick out any particular method for criticism, and perhaps unreasonable to rule out any particular method in any actual context. So, econometrics, it might thereby be supposed, can always be utilised, albeit along with other techniques.

Whether or not Downward and Mearman do reason like this, or others find this line of argument convincing, I repeat that, in any case, some parts of reality are found to be more stable than others. In particular, limited closures of concomitance are found to be abundant. Thus, we can be more directed in the sorts of methods we reasonably apply.

## Fallibilism

A further seeming difference between us is the suggestion of Downward and Mearman that I am somewhat hesitant to accept that the fallibilistic nature of all knowledge itself supports an emphasis on triangulation. Let me briefly elaborate.

Before turning to their ontological argument for triangulation (one with which, as I say, I broadly agree), Downward and Mearman write:

> More generally, fallibilism of theory tends to have two geneses: onto-logical and epistemological. Epistemologically, humans have limited computational capacity to deal with the world, even one of a simple structure, particularly when faced with multiple meanings and incommensurability. Thus, no one theory is likely to be able to capture adequately these aspects. Furthermore, if the object of enquiry (and by extension, the world) is highly complex, it is extremely difficult for any theory to capture its aspects adequately. This concern applies when the social world is held to comprise open

systems, in which, for example, the future is open, because current agency affects future structures in unpredictable ways. Even for a super computer, society is complex and unpredictable. In this light, no one model should be relied upon to give an accurate picture of the object of enquiry. Rather, methodological triangulation requires that in any act of inference to causal claims about an object of enquiry, two (or more) methods with different degrees of openness, are combined.

Clearly all claims are fallible. And reality is complex. This applies to all domains of reality and all sciences, no matter how successful they appear to be.

However, the conclusion that follows, it seems to me, is rather that we must always be alert to the possibility of error, and/or that there may be better ways of doing things. In pursuing our research practices a good deal of caution, humility, reflexivity and honesty is desirable. Where possible and meaningful, repeated trial-and-error experimentation may be called for, and informed criticism sought.

But does it follow thereby that "no one model should be relied upon to give an accurate picture of the object of enquiry"? What if only one model can be supplied that is explanatorily successful, and the model in question is successful indeed? Can we not at least momentarily rely on it? Must we add others just for the sake of having others?

And why suddenly insist that "in any act of inference to causal claims about an object of enquiry, two (or more) methods [be] ... combined"? Why indeed are Downward and Mearman even considering acts of inference to causal claims at the relevant stage of their discussion (when they have yet to introduce their ontological argument drawing on the insights of critical realism)? And if methods are to be combined, and if we assume that Downward and Mearman are really meaning methods that presuppose (rather than possess) different degrees of openness, why in particular combine methods of this sort? Notice that we may use different methods for different tasks: to identify event patterns, to retroduce causes, to eliminate alternatives and so forth; but all may presume a similar state of openness of the system. If there are reasons for combining methods that presupposes different states of openness of the underlying reality, such inferences do not follow especially from recognition that social reality is complex and our knowledge of it fallible.

Methods presupposing different states of openness of the underlying reality are said by Downward and Mearman to be a requirement of the principle of "methodological triangulation". But then what is there that requires that we adopt this principle rather than any other, and in preference to being continually cautious, reflexive and critical, etc.? Certainly, we can stay open to the possibility that triangulation may be useful (just as we are to the possibility that methods of mathematical-deductivist reasoning may sometimes prove useful). But I am not yet convinced that the fallibility of knowledge means we must use methods in combination and more especially in the manner proposed by Downward and Mearman.

Still, as I say, these differences between Downward and Mearman and myself mostly refer only to details of their overall argument. As already indicated, I understand the basic thrust of their contention to be that the ontological conception I defend points to the need for different sorts of methods to be used in combination (whether or not different states of openness are presupposed). This per se is certainly an assessment with which I have little quarrel.

## Final comments

In total, Downward and Mearman and I seem to hold a good deal in common. Certainly there are differences in detail. But in terms of generalities, our positions are similar. If triangulation merely means using different methods or data sets or whatever in combination where appropriate, whether or not we need a term to express this, the practice seems essential.

The term triangulation is appropriate to the navigation case discussed at the outset just because a given "point" or "position" can be determined only when using knowledge of two other points or positions (with the three positions together forming a triangle). To my mind, the term would thus seem more reasonably used in a social science context if this essential feature of the navigational example (of a third result or "point" depending on knowledge of two others) carried over. Perhaps indeed the term would thus be better employed to indicate not merely that different methods are being used in combination but rather that something like dialectical reasoning is involved. For in dialectical reasoning two prior "points", our initial understanding and a revealed contradiction, are both required if the third "point", the dialectical resolution, or superior understanding, is to be achieved.

But, of course, this sort of reasoning already possesses a label. And with the navigational example seen to be a rather mechanical special case, I think that rather than substitute triangulation for the procedure in question we should stick with the category of dialectic.

## Notes

1   It is only approximate where, or because, the curvature of the earth makes a difference.
2   Thus Downward and Mearman observe:

> A common reason for combination of data types is that the main source of data is incomplete. For example, the Bank of England uses survey and

anecdotal evidence from its Agents as the most up to date picture of economic conditions. This compensates for the inevitable lag in official quantitative data

3  Thus Webb *et al.* (1966), suggest that, "Once a proposition has been confirmed by two or more independent measurement processes, the uncertainty of its interpretation is greatly reduced. The most persuasive evidence comes through a triangulation of measurement processes" (p. 3).

4  Just as a cloth may be useful for cleaning a glass window but is of an entirely different nature from the window, or a knife is useful for cutting cheese but possesses quite different properties, so typically methods of social analysis have different properties from the objects being analysed. Using the same terminology for properties of method and object of analysis is no more sensible than calling aspects of the cloth hard because a glass window is hard or the knife tasty or yellow just because the cheese is.

5  In a passage just prior to this one they write: "Lawson (1999) clarifies this position, arguing that econometrics is perfectly permissible providing that it is used in closed systems; however, given that these are held to be unlikely to occur, econometrics is likely to have extremely limited use."

# References

Bigo, Vinca (2006) "Open and Closed Systems and the Cambridge School", *Review of Social Economy*, 64(4), December, pp. 493–514.

Denzin, N.K. (1970) *The Research Act in Sociology*, Chicago, IL: Aldine.

Lawson, Tony (1997) *Economics and Reality*, London and New York: Routledge.

Lawson, Tony (1999). "Connections and Distinctions: Post-Keynesianism and Critical Realism", *Journal of Post Keynesian Economics*, 22(1), pp. 3–14.

Lawson, Tony (2003) *Reorienting Economics*, London and New York: Routledge.

Webb, E.J., Campbell, D.T., Schwartz, R.D. and Sechrest, L. (1966). *Unobtrusive Measures: Nonreactive Measures in the Social Sciences*. Chicago, IL: Rand McNally.

# 9   Irrelevance and ideology

*Bernard Guerrien*

There are plenty of interesting ideas in Lawson's book about how economic theory and practice need to be "reoriented". I agree with him that economics must start from observation of the world where we live. I must say, however, that I do not see why Lawson needs the special word "ontology" to designate an "enquiry into (or a theory of) the nature of being or existence" (p. xv). Nor am I convinced by his "evolutionary explanation" – in Darwinian terms – of the "mathematising tendency" in economics (Chapter 10).[1] But I do not want to discuss these complex subjects here. I am only going to consider Lawson's main criticism of neoclassical economics: its "lack of *realism*". I think that it is not the appropriate objection: *all* theories lack realism, as they take into consideration only some aspects of reality. Everyone agrees on this, even neoclassical economists. The real problem with neoclassical theory is not its "lack of *realism*" but the "ideology" (a word Lawson never uses) that it smuggles in and carries with it.

## Lack of realism and *homo œconomicus*

If economics needs to be "reoriented", it is because its present orientation is wrong. What precisely is wrong with its orientation? If you read Lawson's book (2003), it is wrong partly because of the assumption about man that it adopts. Man is assumed to be "rational", "omniscient", "selfish without limit" and so on. For example, in the section called "Fictions", in the first chapter about modern economics, Lawson writes: "Assumptions abound even to the effect that individuals possess perfect foresight (or, only slightly weaker, have rational expectations), or are selfish without limit, or are omniscient, or live for ever" (p. 18). Or, to quote him again:

> Just as a class of assumptions, such as rationality or total greed, always appear in order to render the human agent atomistic, a further set of assumptions, like a given number of agents or three goods and two periods, are always in place serving to fix the bound-

aries of the analysis, to isolate the set of atoms on which the analysis focuses.

(p. 19)

According to Lawson then, the fundamental "lack of realism" consists in considering individuals as "atoms", and as "isolated":

> The reasons for the fictitious nature of modern economics, then, are clear. To the extent that human beings as well as society are, in reality, complex, evolving and open, a methodology which necessitates that the subject-matter addressed is everywhere atomistic and isolated is likely very often to throw up accounts of human individual and collective behaviour that are fictitious and rather superficial, to say the least.

(p. 19)

The problem with this objection is that a neoclassical theorist would agree with it. He would argue that he is considering only a special aspect of human behaviour: the fact that people try to pay less (rather than more) for a given good, or try to get more satisfaction (rather than less) from given resources. They then try to derive or to "deduce" (to use a word that Lawson doesn't like) certain *ceteris paribus* consequences from this assumption.

Actually, almost all economists, classical, neoclassical or others, agree that humans are not completely selfish, or greedy; but they say that this is not the aspect of human behaviour they are reasoning about. It is the other aspect they are focusing on, and who can deny that self-love exists? Even Marx supposes that the capitalists' motive is profit,[2] and that workers try to get a better life. This is all that is meant when neoclassical theorists assume that people are rational.

On the other hand, neoclassical theorists *do not* assume that people are "omniscient", because this would be nonsense (consequences of my decisions depend of others' decisions, which depend, at least partly, on my decision).[3] Sometimes, not often, they suppose that people have an infinite life. This is an approximation that can be accepted: in general, when we take a decision concerning present and future, we do not think about death (we suppose that we will still live a long time). This is "unrealistic", for sure, but not enough to say that the theory is irrelevant, or without interest.

Actually, the main problem with "modern economics" (neoclassical theory) does not stem from the type of man (the infamous *homo œconomicus*) that it supposes, but from the type of "social structures" that are supposed or implied. The problem with these social structures is not exactly that they *lack realism* but that they are *totally irrelevant*.

## "Modern economics" and social structures

Tony Lawson also insists on the importance of what he call "social systems", or "social structures", or "structured processes of interaction" (p. 43), and he is right in doing so: human (rational) action can be determined – for *logical reasons* – only if rules and context are unambiguously defined. One of his main objections to "modern economics" is that it is "atomistic" – that people take their (optimal) decisions in an "isolated" way; it would seem then that for Lawson, no "social structures" are implied in neoclassical models (one more example of their "lack of realism"). But social structures *are implied*, and it is a pity that Lawson never mentions them, as they are the real Achilles' heel of neoclassical economics – and, more generally, of methodological individualism. This is because it is not enough to say that people are rational, and that they "optimise". Even in the simplest model – bargaining – it is supposed (as a minimal requirement) that people don't use force (that trade is voluntary). But bargaining results depend on a lot of factors, such as bargainers' psychology, resources, impatience, etc. To obtain a determinate result (or prediction), more "social structure" is needed. Consider the neoclassical benchmark model, perfect competition. It supposes a very special and strange "social structure": households and firms are *obliged* to "take" prices, given by an auctioneer, and to inform him of their supplies and demands at these prices; they *are not allowed* to bargain and trade directly among each other, even if the auctioneer has found equilibrium prices. Now, one could say that this model "lacks realism". But, wouldn't it be more appropriate to say that it describes a completely different kind of reality, or social structure – that it describes not a market but a centralised economy, with specific rules and institutions?

Neoclassical economists (and, unhappily, almost all heterodox economists) *never* present perfect competition in this manner: they speak, as Lawson does, of "atoms", "many agents" and so on. They prefer to discuss the lack of realism of *homo œconomicus* rather than about the total irrelevance of the social structures *implicitly assumed* in their models.

## What about ideology?

Lawson also discusses econometrics, especially the "Lucas critique". But here again, the problem *is not* with econometrics – nor the "realism" of its *statistical* assumptions; it is with the "social structure" that Lucas and others suppose, in their models, as they reduce the whole economy to a "representative" agent's choice – or to a "young" choice in an overlapping generations model. This obviously is *nonsense*, as it is also to discuss econometric tests about these models (even if you obtain $R^2 = 0.99999$). The same can be said about "Real Business Cycle" and "Computable General Equilibrium" models. The question is, again: how such intelligent people can propose – and endlessly study – such *stupid* models? I only see one reason for that: *ideology* (intuitive beliefs that render them blind). Here, the belief alluded to is that "market mechanisms" (whatever that may mean) produce "efficient" results – if you abstract from "frictions", "failures", etc. (ignoring these "imperfections" being, for neoclassical theorists, the principal reason of "lack of realism"). As there is a strong link between competitive equilibrium (that is, with auctioneer, etc.) and efficient states – link given by the two Welfare Theorems – then competitive equilibrium *must be* identified with "perfect market" (as both are supposed to be efficient). In some books (especially those on growth, in the "macro" mood – as those of Romer (2001) and Barro and Sala-I-Martin (2004), perfect competition and an "omniscient" "representative agent" (or planner) choice are presented as giving the same results. How can a normal person make any sense of this?

Identifying the real reasons why the standard, dominant theory is *totally irrelevant* is an unavoidable first step, before proposing some other – completely different – alternative theory, whatever theory one may wish to propose. For that, you do not need complicated "methodological" or "epistemological" or "ontological" debates.

## Notes

1 Quite curiously, Lawson refers to Richard Dawkins' theory of evolution, which seems to be inspired, at least partly, by neoclassical theory (the title of Dawkins' popular book is *The Selfish Gene*, and sometimes he writes that genes have "utility functions").
2 Bourdieu (1986) does the same thing but with an enlarged vision of capital (which includes "culture" and networks).
3 The only interesting aspect of game theory is that it insists on this point: even when there is common knowledge about players' characteristics and the rules of the game (issues, payoffs, etc.) – that is, "omniscience" – each rational player's decision depends on his *beliefs* about others players' decisions.

## References

Barro, Robert and Xavier Sala-I-Martin (2004) *Economic Growth*, Cambridge: MIT Press.
Bourdieu, Pierre (1986) "The forms of capital", in J.G. Richardson (ed.) *Handbook for Theory and Research for the Sociology of Education*, Westport, CT: Greenwood Press, pp. 241–258.
Dawkins, Richard (1989) *The Selfish Gene*, Oxford: Oxford University Press.
Lawson, Tony (2003) *Reorienting Economics*, London: Routledge.
Romer, David (2001) *Advanced Macroeconomics*, New York: McGraw-Hill.

# 10 The mainstream orientation and ideology
## Reply to Guerrien

*Tony Lawson*

Bernard Guerrien's thoughtful short comment is to the point and raises issues vital to understanding the situation of modern economics. Guerrien and I agree that modern economics is not in a state of good health. However, we offer different diagnoses of what is wrong.

We both find mainstream theories to be less than realistic. Guerrien indeed suggests that models are so unrealistic as to be (better described as) irrelevant. We part company, though, both in our assessments of what it is that is unrealistic about mainstream theorising and, most especially, in our explanations of this lack of realisticness (whatever its form).

According to Guerrien, the explanation of the mainstream disregard for being realistic is ideology, a term, he notes, that I rarely mention. In so locating the problems of the mainstream Guerrien further suggests that my concern with philosophical issues, and in particular ontology, is largely irrelevant, both for a critical analysis of the problems of the mainstream, and for constructing an alternative.

My response is to agree with Guerrien that we do indeed diagnose the problems of the mainstream differently, both in terms of symptoms and causes. But, although Guerrien is right that I rarely mention ideology, I suggest that, given his particular understanding of the term, my own (ontologically informed) explanation of the mainstream's problems is just as much an account of ideology as Guerrien's, albeit a rather different one. I also believe it to be a more sustainable one. Let me briefly elaborate.

## A summary of Guerrien's position

I start by briefly summarising Guerrien's position, as I understand it. According to Guerrien I locate the problems of modern mainstream economics in its unrealistic theories and in particular in its accounts of human beings.[1] Specifically, I argue that the mainstream everywhere portrays "individuals as 'atoms' and as 'isolated'".

Guerrien is of the view that the mainstream would happily accept this characterisation. He also seems to feel that describing the mainstream in this fashion is not a real criticism, just because the mainstream is using unrealistic assumptions about individuals merely to get at behaviour under a single aspect. The real problem with the mainstream, according to Guerrien, is its account of social structures. It is this, in particular, that is thought to be so unrealistic as to be best described as "totally irrelevant".

Guerrien notes, too, that I critically discuss econometrics and other modelling methods. However, he seems convinced that the problem is not modelling per se but the actual models created, and, in particular, the accounts of social structures that mainstream modellers implicitly accept.

Why do mainstream practitioners produce models of (or presupposing implicit accounts of) social structure that are so unrealistic as to be described by Guerrien as "stupid"? Guerrien's answer is ideology:

> The question is, again: how such intelligent people can propose – and endlessly study – such *stupid* models? I only see one reason for that: *ideology* (intuitive beliefs that render them blind). Here, the belief alluded to is that "market mechanisms" (whatever that may mean) produce "efficient" results – if you abstract from "frictions", "failures", etc. (ignoring these "imperfections" being, for neoclassical theorists, the principal reason of "lack of realism").

So, in Guerrien's view, the problem with the mainstream is its account of social structure, not its theorising of individual agents. And the explanation is ideology, specifically the desire to show that a market economy produces "efficient results", a topic that I fail to consider. A consequence, Guerrien concludes, is that if we want to understand and improve matters, we can avoid getting involved in "complicated 'methodological' or 'epistemological' or 'ontological' debates'".

## An alternative view

In response let me first acknowledge that it is indeed correct to represent me as arguing that a mainstream problem is that its theories and models are highly unrealistic. This I believe is the most immediate manifestation of that project's state of ill health. I also argue, as Guerrien again correctly points out, that a common feature of all these unrealistic mainstream theories is that they comprise accounts of isolated atoms. So far, then, I accept Guerrien's characterisation. However, the implicit ontology of systems of isolated atoms covers the whole agency/structure set up; it is not merely an account of human agents that I am criticising as unrealistic here. Let me briefly expand on this.

By atoms, I mean not something small, of course, but entities that have the same independent and invariable effects whatever the context. By isolated I mean that the agent or groups of agents under analysis are contained (or sealed off) within social systems where, or so that, their actions are unaffected by activities going on elsewhere. These two assumptions together, given an appropriate social setting, allow the prediction or deduction of outcomes. The atomistic entities if triggered always respond in the same way. And system isolation ensures that factors not explicitly theorised are not allowed to intervene and affect the outcome of interest and so prevent it from being predictable.

Now, of course, structure must be included to get an analysis going. This certainly includes any (possibly implicit) account of social context, as Guerrien correctly notes. But it equally applies to the atomistic agents of the model. I nowhere claim that the agents must be human individuals, even if it is the case that the latter are indeed typically portrayed as atoms. In fact, the atomistic entities of mainstream models may be firms, or universities, or even collectivities (see for example Alan Kirman, 1989, p. 136). But even when (as is typically the case) the atoms are human individuals, they too, like the social contexts of action, must (implicitly) be given some structure. If they optimise something, they must implicitly possess the capacity to optimise (that something); if they follow rules they must possess the capacity to do so, etc.

Guerrien is surely correct to emphasise that the implicit accounts of social structure that we find in these mainstream exercises are not very realistic; they are indeed very far from being so. I think Guerrien makes an important contribution in drawing this out. Where we disagree is that Guerrien seems to think that I am uncritical of mainstream implicit accounts of social structure, whilst he himself seems uncritical of conceptions of human agents in these models. He seems to suppose that the latter are not especially unrealistic, or if they are, that this really does not matter much.

But the situation is entirely symmetrical concerning agency and structure. The total account is distorted, and it is always the case that conceptions of individuals and structures are intertwined. It is the total agency/structure framework that is a fiction, that is deformed in such a manner as to achieve a closed system (i.e. a predictable world) of isolated atoms.

In other words, in mainstream models, the (implicit account of) social structure is made to conform with the conceptions of agents, and vice versa, so that deducible outcomes are feasible. Thus, (pre-given) human agents with the capacity to optimise are implicitly situated in (fixed) social contexts where there "exists" an (typically unique) optimal outcome. If the agents (passively) follow fixed rules, the implicit social context is one in which such behaviour necessarily leads to determinate outcomes, and so on (see especially chapter 8 of *Economics and Reality* (1997b) on all this).

I could go on at length on this topic (see for example chapter 2 of

*Reorienting Economics*). But there is probably little need. For although we emphasise different features, Guerrien and I agree on the basics: that the mainstream conceptions are, one way or another, most of the time, quite unrealistic, so much so as to be irrelevant. The real, or more fundamental, difference between Guerrien and me arises with our respective explanations of this situation. So, let me concentrate on the latter.

This "real difference" between us, according to Guerrien, is that he detects an ideological stance taken by the mainstream whilst I do not. But I believe this assessment of where we disagree is not quite right; given Guerrien's conception of ideology we both take such a view. The real difference, rather, concerns our respective assessments of the content of the ideological stance in question. Before proceeding, it is important to be clear what is being meant here by the category of ideology.

## Ideology

Let me recall that Guerrien's conception of ideology is stated as follows: "I only see one reason for that: *ideology* (intuitive beliefs which render them blind)". This is Guerrien's only elaboration of his understanding of the term. I assume by it that Guerrien means something like a certain set of beliefs held by a community that are so intuitive in their appeal that their holders are blinded to the possibility that the beliefs in question might be wrong or even open to valid criticism.[2]

This is a reasonably common or popular conception of ideology,[3] although by no means the only interpretation[4] of this contested and often inconsistently[5] employed term, and an interpretation that is very different from its original meaning.[6] This is not the place to embark on a critical inquiry into the nature or meaning of ideology more broadly conceived, and in any case, in wishing to respond to Guerrien, it is enough, and indeed most relevant, to stick to his interpretation here.

Guerrien, then, is suggesting that there are one or more beliefs held by the mainstream that are treated as beyond question, but responsible for that project's limited relevance. What is this belief or set of beliefs? As we have already seen, Guerrien's specific thesis is that mainstream theories are chosen or constructed in such a manner as to guarantee a political result, namely that markets are (found to be) efficient in some way. It is a form of conspiracy theory. In fact Guerrien makes a link between equilibrium theorising and "perfect markets". For immediately after the passage reproduced earlier he writes:

> As there is a strong link between competitive equilibrium (that is, with auctioneer, etc.) and efficient states – link given by the two Welfare Theorems – then competitive equilibrium *must be* identified with "perfect market" (as both are supposed to be efficient). In some books (especially those on growth, in the "macro" mood – as those of

Romer and Barro and Sala-i-Martin), perfect competition and an "omniscient" "representative agent" (or planner) choice are presented as giving the same results. How can a normal person make any sense of this?

My response is to question the supposition that this conception of the efficiency of markets or perfect competition still constitutes a set of beliefs widely accepted by the mainstream community, if it ever did. At least I do not think this conception plays much of a role in motivating what goes on in the economics academy, which is the focus of our discussion here. Perhaps some academic economists do hold such views, but certainly not all. Mainstream journals are even open to certain "analytical Marxists" and others who seem happy to criticise the market mechanism. And just as much to the point, the substantive content of mainstream theorising is far wider and more dynamic than a fixed focus on market mechanisms, or on conceptions of competitive equilibrium and claims that they lead to efficiency, and such like.

Certainly, few commentators on these matters seem any longer to accept an assessment of the mainstream along the lines proposed by Guerrien. In fact, various close observers/investigators of mainstream substantive contributions have recently swung so far the other way that they not only do not characterise the mainstream as ideological at the substantive level, but actually portray the mainstream project as pluralist (see for example David Colander *et al.*, 2004[7] or John Davis, 2005).

Also to the point, many of those who have contributed to modelling competitive equilibrium have all along resisted the claim that that equilibrium theory be used to draw conclusions about the real world, whether in terms of efficiency or whatever. Thus, Frank Hahn writes:

> it cannot be denied that there is something scandalous in the spectacle of so many people refining the analyses of economic [equilibrium] states which they give no reason to suppose will ever, or have ever, come about. It probably is also dangerous. Equilibrium economics [...] is easily convertible into an apologia for existing economic arrangements and it is frequently so converted.
>
> (1970, pp. 88–89)

Elsewhere, Hahn reveals in rather dramatic fashion what he feels should happen if people contemplate using such models for policy: "When policy conclusions are drawn from such models, it is time to reach for one's gun" (Hahn, 1982, p. 29).

So where does this leave us? Guerrien's specific account of ideology may capture a tendency present in the discipline but it does not begin to explain the range of unrealistic contributions supported, some of which even purport to criticise, but most of which do not concern themselves with, the market mechanism. To understand why mainstream economics is so generally unrealistic, it is necessary to locate the explanation elsewhere.

## The insistence on formalism as ideology

However, this does not mean that an ideology is absent from mainstream deliberation. My own explanation reveals a form of ideology too, but is, I believe, a rather more sustainable account than Guerrien's. In my assessment the immediate cause of the manifest problems of the modern discipline is the widespread, uncritical, almost unthinking, attachment of mainstream economists to methods of mathematical-deductive explanation (in a context where these methods are mostly inappropriate), and the accompanying insistence that they be everywhere employed.

This blind faith in the appropriateness of always using mathematical-deductivist methods is a problem just because the implicit ontology of isolated atoms, that such methods presuppose, is inconsistent with the way social reality is found to be. For it is easy enough to show (via philosophical–ontological analysis) that social reality is open structured, processual, highly internally related, characterised by meaning, value and so on (see *Reorienting Economics*, chapter 2).

An advantage of my own rendering of the mainstream as uncritically committed to the application of mathematical methods in economics, is that it (seemingly uniquely) captures characteristics that remain invariant to that project's numerous flits in fads and fashions. Certainly, it is undeniable that the mainstream insists everywhere that mathematical methods be used.

Even the examples of ongoing change, diversity, novelty, complexity, evolution and multidimensionality, etc., highlighted by David Colander *et al.* (2004) (in their characterising the mainstream as pluralist) are occurring within the framework of formalistic modelling.

In fact, Colander *et al.* have noticed this aspect of "the changing face of mainstream economics" themselves (as I note in my response to Davis elsewhere in this volume). I am not sure they fully appreciate the significance of their observation (they give it little emphasis) but in any case they acknowledge that: "modern mainstream economics is open to new approaches, as long as they are done with a careful understanding of the strengths of the recent orthodox approach and with a modelling methodology acceptable to the mainstream" (2004, p. 492). The insistence on mathematical-deductive modelling prevails in all cases; the essential feature of the recent and current mainstream remains intact.

This mathematical emphasis has been dominant for quite a while now. Above I note Hahn's seemingly open-minded and reflective interpretation of the value of focusing on models of competitive equilibrium.

But if Hahn is receptive to criticism of an overemphasis on the equilibrium conception, this seemingly pluralistic attitude does not carry over (at least in his public pronouncements and writings)[8] to a tolerance of criticism of the mainstream insistence on employing methods of mathematical modelling. Rather Hahn, as I also point out elsewhere in this book, dismisses any suggestion that emphasis on the mathematics may be misplaced declaring it "a view surely not worth discussing" (Hahn, 1992a, p. 18); and he further counsels that we "avoid discussions of 'mathematics in economics' like the plague" (Hahn, 1992a; see also Hahn, 1992b).

Parenthetically, I believe a further advantage of my account (in addition to its explanatory power) is that it is more charitable in its interpretation of mainstream ideology. Guerrien, as we have seen, asks of the mainstream: "how such intelligent people can propose – and endlessly study – such *stupid* models?" His answer is ideology, and in setting out what he supposes are the responsible set of ideological beliefs, he asks the further question: "How can a normal person make any sense of this?"

Implicit in this latter remark is the assessment that the set of beliefs he imputes to the mainstream are rather obviously untenable. This is surely so. But equally surely the mainstream are reasonably "normal" too. Moreover, as Guerrien himself notes the mainstream are mostly *aware* of the unrealistic nature of their constructs. Thus to persist with them on the basis of "intuition" or anyway without question does seem rather bizarre. At best, it imputes to them essentially dishonest motives, a willingness knowingly to distort their conceptions of reality in order to "find" support for the (efficiency of the) market system.

My own explanation puts things in a different, and I believe more charitable, light. The emphasis on mathematics in science more widely has a reputable history of success. Whilst the sorts of unrealistic theories economists formulate have never proven to be explanatorily useful in any context, methods of mathematics have an impressive record across the natural sciences.

And just as much to the point, once we view the mainstream ideology as relating (understandably if erroneously) to the employment of only (or almost only) methods of mathematical modelling, the perseverance of fictions at a substantive level is seen no longer as a matter of trying to achieve a particular conclusion, but an unfortunate and unforeseen consequence of proceeding in a manner widely regarded as rigorous and preserving of standards.

Moreover, with a failure of mainstream economists to carry out ontological analysis the hope can be retained by these practitioners that successful theories of realistic scenarios can be achieved sooner or later, that the current substantive claims (which are always in flux) are merely temporary stand-ins.

Indeed, we can easily detect this attitude in the public commentaries of the more reflective mainstream contributors. Thus, the "theorist" Alan Kirman writes:

> The argument that the root of the problem [...] [is] that we are confined by a mathematical strait jacket which allows us no escape, does not seem very persuasive. That the mathematical frameworks that we have used made the task of changing or at least modifying our paradigm hard, is undeniable but it is difficult to believe that had a clear well-formulated new approach been suggested then we would not have adopted the appropriate mathematical tools.
>
> (1989, p. 137)

And the respected econometrician Edward Leamer notes a "wide gap between econometric theory and econometric practice" but fails to resolve the noted inconsistencies, writing: "Nor do I foresee developments on the horizon that will make any mathematical theory of inference fully applicable. For better or for worse, real inference will remain a highly complicated, poorly understood phenomenon" (Leamer, 1978, p. vi). The idea that there may be relevant non-mathematical theories of inference is never contemplated.

I suggest, then, that the explanation I put forward is not only more explanatorily grounded than Guerrien's but better helps us understand why indeed the mainstream activity can be described as misguided rather than disreputable.

According to this explanation, the problem induced by the mainstream's ideological orientation is ultimately ontological, and sustained by the discipline's further orientation of ontological neglect. It thus follows that Guerrien's worries about ontology being a distraction are also misplaced. Rather, if the explanation advanced here (and defended at length in *Reorienting Economics*) is correct, it follows that an emphasising of ontological issues is likely to be as efficacious a recourse as any to freeing up the economics academy, that is, to overcoming the mainstream's ideological barrier to relevance.

## Developing the explanatory critique

As I say I think the explanation I advance is more sustainable than Guerrien's alternative. But even if correct, the process of explanation (or explanatory critique)[9] ought not to (and does not) stop here. For something must explain the mainstream emphasis on mathematical modelling, even if acknowledged as a form of ideology.

By way of ontological critique I have shown that the current emphasis on formalism is unreasonable. But this critique (and even further persistent explanatory failure) of the mainstream project is never going to convince everyone. The question arises, then, as to whether we can improve matters, by in turn getting at the causes of the misplaced emphasis on mathematical formalism.

In chapter 10 of *Reorienting Economics* I set out an account of how I think mathematical-deductivist methods have become so dominant in Western academies. The account provided is a broadly evolutionary one in which the cultural awe in the successes of mathematics, the erroneous belief that formalism is essential to natural science, as well as the political environment facing (sponsors of) academics, have "conspired" to allow this situation to come about. However, I do not explain why the mathematising project *remains dominant* in economics *in the face of repeated failure*. Rather, I suggest that a psychological explanation is likely required, one perhaps focusing on the non-gender-neutral composition and orientation of the typical economics academy.

It is, as I say, important that such an explanatory project be pursued in order to understand why the mathematising project remains so dominant. But in addition, if the hypothesis of a continuing misplaced emphasis on formalism can be shown to have intelligible causal conditions, we can have even more faith in it constituting a correct assessment of the state of modern economics.

As it happens, a psychological explanation along the sorts of lines just described has recently been advanced, in a paper by Vinca Bigo (2007). Her argument, in brief, is that as infants we do not immediately recognise our separation from others or our mortality. When we do start to appreciate our true situation, this can involve varying degrees of trauma or anxiety. Now in all cases of anxiety, coping mechanisms are developed involving, in extreme cases, fantasies that deny or trivialise what is "lost". Thus, separation from others often results in dichotomies of superiority (of us over "others"), whilst awareness of mortality often results in our holding on to practices that have built into them presumptions that we can, after all, control/predict the future.

The development of boys and girls in all this is radically different, with boys more prone to developing coping mechanisms involving the fantasy of controlling the future. The reasons for this (which I cannot possibly detail here) are connected to the fact that most carers of little children are women. Little girls thus identify with their carers in ways that little boys do not; whilst boys take a distance and seek autonomy in ways that little girls tend not to. This affects the ways that little boys and girls respond to any difficult or traumatic situations in which they find themselves. As I say, I cannot go into the details of this intriguing research here, but it carries the implications that the problems of modern economics may ultimately lie in a chain of path dependent events ultimately underpinned by patriarchy; and that any lasting solution comes with a rather radical transformation of child raising, for example by having male as well as female carers as the norm.

In any case, I think that this is the sort of direction in which the explanatory endeavour discussed above likely takes us. In principle, there may be no end to this process of uncovering deeper explanations. But it is clear that an understanding of a phenomenon at one level is greatly improved by gaining some awareness at least of the causal process most directly underpinning it. In the social world, ideology is frequently going to figure, especially where false beliefs are prominent and sustained. But it is just as important in turn to seek the conditions of any such ideology, and so on.

## Final comments

In his stimulating short note, Bernard Guerrien acknowledges that modern economics needs reorienting but argues that the ultimate cause of its problems is ideology. I do not disagree with Guerrien that ideology is a problem, but I assess the content of that mainstream ideology differently. According to Guerrien, the ideological problem in question is an unreasonable persistence with conceptions that (are constructed to) show the market mechanism to be efficient. I suggest that this claim, as a universal characterisation of the contemporary mainstream, does not stand up to empirical scrutiny. I argue instead that the problem of ideology is the mainstream's insistence that mathematical methods be everywhere employed.

I further speculate that the reason for the prevalence of this particular ideology in the face of persistent explanatory failure is likely (at least in part) a matter of psychology. Although psychological analysis, focusing on mainstream motivations, is something I have hardly touched upon in my own research, I strongly suspect that it constitutes a project whose pursuit, now ongoing, is vital for understanding the state of the economics academy.

## Notes

1 Actually Guerrien writes: "I am only going to consider Lawson's main criticism of neoclassical economics: its "lack of *realism*." At risk of seeming overly pedantic, I should perhaps emphasise that neither in *Reorienting Economics*, nor elsewhere, do I concern myself with something called "neoclassical economics"; and nor, in criticising modern economics, do I make use of the expression "its lack of realism". Rather the economics project on which I focus my criticism is one I consistently refer to not as neoclassicism but as contemporary *mainstream economics*. For I have found the term neoclassical not to be especially appropriate or helpful. And rather than suggest that mainstream theories lack realism, I have preferred to say that they lack *realisticness*, or are implausible, or some such. In this, I simply follow standard philosophical terminology, and reserve the category of realism to denote a class of philosophical theories. These are theories committed to a real world existing at least in part independently of us, and to the possibility of our

acquiring knowledge of (aspects of) it under some descriptions. From this perspective to talk of a specific substantive theory's "lack of realism" is effectively a category mistake. What is needed is a terminology to describe certain properties of substantive theories. For this, as noted, I have tended to employ terms like realisticness or plausibility, or else I tend to write of the concern with fictitious constructs, and such like. Of course, this latter point does not in anyway undermine Guerrien's suggested critique. I shall though proceed as if Guerrien uses the expression lack of realisticness rather than lack of realism, etc.

2   It is perhaps worth remembering that in supposing most people in a community think alike about certain matters, and even "forget" that there are alternatives to the current state of affairs, we also arrive at Antonio Gramsci's concept of *hegemony*.

3   Thus, we might note, for example, that the internet encyclopaedia, Wikipedia, puts it as follows:

> Every society has an ideology that forms the basis of the "public opinion" or common sense, a basis that usually remains invisible to most people within the society. This dominant ideology appears as "neutral", holding to assumptions that are largely unchallenged. Meanwhile, all other ideologies that differ from the dominant ideology are seen as radical, no matter what the content of their actual vision may be.

4   Terry Eagleton (1991, p. 2), for example, lists the following interpretations found in the recent literature: a process of production of meanings, signs and value in social life; a body of ideas characteristic of a particular social group or class; ideas that help to legitimate a dominant political power; false ideas that help to legitimate a dominant political power; systematically distorted communication; that which offers a position for a subject; forms of thought motivated by social interests; identity thinking; socially necessary illusion; the conjuncture of discourse and power; the medium in which conscious social actors make sense of their world; action-oriented sets of beliefs; the confusion of linguistic and phenomenal reality; semiotic closure; the indispensable medium in which individuals live out their relation to a social structure; the process whereby said life is converted to a natural reality.

5   Thus although the notion of ideology as illusion, false consciousness, unreality, upside-down reality, is predominant in the contributions of both Marx and Engels, a second more neutral interpretation is to be found in some parts of Marx's writing, notable in the well-known passage in the *Contribution to the Critique of Political Economy* (1859, pp. 389–390):

> a distinction should always be made between the material transformation of the economic conditions of production [...] and the legal, political, religious, aesthetic or philosophic – in short, ideological – forms in which men become conscious of this conflict and fight it out.

6   The word *ideology* was coined by Count Destutt de Tracy in the late eighteenth century to define a "science of ideas".

7   Thus, in contradistinction to Guerrien we find contributors like David Colander *et al.* (2004) calling attention to what they see as the "changing face of mainstream economics" and criticising heterodox economists for failing to notice such ongoing developments. Specifically, these authors criticise heterodox contributors for adopting an overly "static view of the profession" (p. 486); for referring to the current mainstream as neoclassical; and for missing the "diversity that exists within the profession, and the many new ideas that are being tried out" (p. 487). In fact, Colander *et al.* insist that "Mainstream

economics is a complex system of evolving ideas" (p. 489), and refer to the "multiple dimensionalities that we see in the mainstream profession" (p. 489).

I believe that these critical assessments are mostly correct *if viewed as assessments of the mainstream substantive orientation*. In my view, it has always been unhelpful to refer to a "neoclassical economics", a category rarely clearly defined, and usually misleading. This is a difference between my orientation and Guerrien's noted in note 1 earlier in this chapter. But diversity within the dominant tradition has never been absent, and is still ongoing.

8  See my response to John Davis (under the discussion of pluralism) for a slightly different perspective on Hahn when not making public statements.

9  Let me indicate what I mean by explanatory critique. According to the ontology I defend, everything has a cause. This includes false beliefs and practices that seem patently misguided. In the social realm the causes of false beliefs are themselves typically social, that is, they depend on us. That means that ultimately they can be critiqued and changed.

I want to suggest that the explanation of something that is false or harmful, and the critique of the latter, are one and the same thing. For the reason we seek to identify something as false is in order to expose it; and the very process presupposes the value that it is good to get things right. To identify the cause of the falsity is to become automatically negatively or critically disposed to it, *ceteris paribus*. So to explain something that is undesirable (because false or misguided) is thus simultaneously in effect to critique it; hence the notion of explanatory critique.

I might emphasise, parenthetically, that we have here an account of moving between facts and values, of moving from initial assessments of what is and what ought to be done to further assessments of what ought to be done by finding out more about what is. In other words, what (we believe) ought to (and can) be done *ceteris paribus*, and what we (tend to) do, cannot meaningfully be separated from each other.

# References

Bigo, Vinca (2007), "Explaining Modern Economics (as a Microcosm of Society)", Mimeo: Jesus College, Cambridge.

Colander, David, Holt, R.P. and Rosser Jr, J.B. (2004). "The Changing Face of Mainstream Economics", *Review of Political Economy*, 16(4), pp. 485–500.

Davis, John B. (2005). "Heterodox Economics, the Fragmentation of the Mainstream and Embedded Individual Analysis", in R. Garnett and J. Harvey (eds), *The Future of Heterodox Economics*, Ann Arbor, MI: University of Michigan Press.

Eagleton, Terry (1991) *Ideology: An Introduction*, London: Verso.

Hahn, Frank H. (1970) "Some Adjustment Problems", *Econometrica*, 38, January; reprinted as pp. 1–17 in Frank Hahn (ed.), *Equilibrium and Macroeconomics*, Oxford: Basil Blackwell.

Hahn, Frank H. (1982) *Money and Inflation*, Oxford: Basil Blackwell.

Hahn, Frank H. (1992a) "Reflections", *Royal Economics Society Newsletter*, 77.

Hahn, Frank H. (1992b) "Answer to Backhouse: Yes", *Royal Economic Society Newsletter*, 78, p. 5.

Hahn, Frank H. (1994) "An Intellectual Retrospect", *Banca Nazionale del Lavoro Quarterly Review*, pp. 245–258.

Kirman, Alan (1989) "The Intrinsic Limits of Modern Economic Theory: The Emperor has no Clothes", *Economic Journal* 99(395), pp. 126–139.

Lawson, Tony (1997a) "Situated Rationality", *Journal of Economic Methodology*, 4(1), pp. 101–125.

Lawson, Tony (1997b) *Economics and Reality*, London: Routledge.

Lawson, Tony (2003) *Reorienting Economics*, London and New York: Routledge.

Leamer, Edward E. (1978) *Specification Searches: Ad hoc Inferences with Non-Experimental Data*, New York: John Wiley and Sons.

Marx, Karl (1859) "Preface to a Contribution to the Critique of Political Economy", in David McLellen (ed.), *Karl Marx: Selected Writings*, Oxford: Oxford University Press, pp. 388–391.

# 11 On the problem of formalism in economics

*Geoffrey M. Hodgson*

## Modern economics is sick

In his *Reorienting Economics*, Tony Lawson cites this magnificently appropriate quotation by Mark Blaug (1997, p. 3):

> Modern economics is sick. Economics has increasingly become an intellectual game played for its own sake and not for its practical consequences for understanding the economic world. Economists have converted the subject into a sort of social mathematics in which analytical rigour is everything and practical relevance is nothing.

I believe that on this issue, Lawson, Blaug and I are in agreement: the victory of technique over substance is a chronic problem within modern economics. Although the victory of formalism can be dated to the 1950s (Blaug 1999, 2003), by the 1980s the problem had become much more serious. Because mathematics has swamped the curricula in leading universities and graduate schools, student economists are neither encouraged nor equipped to analyse real world economies and institutions. Arjo Klamer and David Colander (1990, p. 18) reported a survey which showed that only 3 per cent of graduate students on top US economics programmes perceived 'having a thorough knowledge of the economy' to be 'very important' for professional success, while 65 per cent thought that 'being smart in the sense of problem-solving' is what matters and 57 per cent believed that 'excellence in mathematics' was very important.

In 1988 the American Economic Association set up a Commission on the state of graduate education in economics in the US. In a crushing indictment, the Commission expressed its fear that 'graduate programs may be turning out a generation with too many *idiot savants* skilled in technique but innocent of real economic issues' (Krueger *et al.*, 1991, pp. 1044–5). Alan Blinder (1990, p. 445), a member of the Commission, commented:

> Both students and faculty find economics obsessed with technique over substance ... the many macro and micro theory exams the

> Commission examined ... tested mathematical puzzle-solving
> ability, not substantive knowledge about economics ... Only 14
> percent of the students report that their core courses put substantial
> emphasis on 'applying economic theory to real-world problems.'

Alarm bells concerning technique displacing substance in economics
have been sounding for many years (Ward, 1972). However, although
mainstream economics has made some significant theoretical advances
in the 1990s, including an increasing adoption of institutional and evolutionary themes, the situation concerning formalism has not got any
better.

Perhaps the most serious emerging problem is that the graduate students of the 1980s and 1990s, who are skilled in technique but who have
an impoverished understanding of economic principles and their history,
are now beginning to achieve positions of seniority and influence in the
university departments, associations and journals of the economics profession. Their growing power and influence will ensure that formalism
further consolidates its overwhelming hegemony, to the detriment of
wider-ranging conceptual and methodological enquiry. This problem is
particularly serious in Britain and America, where formalism has
achieved its earliest and most complete victory. But the process is
delayed rather than absent elsewhere.

Both Blaug and Lawson face the problem of formalism head-on. But,
as I shall elaborate below, their evaluations differ. Blaug complains that
formalism has been associated with a detachment of economics from
substantial and practical issues. Lawson's (1997, 2003) attack is more
extensive and radical. He develops at length a methodological critique of
what he calls 'deductivism' and identifies this as the root of the formalist
malady. One of my main purposes here is to examine some prominent
aspects of Lawson's critique of formalism. I shall argue that his stance is
too limiting, with the expected outcome that mathematical and econometric tools will be illegitimate except under 'seemingly rare' (Lawson,
2003, p. 21) conditions.

## Tony Lawson's critique of formalism

Lawson affirms that the systems addressed by the social sciences are
open, in that they are subject to multiple extrinsic and intrinsic distur-
bances. This makes the task of prediction either difficult or impossible.
For Lawson (1997, p. 288), 'event prediction is usually infeasible' and 'in
any case not required for a successful science of economics'.

Lawson (1997, pp. 16–17) argues that 'deductivism' presumes 'event
regularities' or 'constant conjunctions of events or states of affairs' with
regularities of the form 'whenever event x then event y'. Philosophically,
this is a rather atypical definition of deductivism, because it refers to

empirical regularities concerning events rather than logical deductions concerning propositions. He seems to suggest that logical or mathematical constructions, if they are to be of relevance or use, must be some kind of map of reality at the level of events. For example, Lawson (2003, p. 22) writes of the importance of a ' "fit" with reality'.

From this stance, his critique of the use of formalism in economics readily follows. Social reality is an open system, generally lacking in 'constant conjunctions of events'. By contrast, formal models cannot be open to an indefinite number of additional relations or variables. In either a strict or a stochastic sense, such formal models generate regularities in the form: if $x$ then $y$. Such event regularities are highly limited in the social realm. Accordingly, there is a general mismatch between formal models and reality. If economics is to progress, then formal modelling must be limited to those cases where such regularities pertain, and these appear to be rather rare.

In the absence of formal models, what does the theorist do? Lawson realizes that no theory (formal or discursive) can proceed without some degree of abstraction: it is impossible to consider all elements and interactions at once. Indeed, he develops his methodological notion of abstraction at length. But here he faces a difficulty. If abstraction is necessary, and it involves the limitation of the sphere of consideration and the exclusion of additional relations or disturbing forces, then doesn't this too imply the assumption of a closed system? Stephen Nash (2004) has recently argued in the affirmative, suggesting that Lawson too must assume conditions or forms of closure. To some extent, however, Lawson (1997, p. 236) anticipates this objection. He proposes a distinction between 'abstraction' and 'isolation' in the following terms:

> When we focus upon varying productivity performances here, conditions of work there, rising or falling unemployment rates, and so on, we do not suppose that these features we choose to emphasise exist in isolation, even as a temporary, heuristic, measure. To do so is to assume a totally different world from the one in which we live, and one that has no bearing upon it.... In short, there is literally a world of difference between leaving something (temporarily) out of focus and treating it as though it does not exist. The achieving of an abstraction and treating something as though it existed in isolation are not the same thing at all.

He uses this distinction to protect his argument against the objection that his method of abstraction also implies the assumption of closure; he argues that abstraction does not imply closure but isolation does. With some important nuances and qualifications, Lawson (1997, pp. 131–3) associates the notion of isolation with the work of Uskali Mäki (1992, 1994) and contrasts isolation with his own concept of abstraction.

However, I shall argue later below that the distinction is, at least in prominent practical instances, difficult to sustain. Lawson takes a relatively extreme position in his attitude to formalism in economics, even among critics of mainstream economics, and even among the school of 'critical realists' to which he belongs. For example, critical realists such as Paul Downward (2000) have defended a more frequent use of some econometric techniques. Lawson points to very few concrete instances where econometrics has been appropriately deployed; Downward points to several. And the critical realist Erik Olin Wright (1994, pp. 183–9) has strongly supported the use of 'explicit abstract models, sometimes highly formalized as in game theory' and other 'rational choice models'. Although of course an extreme position such as Lawson's is not necessarily inappropriate or wrong, it does invite repeated criticism.

Perhaps a consequence, in Lawson's later writing, there has been a slight shift of tone and emphasis, if not substance as well. For example, Lawson (1999, pp. 7–8) proposes that from the fact that 'the world is open and structured, it does not follow' that economists 'ought thereby not to engage at all in formalistic methods such as econometrics'. He continues:

> The possibility of successes with the latter requires local closures.... Critical realism thus cannot and does not rule out *a priori* their limited occurrence. Rather, critical realism adopts an essentially *ex posteriori* orientation ... the opponent is the advocate of any form of *a priori* dogma.

With some amendments, Lawson (2003, pp. xix, 27, 178–9) repeats a similar argument in several places in his latest book. Again and again he insists that he is not against the use of econometrics or models in principle, but that they are of highly limited use given the closure conditions upon which they depend. He writes that 'a blanket rejection of econometrics, or indeed of any other method, is not a stance that is, or could be, sponsored in critical realism'. What is opposed is not econometrics but 'the *reduction* of economics to formalistic analysis'. But he then goes on to say that the 'application of formalistic methods requires certain (closure) conditions constituting special configurations of social reality that (unsurprisingly from the perspective sustained) have turned out to be rather rare'. In a recent essay, Lawson (2004) again repeats his insistence that he is not 'anti-mathematics'. But his expectation remains that the conditions for its effective and proper use would be rare.

In these passages at least two features are emphasized. The first is a strong, sincere and repeated claim of anti-dogmatism concerning whether or not mathematics can or should be used. But he lays down criteria for its use, including the requirement of (approximated) local closure. As a result of these criteria, the specific measure of his own anti-dogmatism, in practice rather than in intention, is how far he would admit that open systems might appear (or be approximated) in reality. Lawson argues that his critical realist perspective suggests at the outset that they are 'limited' or even 'rather rare'. Accordingly, the ontological arguments in Lawson's critical realism lead him right away to expect that the possibilities for formalism are highly restricted. This sets limits on his anti-dogmatist stance, despite his pronounced anti-dogmatist intentions. Although Lawson imposes no absolute normative ban on the use of mathematics, his arguments limit its legitimate use to 'rare' circumstances only.

Generally, one can also ask if a pervasive anti-dogmatism were possible. The need for some dogmatic presuppositions must be acknowledged by any philosopher or theorist. The removal of all dogma would mean a disabling nihilism of universal scepticism. In such circumstances, no theory could be established. Similarly, human activity would become paralysed if we ceased to believe in the essential dogma that most of the natural regularities and social institutions of today will survive until tomorrow. We often admire anti-dogmatism as a commendable personality trait, but philosophy of science suggests that some considerable degree of dogmatism is unavoidable.

The second feature is the proclamation of 'an essentially *ex posteriori* orientation', although what precisely is meant by this is insufficiently clear. Critical realists rightly emphasize the importance and priority of ontological commitments. Consider fundamental ontological commitments such as 'ubiquity determinism' (Bhaskar, 1975, pp. 70–1), which means that every event is deemed to have a cause. We have known at least since the days of David Hume that it is impossible to deduce causes a posteriori from our experience of events. It is in the very nature of such primary ontological commitments that they are neither based on nor deduced from evidence or experience. One of the crucial aspects of the philosophical assault on positivism in the middle of the twentieth century was the reaffirmation of the importance of such prior ontological commitments, which cannot be established by appeal to evidence or experience alone (Quine, 1951; Caldwell, 1982). So one is left wondering what 'an essentially *ex posteriori* orientation' means, and how it can be reconciled with an insistence on the primacy of ontology.

Again I detect a slight post 1997 shift of tone and emphasis when Lawson (2003, pp. 20–1) openly discusses the possibility that econometrics might be of use in some instances:

> Clive Granger has argued convincingly that it is possible to use econometrics to provide relatively successful short-run forecasts of phenomena such as electricity loads and peaks in regions wherein one factor, temperature, or more specifically the extreme cold, dominates behaviour.... The point remains, however, that the sorts of

conditions in question appear *a posteriori* not to be typical of the social realm. Rather, as I say, social reality is found to be a quintes-sentially open, structured, dynamic and highly internally related system, amongst other things, whilst the conditions for achieving a local closure are seemingly rare.

This is the only example I can find where Lawson has pointed to a spe-cific piece of econometric analysis and acknowledged its legitimacy. Note, however, the strictness of the key condition involved. According to this passage, for econometrics to be applicable, 'local closure' must be actually achieved, not merely approximated. However, it is clearly the case a posteriori that electricity consumption (even in cold regions) is a feature of an open rather than a closed system. For instance, electricity consumption is generally affected by its price. Such prices are heavily influenced by global market conditions. Global markets are far from being closed systems. Granger did not provide an example that estab-lishes local closure. By the logic of his own argument, Lawson should have deemed econometrics to be inapplicable to this situation as well. His single claimed example of the legitimate use of econometrics turns out to be illicit according to his own key criterion.

Indeed, if we require that formal models can only be applied in con-texts where local closure is actually achieved, then this would mean that such models were inappropriate in other sciences and disciplines, such as biology, physics or engineering. Generally, in multiple contexts, in both the natural and social world, such closures are absent, as Roy Bhaskar (1975) as well as Lawson himself have emphasized. If formal models require strict local closure, then formal models are never appro-priate. But this would overlook the achievement of mathematical models in some sciences. It may be suggested that local closure is sometimes approximated in physics, and because of this some formal models can be of use. But models and simulations have also been used with some success in biology and evolutionary anthropology, which face a degree of complexity and openness comparable to that found in human societies (Murray, 1989; Boyd and Richerson, 1985).

At least in recent seminar presentations, Lawson has amended his position still further, by proposing that econometrics might apply when local closure is 'approximated in reality'. This formulation contrasts with that in his two (1997, 2003) books, which generally insist that local closure conditions must actually apply for formalism to be viable. From his amended standpoint, admitting a degree of approximation to closure, it would be possible to admit the Granger example as a case of the legitimate application of econometric techniques. The general problem for Lawson in applying this revised criterion more widely is that the degree of acceptable approximation is left unspecified. In general, once the insistence on the actual achievement of local closure is removed, and approximations to closure are admitted, then the door to econometrics is unlocked and opened.

## Some key problems and omissions in Tony Lawson's critique

Much of Lawson's discussion of formalism concerns econometrics. He gives insufficient attention to other applications of mathematical techniques, which serve primary purposes other than the prediction or explanation of measurable variables. Such additional applications of formalism include (a) heuristics and (b) internal critiques. I shall address each of these in turn.

The purpose of a heuristic is to identify possible causal mechanisms that form part of a more complex and inevitably open system. Heuristics can be useful without necessarily making adequate predictions or closely matching existing data. Their purpose is to establish a plausible segment of a causal story, without necessarily giving an adequate or complete explanation of the phenomena to which they relate.

An example of a formal heuristic that has been persuasive in economics is the ethnic segregation model constructed by Thomas Schelling (1969). Using a very simple model of housing location, Schelling showed that ethnic segregation can result even from very small feedback effects. Even if people only have a very slight preference for their own ethnic group, this can be enough to cause migration out of mixed ethnic areas, with the end result of segregated ethnic ghettos. The problem is extremely simple, and hardly realistic in its detailed assumptions. However, making the model more complicated and 'realistic' would be beyond the point, partly because it is obvious that similar outcomes might result from a more complicated model. Instead, the Schelling model points to a credible mechanism that shows that ethnic segregation does not necessarily depend upon the actions of bigoted racists. Such racists exist in the real world, so their inclusion in the model would make it more realistic. But this would defeat the object of the model, which is to show that segregation might result even without them. The model abstracts from the more forceful versions of racism that we find in the real world to establish this key point. In this case, the power of the model is helped by its unrealisticness. The power of the model lies in its capacity to abstract a plausible but hitherto neglected causal mechanism.

In a very useful discussion of such 'credible worlds', Robert Sugden (2000) asks probing questions concerning the role and 'realisticness' of this and other heuristic models in economics. These heuristic models have the paradoxical claim that they are literally unrealistic yet they seem to illuminate important aspects of reality. Using the Schelling model alongside George Akerlof's (1970) famous article on the 'market for lemons', which again claims to establish meaningful propositions about the world on the basis of an admittedly unrealistic model, Sugden (p. 28) describes these models as 'credible counterfactual worlds' that give 'some warrant for making inductive inferences from model to the real world'.

In no case can the construction of a heuristic or counterfactual model clinch the argument concerning the causal mechanisms that actually exist in the real world. However, what they sometimes do show – as in the case of the Schelling model – is that outcomes might not necessarily result from the causal factors that may be presumed at first sight. To complete the argument, further theoretical development and empirical enquiry are always required. I have suggested above that heuristics are appropriate if they successfully abstract an important causal mechanism in reality. Accordingly, heuristics relate to the very process of abstraction that Lawson himself highlights. But Lawson suggests that heuristics are isolations rather than abstractions. So here I must return to Lawson's (1997, p. 236) attempted distinction between isolation and abstraction, as quoted above. According to him, the key difference is 'between leaving something (temporarily) out of focus and treating it as though it does not exist'. Again take the Schelling model as an example. Schelling himself accepts that bigoted racists exist, yet he leaves them out of his model. The purpose of the model is not to excuse or deny racism, but the more severe forms of racism are deliberately removed. Nevertheless, the model is extremely and worryingly persuasive.

No one to my knowledge, including Schelling himself, has suggested that such as model is a complete or adequate causal representation of the processes underlying the emergence of ethnic segregation in reality. The model is simply a heuristic step along the road towards that more complete end. More generally, no sensible mainstream economist would deny that the world is open, and no adequate presentation of a formal model would omit to mention that other (omitted) causal mechanisms exist.

Ultimately, Lawson's attempted distinction between abstraction and isolation hinges on the precise meaning of notions such as 'treating [that which is left out of the picture] as though it does not exist' and the implied distinction between a 'temporary heuristic' and 'leaving something temporarily out of focus'. Yet Lawson is insufficiently precise here. If I 'focus' on the workings of a national economy (perhaps without building a mathematical model) and ignore its trade with other nations, then in what sense might this qualify as a temporary account, rather than a presumption that such exports and imports do not exist? Surely, some verbal statement would be required, acknowledging the existence of international trade, explaining its omission from the current discussion and suggesting that further work must be done to incorporate it into the analysis. But this is also the kind of necessary qualification that we should expect from the best presentations of heuristic models. On the other hand, it would be impossible to mention all the things that we have left out of the account. In this sense all theory is 'temporary'. But do such unmentioned omissions amount to treating some causal linkages as though they do not exist? If this were the case, then every theory, including non-formal, discursive theory, by Lawson's criteria is a failure. Once we try to apply Lawson's criteria, then their insufficiency and vagueness become apparent, and his attempted distinction between abstraction and isolation is revealed as highly problematic.

A crucial point here is that in economics we should not and cannot judge models in isolation. Lawson treats any model as if it were alone an intrinsic claim to be a partial map of the world. Yet the meaning of any heuristic model depends upon an interpretive framework that is not contained in the formalities of the model itself. If heuristic models are suitably hedged and qualified, in the manner suggested above, then these qualifications form part of the interpretative apparatus for the model. If heuristic models are treated within an adequate interpretative context, then such heuristic packages can successfully defend themselves against they charge that they treat other aspects of reality as though they do not exist.

By contrast, Lawson himself isolates formal models from their interpretative contexts, treating these as if they do not or need not exist, and denies the validity of even 'temporary' heuristic models per se. The strictures of appropriate contextualization that Lawson rightly requires of discursive theory should apply to his treatment of formal models as well. Bringing the interpretative framework of a heuristic model into the picture is highly important in appraising the problem of excessive or misplaced formalism in economics. An alternative diagnosis emerges, in which the malady is not the use of formalism as such but the inadequacy and underdevelopment of the interpretative context in which they are placed. Technique can take priority over substance as a result of the relative neglect of interpretative context. An adequate interpretative framework would depend on the discussion of the genesis, meaning and methodological significance of key concepts that are involved in the model or its interpretation. This is never a small task, and if done properly it will be at least as weighty as the formal technique of the model itself. Yet in modern economics such interpretative and conceptual matters are often marginalized and underdeveloped. I contend that this is one of the main problems with formalism in economics today.

While Lawson implicitly treats formal models as if they were claims to map the world, his explicit metaphor is more frequently of the model as a tool. For example, Lawson (2003, p. 12) notes the ontological mismatch between formal models and reality and suggests that this is grounds to question their use: 'Few people ... would attempt to use a comb to write a letter ... or a drill to clean a window.' This argument is not as illuminating as it may seem at first sight. Of course, we would use a pen to write a letter and a clean cloth to clean a window. Yet the ontology of pens is very different from that of letters, and likewise there is a big ontological difference between clean cloths and dirty windows. So there is nothing in this appropriateness-of-tools argument that rules out, for instance, using closed models to help understand an open reality.

I now turn to the second use of formalism that is neglected by Lawson: that of an internal critique. Generally, the impact of an effective internal critique is negative rather than positive; it shows the limits of an existing theory rather than building a new one. It is nevertheless important. Consider the example of the critique of mainstream capital theory by Piero Sraffa (1960) and others. By developing a model with disaggregated rather than aggregated physical capital, Sraffa showed that the measure of capital could not be independent of profits, wages or prices. Consequently, any attempt to explain the latter by means of an aggregated capital variable must assume that which it has to explain. The validity of this argument was later accepted by Paul Samuelson and others (Harcourt, 1972). It meant that several of the models and arguments used in the mainstream theory of capital and distribution were either invalid or dependent on highly restrictive assumptions.

A demonstration that a widely adopted approach depends on restrictive or even implausible assumptions is a key feature of many of the successful and significant internal critiques that we find in economics. Other examples include works by Rolf Mantel (1974) and Robert Rowthorn (1999). Mantel and several other theorists showed that even with the assumption of individual utility maximization, the excess demand functions in an exchange economy can take almost any form, and there is thus no basis in standard general equilibrium theory for the assumption that they are generally downward sloping. Their work proved very influential in bringing the microfoundations project in general equilibrium theory to an end (Rizvi, 1994). Rowthorn showed that prominent models used by governments in macroeconomic policy making are based on highly restrictive and unwarranted assumptions.

Such critiques do not themselves provide new theories, although they may suggest some appropriate measures and establish some relevant pointers. By their nature, internal critiques are not claims to map the real world. Instead, they are attempts to show that other theories are inadequate or overly restrictive in regard to the kind of world to which they relate. I have not come across an adequate discussion of the role of internal critiques in Lawson's work, despite their prevalence the Cambridge tradition of economics that used to be well established in his university department.

Significantly, neither heuristics nor internal critiques are attempts to map the world with a model. Accordingly, insofar as they are of some scientific use, severe doubt is cast on Lawson's central argument that the adoption of a particular model involves explicit or implicit assumptions about the ontology of the social world. By contrast, it would seem that some models are of use, even if there is a significant misfit with reality. If so, then Lawson's main argument falls.

## Conclusion

In regard to formalism, many economists propose the extreme view that it is the principal and necessary means by which economics becomes rigorous and scientific, and thus the dominance of formalism is a positive sign of success. Lawson takes a position near the other extreme. He argues that formalism is justified in 'rare' circumstances only, where local closure exists or is approximated. I propose that both attitudes to formalism are flawed, partly because they both downplay its necessary interface with interpretative structures.

Yet while Lawson and the mainstream are at odds, there are some shared presuppositions. Many mainstream economists assume that their models are sufficient to represent the world, neglecting the interpretative discourses required to make such a claim meaningful. Lawson too believes that the adoption of a formal model intrinsically upholds some substantial claims concerning the nature of reality. I believe that both positions are false.

If modern economics is sick, then what is the nature of the sickness? A good answer to this question is required to help us find an appropriate remedy. Lawson's medicine is to require the application of formalism only when local closure is achieved or perhaps approximated. However this remedy virtually ends up as an inversion of the disease itself, and I have argued that it is based on a faulty diagnosis.

Especially in his recent writing, Lawson has insisted that he is not against formalism as such, and he has no dogmatic prescription concerning its use. However, I am aware of only one example of a piece of econometrics that Lawson has deemed as legitimate, and even here to admit it he has to fudge the criterion of strict closure declared in his 2003 book. More recently (but until now only verbally as far as I am aware), he has relaxed this criterion to allow econometrics to be used when closure is approximated, rather than actually achieved.

The consequent challenge for Lawson is to be more specific about the degree of approximation and to point to still further examples of the legitimate use of mathematical models in economics. Until this is done, Lawson remains in the extreme position of admitting as legitimate only one specific case, among hundreds of thousands of examples that are available to us.

Middle ground solutions are not intrinsically warranted simply because they are middle ground. But part of the tragedy of modern economics is that they have so far received limited attention and consideration, with notable exceptions such as a recent article by Victoria Chick and Sheila Dow (2001).

I suggest that the problem with formalism is not the general inappropriateness of formalism itself, but it is the problem identified by Blaug in the quotation near the beginning of this article. Blaug sees the kind of formalism in modern economics as 'an intellectual game played for its own sake' rather than for its use in explaining and engaging with the real economic world. Blaug complains that in modern economics 'analytical rigour is everything and practical relevance is nothing'. Again the solution here is not necessarily to confine formalism to the very rare conditions of actual or approximated closure, but to ensure that concerns for practical relevance come to the fore. Formal techniques should be the servants rather than the masters of scientific enquiry.

It is also worth bearing in mind that there is an example of a social science in which formal methods and models have hitherto been put to little use, apart from statistics. Yet this discipline is widely acknowledged to be in a state of severe disorder, especially concerning its core presuppositions, its self-identity and boundaries, and its relations with other disciplines, particularly economics and biology. This afflicted social science is sociology. The persistence of its acute scientific maladies alongside its relatively infrequent use of formalism indicates that additional problems exist within the social sciences today. These include the postmodernist affirmation that one theory is as good as another, the frequent choice of a theory on ideological rather than scientific grounds and an occasional self-inflicted blindness concerning the biological aspect of human nature and its significance for the study of human society.

Despite our differences of view, I wish to emphasize that both Lawson and myself, and others here cited including Blaug, Chick, Dow and Mäki, adopt a realist philosophical perspective. Realism acknowledges that a world exists beyond our perceptions. Realists uphold that, to be adequate, sciences including economics should not be self-contained logical games but attempts to address and understand aspects of the real world. Accordingly, there is no room for a philosophy of science in which 'anything goes'. There is a shared realist imperative: to understand the real world.

However, I argue here that there is a place for mathematics in economics, even when conditions of closure are absent or fail to be approximated. I have emphasized the greater importance of the interpretative structure within which the theory is placed. The pressing agenda issue for further discussion and enquiry in this area is to explore the inadequately explored middle ground between the unacceptable extremes of unreflecting worship and (at least expectational) denial of formal models and methods.

# Acknowledgement

The author wishes to thank Mark Blaug, Sheila Dow and Tony Lawson for very helpful comments on an earlier version of this chapter.

# References

Akerlof, George A. (1970) 'The Market for "Lemons": Quality Uncertainty and the Market Mechanism', *Quarterly Journal of Economics*, 84(3), August, pp. 488–500.

Bhaskar, Roy (1975) *A Realist Theory of Science* (1st edn) (Leeds: Leeds Books).

Blaug, Mark (1997) 'Ugly Currents in Modern Economics', *Options Politiques*, 18(17), September, pp. 3–8.

Blaug, Mark (1999) 'The Formalist Revolution or What Happened to Orthodox Economics After World War II?', in Backhouse, Roger E. and Creedy, John (eds) *From Classical Economics to the Theory of the Firm: Essays in Honour of D. P. O'Brien* (Cheltenham: Edward Elgar), pp. 257–80.

Blaug, Mark (2003) 'The Formalist Revolution of the 1950s', in Samuels, Warren J., Biddle, Jeff E. and Davis, John B. (eds) *A Companion to the History of Economic Thought* (Malden, MA and Oxford, UK: Blackwell), pp. 395–410.

Blinder, Alan (1990) 'Discussion', *American Economic Review*, 80(2), May, pp. 445–7.

Boyd, Robert and Richerson, Peter J. (1985) *Culture and the Evolutionary Process* (Chicago, IL: University of Chicago Press).

Caldwell, Bruce J. (1982) *Beyond Positivism: Economic Methodology in the Twentieth Century* (London: Allen and Unwin).

Chick, Victoria and Dow, Sheila C. (2001) 'Formalism, Logic and Reality: A Keynesian Analysis', *Cambridge Journal of Economics*, 25(6), November, pp. 705–21.

Downward, Paul (2000) 'A Realist Appraisal of Post-Keynesian Pricing Theory', *Cambridge Journal of Economics*, 24(2), March, pp. 211–24.

Harcourt, Geoffrey C. (1972) *Some Cambridge Controversies in the Theory of Capital* (Cambridge: Cambridge University Press).

Klamer, Arjo and Colander, David (1990) *The Making of an Economist* (Boulder, CO: Westview Press).

Krueger, Anne O. *et al.* (1991) 'Report on the Commission on Graduate Education in Economics', *Journal of Economic Literature*, 29(3), September, pp. 1035–53.

Lawson, Tony (1997) *Economics and Reality* (London and New York: Routledge).

Lawson, Tony (1999) 'Connections and Distinctions: Post Keynesianism and Critical Realism', *Journal of Post Keynesian Economics*, 22(1), Fall, pp. 3–14.

Lawson, Tony (2003) *Reorienting Economics* (London and New York: Routledge).

Lawson, Tony (2004) 'On Heterodox Economics, Themata and the Use of Mathematics in Economics', *Journal of Economic Methodology*, 11(3), September, pp. 329–40.

Mäki, Uskali (1992) 'On the Method of Isolation in Economics', *Poznan Studies in the Philosophy of the Sciences and the Humanities*, 26, pp. 319–54.

Mäki, Uskali (1994) 'Isolation, Idealization and Truth in Economics', *Poznan Studies in the Philosophy of the Sciences and the Humanities*, 38, pp. 147–68.

Mantel, Rolf R. (1974) 'On the Characterization of Aggregate Excess Demand', *Journal of Economic Theory*, 12(2), pp. 348–53.

Murray, J.D. (1989) *Mathematical Biology* (Berlin: Springer).

Nash, Stephen J. (2004) 'On Closure in Economics', *Journal of Economic Methodology*, 11(1), March, pp. 75–89.

Quine, Willard van Orman (1951) 'Two Dogmas of Empiricism', *Philosophical Review*, 60(1), January, pp. 20–43. Reprinted in Quine, Willard van Orman (1953) *From a Logical Point of View* (Cambridge, MA: Harvard University Press).

Rizvi, S. Abu Turab (1994) 'The Microfoundations Project in General Equilibrium Theory', *Cambridge Journal of Economics*, 18(4), August, pp. 357–77.

Rowthorn, Robert E. (1999) 'Unemployment, Wage Bargaining and Capital-Labour Substitution', *Cambridge Journal of Economics*, 23(4), July, pp. 413–25.

Schelling, Thomas C. (1969) 'Models of Segregation', *American Economic Review*, 59(2), pp. 488–93.

Sraffa, Piero (1960) *Production of Commodities by Means of Commodities: Prelude to a Critique of Economic Theory* (Cambridge: Cambridge University Press).

Sugden, Robert (2000) 'Credible Worlds: The Status of Theoretical Models in Economics', *Journal of Economic Methodology*, 7(1), March, pp. 1–31.

Ward, Benjamin (1972) *What's Wrong With Economics?* (London: Macmillan).

Wright, Erik Olin (1994) *Interrogating Inequality: Essays on Class Analysis, Socialism and Marxism* (London: Verso).

# 12 On the nature and roles of formalism in economics
## Reply to Hodgson

*Tony Lawson*

Geoffrey Hodgson and I have debated numerous issues over the years (not least the nature of old institutionalism and how its contributions are best interpreted), mostly in seminars or over a drink or two. Whether we agree or disagree, I find that Hodgson's views are always interesting and usually very substantial. The issue of formalism seemingly opens up a new area of debate between us. In characteristic style Hodgson's various contentions in his current piece are wide-ranging, thought provoking and backed up by numerous authoritative sources. Thus, it is necessary to do quite a bit of work to show why I nevertheless think Hodgson fails to make too much of a case against my position.

Hodgson's main thesis is that my critique of mainstream mathematical modelling is overly restrictive in the way I imagine models to be useful. Formalistic models can provide insight in numerous ways that I fail to contemplate, and Hodgson is concerned to indicate some of these.

This topic of the alternative roles for formalistic models is actually something I explore at length in *Economics and Reality*. Its consideration takes Hodgson to discussions of methods of abstraction, theoretical isolation, heuristics and so forth, all issues on which I have previously found a need to say much, but which do perhaps get too little coverage in economic methodology in general. As it happens, I believe that much of what Hodgson has to say on these issues cannot be sustained. But his commentary does provide an opportunity to give my take on these neglected issues a further airing, and perhaps to develop them further.

There is a further related, if ultimately secondary, issue I should also address. Overall, I think there is a danger that Hodgson's contribution conveys the (false) impression that I am opposed to formalism per se. This is such a misunderstanding that I need first to get it out of the way before addressing the central topic here, the manner in which formal models might usefully be employed.

## Orientation to formalism

Whatever Hodgson's intention, it seems to me likely, as I say, that the dominant impression conveyed by his piece is that my stance is somehow an anti-mathematics one. Hodgson does not attribute such an orientation to me directly; in brief asides, indeed, he even acknowledges that this is not an accurate statement of my position. However, he pursues several lines of argument that, I fear, will mostly encourage the uninformed reader to suppose that I am after all opposed to the use of mathematical formalism per se. Little could be further from the truth. Rather I am opposed to the abuse of mathematical formalism, and such abuse is, I believe, typical of the situation in much of modern economics.

What line of argument of Hodgson's do I have in mind? At the start of his commentary Hodgson reproduces a passage by Mark Blaug of which I have previously made much use. In it Blaug suggests that "Modern economics is sick", noting that "Economists have converted the subject into a sort of social mathematics in which analytical rigour is everything and practical relevance is nothing" (Mark Blaug, 1997, p. 3).

Now the reason I quote this passage is simply that I both agree with it, and I find it significant because Blaug once seemed sympathetic to the mainstream. However, Hodgson asserts that Blaug and I make different evaluations, with my position being "more radical". My own view, though, is that, to the contrary, Blaug's position is simply a summary of a critical assessment that I have spent much time defending. Indeed, I would describe my own position on the use of mathematics as anything but radical; it is simply informed by an appreciation of mathematics. I neither support its universal application in economics as an a priori stance nor its universal rejection as an a priori stance. Rather I recognise that all tools, including mathematical ones, are limited in their scope of application (I believe that the appreciation of a tool is bound up with an awareness of its limitations), and that the relevance of mathematics in any specific application depends on the context-specific merits of the case.

I am perplexed, therefore, to find that Hodgson portrays me as an extremist on such matters:[1]

> In regard to formalism, many economists take the extreme view that it is the only means by which economics becomes rigorous and scientific, and thus the dominance of formalism is a positive sign of success. Lawson takes a position near the opposite extreme. He argues that formalism is justified in "rare" circumstances only, where local closure exists (or is approximated). I propose that both attitudes to formalism are flawed.

And Hodgson ends with the following plea:[2] "The pressing agenda issue for further discussion and enquiry in this area is to explore the inadequately explored middle ground between the unacceptable extremes of unreflecting worship (and at least expectational) denial of formal models and methods."

Hodgson's talk here of extremes is misleading if not incoherent. At one supposed extreme is the view that formalism "is the only means by which economics becomes rigorous and scientific"; at the other is the view that the use of "formalism is justified in 'rare' circumstances only". Clearly, such views need not even be incompatible let alone opposite extremes. Of course, I have argued extensively against the former view that formalism is essential to science or rigour. But one could (mistakenly) hold to such a view (that formalism is after all essential to science), conclude that formalism has but limited application to the social realm and infer thereby that a scientific economics has limited scope.

As I say, this is not my position (my own position to the contrary is that a science of economics is entirely feasible whatever the scope for formalism).[3] But it is logically feasible, and indeed is accepted by many hermeneuticists and others who do accept the implicit conception of science in question, but reject its relevance to the study of society (see Lawson, 1997, chapter 10).

In truth the (mainstream) view that formalism "is the only means by which economics becomes rigorous and scientific" is just a mistake, not an extreme view or form of practice. The real sense in which the mainstream is extreme lies in its insistence that we all must always adopt mathematical-deductivist methods of a certain sort, irrespective of how explanatorily successful they are (in potential or practice). If there is an opposite extreme to this it is the insistence that such formalistic methods be always rejected irrespective of how explanatorily successful they are. I doubt anyone accepts such a position.

Why then does Hodgson suggest that I am at an opposite extreme to the mainstream? I have to admit to being unsure about this. Perhaps I have just not expressed myself with sufficient clarity.

It is true that, in attempting to identify conditions under which certain methods of mathematical-deductivist reasoning are *guaranteed*, I have suggested that they seem rarely to have come about in the social realm. But this is a long way from an a priori rejection of formalism, from an insistence that formalistic methods be rejected irrespective of how explanatorily successful they are.

Actually, it may be useful if I elaborate a bit on this issue. For although it seems to me that the orientation I adopt is reasonable, Hodgson actually interprets it as setting limits to what he calls "my claim of anti-dogmatism". Perhaps this explains his misunderstanding. Let me briefly elaborate.

## Dogmatism and identifying the conditions of closures

First, I must examine what is meant here by dogmatism, or dogma. I do use the term dogma in *Reorienting Economics*, though only occasionally. In fact, I use it twice, in each case to describe the doctrine, advanced by mainstream economists without grounds, that certain sorts of methods only should always be followed.

Thus in the preface to *Reorienting Economics* I write:

> Rather, the primary object of my criticism is as stated. In its most general formulation, my opposition is directed at any kind of *a priori* dogma. The realist approach I defend is contrasted with any kind of ungrounded insistence that certain methods only, or almost only, should be followed.
>
> (Lawson, 2003)

And in chapter 7 I write:

> Rather the opponent is the advocate of any form of *a priori* dogma. In the context of modern economics specifically, the primary target is ... the current mainstream *a priori* insistence that formalistic modelling is the only proper, and a universally valid, method for modern economics, along with its effective prohibition on alternative approaches.

No doubt dogma and dogmatism have various meanings. But it is surely clear that in using it to describe mainstream practice I am here simply taking dogma to be doctrine that is not defended but accepted on authority as unquestionable. Dogmatism as I am interpreting the practice, then, is just the act of accepting dogma, that is, of adhering to something on the basis of authority alone and treating it as beyond question or criticism.[4] Clearly, it is something similar to Guerrien's notion of ideology discussed previously in the current volume.

Now, of course, in suggesting that the dogmatic stance of modern mainstream economists be rejected I do not want to imply that all doctrines can always be meaningfully challenged.[5] And I am well aware that in acting at any point in time it is practically impossible to subject all beliefs that condition an action to critical scrutiny at that moment. But I do believe that everything that can be challenged should be treated as *open to critical scrutiny in principle* whether or not the latter is forthcoming. And I certainly believe the mainstream insistence that methods of mathematical formalism be everywhere utilised ought to be open to question and criticism by all. As I say, it is the mainstream refusal to consider the possibility that formalistic methods may actually be limited in their scope of legitimate application that I have suggested is dogmatic.

However, Hodgson suggests that my pointing to such limitations reveals the limits of my anti-dogmatism in practice. How does he reach this view? He writes:

> In these passages [by Lawson] at least two features are emphasized. The first is a strong, sincere and repeated claim of anti-dogmatism concerning whether or not mathematics can or should be used. But he lays down criteria for its use, including the requirement of (approximated) local closure. As a result of these criteria, the specific measure of his own anti-dogmatism, in practice rather than in intention, is how far he would admit that open systems might appear (or be approximated) in reality. Lawson argues that his critical realist perspective suggests at the outset that they are "limited" or even "rather rare". Accordingly, the ontological arguments in Lawson's critical realism lead him right away to expect that the possibilities for formalism are highly restricted. This sets limits on his anti-dogmatist stance, despite his pronounced anti-dogmatist intentions. Although Lawson imposes no absolute normative ban on the use of mathematics, his arguments limit its legitimate use to "rare" circumstances only.

Hodgson's logic here is not compelling. Let me momentarily leave aside the seemingly emotive topic of the use of formalistic methods in economics. As I say, I am opposed to dogmatism in the form of any authoritative assertion that only one set of research methods can ever be used in economics. Suppose, though, that having made this declaration, I also make the suggestion that the conditions under which, say, electron accelerators or stethoscopes are useful in economic research rarely crop up. Would Hodgson maintain that I am thereby once more setting limits to my otherwise anti-dogmatic stance? I doubt it. Certainly I hope not. For in such examples it is surely clear enough that it is neither I, nor my arguments, that limit the use of electron accelerators or stethoscopes to "rare" socio-economic situations; rather it is the world, the nature of social reality, that sets the limits to the conditions under which the tools in question are useful. Seeking to identify or theorise these conditions has nothing per se to do with dogmatism or anti-dogmatism.[6]

The point is that the mathematical methods used by economists are themselves just tools. My claim is merely that the conditions in which they are useful seem not to have occurred much in the social realm.

I may be quite wrong in this assessment. But that does not yet set limits to my anti-dogmatism. It would be dogmatic of me, perhaps, if I used this assessment to advise that formalistic methods be everywhere excluded from the economist's toolbox. But I have never suggested this. My position is always that all methods (that anyone seriously proposes) be retained to some degree, not least because even ontological arguments seeking to uncover their spheres of usefulness are fallible.

For example I write in *Reorienting Economics*:

> In so concluding I am not at all suggesting that formalistic modelling methods should not exist among the battery of options available. All knowledge is fallible, including ontological theorising. And even accepting the ontological perspective systematised and defended in the chapters, which follow, there may yet be some (greater) scope of application for methods of mathematical modelling than so far uncovered. But just as significantly, although ontology can provide some directionality to social theorising, one of its most useful functions, and perhaps its primary one, is actually to open up analysis. This is precisely its role here. My aim with the discussion of this chapter is not to narrow down the range of methodological options by attempting to prohibit a particular method. Rather it is to widen the range of possibilities through criticising the fact that, and manner in which, the particular method in question is currently and unthinkingly universalised.
>
> (Lawson, 2003, chapter 1)[7]

The surprising aspect of all this is that Hodgson's assessment of my position is thought to carry plausibility. To the extent that it is, I suspect it has more to do with some rhetoric that likely misleads. Consider the final sentence of his passage reproduced above. Here Hodgson writes: "Although Lawson imposes no absolute normative ban on the use of mathematics, his arguments limit its legitimate use to 'rare' circumstances only."

I have already noted that it is not my argument but the nature of social reality that serves to limit the legitimate use of any methods. The point to which I want to draw attention here, though, is the first part of the sentence: "Although Lawson imposes no absolute normative ban on the use of mathematics",[8] and in particular Hodgson's use of terms like "imposes", "absolute" and "ban", which seem to create a smell of dogmatism. Even use of the term "normative" in this context adds to this effect (it is difficult to imagine a non-normative ban).[9]

Now I hope it is clear that I am not in a position to impose anything, whether or not I want to; that I would not like to be in such a position; and even more to the point I want nothing banned, whether absolutely or partially. Such sentence constructions mislead and I fear hinder serious argument.

It is true that I argue that regularities (real or imaginary) of the form "whenever event (or state of affairs) x then event (or state of affairs) y" (or stochastic near equivalents) are a necessary condition if formalistic deductivist methods of the sort economists seek are to be utilised. Systems in which these regularities occur I refer to as closed. But I seek to identify the conditions under which such event regularities are *guaranteed*. I may be wrong in my analysis. And in any case, my analysis does not preclude the possibility of their occurring in other conditions. So however we look at it I am hardly laying down criteria for the use of mathematical-deductivist methods, merely trying to understand something about the conditions of their likely successes, if any.

Basically I am trying to help clarify the nature of the situation in modern economics. Whether I speculate that closed social systems are more likely, or less likely, or just as likely, in the future than in the past, this hardly counts as an "admission", and again clearly has no bearing on my position vis-à-vis dogmatism.

## Successful econometrics?

If in *Reorienting Economics*, I observe that examples of successful deductivist, including econometric, modelling seem not to have occurred especially often in the social realm, I do *not* contend that there could never be any limited success stories. Indeed, I suggest possible examples of past successes. However, presumably because he reads me as seeking to banish the use of econometrics, Hodgson seems to regard this as a logical slip. Let me quickly indicate why this too is not the case.

Very briefly, the reason my noting a (conceivably) successful econometric exercise is not a logical slip is simply that there is nothing in the conception I defend that suggests that a closure (or indeed any configuration) could not occur. I may yet be committing an empirical mistake; I may have assessed the econometric contribution to which I referred in an overly positive manner. But this has nothing to do with the logic of my overall argument.

Remember that a closed system is simply one in which an event regularity of sorts occurs. In particular, a closure is not the same as, and cannot be reduced to, the closure *conditions*. Closure conditions are sufficiency conditions, those that *guarantee* an event regularity; they are not strictly necessary for it. In principle, an event regularity could even emerge by accident, with differing causal factors underpinning any set of found-to-be-correlated events.[10]

More to the point, remember too that in perhaps all "applied" or empirical contexts where measurement is involved (including the well-controlled experiment), the relevant form of closure is a *stochastic* one (see Lawson, 1997, p. 76) not a *deterministic* one. A stochastic closure is a system in which a regularity occurs, connecting or covering a set of random outcomes or "variables". Specifically a regularity holds between the conditional mean value of any one "variable" (conditional upon the realised outcomes of the others) and the realised values of the remaining "variables". Notably, such a scenario can include a stochastic component capturing not only any measurement error but also the effects of any relevant factors or conditions that are unobserved (or otherwise excluded from explicit analysis).

Clearly if the conditional distribution of the latter component (and so of the dependent or response variable) is small, the regularity involved, because closely approximating a deterministic regularity, will, if successfully identified, and non-spurious, be useful for predictive purposes. It was such a stochastic closure that (for particular reasons set out in *Reorienting Economics*) I was presuming had been (unusually) uncovered in the econometric exercise to which I referred.

Hodgson recalls that in a seminar discussion somewhere, I referred to a local closure being "approximated in reality", facilitating the use of econometrics. Unfortunately, I do not remember the occasion or context. But I assume that if I made such a remark, I had in mind a stochastic closure closely approximating (or constituting a stochastic near-equivalent of) a deterministic one. The standards of approximation will be those laid down by econometricians.

I admit that I do not expect social reality to throw up very often such conditions as guarantee stochastic closures of this sort (that are not completely spurious,[11] and employing econometricians' own context specific assessments of acceptable approximations); and nor do they seem frequently to have occurred. That is why, as Hodgson also notes, I am able to provide very few examples of apparent successes. But if they occur, or more to the point, if I assess (fallibly) that they have occurred, this per se says nothing about the logic of my overall argument.

Notice, too, that the position I am defending, despite Hodgson's suggestion to the contrary, in no way encourages the current emphasis on formalistic modelling, even in respect to econometrics. The situation of modern econometrics is not that econometricians are everywhere manipulating criteria whereby stochastic closures might be said to be close approximations to deterministic ones, in order that the current heavy emphasis on formalism wrongly appears justified. Rather this heavy emphasis continues in the absence of widespread successes as measured by these (conventional) criteria, and indeed in the absence of any other apparent justification.

So, in sum, I hope it is clear that by my giving some qualified support for a particular econometric exercise (whether or not the support is warranted in this particular instant), I am thereby neither revealing a logical inconsistency in my argument nor supporting the current *emphasis* on formalism.

But equally, to return to the broader theme (and as my support for the particular exercise just discussed further illustrates), *I am nowhere opposing the use of formalism per se either.* As I have repeatedly stressed, my objective in my critical assessments of the state of modern economics, is to understand why certain research methods have generally failed or occasionally (seemingly) proven successful. Whatever else my project may entail, it has nothing to do with seeking to narrow down the range of research practices on offer. Ultimately, indeed, as I have argued earlier, my findings in fact support just the opposite stance, of expanding the options available and recognised as viable.

## Previous statements

Perhaps the reader unfamiliar to my contributions will suspect that there is no smoke without fire, that the overall or basic position I am here accepting is so far from that seemingly attributed to me by Hodgson, that I must myself be saying things now that are inconsistent with the broad message of previous contributions. In case this is so, I hope I can be permitted to reproduce here a few (of the very many) relevant passages.

In *Reorienting Economics* I write:

> Let me elaborate a little on my orientation to formal modelling. Although parts of this book, and most specifically chapter 1, are critical of the way formal modelling methods are taken up in modern economics, I hope by now the highly conditional nature of my criticism is apparent. It is not, and has never been, my intention to oppose the use of formalistic methods in themselves. My primary opposition, rather, is to the manner in which they are everywhere imposed, to the insistence on their being almost universally wielded, irrespective of, and prior to, considerations of explanatory relevance, and in the face of repeated failures.
>
> (2003, p. xix)

Elsewhere in a paper in the *Journal of Economic Methodology* I am just as explicit. Here I write (in response to comments by Julian Reiss): "*My argument is not at all an anti-mathematics one; and it never has been*. I have only ever criticised the way (certain) mathematical methods tend to be used in modern economics"[12] (2004, p. 337; emphasis in the original).

After a lengthy discussion of my views on the use of mathematics in economics I summarise my position as follows:

> In short, I do not denigrate the use of mathematics. I do, though, believe that the sorts of mathematical-deductivist methods mainstream economists mostly use presuppose an implicit worldview that is not especially typical of social reality. I also suggest that many of the widely acknowledged failures of the discipline arise just because these methods are being applied in conditions for which they are not especially appropriate. In consequence, in *Reorienting Economics* I argue for a more pluralistic orientation to social theorising, and spend time demonstrating that alternatives methods of relevance do exist. In this I do not suggest that formalistic methods be excluded for the methodological options on offer. But I do insist that methods of mathematical-deductivist reasoning (like any other tools)

have limits to their usefulness, and that this be recognised and respected. However, I see this as a pro-, rather than an anti-, mathematics position.

(2004, pp. 337–339)

I hope I have said things with sufficient clarity, not to mention repetition, to dispel any worry that I am somehow opposed to the use of mathematical formalism as an a priori disposition.

## The roles of formalistic models in economics

I turn, then, to the matter that I take to be Hodgson's central concern, the manner in which mathematical models can be useful to social illumination. Unfortunately, before we can get to points of substantive disagreement, there are, even here, one or two important issues of interpretation on which Hodgson does not get me right.

In developing his comments on how models can be used Hodgson suggests that I supposedly commit the mainstream error of viewing models as somehow mappings on to, or in correspondence with, reality:[13]

> [Lawson] seems to suggest that logical or mathematical constructions, if they are to be of relevance or use, must be some kind of map of reality at the level of events. For example Lawson (2003, p. 22) writes of the importance of a "'fit' with reality".

I *do* write on the idea of models as mappings of, or as corresponding to, reality. But I defend precisely the opposite position to that which Hodgson imputes to me. What I actually write is the following:

> It seems likely that [many] [...] economists are in effect holding, if implicitly, to conceptions of knowledge and truth as relations of identity or, more generally, correspondence.[14] Certainly the widespread use of the terminology of economic models is consistent with this – as if the latter are somehow smaller, scaled down, or otherwise simplified, versions or mappings of the original. Economists frequently talk of "mappings" in connection with their modelling, often remarking that any map drawn to a scale of one-to-one would be as complicated as whatever it is supposed to represent, and thereby useless. From this perspective it follows that because of the complex nature of social reality any feasible mapping is never isomorphic. In consequence, the argument seems to run, all models are inevitably distortions; true models or theories are most unlikely to be obtained.
>
> Whether or not any economist holds to this line of reasoning completely (or explicitly), or would express things quite so starkly, it is

worth considering this position here anyway as an obvious point of reference. And it should be apparent from everything that has gone before that any conception of knowledge and truth along the lines indicated, i.e., as relations of correspondence between discourse and extra-discursive reality, is profoundly misleading.

(1997, chapter 17, p. 238)

Rather than employing the misleading imagery of mappings in my argumentation, I refer over and again to the ontological preconditions of formalistic-deductivist methods, and question whether they hold in the social realm. Rarely do I use the word "fit", and where I do it is clear that this is precisely my meaning in using the term. Even the passage to which Hodgson explicitly refers is followed by one indicating that "fit" is to be interpreted in terms of the presence of ontological preconditions:

> But "fit" with reality matters too. The problem with the mainstream stance is that the ontological preconditions of its formalistic methods appear to be not only not ubiquitous in the social realm, but actually rather special occurrences. If we knew both that social life was every-where atomistic, and also that for any type of outcome we could effectively isolate a fixed set of causes (treating all other causal processes as a kind of stable, non-intervening or homogeneous back-drop), we would have grounds for feeling confident in the emphasis that mainstream economists place on the sorts of deductivist methods they use. However, our best ontological analysis suggests that closures are a special case of social ontology, whilst our *a posteriori* experience is that this special case seems not to come about very often at all.
>
> (2003, p. 22)

Actually I use the word "fit" twice in *Reorienting Economics*. In the other instance I indicate precisely what I mean:

> "As a result the possibility of a lack of ontological fit (a mis-matching of the presuppositions of these modelling methods with [the nature of] those features of social reality being investigated) does not arise. Yet, as I say, methods of mathematical-deductivist modelling, like all methods, do have ontological presuppositions. And my assessment, simply stated (and defended below), is that these preconditions of mathematical-deductivist methods appear not to arise very often in the social realm."
>
> (2003, p. 12)

## Heuristic and internal critique

An equally surprising assertion made under this head is that I concentrate my critique on econometrics[15] and in doing so fail to consider whether formalistic models might be used for heuristic purposes or as vehicles for internal critiques. As much of the discussion below is about, and draws upon, my account of heuristic as set out in *Economics and Reality* I will not add anything on this topic for the moment. But I should perhaps say something at this point about internal critique.

Now an internal or immanent critique (which I actually discuss fairly extensively in *Economics and Reality*) proceeds by way of working from certain internally accepted features of a project or paradigm, and pointing out that they lead to problems, inconsistencies or limits elsewhere within the project or paradigm, conceived on *that project's own terms*.[16]

As I say, Hodgson advances the idea that formalistic models might be used for making internal critiques. Now in *the context of modern mainstream economics* no one could presumably fail to recognise this, simply because the mainstream is everywhere couched in terms of mathematical formalism. The insistence on mathematical-deductive methods is the essence of that project. The possibility, to which Hodgson points, arises just as a consequence of the mainstream problematic insistence on formalistic methods.[17] Indeed, as most mainstream contributions advance by precisely addressing perceived (internal) weaknesses, or inconsistencies or limitations of preceding contributions, most mainstream contributions themselves constitute or contain internal critiques. There is no great insight here.

Of course, heterodox economists will likely employ formalistic models for purposes of seeking more destabilising critiques than will mainstream economists themselves. And I do not at all want to belittle their achievements on their own terms. Why then do I not join in (more than I do)?[18] The answer is simply because I do not think such critiques lead to any necessary advance in terms of illuminating the world in which we actually live. Mostly they lead to the internal shoring up of an irrelevant conceptual system. And even when a framework is radically transformed or replaced, it almost always is so by an equally irrelevant alternative formalistic system. Witness the recent turn to evolutionary game theory, agent based modelling, complexity theory and so forth, following the demise of general equilibrium analysis and the like. Does anyone really suppose that these are providing advances in understanding social reality? Some commentators do seek to interpret such developments as examples of mainstream pluralism. But in spirit they are no such things. And at the methodological level, in particular, they are quite the opposite. At best they are manifestations of the mainstream flexibility to move from one highly questionable mathematical conception to another.

Is there no scope for progress via internal critique involving formalistic methods? It seems to me that the best bet for those keen on internal critiques utilising formal models is precisely to keep plugging away in the hope that mainstream practitioners eventually grow tired of shoring up existing, or seeking new, formalistic systems (for I doubt that the options by way of formalistic systems will run out), and are willing to turn to something else. But I am not optimistic it will happen.

Is there any better alternative way to proceed? If the problem is that by making an internal critique of (elements of) one mathematical-deductivist approach, mainstream economists merely readjust it or invent an alternative one, the surest way to make real progress, it seems to me, is to orient the internal or immanent critique at features *common to (or presupposed by) the variety of mathematical-deductivist methods or projects* associated with mainstream economics. It is to carry out an immanent critique of the mathematical-deductivist approach to social theorising itself. This anyway has been my approach.

Mainstream economists recognise that event regularities are required (or need to be posited) if their methods are to have application (see e.g. Maurice Allais, 1992, p. 25). It is widely recognised that such regularities (whether deterministic or stochastic) rarely emerge in the social realm. What I have shown is that such regularities, if they are to be guaranteed, require conditions (a closed world of isolated atoms) that are rather unlikely to hold in the social realm. Thus methods that presuppose them (if success is to be guaranteed) are questionable, and the reason for the continuing failure of a project that insists on them is evident.

This is indeed an internal or immanent critique just because (or to the extent that) in footnotes, introductions, public speeches, rhetorical asides and so forth, mainstream economists talk in a manner that presupposes worldviews according to which social reality is anything but closed and atomistic. The problem is an apparent lack of awareness that their methods prohibit the sorts of theorising that conforms to their implicit broader perspectives.

Still here I am straying rather from the issue. Hodgson seems to suggest that I fail to notice, or consider the possibility, that mathematical-deductivist methods can be used for purposes of internal critique in the context of modern economics. My response is to observe that no one could fail to recognise this possibility, for it mostly exists just because that project is itself intrinsically mathematical. My worry, though, is that the sorts of critiques possible will likely leave this overall and unhelpful mainstream emphasis or orientation (as opposed to specific mainstream examples) untouched. It is for this reason that I have adopted an alternative approach that reveals the limitations of the mainstream deductivist project as a whole. Of course, there is more to effecting change than getting it right (irrespective of whether or not my arguments are correct). If Hodgson believes that continually chipping away via internal critiques employing mathematical methods will prove more effective in the long run, whatever the intellectual case, then let him chip away (also see John Davis' commentary in this volume and my response). For reasons I have given, though, if a more realistic economics is the objective, I am not optimistic that the outcome will be worth the effort.

## Points of substantive disagreement

Now that the main misunderstandings at least have been cleared out of the way I can turn to those of Hodgson's comments that, in part at least, do point to some real substantive differences between us.

A central plank of Hodgson's critique is the charge that the distinction I draw between methods of abstraction and theoretical isolation does not hold. Or rather Hodgson claims "the distinction is, at least in prominent practical instances, difficult to sustain". I believe, to the contrary, that the distinction (elaborated below) is very easy to sustain, and that it is vital to social analysis that we do sustain it.

Why does Hodgson single out this particular issue? The answer is not totally clear to me. Hodgson notes that I regard abstraction as both unavoidable and useful but that I am rather wary of the method of theoretical isolation, associating it implicitly with the mainstream. I think Hodgson's goal is to persuade that the sorts of methods that I advocate (and more especially abstraction) face essentially the same problems as those confronting the mainstream. In other words, Hodgson seems to be working on two fronts. On the one hand he wishes to suggest that formalistic methods can be more useful than I allow. On the other hand he wishes to convey the impression that any alternative methods that I have advocated share any difficulties that can be associated with formalism.

I say this because I notice that his discussion of these matters is preceded by a commentary on my own critique of the mainstream insistence on using mathematical-deductivist methods. Specifically, Hodgson notes my criticism of the mainstream turns on their reliance on methods that presuppose a closure, in order to analyse open systems. Hodgson clearly hopes to undermine this critique. And his strategy in this entails seeking to persuade the reader that methods that I advocate also presuppose a closure. For if the latter were the case, Hodgson seems to suppose, then my critique of the mainstream would be seen to be unsuccessful, at least in the sense of my failing to propose anything better. Hodgson notes that I distinguish the method of theoretical isolation from abstraction and that I associate closures mostly with the former. At the same time I emphasise that abstraction allows us to investigate open as well as closed systems, and, specifically, that it does not force us to treat open systems as though they are closed. Thus Hodgson perceives a need to undermine the distinction between abstraction and theoretical isolation.

Now, curiously enough, if my assessment of Hodgson's motivation is correct here he does not actually need to seek to dissolve the distinction between methods of theoretical isolation and abstraction. For I do not deny that closures of some sort are often important to the (dialectical sort) of explanatory analysis that I have often emphasised. However, I do find that the closures that have proven most relevant are not of the sort that mainstream economists tend to seek. Mainstream economists are interested in *closures of causal sequence*, those (if any) in which one (set of) event(s) or state(s) of affairs stands in the causal sequence of another (for example, household disposable income standing in the causal history of household expenditure patterns). The sort I think are typically more useful to explanatory social analysis are (a subset of) *closures of concomitance* (see Lawson, 2003), and specifically those that hold when specific features of a domain of reality share a similar causal history and so can be expected to turn out roughly the same (when the price of postage stamps increases in London it also does so in Cambridge; the amount of rain that falls in a square metre of my front garden on any given day, is much the same as falls in the same area in my back garden [and in my neighbour's]).

Moreover, for mainstream economists the goal of seeking closures is to predict and thereby control. In contrast, closures are of most use to the very different sorts of (dialectical) explanatory procedures I defend precisely when they unexpectedly break down, when the stretch of reality under consideration in fact ceases to be closed (to support an event regularity). There is much to be said here (see especially chapter 4 of *Reorienting Economics*). Certainly the methods I believe to be most useful to explanatory analysis are very different from the deductivist modelling efforts of the mainstream.

If Hodgson really wants to suggest otherwise it is here he ought to pitch his critique. But he does not. Instead he notes my positive exploration of the method of abstraction. As I say, I can only suppose it is because he thinks that he can somehow undermine my own explanatory emphasis by showing that abstraction and theoretical isolation cannot be easily rendered distinct that it is here he concentrates his attack. Because I believe the distinction that Hodgson's attempts to dissolve is nevertheless vital to social analysis (if not actually the one Hodgson best needs to attack), I must now defend it anyway. This is the focus of the discussion that follows.

## Abstraction and theoretical isolation

Before turning to the details of Hodgson's criticism I should recall what I take the distinction between abstraction and theoretical isolation to be.

I interpret abstraction, here as always, according to its traditional meaning of focusing upon certain aspects of something to the (momentary) neglect of others. It is a process of focusing on some feature(s) of something(s) while others remain in the background. For example, in considering the ability of copper to conduct electricity well I may focus upon its atomic structure and thereby abstract from its colour, texture, malleability and so on. It follows that there is always something that is abstracted *from*. That which is abstracted from is the *concrete*. One significant purpose of abstraction is to individuate one or more aspects, components or attributes and their relationships in order to understand them better.

Hodgson notes that in referring to the method of theoretical isolation I draw on the work of Uskali Mäki. This is correct; the method is not one I myself defend or have sought to develop. Let me then restate the conception of it I set out in *Economics and Reality*, which makes reference to Mäki's (1992) conception, and seems to be Hodgson's notion. There I write of it:

> According to Mäki, [the method of theoretical isolation] is a method "whereby a set of elements is theoretically removed from the influence of other elements in a given situation" (1992: 318). Mäki adds that "In an *isolation*, something, a set X of entities, is 'sealed off' from the involvement or influence of everything else, a set of Y entities; together X and Y comprise the universe" (ibid.: 321). Of course, even in experimentation no such isolation occurs literally, only physical re-arrangement. But the aspect of all this that I find most problematic is Mäki's notion of *theoretical* or *ideal isolation*, an apparently "traditional forceful procedure ... in economics" wherein no material re-arrangement is involved at all. Rather "a system, relation, process, or feature ... is closed from the involvement or impact of some other features of the situation" by way of "an intellectual operation in constructing a concept, model or theory" (ibid: 325). In fact, Mäki goes further and distinguishes "internal" and "external isolation": "In an *internal isolation*, one isolates a system from influences coming from within the system, while *external isolation* closes a system from influences that have sources which are external to the system". Mäki adds that both "internal and external isolation are relevant in economics" (ibid.: 326).
>
> (1997, pp. 131–132)

The distinction before us is easy enough to grasp. To abstract is to focus on aspects of something whilst *not* assuming the non-existence, or non-impact, of features not focused explicitly upon (that are abstracted from). To isolate theoretically is precisely to treat those aspects not focused upon as non-existent, or at least as sealed off, as having no systematic influence.

The difference between the two is easily demonstrated if we consider an aspect of some team game, say football or hockey, on television.

Suppose, we see on the television screen a player, say a footballer, running with the ball down the side of the pitch, towards the end at which the opponents goal is situated. If we are abstracting we will be interpreting this footballer's actions in a manner that takes into account the fact that supporting players on the same side will be moving in the same direction, and defenders of the opponents' team will be facing up to make a challenge. If instead we treat these other players as somehow sealed off from the action, as momentarily non-existent, then we are using the method of theoretical isolation. Clearly this creates a different world from the actual one addressed via abstraction. In the isolationist's world as described, if scoring is the player's objective all he or she has to do is take the ball to the goal and kick it between the two posts. There will be no opposition, because all other players not focused upon are assumed to have no impact.

A sports example such as this is useful because the game is clearly an internally related whole. The parts, the various movements of individual players, only get their meaning from the whole, so that any attempt to interpret one bit whilst ignoring the rest must fail if it is meaningful at all. I throw in the TV screen just to get the abstractionist and the isolationist to focus on the same part.

Clearly abstraction, but not theoretical isolation, will be relevant wherever the whole is not just the mechanical sum of parts. Composers, surgeons, artists as well as social theorists deal with internally related wholes. As such abstraction, not theoretical isolation, will be the appropriate method of analysis.

Now it should be clear, although it is worth emphasising it anyway (not least because this may be a source of the confusion), that these two methods, *though distinct*, are not strict alternatives. Because the world in which we live is so complex, abstraction is always involved. It will be so even where an isolationist approach is adopted (indicating that the presumption of "isolation", or being sealed off, can only ever be a relative one). For example, in considering the sports game above, in the scenarios of *both* the abstractionist and the theoretical isolationist, the causal force of gravity is presupposed, but abstracted from. That is, in each case gravity is not mentioned or analysed but accepted as acting; it is not assumed to be sealed off or inoperative; in neither case are the players treated as being propelled into outer space.[19]

In contrast the method of isolation has very restricted conditions under which it is relevant or anyway useful. The paradigm case is provided by a situation of controlled laboratory experiment. Here a mechanism is physically insulated from countervailing features in order to be empirically identified: an event regularity is generated correlating the triggering of the mechanism and its unimpeded effects. Once more abstraction will be involved. We may momentarily concentrate on the "isolating" of the mechanism, then on the triggering of it, then on some of its effects. We may at all times abstract from, colour, smell, sound, cost of apparatus and so forth; but then again we may not: it all depends on the context.

Of course, the controlled experiment represents a physical not a theoretical isolation. But a theoretical isolation is a process of imagining what would occur if a physical isolation could be achieved. A theoretical isolation is indeed a thought experiment. And where physical conditions are such as to inhibit in principle (as opposed to providing practical difficulties for) the physical isolation of certain features, then it seems that the method of theoretical isolation is without utility.

For example the interconnectedness and mutual constitution of the numerous different features of social reality are such that it is impossible to experimentally isolate individual components, such as money, firms or markets, and examine how they so operate when isolated from each other and from everything else. Equally, it is meaningless to *theorise* these features as if sealed off from the influence of each other and everything else. Of course, stated explicitly, this all seems obvious. Nevertheless such isolationist procedure dominates the specific methodological practices of modern economics.

If it seems clear enough that abstraction and theoretical isolation are indeed rather distinct (albeit not strict alternatives), I must now turn and examine how Hodgson argues to the contrary. There are essentially three strands to Hodgson's endeavour. First, seemingly accepting that closure is presupposed by the employment of methods of theoretical isolation, Hodgson seeks to associate closure with abstraction too. Second, drawing on Schelling's (1969) analysis of "racial" segregation, Hodgson seeks to show that the use of heuristics, clearly presupposing the method of isolation, is equivalent to the process I describe under the heading of abstraction. Third, Hodgson claims that the distinction I draw between the methods of abstraction and isolation is too vague to be of practical import. Let me run through each of these charges in turn indicating why I believe each to be unsustainable.

### Abstraction and closure

How first does Hodgson argue that abstraction presupposes closure? In truth, he does not; that is, he does not provide an argument. Rather he asks the question: "If abstraction is necessary, and it involves the limitation of the sphere of consideration and the exclusion of additional relations or disturbing forces, then doesn't this too imply the assumption of a closed system?" And he gets Stephen Nash to answer it for him: "*Stephen Nash (2004) has recently argued in the affirmative, suggesting that Lawson too must assume conditions or forms of closure.*"

Hodgson adds nothing to this, though he perhaps believes that his case is bolstered through his suggesting that I use the distinction (between abstraction and theoretical isolation) as a form of protection: "[Lawson] uses this distinction to protect his argument against the objection that his method of abstraction also implies the assumption of closure; he argues that abstraction does not imply closure but isolation does."

Now whatever else Stephen Nash (2004) does or does not do, as far as I can see he nowhere mentions abstraction, let alone argues that it presupposes a closure. Nash does suggest that the explanatory method I advance presupposes closures (something I have already acknowledged above), but fails to draw a distinction between closures of concomitance and closures of causal connection and so to appreciate that it is the former variety that are significant for the explanatory approach I defend. He further fails to note that (perceived) closures are significant precisely when they break down. But this is all beside the point. The topic of abstraction is not addressed.

If there is no argument advanced either by Hodgson or by Nash, there is seemingly none (here) to which I must determine a response. And to the point it should be very clear from all that has gone before that of course abstraction does not imply closure. At least it does not if by abstraction we mean focusing on a part of a whole whilst leaving the rest of the whole momentarily out of focus, and if by closure we mean, as I do throughout, a system supporting an event regularity. Clearly, abstraction can be applied to all types of systems, to those that support strict event regularities, to those that support partial ones and equally to those seemingly not supporting any. It can be applied to matters that are real or fictitious. If I talk only about the horn (or white colour, or billy-goat beard, or lion's tail, or cloven hoofs) of a unicorn, I am abstracting in the context of discussing a fiction. To say of the social system, or of any specific part of it, that it is fundamentally open is to abstract. To suggest that abstraction presupposes closure is simply to misunderstand one or other or both of the two terms.

### The use of heuristics is equivalent to the method of abstraction

A second point of difference between us concerns the way in which Hodgson believes that formalistic models might serve as heuristic devices. Once more Hodgson is concerned to connect abstraction to theoretical isolation. The latter method is closely connected to the notion of heuristics as used in economics, and this seems to account for Hodgson's concern to relate the latter in turn to abstraction. Here the analysis gets more interesting. Hodgson writes:

> The purpose of a heuristic is to identify possible causal mechanisms that form part of a more complex and inevitably open system. Heuristics can be useful without necessarily making adequate pre-

dictions or closely matching existing data. Their purpose is to establish a plausible segment of a causal story, without necessarily giving an adequate or complete explanation of the phenomena to which they relate.

It is this belief that appears to ground Hodgson's suggestion, which I am disputing, that the use of heuristics and abstraction are closely related if not equivalent, that "heuristics relate to the very process of abstraction that Lawson himself highlights".

Hodgson's contention that the "purpose of a heuristic is to identify possible causal mechanisms", is, I believe, simply wrong (at least if I am interpreting him correctly, a matter to which I return in due course). It may well be the case that heuristics can be useful for some yet-to-be-explicated purposes "without necessarily making adequate predictions or closely matching existing data". But their contribution is not "to establish a plausible segment of a causal story". Rather any usefulness they possess, or so I shall argue, can stem only from the fact that a plausible segment of a causal story has already been established.[20]

However, I realise that this last claim is likely to be contentious; that others too will likely be uncomfortable with it. So let me defend it at length. It is in the context of suggesting that heuristics achieve the same outcome as abstraction that Hodgson refers to Schelling's (1969) model of "racial" segregation (to illustrate his argument). This latter focus is useful in that, unlike many economic contributions, Schelling's analysis does indeed seem to carry insight and be somewhat persuasive. This, no doubt, is why Hodgson draws upon it. So eventually below I run through my argument referencing Hodgson's example of Schelling as is relevant.

### Heuristic and the method of successive approximation

First, though, I should establish the meaning of the term heuristic. Of course, specific categories can be made to mean anything we want them to. But all have a context, and most have a history. The term heuristic originally meant something like "serving to find out". How the latter is interpreted does vary according to context. In education it usually relates to a system in which pupils are trained to find out things for themselves. In philosophy and science it most commonly means a rule of thumb that has been found to be useful in making progress towards solving a problem. A heuristic computer program is one that begins with only an approximate method of solving a problem within the context of some goal, and then uses feedback from the effects of the solution to improve its own performance.

It is worth emphasising that in all such cases, the heuristic (the method, system or whatever) is observed to work; it is found successfully to serve some process of finding out. If something new is proposed as a heuristic device there is presumably an expectation at least that it will serve its intended purpose.

The way the term heuristic is usually employed in economic method-ology is bound up with developing theories by way of relying on assumptions or conceptions believed to be false.[21] Heuristic assumptions are often said to be those that are used to simplify the analysis as a first step with the expectation (or perhaps, with hindsight, with a knowledge) that the picture is to be (or has been) rendered more realistic through complicating it at a later stage.

Such a process of gradually complicating the picture with the aim of making it more realistic is presumably what Hodgson has in mind when he notes that "heuristic models ... are literally unrealistic" and he writes that Schelling's "model is simply a heuristic step along the road towards that more complete end". In a later version of his paper (presented at the Cambridge Realist workshop in November 2005) Hodgson also refers approvingly to Musgrave (1981) who in fact provides the classic state-ment of the stepwise procedure in terms of heuristic devices or assump-tions:

> "[A scientist] may wish to *develop* ... a theory in two stages: in the first stage he takes no account of factor F, or "assumes" that it is neg-ligible; in the second stage he takes account of it and says what dif-ference it makes to his results. Here the "assumption" that factor F is negligible is merely a heuristic device, a way of simplifying the logical development of the theory. Let us call such assumptions *heuristic assumptions.*
>
> (1981, p. 383)

It is thus easy to see how the method of theoretical isolation "whereby a set of elements is theoretically removed from the influence of other elements in a given situation" (Mäki, 1992, p. 318) relates to the making of heuristic assumptions in economics. For both advance knowing that significant causal influences (and perhaps other significant features) are omitted.

The stepwise approach of moving from initial conceptions of isolated features to a more realistic or complete theory is often referred to as the method of successive approximation, particularly when there are (pos-sibly many) more than two steps involved. It is something I discuss explicitly in *Economics and Reality*, where I look at the practice of accept-ing certain sorts of believed-to-be-false assumptions as a "heuristic device in a step-wise process of moving from simplified or ideal concep-tions to others of greater complexity and so, it is supposed, realisticness" (Lawson, 1997, p. 127). What is required here is some analysis of heuris-tic assumptions interpreted as unrealistic claims, and how they serve to facilitate theory development.

Hodgson himself does not give any analysis of why, or when, a conception regarded as unrealistic might be illuminating. He does, though, appear to suggest that it might be provided by Robert Sugden's (2000) account of "credible worlds", which also makes reference to Schelling's (1969) contribution. Sugden's idea is that if a model captures a "credible counterfactual world" we apparently have some inductive warrant for its relevance to our world. Hodgson writes:

> Robert Sugden (2000) asks probing questions concerning the role and "realisticness" of this and other heuristic models in economics. These heuristic models have the paradoxical claim that they are literally unrealistic yet they seem to illuminate important aspects of reality. Using the Schelling model alongside George Akerlof's (1970) famous article on the "market for lemons", which again claims to establish meaningful propositions about the world on the basis of an admittedly unrealistic model, Sugden (p. 28) describes these models as "credible counterfactual worlds" that give "some warrant for making inductive inferences from model to the real world".

Inductive inferences concerning states of affairs are problematic at the best of times. But even overlooking this, we are entitled to ask: what does it mean to talk of "credible counterfactual worlds"? It appears to be accepted that worlds such as that described by Schelling could not come about. So in what sense are they credible? We surely need to know this if Hodgson's reference to Sugden is to help us understand when or why some conceptions that are acknowledged as unrealistic remain useful.

It so happens, as I say, that in *Economics and Reality* I set out an analysis of possible heuristics and related issues that can make sense of all this. This is something to which I now need to return. Let me give a brief summary.

### Conditions of success of these methods

In *Economics and Reality*, in fact, I argue that two conditions are essential (though by no means sufficient) to the success of this method of successive approximation (relying on heuristic assumptions as interpreted by Musgrave and others). These are:

> 1  that the factors considered in "isolation" be real causal factors, structures and/or transfactually acting mechanisms or tendencies; and
> 2  that the effects of the factors so considered in "isolation" combine or interact mechanically.

> (Lawson, 1997, p. 129)

These conditions, and the need to satisfy them, are easily grasped. Basically the idea is to move from an understanding of a part of a causal story to an understanding of more, or of all, of it.

This requires, first, that the features (treated as) isolated in thought be causal mechanisms and that the nature of the causal parts, or individuals, viewed in isolation as a first step, are not knowingly portrayed incorrectly. In other words, it is essential that the intentional fictionising concerns *not* the manner of acting of the parts considered separately (in isolation) but only the (heuristic) assumption of their acting in isolation from (some) other factors affecting the total outcome.

Of course, this requirement, in its turn, presupposes that the way a causal mechanism operates as it is found in reality is the same as it would operate in "isolation from (some) other factors affecting the total outcome" (or under the conditions assumed in the heuristic exercise).

Notice too, that this requirement rules out the vast majority of theoretical conceptions that are bound up with modern mainstream formalistic modelling.

A second condition that must typically be satisfied if we are successfully to utilise the method of successive approximation (or heuristics), that is if we are to achieve an understanding of the whole by way of considering the workings of parts considered in isolation, is that the effects of the different parts or causal elements can be aggregated, that is combined additively or mechanistically. In contrast, if there are, say, emergent powers of the more complex entity or whole irreducible to those of its parts considered separately, then it is not clear that it is especially useful to proceed by seeking to understand (or speculating about) how each part might act in isolation.

Notice too, that to make sense of the first condition (that the way a causal mechanism operates as it is found in reality is the same as it would operate in isolation from [some] other factors affecting the total outcome) we need the notion of transfactuality. Something is said to be acting transfactually when it is having its effect *whatever the actual outcome*. Gravity is pulling my computer keyboard to the floor even as my desk acts to counteract this force and leave the keyboard at rest (relative to myself) in front of me. In other words, the keyboard does not need to be dropped in an experimental vacuum for gravity to have its effect. Similarly, the aspirin acts to offset my headache even if my noisy environment and heavy drinking countervail its effects and leave my head in a worse state. Such factors as gravity and the aspirin, when triggered, act not counterfactually but transfactually. We can talk not just of how they would (counterfactually) act in different non-actual but ideal circumstances, but also of how, when triggered, they are continually transfactually acting, whatever other forces are in play. The category of a tendency is reserved for the effects of forces that are acting transfactually, i.e. whatever the actual outcome.[22] It is when a mechanism is insulated from countervailing factors that (as in a well-controlled experiment) its tendencies and the outcome produced coincide.

Although advocates of the method of successive approximation, or the making of heuristic assumptions, typically do not identify the two noted conditions for the method of successive approximation to be successful, they can be seen to be built into their illustrations. Consider the classic exposition of Alan Musgrave, concerning Newton's analysis of inter-planetary motion:

> When Newton sought to discover what his theory predicted about the solar system, he first neglected inter-planetary gravitational forces by "assuming" that there was only one planet orbiting the sun. He proved that, if his theory was correct, the planet would move in an ellipse with the sun at one of its foci. This assumption was not a negligibility assumption: Newton knew that planets would sometimes have detectable gravitational effects on one another. Nor was it a domain assumption: Newton was not saying that his theory only applied to one-planet solar systems. You miss the point if you object that Newton's assumption is false, because our system has more than one planet. You also miss the point, though less obviously, if you object that the *consequence* of Newton's assumption was false, because planets do not move exactly in ellipses. The consequences drawn from heuristic assumptions do not represent the precise predictions of the theory in question; rather, they are steps towards such precise predictions.
>
> (1981, p. 383)

Clearly, the method of successive approximation is found to be successful in the case of Newton's analysis of inter-planetary motion, both because it is real (gravitational) tendencies that are so considered (in isolation), tendencies that seemingly operate transfactually whatever else is going on, and also because gravitational tendencies do appear to combine mechanically.

Equally clearly, however, the conditions in question, and in particular the requirement that causes combine mechanically, do not hold in general. Perhaps their lack of universality is most readily apparent if we think of chemical reactions and combinations. But mechanistic combining is hardly typical of social phenomena either. For example the network of social relations so central to social life cannot meaningfully be broken down into parts with some bits treated as though existing in isolation before others are eventually added back in. It makes no sense at all to treat any feature in isolation from another to which it is essentially related. In studying family behaviour, say, it is clearly quite irrelevant to study conceptions of parental mechanisms apart from conceptions of the nature, including needs, of children or the mutual relationship in which parents and children stand. Equally, it is incoherent to consider the situation of landlords/ladies in isolation from (conceptions of) tenants, or conceptions of employers in isolation from those of employees, and nor does it make sense to consider capitalist firms, markets and money in isolation from each other, and so on.

## Pure and applied explanation

There is a further point I want to pull out from all this, one that can perhaps be made in the clearest way if I first distinguish *pure* from *applied* modes of explanation. Briefly put, pure explanation is concerned with identifying and understanding causal mechanisms; applied explanation is concerned with working out how already known mechanisms conspired to bring about some concrete real world event or state of affairs (see e.g. Lawson, 1997, chapter 15). For example meteorologists pretty much know the separate causal mechanisms that govern weather patterns; much of the pure explanatory component has been done. Each day, though, at least in the UK (and probably everywhere else after some novel weather pattern has been experienced) an applied explanatory endeavour is initiated: the object becomes to explain the pattern of behaviour just experienced utilising an understanding of causal mechanisms already available (and drawn upon in explaining every other day's weather patterns).

The point of drawing attention to this latter distinction here is to emphasise that, to the extent that the method of successive approximation, or the making of heuristic assumptions as understood here, have relevance at all in scientific methodology, it is as a component of applied, not pure, explanation. The method in question can be put to work only after the pure-explanatory work has been done. For example, the heuristic assumption that only causal mechanism $X$ is in play (or need be considered), albeit as a first step, presupposes that causal mechanism $X$ has already been uncovered.

Thus in Musgrave's analysis, Newton's goal is not to construct a theory of gravitational forces. This he already possessed. Rather the purpose (we are informed)[23] was to show in a stepwise manner how his theory could ultimately correctly predict inter-planetary movement.

## Grounding counterfactuals

The reason I draw attention to this distinction is to indicate that it is only *after* a causal hypothesis of interest is obtained, that is after the pure-explanatory stage, that it may be legitimate for counterfactual insights concerning it to be generated. In other words, a statement about a tendency that is transfactually in play will often license a subjunctive conditional about what would have happened at the level of the course of events if the system had been insulated from the activities of (some) other actually operative mechanisms, or indeed if it had been in any other state.

How we obtain our understanding (or hypotheses) of causal mechanisms of interest is itself a complex process that I discuss at length elsewhere (see especially, Lawson, 2003, chapter 4; but also see my responses to Caldwell and Ruccio in this volume). Contrast explanation will often be important (operating under a logic of analogy and metaphor amongst other things). But it may be merely that we abduct insights obtained in other spheres (as I think may be the case of Schelling's analysis – see below).

I think it is this overall framework or understanding that Sugden is edging towards with his notion of "credible counterfactual worlds". If a mechanism does act transfactually it licenses a hypothetical statement about how things might be in a different world. Descriptions of the different worlds from our own may be more or less realistic. There is a sense in which alternative worlds seem more credible if the only unrealistic aspect is the absence of actual mechanisms, as opposed to claims about how identified mechanisms do, or could, actually work. This, I suspect, is the basis for Sugden regarding such a counterfactual world as in some sense credible, despite never being expected to occur.

But if it is, notice that it is not the fact of "credible counterfactual worlds" that give "some warrant for making inductive inferences from model to the real world", as Hodgson, following Sugden, puts it. Rather it is a prior understanding of the real world that licenses subsequent claims about certain counterfactual "worlds" appearing credible.

Notice too, that no matter how insightful a counterfactual analysis of this sort might be, a comprehensive understanding of the causal process under study cannot typically be captured or conveyed in this manner. Rather, to obtain a full (and indeed ultimately practically useful) understanding of the situation, tendency statements must be interpreted as categorical and indicative, to the effect that, if triggered, a mechanism is really in play whether or not its effects are fully manifest.

In other words, to focus only on actual outcomes in counterfactual scenarios (real or impossible) is typically to miss the main insights available. For if a mechanism licensing a focus on "credible counterfactual worlds" is indeed operative, then it is it is having its effects anyway (transfactually); there is a tendency continuously in play in our actual world, whatever the outcome. And this can be acted on. For example policy can consequently be devised to reinforce or countervail such a tendency as required.

## The dominant-mechanism special case

Of course, if a domain of reality is such that a causal mechanism focused upon (and treated as acting in isolation as a first theoretical step) is not only stable but dominating of other causal factors (and especially if all mechanisms in play do combine mechanistically) it is likely that event patterns that the theory predicts are recognisable in the outcomes actually achieved. But where this is so, the method fares well not because false claims are providing insight in some mystical fashion, but because the conceptions of mechanisms acting in relative insulation from counteracting others are not that unrealistic after all (and so barely qualifying as heuristics). Of course, it was in part to deal with such scenarios that I introduced the notion of demi-regularities or demi-regs.[24]

In other words, isolationist methods appear most legitimate and insightful (though their ability actually to add much is questionable) precisely in situations where a causal mechanism is so dominant it is (momentarily) effectively insulated from the countervailing effects of other factors. That is, methods of theoretical isolation are legitimised and express reality in a recognisable fashion precisely on occasions where the isolation is not merely "theoretical" but effectively actual. Needless to say, to suppose that such occasions license the ubiquitous reliance on such methods is to overlook the rarity of the former.

An example of such a special case is the celestial patterning addressed by Newton and referred to by Musgrave. Indeed, I suspect that Newton was as much concerned to explain a demi-reg (the approximate ellipse traced out by the paths of many planets) as to launch a project of successive approximation (in conditions where the mathematics of dealing with the movements of more than two planets had yet to be developed, and indeed was achieved only after Newton's death). The celestial pattern arises because of rather *peculiar* conditions that hold in the case of the planets, in that both their intrinsic states as well as the extrinsic forces acting upon them are, in relevant respects, sufficiently stable, at least over the time period with which most people are usually concerned, i.e. over human lifespans. Properly interpreted, Newtonian mechanics posits theories of how bodies (tend to) act; celestial phenomena function merely as evidence of the postulated tendencies. Thus, if the intrinsic or extrinsic states of the planets in our solar system were not so stable but were to change in some way, perhaps a massive meteor were to pass through the solar system, then such a mechanics would entail a consequent disruption of the familiar celestial phenomenal patterns.

The point is that although the celestial example is spectacular in nature, it represents a relative rarity in constituting a spontaneous demi-reg of its sort. No doubt it is precisely its spectacular nature that accounts in some part for the general failure from Laplace onwards to realise that the situation *is* relatively uncommon, to appreciate that the celestial demi-reg, or near closure supporting it, is far from being indicative of the phenomenal situation that can be expected to prevail more or less everywhere. This failure, in turn, appears to be largely responsible for the widespread, if tacit, acceptance, formerly in philosophy, and currently in the social sciences in particular, of a ubiquity of constant conjunctions of events in nature, and thus of the doctrine of the actuality of "causal" laws. It no doubt also encourages the idea that methods of theoretical isolation, or of successive approximation, or of heuristics and such like, have ubiquitous relevance, when in fact conditions under which they are relevant, certainly as they are formulated in modern mathematical-deductivist economics, appear to be circumscribed indeed.[25]

## *Schelling*

We are finally in a position to interpret the contribution of Schelling. And we can now appreciate that Schelling's analysis can be expected to be insightful if it captures a real mechanism that operates transfactually, that is, that produces tendencies towards "racial" segregation, whatever else is going on.

As I understand Schelling's (1969) analysis, the basic idea is as follows. In a context in which:

1   individuals perceive themselves as belonging to one or other of two mutually exclusive and exhaustive groups and
2   (at least a significant number of) individuals prefer not to be located in a situation where they are dominated or overwhelmed by members of the "other" group, and
3   space that can be occupied is confined or restricted, or where group-ing of some kind must (for whatever reason) occur,

there will be a tendency towards (some) segregation.

I doubt this was ever news. Indeed, do we not all experience situations in which a tendency of this sort is so dominant that it is even actu-alised. I certainly have, and regularly. My earliest memories include glimpses of physical education lessons in primary school where the teacher regularly asked the class of about thirty children to form four or so groups. Invariably, as I recall, the groups were wholly male or wholly female but not mixed. Today, I cannot but notice that in my workplace (Cambridge) coffee room, the "support staff" invariably avoid sitting next to "academic staff" except on occasions (such as outside of lecture term) when the number of academics present is much reduced (and indeed no greater than the number of support staff).

Schelling's contribution, I think, is to suggest that the mechanism in question – basically a preference not to be dominated by perceived "others" in a confined space – is relevant to understanding racial segre-gation in the US, at least at a certain moment and place in history. He points out that for purposes of the US census individuals are (or were) classified as white or as black, and that many at least view themselves in this fashion. Now to the extent that a majority (and perhaps almost all) individuals prefer not to be overwhelmed by others of a different "colour", and there is a restricted area in which some population is located, we have reason to expect a tendency to racial segregation.

Schelling suggests several more concrete claims that seem likely, realistic and consistent with his basic more abstract conception. Thus he mentions mechanisms whereby "Whites may prefer to be among whites and blacks among blacks" (p. 489), or "whites may prefer the company of whites, while blacks don't care" (p. 489) or whereby "Whites and blacks may not mind each other's presence, even prefer some integration, but [where there is] … a limit to how small a minority either colour is willing to be" (p. 489).

Schelling, though, does not develop an ontology of transfactual tendencies as set out above. Instead, he writes as though countervailing factors are absent and tendencies in play will all be realised (as outcomes or movements). For example:

> Whites and blacks may not mind each other's presence, even prefer some integration, but, if there is a limit to how small a minority either colour is willing to be, initial mixtures more extreme than that will lose their minority members and become one colour; those who leave may move to where they constitute a majority, increasing the majority there and causing the other colour to evacuate.
>
> (p. 489)

Clearly, this passage is easily rewritten in terms of tendencies and greater contingency ("tend to lose" in place of "lose", etc.). When it is, it is this revised formulation in terms of tendencies that licenses the passage as written (not the other way round).

Of course it may be that Schelling believes that "colour preferences" dominate all countervailing factors. If so then his formulation might be accepted as it is, as a claim intended to be realistic with respect to the real world.

### Schelling and counterfactuals

Alternatively, the implicit claim that *only* "colour preferences" are effective (or that they dominate) can be interpreted as a heuristic assumption. Proceeding on this interpretation seems legitimate, although the point of it is not clear. The language of tendencies conveys all the insights that could be so expressed (and indeed more). The aim could be to do as Musgrave suggests and add in complicating factors bit by bit. But then we would need to know that the effects of Schelling's mechanism, and of those yet to be identified, aggregate in a mechanical fashion. I see no reason to expect this and Schelling reveals no inclination to proceed in this fashion.

Instead, Schelling continues by imagining yet more concrete or detailed scenarios that conform *not at all* to the world in which we live or to one we could reasonably expect to occur. He constructs fictitious set-ups (e.g. "a line along which blacks and whites [...] have been distributed in equal numbers and random order" [p. 489]), and assumes that individuals can move freely (and repeatedly move) according to fixed rules, identical for everyone, without costs or countervailing forces of any kind, and so forth.

I am not at all sure that this additional analysis provides any insight other than to the very specific properties of the very particular set-ups or "models" considered. Any understanding concerning the real world is already contained in the analysis of tendencies. What is going on is that the concern with modelling for its own sake at this point takes over.

Interestingly enough Schelling (1969) does not actually construct any *mathematical* model as such. As a result, Hodgson's claim that Schelling's contribution is a demonstration of the benefits of "a formal heuristic" is erroneous from the outset. Still there is little doubt that the just discussed assumptions introduced by Schelling facilitate or encourage a mathematical modelling approach. And it is also clear that whatever the precise nature of Schelling's own early piece it eventually stimulated many papers of a more formalistic kind.

The point to emphasise, though, is that these later papers, or modellers, did not generate the insights we associate with Schelling, but rather they drew upon them in an attempt to legitimise their modelling endeavour. Any new insights obtained concerned merely the properties of the (increasingly complex and unrealistic) formalistic models. Assumptions are made just to get certain desired patterns or results (elegantly) to emerge.[26]

If I am correct in my analysis of all this the question that clearly arises is "why bother?" Why the interest in models for their own sake? The answer, of course, is the situation I have been actively attempting to counteract throughout much of my writing: the widespread idea that mathematical modelling is in itself a necessary feature of any respectable economic theorising.

### Heuristics and causal mechanisms

Let me at this stage return to Hodgson's particular critique. It will be remembered that according to Hodgson: "The purpose of a heuristic is to identify possible causal mechanisms that form part of a more complex and inevitably open system." I have shown that, to the contrary, the heuristic assumptions can go to work in economic methodology only after causal mechanisms of interest have already been identified or at least hypothesised. Schelling (1969) I have suggested illustrates just this.

After setting out his own outline of Schelling (1969) Hodgson adds:

I have suggested above that heuristics are appropriate if they successfully abstract an important causal mechanism in reality. Accordingly, heuristics relate to the very process of abstraction that Lawson himself highlights. But Lawson suggests that heuristics are isolations rather than abstractions. So here I must return to Lawson's (1997, p. 236) attempted distinction between isolation and abstraction, as quoted above. According to him, the key difference is "between leaving something (temporarily) out of focus and treating it as though it does not exist". Again take the Schelling model as an example. Schelling himself accepts that bigoted racists exist, yet he leaves them out of his model. The purpose of the model is not to excuse or deny racism, but the more severe forms of racism are deliberately removed. Nevertheless, the model is extremely and worryingly persuasive.

Here Hodgson seems to make the same mistake as before. Let us be clear. Where a causal mechanism is in play we can focus momentarily upon it, and leave countervailing factors and so forth aside. If the causal mechanism is of a sort that it will have these effects whatever the context, i.e. whatever the relations in which it stands to other causal structures, then clearly it follows that the way it would operate in isolation is equivalent to the way it will operate as we find it in the real world. In such a scenario, it is not illegitimate, and there may be some utility, if, as a first step to an analysis, we adopt the heuristic assumption that the causal factors left out of focus do not exist, or are sealed off. This will clearly be especially the case if the omitted factors appear insignificant compared to the factor on which we focus.

But to describe this situation with the words: "heuristics are appropriate if they successfully abstract an important causal mechanism in reality" is to get things the wrong way round. A correct statement is rather of the sort that "heuristics are appropriate (if at all) where an isolatable causal mechanism has already been abstracted". And from this it does not quite follow, as Hodgson would have it, that "Accordingly, heuristics relate to the very process of abstraction that Lawson himself highlights." Rather it follows only that the appropriate use of heuristics *depends* (like everything else) on the very process of abstraction that I highlight.

The heuristic, in the given context, is the assumption that factors out of focus have no effects, that they can be treated as sealed off or non-existent, that the mechanism in focus is acting in (relative) isolation. It is thus indeed the case that "heuristics are isolations rather than abstractions".

In the second part of the passage Hodgson writes that although Schelling ignores factors such as "bigoted racists" Schelling's "model is extremely and worryingly persuasive".

I myself am not sure how useful it is to treat Schelling's mechanism as a heuristic first step, as I have already indicated. But whether or not it is useful to do so, any insight to Schelling's analysis arises only because it first captures a case (albeit a special one) of a mechanism that can be regarded as realistic. Why any persuasiveness thereby imparted should be worrying I do not know. Moreover, the consequences of some individuals holding racist views are likely incorporated anyway; certainly Schelling does not examine or distinguish the various grounds for preferences regarding racial segregation, so there is no reason to suppose that bigotry is excluded.

Now I am well aware that I have only provided an interpretation of what is going on and that it is open to contestation. But I do believe I have set out a defence of a framework that can render coherent the various issues before us. Certainly, I do not find much that is coherent in Hodgson's few criticisms; and nor actually am I aware of an equally coherent alternative framework provided elsewhere. Hodgson is very wide of the mark indeed when he suggests that I do not consider the possible heuristic value of formal models, and that I ignore the role of context. At the very least, I think we must accept that if there is insight to be gained from treating formal models as heuristic devices the case for this has yet to be made. If Hodgson feels compelled to establish this point I think he must first do a bit more work. In any case there is nothing here to encourage the view that abstraction is the same as theoretical isolation.

### An alternative interpretation

Let me, though, add a qualification to all this. For many reasons it is vital to be charitable in debate, and perhaps there is a more charitable reading of what Hodgson is saying. The preceding discussion does seem to me to be the most accurate reading of Hodgson, in that he writes that the "*purpose* of a heuristic is to *identify* possible causal mechanisms", and that the "*purpose* [of heuristics] is to *establish* a plausible segment of a causal story, without necessarily giving an adequate or complete explanation of the phenomena to which they relate", and so forth. And I did want to respond to what seems to be the most comprehensive as well as accurate interpretation of Hodgson's position. But it is possible that Hodgson is simply suggesting that when we make heuristic assumptions and consider features as if in isolation it is important that those features treated as isolated be real causal mechanisms. That is, it is feasible that Hodgson is *not* at all suggesting that heuristic is somehow bound up with the process of *identifying* a causal mechanism but rather that heuristic (to be successful) needs to be employed in an analysis in which a mechanism has *already been identified*.

If this is the correct interpretation of his position, Hodgson has seemingly expressed himself rather misleadingly, but at least this would be a claim on Hodgson's part that seems sustainable.

However, the nature of my response is still much the same (albeit I could perhaps have made it significantly shorter). Specifically, it remains the case that it is an achieved understanding of the actions of a transfactually active causal mechanism that licenses the subjunctive conditional or counterfactual, that sets the boundaries of, and illuminates, "credible counterfactual worlds"; it is not the other way round. And fundamentally, it still does not follow that theoretical isolation or "heuristics relate to the very process of abstraction" in the sense of being much the same thing.

For sure, to consider a transfactually active mechanism as if it were isolated from countervailing factors involves abstraction. But to assume thereby that this method of isolation, or the use of heuristics involved, is the same as abstraction (even if the focus is a scenario of a single dominant mechanism in operation), is simply a mistake. Abstraction, as earlier noted, is involved in theorising both the real and the fictional, the open and the closed and equally both the isolated and non isolated; indeed it is a part of all forms of conceptualisation or theorising. To conclude that because abstraction is involved in some special case it thereby reduces to, or is somehow intrinsically bound up with, that special case is a conflation that simply does not bear considering further.

So, in short, we can see that, whichever way Hodgson is arguing it, the distinction between abstraction and theoretical isolation cannot be dissolved and in fact (especially given the apparent rarity of the conditions in which the latter is likely useful) remains vital to successful explanatory endeavour.

*The distinction drawn between abstraction and theoretical isolation is insufficiently precise*

Hodgson's third charge is that the distinction I draw between abstraction and theoretical isolation is insufficiently precise. I hope, though, that is by now clear that this is not so, and that I have said enough to demonstrate that the two methods are indeed irreducible one to the other. Still let me go through Hodgson's last strand of argument to illustrate this one more time.

Hodgson considers a case in which some factor X (trade with other nations) is ignored (in an analysis of the workings of a national economy), and questions whether ignored meaning being-not-mentioned (abstraction) is not the same as ignored meaning treated-as-having-no-influence or not-existing (theoretical isolation).

He writes of the former (abstractionist) scenario:

> Surely, some verbal statement would be required, acknowledging the existence of international trade, explaining its omission from the current discussion and suggesting that further work must be done to

incorporate it into the analysis. But this is also the kind of necessary qualification that we should expect from the best presentations of heuristic models.

Actually, I think it is typically only in the case of theoretical isolation that mention of specific omissions is warranted. Analysis never starts from complete ignorance; much is always taken for granted but remains unstated. As I noted earlier, most social theorists take gravity as given (they abstract from it) in social analysis, but rarely acknowledge or explain that omission. If in contrast they wanted to assume its effects were absent or sealed off, this would most certainly warrant a mention, and an explanation. For under such a heuristic assumption our planet (if indeed there was one at all) would be very different indeed.

In similar fashion, when an economist discusses aspects of an economy such as the UK, its trade with other nations might not get a mention (be abstracted from); but it would nevertheless be presupposed. The focus may be on the workplace, say on improving work security, or on gender mainstreaming in employment strategy. In each such case trade may not be mentioned (it may be abstracted from); because most social theorists take for granted the fact that the UK is a trading nation. But if trade were assumed away, rather than treated as a background causal factor, this once more would certainly warrant a mention and an explanation. For life in the UK, under such an assumption, would be very different indeed from life in the UK as we currently know it.[27] There is no support here for the thesis that abstraction and theoretical isolation cannot be distinguished.

Hodgson continues:

> On the other hand, it would be impossible to mention all the things that we have left out of the account. In this sense all theory is "temporary". But do such unmentioned omissions amount to treating some causal linkages as though they do not exist? If this were the case, then every theory, including non-formal, discursive theory, by Lawson's criteria is a failure. Once we try to apply Lawson's criteria, then their insufficiency and vagueness become apparent, and his attempted distinction between abstraction and isolation is revealed as highly problematic.

The first two sentences here are surely correct. But it does not at all follow that not to mention a causal linkage is thereby, of necessity, to treat it as not existing, or as being sealed off. As I say, it is not at all the case that a social analysis that neglects to mention the gravitation is necessarily operating thereby under the assumption that gravity does not exist. That is one reason abstraction is so useful.

In short, it is clear that there is nothing in all this that in any way threatens the distinction between abstraction and theoretical isolation or renders it "highly problematic". It may well be that the method of isolation is found to have little utility. But the distinction in question, between the practice of not focusing on something and assuming its effects are somehow absent or sealed off, remains as clear and vital to social theorising as ever.

## Concluding comments

Despite the emphasis that mainstream economists place on methods of formalistic modelling (or perhaps because of it), they make relatively few attempts to justify their orientation. This is surely a significant absence leading in and of itself to an impoverishment of the discipline, whatever else might be going on. Hodgson's spirited intervention to make a substantial defence of forms of formalistic modelling, and/or the manner in which mathematical-economic models might fruitfully be interpreted or utilised, is thus to be welcomed. He performs an important service. For reasons given, however, I am not convinced by Hodgson's efforts so far. But knowing Hodgson, I suspect he will persevere further in this, and I am confident we will all be the better for it, whatever may be the conclusions that are reached along the way.

## Addendum

At the end of 2006, after I had completed the foregoing response to his *post-autistic economic review* piece, Geoffrey Hodgson kindly presented me with a copy of his new book *Economics in the Shadows of Darwin and Marx*. It contains a revised longer version of his *PAE review* paper. In this longer version, Hodgson expands some of his arguments and adjusts some of his rhetoric. But I find nothing in it to give me reason to revise or qualify anything written above.

However, Hodgson does introduce one seemingly new line of argument in his later text. There is an extra section tagged on asking whether economists should be allowed to embrace false assumptions. This contains an additional criticism of me:

> Lawson (2002, p. 76) warns against false assumptions, proposing that if they are allowed "it is clearly possible to derive any conclusions whatsoever – true ones or false ones – simply by deductive logic". The argument is wrong. If I make the (false) assumption that "the economy consists of just two goods" then there is no way we can deduce from that proposition alone that the economy consists instead of four, five or a million.
>
> (Hodgson, 2006, p. 128)

But my argument is *not* wrong. What is wrong is Hodgson's representation of it. The first sentence in this passage makes reference to the claim (by me) that a specific suspect *practice* (allowing false assumptions) makes it feasible for the modeller to generate any conclusions. The contention ridiculed in the third sentence is that any specific suspect *model* can be used to generate any conclusions. The mistake, Hodgson's not mine, is to suppose that the latter contention follows from the former.

Let me be clear. I do point out that if false assumptions are allowed, then for *any* conclusion X, I can always find some allowable set of assumptions Y, from which X can be deduced. For example if (to use Hodgson's construction) the desired conclusion X is "the economy consists ... of four, five or a million [goods]", then I can assume (1) the number of goods in the economy is the same as the number of days in a week; and also (2) the number of days in a week is four, five or a million. The desired result follows by deduction. But if the suspect *practice* in question (of allowing assumptions thought to be false) allows me to generate any result, it does not at all follow that once I specify some particular *model* H (e.g. "the economy consists of just two goods") that any conclusion (such as X) can be drawn from it alone. Hodgson's charge simply rests on a non-sequitor.

In Lawson (2002), I do give illustrations. In fact, at the point where Hodgson paraphrases me I write:

> Now if, and once, falsity (in this broad sense) of assumptions is allowed, it is clearly possible to derive any conclusions whatsoever – true ones or false ones – simply by deductive logic. Thus suppose I want to deduce the (apparently true) proposition that "all ravens are black". One way I might do it is by including in my assumptions, the propositions: "all ravens are vegetables" and "all vegetables are black". Clearly my desired conclusion follows by deductive logic. In similar fashion if I want to deduce that "agent X does Y", I need only assume (i) that a situation prevails in which it is rational (in a specific sense) for a situated agent X to do Y, along with the assumption (ii) that X always acts rationally in the specified sense. The assumptions about the situation and human capabilities and their exercise need not be realistic, merely facilitating of mathematical modelling tractability. What could be more trivial and more pointless?

Of course, my focus in the paper in question is specifically on strategies of mathematical-deductivist modelling. It is in this context that I look at the consequences of the practice of allowing assumptions considered by everyone to be false. The reason I do so, it should be clear, is precisely that, given the nature of social reality, the mainstream insistence on a formalistic modelling orientation regularly necessitates the reliance on such accepted-as-false assumptions. My point is that because the construction of such assumptions is considered legitimate *practice* (i.e. the restriction of being realistic is removed), the mainstream "theorist" or modeller can always find some way of generating a particular desired result.[28]

In any case, I hope it is now clear enough that in Lawson (2002) I am, at the relevant stage of the discussion, not at all concerned with the properties of any specific model.[29] As I say, the mainstream insistence on a formalistic modelling strategy in economics requires that a reliance upon thought-to-be-false assumptions be an allowed practice. I am merely pointing out how easy it is to generate any desired conclusions once such a practice (that Hodgson seems to be encouraging) is sanctioned, and questioning the value of such activity.[30]

## Notes

1 In this way, Hodgson claims the middle ground for himself without having to do the ontological groundwork. Thus having noted these supposed extremes Hodgson associates himself with "middle ground solutions" on such matters, and connects this back to his original reference to the passage from Mark Blaug:

> I suggest that the problem with formalism is not the general inappropriateness of formalism itself, but it is the problem identified by Blaug in the quotation at the beginning of this article. Blaug sees the kind of formalism in modern economics as "an intellectual game played for its own sake" rather than for its use in explaining and engaging with the real economic world. Blaug complains that in modern economics "analytical rigour is everything and practical relevance is nothing". Again the solution here is not necessarily to confine formalism to the very rare conditions of actual or approximated closure, but to bring concerns for practical relevance to the fore. Formal techniques should become the servants rather than the masters of scientific enquiry.

2 In a recent presentation at the Cambridge Realist workshop this passage is revised to read as follows:

> We need to investigate the inadequately explored middle ground between unacceptable extreme stances that either treat mathematics as the sine qua non of theory, or practically exclude it in all but "rare" cases. I advocate this middle ground position, not because central areas are intrinsically or universally superior to extremes, but because the extremes in this case jointly downplay the necessary interpretative structure of any formal theory.

3 Thus in *Reorienting Economics* I write:

> For many modern economists, in fact, mathematical deductive reasoning is regarded as essential to science. It follows, for this group, that to relax the existing emphasis on mathematical methods is effectively to give up on the possibility of economics as science.
>
> One reasonable response to this line of reasoning is to question why economics has to be a science. Many critics indeed have rejected the possibility

of economics as science. But in fact this is not my orientation. To the contrary, my concern is more with the recovery of economics as science. Ontology helps us better understand the nature of science, and, as we shall see, to appreciate that mathematics is not essential to it. To suppose that scientific practice reduces to, or even necessitates, mathematical formalism is once more erroneously to universalise a priori a special case (in this case a particular form of scientific practice) as we shall see in due course.

(2003, pp. xx–xxi)

4 Can it be doubted that the practice of mathematical-deductivist modelling is treated this way in the academy? I suspect Frank Hahn captures the ruling sentiment well when he insists of any suggestion that the reliance on formalism may be problematic that it is "a view surely not worth discussing" (Hahn, 1985, p. 18). In fact, Hahn later counsels that we should "avoid discussions of 'mathematics in economics' like the plague and give no thought at all to methodology" (Hahn, 1992a; see also Hahn, 1992b).

5 Hodgson seems to suppose that I believe the contrary, but does not say why. Of course I do not. I believe that I have sense experiences that are of a real world in which I live (not, for example, that I am fooled into supposing this is the case by some evil demon that is sending false signals directly to my brain). Yet I do not know how to subject this belief to critical scrutiny.

6 A radical constructivist might demur, but Hodgson declares himself a realist in the same vein as myself.

7 Or as I write elsewhere in the same book:

The last thing I wish to do is support any efforts to prohibit forms of activity, or limit the range of methodological options.

I do not deny that I am rather pessimistic about the prospects of significant success with mathematical methods in economics. In the light of the conception of social ontology defended in the chapters below, along with the assessment made of the ontological presuppositions of formalistic modelling methods, I find it not at all surprising that these latter methods have fared somewhat poorly. But in acknowledging my pessimism, I do not oppose a share of resources being used in endeavours to study social material mathematically. Amongst other things, all knowledge is fallible, as I have already stressed, so that, in particular, the grounds of my pessimism may yet prove erroneous. Rather, the primary object of my criticism is as stated. In its most general formulation, my opposition is directed at any kind of a priori dogma. The realist approach I defend is contrasted with any kind of ungrounded insistence that certain methods only, or almost only, should be followed. Such an insistence seems especially unfortunate when, as currently, the methods laid down persistently perform rather badly, whilst that unhappy performance can be explained.

(2003, pp. xix–xx)

8 Whether or not Hodgson is conscious of the fact, by the very act of (unnecessarily) denying that something applies to me he is conjuring up the possibility that it might, or that something similar might. If I started a sentence with the words "Although person X is not an absolute imbecile (or, say, philosophical novice)..." the nature of the expectation/impression I would be seeking to convey is clear. Similarly it is easy to (or rather it is difficult not to) take Hodgson to be suggesting that I impose at least a partial ban on the use of mathematics. And this affects the way in which the remainder of the sentence – "his arguments limit its legitimate use to 'rare' circumstances only" – is received.

9 We might also consider the first part of the passage in question. Here Hodgson writes (with emphasis added by me):

> In these passages at least two features are emphasized. The first is a strong, sincere and repeated claim of anti-dogmatism concerning whether or not mathematics can or should be used. But *he lays down criteria for its use*, including the *requirement* of (approximated) local closure. As a result of these criteria, the specific measure of his own anti-dogmatism, in practice rather than in intention, is how far he would *admit* that open systems might appear (or be approximated) in reality.

It is the emboldened terms that I wish to draw to attention. I assume Hodgson means "closed" and not "open" in the last sentence. In any case I do not seek to lay down criteria under which something may be used. Rather I seek to identify conditions under which success with the methods in question are guaranteed. That is all. It is these, in my assessment, that may rarely figure in the social realm.

10 Of course, as I discuss in *Reorienting Economics*, the latter scenario is unlikely. But however unlikely, such a situation remains logically feasible; it simply does not follow that a closure, even a deterministic one, *could not* occur if generally operative causal mechanisms are not all explicitly accounted for.

11 Of course, this has not prevented econometricians producing thousands of models. But we all know that, especially with time-series analysis, if we experiment by running very many regressions (some econometricians run literally tens of thousands of regressions on a given data set), exploring all imaginable functional forms (or data transformations), it is usually possible to find a within-sample relationship that is close fitting by conventional criteria, whatever the latter may currently be. In this case, a stochastic closure of sorts is identified. But I do not suppose anyone believes many of the results (in the form in which they are presented, whether or not they are published). The theory and assumptions behind the methods of statistical inference employed to identify the relationship are repeatedly contravened (rendering the interpretations typically attached to such empirical results invalid). In addition, the right hand side "independent" variables are usually not at all those that can reasonably be claimed to stand in the causal history of the dependent variable. Most telling of all, perhaps, is that as soon as new observations are obtained, previously "identified" relationships of this sort are almost uniformly found to break down.

Econometricians, of course, know all this (even if they continue with their project on grounds other than realisticness or believability – see Vromen, this volume). Edward Leamer (1978), for example, talks of the inconsistencies in the theory and practice of econometrics, and of the "priests" who produce the theory to inform econometric practice, and the "sinners" who misapply the theory in practice. He even notes that these are the same people on different occasions. He notes too that "Sinners are not expected to avoid sins; they need only confess their errors openly" (Leamer, 1978, p. vi). He further notes that, where realisticness is the issue, "hardly anyone takes anyone else's data analysis seriously" (1983, p. 37).

12 The broader passage forming the context in which the passage in the text is set reads as follows:

> Notice, too, that I do not suggest that the methods of mathematic-deductive modelling which mainstream economists wield can never have an appropriate application. To the contrary, I suggest in *Reorienting Economics* that the perspective I adopt can identify the sorts of conditions in

which success is likely and so explain such successes as occur (see e.g. p. 20). And nor do I suppose that mainstream economists do nothing but mainstream economics; indeed I expressly deny that this is so (see e.g. p. xxi) [...] Let me ... [stress] that I fully agree that "there is no necessary link between mathematics and bad practice". Indeed, I cannot emphasise my agreement with this statement too strongly. *My argument is not at all an anti-mathematics one; and it never has been.* I have only ever criticised the way (certain) mathematical methods tend to be used in modern economics. Indeed it is precisely the belief that mathematics ought not to be applied without due care and consideration, coupled with a conviction that in modern economics it too often is so, that explains the direction of much of my writing. If you like, my concern is that much of economic modelling appears somewhat analogous to a violin being used as a drumstick. To suggest that this may be "bad practice" is in no way to devalue the violin, or to deny it a place in the orchestra.

Nor do I limit mathematics to deductivist modelling. Actually if what economists do is mathematics, it is a form of applied mathematics; it is the application of mostly already worked out mathematical systems And if it is ever appropriate to "associate" a method with an ontology I see no reason to suggest that some mathematical methods could not be associated with a causalist ontology.

If *I do* not, *then, limit mathematics to methods of deductivist modelling I do* contend that the sorts of modelling methods mostly utilised by modern economists are deductivist in nature.

(Lawson, 2004, pp. 337–8; emphasis in the original)

13  In a revised version of Hodgson's paper presented at the realist workshop on 14 November 2005, the relevant passage is formulated as follows:

Lawson suggests that logical or mathematical constructions, if they are to be of relevance or use, must be some kind of map of reality at the level of ongoing events. In one passage Lawson [...] writes of the importance of a "'fit' with reality," suggesting that all theory has to somehow correspond with the real world.

14  This conception is presumably influenced by the positivistic conflation of knowledge with direct experience and reduction of reality to events and states of affairs given in experience.

15  Hodgson thus writes:

Much of Lawson's discussion of formalism concerns econometrics. He gives insufficient attention to other applications of mathematical techniques, which serve primary purposes other than the prediction or explanation of measurable variables. Such additional applications of formalism include (a) heuristics and (b) internal critiques. I shall address each of these in turn.

As it happens, in *Economics and Reality* I address very many different ways in which it might be thought that mathematical modelling can contribute to social illumination. Only one of the chapters (chapter 7) focuses on econometrics. Chapter 9 deals explicitly with defences that accept some goal other than tracking measurable variables, and, unsurprisingly, I do there discuss the possible heuristic role of formalistic models at some length (see below).

16  Thus it is not clear that Hodgson's examples – those that reveal that models are based on restrictive or unwarranted assumptions – are after all critiques of this form.

17 Moreover, certain critiques that do not at all require mathematical models for a point to be made are often put in that form just in order to get a hearing. Hodgson references Sraffa's contribution. But Sraffa's essential point is that the meaning/interpretation of an integral element of a system will (or can) depend on the system as a whole. He made the same point to Wittgenstein (in the context of language systems – and causing Wittgenstein to rethink significantly his position) but without the need/constraint of using mathematics to convey his message. Moreover, in the latter case Sraffa seems to have had the more persuasive impact.

18 I have engaged in this sort of activity myself a good while ago. See for example, Lawson, 1981.

19 In other words, in cases where isolationist methods are adopted, and it is assumed that some factor X operates in isolation, it will be clear from the context of analysis that some (and which) factors are being treated as operative but unmentioned as opposed to being sealed off.

20 In other words, I am suggesting that any insight attached to a formal model is typically not the result of the modelling or heuristic exercise itself but derived first in a different context. For a mainstream economist, the overriding objective is to produce a mathematical model. Obviously, modellers are uncomfortable with the charge of irrelevance, so attempts will be made to render models as realistic as possible; real insights will be tagged on wherever feasible. But as I say, I believe the real insights are typically independent of, and indeed achieved prior to, the construction of the mathematical model.

21 This is the conception shared by others who work in this field. For example, Steve Keen (2001) recently considers heuristics emphasising clearly that "A heuristic assumption is one which is known to be false, but which is made as a first step towards a more general theory."

22 Notice that the point of a controlled experiment is to insulate some real causal factor (in order better to identify empirically, or, just as commonly, to empirically verify [or not], the manner in which a mechanism works). Significantly, however well the mechanism is insulated (and insulation will rarely, if ever, be perfect) knowledge of the mechanism's workings will often allow us to say that, and how, it will operate outside the experiment, in the open system of complex interacting reinforcing and countervailing forces. Clearly it is because many mechanisms act transfactually that we can successfully apply knowledge achieved in the (controlled) experiments, where event regularities are produced, to conditions where event regularities are absent; for the result achieved apply first and foremost to transfactual tendencies not to highly restricted and rare event regularities.

23 Actually, I am not so sure of Musgrave's explanation of Newton's intentions (see below), even if, as in this case, the conditions for method of successive approximation to be successful appear to be satisfied.

24 Which in *Economics and Reality* I characterised as "a partial event regularity which *prima facie* indicates the occasional, but less than universal, actualization of a mechanism or tendency, over a definite region of time-space" (see also *Reorienting Economics*, chapter 4). In Lawson 1997 I suggested that a demi-reg:

> indicates the likely effects of a causal mechanism that frequently but not uniformly are actualised over a particular region of time-space. The patterning observed will not be strict if countervailing factors sometimes dominate or frequently co-determine the outcomes in a variable manner. But where demi-regs are observed there is evidence of relatively enduring and identifiable tendencies in play.

25 Perhaps too it is a focus upon the rare (if sometimes rendered prominent) scenario, wherein some mechanism dominates others (so that that treating it as if acting in isolation is not so different from treating it realistically) that most encourages Hodgson in his view that "the distinction (between theoretical isolation and abstraction) is, at least in prominent practical instances, difficult to sustain".

26 At this point I am minded once again of Frank Hahn's awakening to the nature of this sort of state of affairs (even if Hahn mistakenly supposes that those who recognise it more immediately are disposed to being anti-mathematics [as opposed to being anti- the abuse of mathematics]):

> there is [...] a lesson which has only gradually been borne in on me which perhaps inclines me a little more favourably to the "anti-mathematics" group. The great virtue of mathematical reasoning in economics is that by its precise account of assumptions it becomes crystal clear that applications to the "real" world could at best be provisional. When a mathematical economist assumes that there is a three good economy lasting two periods, or that agents are infinitely lived [...] everyone can see that we are not dealing with any actual economy. The assumptions are there to enable certain results to emerge and not because they are to be taken descriptively.
>
> (Hahn, 1994, p. 246).

27 Any resulting analysis would be extremely different. This absence would mark most of the UK's internal economic institutions, as well as the sorts of political activities undertaken. All goods, including technology, would be home produced. Competition would presumably be internally generated. International pressures affecting security at work policies would be absent. The economy would not (need to) be part of trading blocks. Presumably factors like the European Employment Strategy would have no impact. There would be no scope for policies like export-led growth or import quotas. There is no obvious reason why movements in world commodity prices would have any impact, etc.

28 The specific challenge for formalistic modellers in economics is to start from "results" widely accepted as plausible and to work back to assumptions relating in effect to a closed world of isolated atoms (that such models presuppose) that would allow the desired results to be deduced. Clearly, if the reliance upon thought-to-be false assumptions were discouraged, this would prove very debilitating for any project insisting on employing methods of formalistic modelling in an attempt to illuminate social reality.

29 I feel sure, though, that this is, and always was, entirely obvious. What is happening in all this, I fear, is that Hodgson is being less than charitable in the way he is choosing to interpret and/or represent me (an orientation with which he seems to conclude the relevant chapter of his book). I only hope that this does not overly detract from matters where there is real substantive or philosophical disagreement.

30 I might add that one reason I appreciated Frank Hahn's presence at "theory" seminars in Cambridge is that, when modellers started their papers setting out their axioms and assumptions, Hahn regularly jumped in saying "you are only assuming x, y and z to allow conclusion c to be drawn". At this point, of course, the seminar was effectively over (although those speakers tended laboriously to make their way to the anticipated conclusion "c" anyway).

# References

Akerlof, George A. (1970) "The Market for 'Lemons': Quality Uncertainty and the Market Mechanism", *Quarterly Journal of Economics*, 84(3), August, pp. 488–500.

Allais, Maurice (1992) "The Economic Science of Today and the Global Disequilibrium", in M. Baldassarri, J. McCallum and R. Mundell (eds), *Global Disequilibrium in the World Economy: Central Issues in Contemporary Economic Theory and Policy*, Basingstoke: Macmillan.

Blaug, Mark (1997) "Ugly Currents in Modern Economics", *Options Politiques*, 18(17), September, pp. 3–8.

Hahn, Frank H. (1985) "In Praise of Economic Theory", the *1984 Jevons Memorial Fund Lecture*, London: University College.

Hahn, Frank H. (1992a) "Reflections", *Royal Economics Society Newsletter*, 77.

Hahn, Frank H. (1992b) "Answer to Backhouse: Yes", *Royal Economic Society Newsletter*, 78, p. 5.

Hahn, Frank H. (1994) "An Intellectual Retrospect", *Banca Nazionale del Lavoro Quarterly Review*, XLVIII(190), pp. 245–258.

Hodgson, Geoffrey M. (2006) *Economics in the Shadows of Darwin and Marx: Essays on Institutional and Evolutionary Themes*, Cheltenham: Edward Elgar.

Keen, Steve (2001) *Debunking Economics*, Sydney: Pluto Press and Zed Books.

Lawson, Tony (1981) "Keynesian Model Building and the Rational Expectations Critique", *Cambridge Journal of Economics*, 5(5), pp. 311–326.

Lawson, Tony (1997) *Economics and Reality*, London and New York: Routledge.

Lawson, Tony (2002) "Mathematical Formalism in Economics: What Really is the Problem?", in Philip Arestis and Sheila Dow (eds), *Methodology, Microeconomics and Keynes, Festschrift for Victoria Chick*, London: Taylor & Francis.

Lawson, Tony (2003) *Reorienting Economics*, London and New York: Routledge.

Lawson, Tony (2004) "On Heterodox Economics, Themata and the Use of Mathematics in Economics", *Journal of Economic Methodology*, 11(3), September, pp. 329–340.

Leamer, Edward E. (1978) *Specification Searches: Ad Hoc Inferences with Non-Experimental Data*, New York: John Wiley and Sons.

Leamer, Edward E. (1983) "Lets take the Con out of Econometrics", *American Economic Review*, 73(3), pp. 34–43.

Mäki, Uskali (1992) "On the Method of Isolation in Economics", *Poznan Studies in the Philosophy of the Sciences and the Humanities*, 26, pp. 317–351.

Musgrave, A. (1981) "Unreal assumptions in Economic Theory: The F-Twist Untwisted", *Kyklos*, 34(1:i), pp. 377–387.

Nash, Stephen J. (2004) "On Closure in Economics", *Journal of Economic Methodology*, 11(1), March, pp. 75–89.

Schelling, Thomas C. (1969) "Models of Segregation", *American Economic Review*, 59(2), pp. 488–493.

Sugden, Robert (2000) "Credible Worlds: The Status of Theoretical Models in Economics", *Journal of Economic Methodology*, 7(1), March, pp. 1–31.

# 13 Finding a critical pragmatism in *Reorienting Economics*

*Bruce R. McFarling*

There is an "ology" that pervades the essay in which Tony Lawson (2003) launches *Reorienting Economics*. The preface would lead us to believe it should be ontology. However, while ontology receives starring credit, it is epistemology that plays the starring role.

This first essay is structured into four theses. In his first thesis (2003: 3–8), the focus is on the mode of explanation of modern economics. This is argued to be deductivism, defined as explanation in terms of event regularities. Lawson refers to systems exhibiting event regularities as "closed", which can make his work difficult to read for someone with a General Systems background. For someone more accustomed to thermodynamic or causal closure, it is helpful to mentally translate "closed" as "event-regular" everywhere Lawson uses the term. The argument proceeds that this mode of explanation in terms of event-regular systems leads to the peculiar types of mathematical formalisms with which we are all familiar.

In his second thesis, Lawson points out the ill-health of the "mainstream project" (2003: 8). This consists in large part of remarks taken from mainstream economists that reflect upon this poor state of health. It is conceded that they rarely lay the blame on the peculiar type of mathematical formalism that forms the touchstone of mainstream economics. However, with respect to "ology" sighting, the essential point is Lawson's conclusion:

> there is quite widespread agreement that the modern discipline is not in too healthy a condition, and that whatever explains the fact that the formalistic mainstream project has risen to such dominance . .. it has little to do with this project's record so far in explaining the social world in which we live.
>
> (2003: 11)

In the first two theses, Lawson has been laying the foundation for the critique presented as the third thesis. Yet the foundation for his ontological turn in economics is epistemological. He argues that it is not the content of the theory in the mainstream content that is stable over time, but rather its mode of explanation. To justify an interest in the ontology to follow, he presents a picture of the mainstream project in ill health. Yet the symptom of ill health is that it is not succeeding in explaining.

In the third thesis Lawson enquires what ontology is implied by event-regular systems, and how closely does this match the ontology of social systems. Lawson argues (2003: 13–15) that there is an extremely strong bias (although not an ironclad necessity) towards an atomistic view of such systems, where the individual agents are simple and react in at least stochastically deterministic ways in response to given conditions. There is also argued (2003: 15–16) to be a strong bias toward viewing systems as isolated systems. This argument is easily followed, since a system composed of nothing but deterministic, atomistic agents will not be homeostatic, so that the state of such a system becomes indeterminate if the system is exposed to indeterminate external influences.

Lawson (2003: 16–17) then claims a variety of characteristics of social reality. For example, positions in social reality are internally related, the social realm is structured and it contains value and meaning. As none of the features in this list can be exhibited by a *purely* atomistic and isolated system, it is concluded that much of what economics needs to be explained is incompatible with its implicit ontology.

Lawson (2003: 18–20) argues that this incompatibility is responsible for the constant appearance of the central fictions of mainstream economics. These central fictions are a familiar fixture. They bear a surface similarity to the isolating fictions of scientific theory. For example, a natural scientist will adopt the fiction of a weight dropping through a vacuum to eliminate the real additional influence of wind resistance. However, because deductivism is constructing a theory in a fictitious world that is supposed to correspond to events in the real world, it seems that its fictions cannot be restricted to the absence of forces that are in fact likely to be present. They must also include the presence of fictitious forces to take the place of real world influences that cannot be expressed in an atomistic and isolated system.

While ontology is brought on stage here, it is certainly not appearing solo. The essence of the argument here is that the mainstream mode of explanation is not capable of explaining what Lawson wishes to explain. Certainly, it may be granted that Lawson's wish to explain particular aspects of reality is an ontological concern. However, the capabilities of a mode of explanation is an epistemological concern, and that is certainly the crux of the argument. Without the limited capabilities of the mainstream mode of explanation, the critique falls over. With the limited capabilities there is something of substance to the critique, even if one differs with Lawson's ontology.

The final thesis is the conclusion of the critique. Adherence to a mode of explanation in terms of event-regular systems is the reason for the lack of health, and is indeed the constraint preventing mainstream economics from being scientific. It is argued that even where science deliberately constructs event-regular systems in an experimental setting, it does so to form a cause and effect theory applicable to non-event-regular systems (Lawson 2003: 22–26). The argument may be seen as claiming that the mainstream mode of explanation is not a scientific mode of explanation. Here, too, the argument seems as much epistemological as ontological.

It should be stressed that this argument has substantial merit. Constructing a theory in an abstract event-regular system is not, in fact, the same thing as constructing an experiment – an artificial event-regular system in the real world. In the former case, the event-regular system has no necessary connection with a real world non-event-regular system. In the latter case, the fact that it is constructed in the real world of real components provides the connection with the same components interacting in a non-event-regular system.

While the starring role of epistemology is the strength of the argument, the anonymity of the star is a weakness. Possessing a mode of explanation that implies an inadequate ontology is not necessarily a critical flaw. As long as the explanatory process allows the worst mismatches to be replaced by less severe mismatches, one can hope that the mode of explanation may evolve towards one that implies an adequate ontology.

The central question, therefore, has not changed in a century, because while theoretical stances within the mainstream project have proliferated and shifted ground, essential aspects of its mode of explanation have not changed in a century. That question is, why do mainstream economists not engage in evolutionary science (Veblen, 1898)? Of particular interest for the past sixty years is how a determined effort to subject theories to statistical analysis have left the mainstream project every bit as stalled as it was a century ago.

Lanis and McFarling (2004) point in the direction of one flaw. We construct a highly artificial, highly regular scenario in the context of explaining the degree of disclosure of accountants in the context of different national accounting and economic institutions. However, the scenario we have constructed is non-functional. That is, legal, professional and commercial institutions will establish norms for what *must* be disclosed to provide an adequate report, what *may* be reported, and what ought to be reported in exceptional circumstances and what ought not to be reported.

Any mathematical relation connects elements from its domain to elements from its range. In our artificial scenario, we relate a score on a synthetic index of social attitudes to the degree of disclosure within the accounting institutions of a nation. A functional relation connects either one or many elements from the domain to one element in the range. Any relation that connects either one or many elements from the domain to multiple elements in the domain is therefore non-functional. Regression analysis, where it is used correctly, overcomes the problem of relating to multiple scattered observations by constructing the function in terms of a probability distribution, so that the scattered observations are inter-preted as different samples drawn from the same distribution.

However, the regularity in our scenario is on the bounds on reporting. Even if one viewed this range of discretion as a probability distribution, each shift in the bounds would result in a new probability distribution. The degree of discretion, which will vary from one institutional context to another, implies that the regularity is not functional – it is one collec-tion of institutional norms to many possible degrees of disclosure. There-fore, any effort to fit the best function will necessarily fail. It appears that functional regularity is equivalent to Lawson's event-regularity. We point out several statistical techniques that may be used with better effect – techniques that will only be picked up outside the mainstream project, if Lawson's argument regarding the event-regular epistemology of the mainstream mode of explanation is correct.

In any event, here is part of the answer to the puzzle of why sixty years of determined empirical testing has left the mainstream project stalled. If your tool for finding and correcting mismatches with the real world fits functions to data, you will be left blind when the problem involves a regular relationship that is not a function.

A more specific epistemological query than the mode of explanation is the unit of analysis. Any analytical explanation will involve one or more units of analysis, so that the phenomena to be explained are explained in terms of the unit of analysis. In McFarling (2004), I find that the unit of analysis in a particular corner of the mainstream project to be selection from alternatives, followed by performance. It may be noted in passing that this is essentially the same neoclassical unit of analysis that is ably dissected and subjected to acid critique by Veblen (1898) as part of an increasingly obsolete natural law approach, which he contrasts with a modern, evolutionary approach. However, this unit of analysis was originally unearthed in the work of Posner (1995). Thus, even if much of the theory of the mainstream project is in a state of flux, this unit of analysis clearly exhibits greater longevity.

I then pose the question whether it is possible to arrive at a theory of culture with such a unit of analysis, and argue it is not. If culture acts in part as a restraint on action, then situating culture in the selection will erode those restraints. And if culture is simply embedded in the con-straints on decisions, then culture is a *deus ex machina*, affecting the outcome but not explained by the unit of analysis. Culture cannot be analysed with selection followed by performance as the unit of analysis – it can at best be taken as a given.

What is the point of identifying the unit of analysis? Being informed that the mainstream project is deductivist, based on presumed event-regularities, may make it easier to identify a mainstream economist.

However, it does not go very far in explaining how the mainstream economist is reproduced. The unit of analysis, on the other hand, goes a long way toward explaining the reproductive process. The first thing a nascent researcher needs to learn is what type of questions to ask. And the unit of analysis provides a trio of questions that can be asked about individuals in a wide variety of settings. What selections are faced by this individual? Which one is likely to be selected? And what performance is likely to follow that selection?

The attraction of this unit of analysis is that there are always more puzzles to solve. If you try to provide a complete theory of the economy with a unit of analysis that is blind to important aspects of the economy, each new trial solution will prove to be a misfit when it encounters the affects of one or more excluded aspect. And if the reaction to a misfit is to start over with the same trio of questions, there will always be a permutation of available selections and likelihood of occurrence that has not been tried before.

Given this unit of analysis, a question that arises is whether ontology *can* be used to reorient mainstream economics. Supposed this is your unit of analysis in developing new explanations, and suppose econometrics is your tool for finding out what the problem is with your explanations. How will you react when being told that there are certain features of the social world that do not fit the ontology implicit in your method? You will interpret these features in terms of your unit of analysis.

Indeed, you may devise econometric tests to determine whether the features as you have interpreted them are present in the data you have available. If you get statistically significant results, you may even publish the outcome in a respectable mainstream journal. Yet you are not likely to have made a step towards evolutionary science. When interpreting the features with your unit of analysis, you will omit what is incompatible with your unit of analysis.

Indeed, in McFarling (2004), I find hope in New Institutional analysis. This comes from the argument that the New Institutional unit of analysis is the transaction, followed by performance. Yet there is not necessarily an ontological advance here. Indeed, it may be that New Institutional analysis maintains its credibility within the mainstream project in part by adhering to the same flawed ontology as follows from the neoclassical unit of analysis (though see David Dequech, 2002). However, by placing the selection in the context of a transaction between two individuals, the unit of analysis admits questions regarding relationships between individuals that the neoclassical unit of analysis does not admit. The conclusion is not that New Institutional economics *is* an evolutionary science, but rather that it is not prevented from being an evolutionary science by its unit of analysis.

The dangerous face of epistemology is the invitation to focus on the ways that we understand things. And it is when I consider the mode of explanation in this essay that I come upon a concern. Event-regular systems are classified as closed systems. Everything else is classified as open systems.

One thing this blinds us to is any other kind of regularity. Suppose that an individual has a regular response to a cluster of events, where a response consists of one of a range of actions that are meaningful in that context. Response-regular systems are not necessarily event-regular, but it is a form of regularity. Suppose that an individual has a response that is within regular bounds, with clear discretion within those bounds. Boundary-regular systems are not necessarily event-regular, but it is a form of regularity. Suppose that a system is homeostatic, so that the response to an event is contingent on the discrepancy between the current internal state of the system and the target internal state. A homeostatic system would only approach event-regularity in a perfectly homogeneous environment where events are sufficiently infrequent so that the state prior to the event closely approximates the target state. Yet not only is homeostasis a form of regularity, but a collection of homeostatic systems can create regularity in a wider system.

In other words, in this system of classification, we are to label event-regular systems as closed and all other systems as open, whether or not they exhibit one or several other forms of regularity. If you need event-regular systems to be a reputable mainstream economist, this may suffice to tell us whether a person is pursuing that status or rejecting it in favour of status with some other peer group. However, suppose we accept Lawson's argument that adequate economic theory will normally have to be compatible with an "open" system. We have a simple dichotomy here, and the positive category is the one to be avoided. Reorientation is required because the pursuit of theories of closed systems is and will continue to be fruitless in generating effective explanations. Yet saying that the reorientation will take open systems as the object of theory is to say that it will take "not-event-regular" systems as the ultimate object of theory. It is, in short, simply a restatement of the "though shalt not" dictum, except that this time the "not" has been located inside the term "open".

Thus in trying for a positive statement, Lawson must elaborate on what kind of open system he means. That elaboration appears to be whatever kind of open system is compatible with social ontology and his realist transformational model of social activity. And it is here that the argument appears to become controversial. As Vromen (2004) points out, there is a substantial inconsistency between the qualifications with which Lawson wraps this model, and the ultimate authority that Lawson grants it as a final arbiter between properly and improperly oriented economic theory.

This is the crux of the question of whether ontology or epistemology should have the starring role in this play. If we have the "right" ontology, how did we discover that it is the right ontology? And if we have a way of discovering the right ontology, which is more fruitful to convey: the method of discovery or the ontology itself as received wisdom?

Of course, this is a counterfactual. As strongly suggested by the qualifications that Lawson places on his ontology – that it is "practically conditioned, historical and fallible" (Lawson, 2003: 61) – it would appear that at most we can say that our ontology seems to be the best we can do at the moment. As Vromen appears to be arguing, this is a weak basis for launching a revolution.

The implicit recognition of this is built into the structure of Lawson's first essay. Accepting that the mainstream project is generating a flurry of explanations without succeeding in explaining anything is supposed to generate interest in considering the suitability of the underlying ontology. Epistemology is providing the wedge intended to create an opening. Lawson's particular social ontology is then supposed to enter the gap that is created.

Yet how are we to discriminate between different explanations, once we have reoriented ourselves to open systems? I skip past the ontology of the second essay and the realism of the third to the essay on explanations in social science. Lawson describes a method of forming hypotheses in terms of relative contrasts that are to be expected if a hypothesis is correct. He then argues that "The hypothesis that performs best in terms of empirical adequacy in this sense over the widest range of relevant conditions can, with reason, be accepted as better grounded" (2003: 97).

What we have here, of course, is a pragmatic criterion for judging the epistemological fitness of a mode of explanation and unit of analysis – or units of analysis, since the criterion accepts successful eclecticism as readily as successful and rigorous modes of explanation. Note that this is a basis for a pluralism that extends beyond those approaches that we agree with. We can accept that a mode of explanation is progressing under this criterion even if we think its ontology is flawed and that its conclusions are fallacious. Indeed, one can hope that if it continues to pursue a broader range of successful explanation, it will either eliminate the source of the fallacies, or it will develop an explanation that shows why we have misunderstood the question all along.

This, then, is Lawson's critical pragmatism. I naturally refrain from systematising it, since in that case it would be my pragmatism rather than his. Its core is the epistemology that Lawson works out as a side effect of bridging the gap between his critical realism and a potentially scientific practice of economics. I conjecture that it is narrower in scope than the virtual blank slate offered by the concept of the open system, but broader in scope than the social ontology constructed in terms of his realist transformational model of social activity.

# References

Dequech, David (2002) "The Demarcation between the 'Old' and the 'New' Institutional Economics: Recent Complications". *Journal of Economic Issues*. Vol. 36 (2), June, pp. 565–572.

Lanis, Roman and McFarling, Bruce R. (2004) "Healthy Economics Healing Autistic Accounting Theory: Visiting a Neglected Area of Institutional Economics". *Journal of Economic Issues*. Vol. 38 (1), March, pp. 59–83.

Lawson, Tony (2003) *Reorienting Economics: Economics as Social Theory*, London: Routledge.

McFarling, Bruce R. (2004) "The Clarence Ayres Memorial Lecture: An Institutionalist Reconstruction of Culture". *Journal of Economic Issues*. Vol. 38 (2), June, pp. 339–352.

Posner, Richard A. (1995) "The New Institutional Economics Meets Law and Economics". In Posner, Richard A. (ed.) *Overcoming Law*. Cambridge, MA: Harvard University Press, pp. 426–443.

Veblen, Thorsten (1898) "Why is Economics Not an Evolutionary Science?" *Quarterly Journal of Economics*. Vol. 12 (4), July 1898. pp. 373–397.

Vromen, Jack (2004) "Conjectural Revisionary Ontology". *post-autistic economics review*, Issue No. 29, article 4, 6 December. Online, available at: www.btinternet.com/~pae_news/review/issue29.htm (accessed 2 June 2008).

# 14 Ontology or epistemology?
## Reply to McFarling

*Tony Lawson*

Pride of place in any critique of, or elaboration of possibilities for, economics ought to be (and indeed essentially always is) allocated to epistemology (rather than say ontology). This is Bruce McFarling's central contention. In advancing it, McFarling indicates that by epistemology he means the philosophical activity concerned with explanatory method, criteria and units of analysis. His general critique of *Reorienting Economics* is that I over- (or mis-) emphasise ontology. Although I give star *billing* to ontology, I actually give the starring *role* to epistemology. More specifically:

1   Although I fail to recognise it, epistemology, not (as I claim) ontology, takes the lead role in my critique of the mainstream project of modern economics.
2   A more fundamental critique of the mainstream than my own is achieved by focusing on units of explanatory analysis (which is more clearly epistemological in orientation).
3   When I do advance an alternative explanatory approach to that of the mainstream, ontology barely figures. Further, this alternative is said to constitute a form of critical pragmatism.

I structure my response to McFarling's very interesting commentary by considering each of these three theses in turn (concluding with a brief comparison of my position and that of "classical pragmatism").

Before turning to these matters, though, let me reiterate a relevant point I sought to emphasise in *Reorienting Economics*. This is simply that my fundamental concern is not with the relative potential of ontology compared, say, to that of epistemology or substantive theory. Rather it is to encourage a more explicit systematic sustained concern with (particularly philosophical) ontology in social theorising than has hitherto been the case.

Certainly, ontology has long been neglected. Even with the growth in "economic methodology" as a distinct project from the late 1970s onwards, the emphasis was noticeably epistemological; explicit ontological theorising was almost entirely absent. And an explicit focus has been equally absent from the methodologically oriented heterodox contributions (even if it was always implicit in, and indeed crucial to, the heterodox oppositional stance). Believing this state of affairs to be debilitating of social theory, not least economics, I have put a good deal of effort into arguing for a recovery of (explicit) ontology, and I have defended a specific ontological theory.

Now it is because I believe a serious approach to ontology is likely to bring about a reorientation of economic practices, both as a direct result of the explicit attention to ontology per se, and as a result of consequences drawn for epistemological and other issues, that I have given ontology the primary emphasis. Whether it thereby plays the biggest part in the resulting exercise is something that does not especially concern me.

But certainly, I have never suggested that ontology can go to work in some contextual vacuum, or unaided by other forms of reasoning. Like everything else, ontological study always requires motivation, and the latter will depend upon context. The teasing out of ontological presuppositions always requires something else that bears the presuppositions. Deriving a sustainable ontological conception will itself require points of entry that need to be chosen on some basis; and so on.

If I have given the impression that I suppose otherwise, this is my chance to rectify matters. I do believe myself to have been consistent in this though, albeit perhaps previously failing to give relevant comments sufficient prominence. But, for example, in the preface to *Reorienting Economics* (2003), I included the following cautionary note:[1]

> I might also stress that I am not here proposing that ontology be prioritised in any context-independent sense. I do, though, think explicit and sustained ontological analysis, or its results, can be invaluable, and at this juncture, given the state of the modern discipline, probably essential. But ontology, like all other forms of theorising, is itself a situated, partial, fallible process, producing results that are likely to be transient, at least partially. I thus urge a rounded approach to theorising in economics. I advocate only that developments in ontology and those in method and substantive theorising evolve in tandem, with each informing or otherwise enriching the other, where possible.
>
> (p. xix)

In any case, let me now stress that, in seeking to reclaim ontology for social theorising, especially for economics, I in no way wish to suggest that, by giving it star billing at this time, I am supposing it is the only actor or even the only star involved. However, I do think that the contribution of ontology to *Reorienting Economics* warrants its being billed as a major star. McFarling seems to suggest that even this attribution is mistaken; that ontology neither does nor should take a significant role in *Reorienting Economics*. So, let me turn to the specifics of his argument.

## The nature of my critique of the mainstream

McFarling first notes that the way I motivate an ontological turn in economics is epistemological in nature, consisting in my drawing attention to the mainstream project's continuing record of explanatory failure:

> the foundation for his [Lawson's] ontological turn in economics is epistemological. He argues that it is not … the mainstream content that is stable over time, but rather its mode of explanation. To justify an interest in the ontology to follow, he presents a picture of the mainstream project in ill health. Yet the symptom of ill health is that it is not succeeding in explaining.

Well yes and no. To seek to motivate a reorientation starting from any kind of failure is to presuppose something about how things in the world ought to be different, and (so) could be different. My argument is that, even in an explanatory context, this in part is an ontological assessment.

Moreover, if I do include the predictive and explanatory failing of the mainstream project in my starting point, I also include far more. I also emphasise that the mainstream project is further ridden with theory/practice inconsistencies, lacks a clear idea of where it is heading, continually employs assumptions it knows to be false as claims about features of social reality, lacks the resources (ontological insight) to address many pressing questions and much more. And in raising each of these issues, I am presupposing something about reality that renders these issues problematic.

Still, I do not want to quibble here. I have already accepted that ontology is motivated in part by other context specific considerations.

McFarling's next point is that, although my explanation of the explanatory failure of modern economics as well as of the proliferation of theoretical fictions – turning on the mismatch of its implicit atomistic closed-systems presuppositions with the open, dynamic, highly internally related, etc., nature of social reality – is ontological in nature, even here ontology does not figure "solo":

> [Mainstream economists] must also include the presence of fictitious forces to take the place of real world influences that cannot be expressed in an atomistic and isolated system.
>
> While ontology is brought on stage here, it is certainly not appearing solo. The essence of the argument here is that the mainstream mode of explanation is not capable of explaining what Lawson wishes to explain. Certainly, it may be granted that Lawson's wish to

explain particular aspects of reality is an ontological concern. However, the capabilities of a mode of explanation is an epistemological concern, and that is certainly the crux of the argument. Without the limited capabilities of the mainstream mode of explanation, the critique falls over. With the limited capabilities there is something of substance to the critique, even if one differs with Lawson's ontology.

Here McFarling at least acknowledges that ontology plays a role. But his attempt to diminish it fails. We can agree that the intrinsic capabilities of a mode of explanation are an epistemological concern. But, contra McFarling, I do not think we must accept that this is the crux of the matter. The latter, rather, is whether the domain of reality we wish to illuminate is of such a nature that the intrinsic capabilities of a mode of explanation are at all relevant/appropriate; and this, in part at least, is an ontological issue. Even if the social realm (that domain of reality with which we are primarily interested) is of a nature that is different from the conception I defend in *Reorienting Economics*, the fundamental issue is still whether the capabilities of the explanatory procedures of the mainstream are the appropriate ones *given the way the relevant domain of reality is*. If it is recognised that (philosophical) ontology is not everything, it cannot thereby be sidelined.

McFarling, though, is not content merely to suggest that epistemology is more prominent in *Reorienting Economics* than my explicit emphasis on ontology might suggest. He seems to think that my failure to make this clear somehow constitutes a weakness in my overall argument, masking the possibility that we might make explicit progress without explicit ontology. For he writes:

> While the starring role of epistemology is the strength of the argument, the anonymity of the star is a weakness. Possessing a mode of explanation that implies an inadequate ontology is not necessarily a critical flaw. As long as the explanatory process allows the worst mismatches to be replaced by less severe mismatches, one can hope that the mode of explanation may evolve towards one that implies an adequate ontology.

It may indeed be the case that the initial use of inappropriate explanatory procedures often does *not* matter – just so long as the inaccuracies or limitations experienced are used to help move the explanatory process in a more relevant direction (and McFarling's description of these problems as "mismatches" here seems to indicate that he anticipates a situation in which ontology would be driving the process). This, though, is precisely what does not happen in modern economics, and indeed is constrained from happening.

In the previously quoted passage, McFarling refers to knowledge as an evolutionary process. Darwinism has influenced pragmatism (which I take to be McFarling's preferred philosophical position) in a number of ways of course. And if McFarling is suggesting that knowledge, or the development of modes of inquiry, is in part an evolutionary process, I am inclined to agree with him. But let us remind ourselves what a (Darwinian) evolutionary knowledge process looks like, or at least what it looks like if natural selection is the operative metaphor, and research practices constitute the relevant population.

In *Reorienting Economics* (chapter 5) I develop the PVRS model (or population, variety, selection, reproduction model), as a general conception of which the Darwinian natural section model is a biological token or special case. Fundamentally, there has to be a population containing a variety of traits constituting different and indeed competing, reproducible research practices. And second, there must be an environment that serves to favour (or select) some set of practices over and above others. In the Darwinian case, environmental selection mechanisms are largely independent of the mechanisms producing the new variety to be selected.

McFarling is suggesting, I take it, that even if explicit ontological analysis is absent, as long as a sufficient variety of explanatory research practices is generated, the evolutionary process will likely allow those most appropriate to explaining social reality to be selected.

It may do so. But then again it may not. Evolutionary processes lead us nowhere of necessity. Thorstein Veblen understood this even if he thought an evolutionary process affecting developments in the science of economics would result in an evolutionary science of economics (i.e. the study of the economy as an evolutionary process). Thus, although Veblen rejected teleology, and argued that because, or where, the evolutionary process leads to some trait or practice, etc., becoming dominant, this achieving of dominance did not in itself make that something laudable, he did (erroneously) believe that something laudable, the evolutionary method (or an evolutionary science), was nevertheless becoming dominant in economics. In this, he was simply wrong. Where an evolutionary process leads us depends upon the variety in evidence and the nature of context in which "selection" occurs.

As McFarling notes, mainstream economics has been stuck in a rut for sixty years or so. Certainly there is little evidence of explanatory progress. If we believe that an evolutionary framework or process is nevertheless at work, what could be the explanation of the present unfortunate state of affairs? It can presumably take one or both of the following forms:

1   the environment selects first and foremost on some criterion other than the ability to provide insight or social understanding,

2   the variety generating mechanism, the mechanism throwing out novel practices, has so far failed to produce any adequate ones.

My assessment is that (1) is the dominant explanation of the continuing lack of explanatory successes of the mainstream. McFarling, though, seems to suppose that (2) is the primary explanatory factor. I believe the problem is ultimately located in the misunderstandings and insecurities (and so practices) of those who hold the institutional power to affect greatly the research approaches that are selected (defined as proper and so acceptable) within the economics academy (and who have shown themselves prepared to wield that power). McFarling appears to view the problem as a lack of available alternative explanatory methods. Let me consider each of these conceivable explanations in turn.

## An emphasis on environmental selection

Unlike McFarling, I find that sufficient relevant explanatory alternatives are available. They are used successfully in other branches of social science, and repeatedly advanced by non-mainstream contributors to economics. Veblen's evolutionary method is an example of course. Indeed, I myself have put a good deal of time into developing and emphasising dialectical approaches, such as contrast explanation (or the method of explaining critical contrasts), as explanatorily powerful relevant alternatives. Others have done something similar.

But such is the hold of the mathematical mainstream on the academy, backed up by vested interests in ensuring the mathematical modelling skills continue to be attributed highest status, that these alternatives are so far compulsorily dismissed as insufficiently scientific or not "proper economics" or some such. This is presumably why groups identifying themselves as heterodox are so vocal and persistent in economics (despite, or rather because of, their inability to achieve fair access to vacant university posts. It explains too the emergence of protest movements like *post autistic economics*).

What explains the mainstream prioritising of mathematical-deductivist modelling practices? In my contributions, I single out at least the following three determinants:

1   a pervading belief that (a) economics should be scientific coupled with the equally widespread acceptance that (b) mathematical deductive reasoning is essential to (is basically the language of) science,
2   a pervading belief that mathematical methods are somehow explanatorily neutral,
3   a pervading lack of awareness of (or lack of attention paid to) the nature of social reality and so of the sort of explanatory method appropriate to it.

If (3) were the only constraint, then an evolutionary process, with increasing social illumination and understanding as the criterion of fit, would presumably lead us in the right direction sooner or later. But (3) is not the only problem. (1) and (2) are also in place and affecting the explanatory process. It is easy enough to show both that mathematical-deductive reasoning is not essential to (is not basically the language of) science (1b); and (as already noted) that mathematical methods are not somehow explanatorily neutral (2). From this perspective it is also helpful to reveal the nature of social reality and so of the sort of explanatory method appropriate to it, and so to address explicitly the problem of (3). My response has been an internal engagement with mainstream economists, or at least with younger economists who are entering the profession but open to critical reflection, to redress each of these three misunderstandings.

My experience is not that mainstream economists place no value at all on social illumination. It is rather that they fail to appreciate that the criterion of scientificity they adopt is not only erroneous in itself (if the desire is to emanate the natural sciences), but is met by methods of a sort that, in being insisted upon, are serving only to squeeze out explanatory endeavour of a nature that is capable of facilitating social insight.

The central point here, of course, is that the addressing of each of these three explanations of the mainstream emphasis on formalism (carried through in *Reorienting Economics*) involves ontological analysis in a significant way.[2]

## Insufficient variety of explanatory practices on offer

McFarling, though, seems to believe that the reason an evolutionary approach has not led to greater explanatory progress has little to do with the environment of selection and is more a question of the limited or inadequate supply of viable explanatory approaches. As a result, he sets about suggesting his own preferred explanatory method (see also McFarling 2004). Thus, for McFarling, epistemology in the form of developing an alternative explanatory framework takes centre stage.

But in the current climate (or environment of selection), I doubt that McFarling's, or any potentially fruitful, alternative will have a significant impact. In so speculating, I do not, of course, want to oppose or belittle McFarling's contribution, or indeed any proposed serious alternatives (as I say I have already spent much time developing a dialectical alternative appropriate to open [as well as closed] systems, and in the process seemingly encouraged McFarling to interpret me as giving epistemology the central role). Certainly, I do not wish to suggest that the specific alternative favoured by McFarling is not a useful addition to the social scientists' toolbox; indeed, the more relevant possibilities that are included the better. I merely observe that new contributions tend to carry little weight with the current mainstream unless facilitating of the (largely irrelevant) formalistic manoeuvres with which the project's members are familiar and/or comfortable.

Parenthetically, I cannot help but note that, despite the attention given to epistemology, even McFarling's defence of his alternative method is ultimately, in part at least, ontological. He proposes an approach that does not rely on functional relations connecting the variables capturing events. But his justification for so doing is just that the real world is such that functional relationships are not appropriate to its analysis. McFarling mostly leaves this implicit, but it is presupposed, and more or less explicit in the following summing up:

> In any event, here is part of the answer to the puzzle of why sixty years of determined empirical testing has left the mainstream project stalled. If your tool for finding and correcting mismatches with the real world fits functions to data, you will be left blind when the problem involves a regular relationship that is not a function.

Of course, some of the terminology that McFarling uses serves to mask the full ontological nature of the explanation. But it is easy enough to see that the claim is coherent only if "the problem involves" stands in for something like "the relevant features of reality support", and so forth.

## Units of analysis as the basis for an alternative critique of the mainstream

McFarling's second broad theme is that a more fruitful way to formulate criticisms of the mainstream may be in terms of units of analysis. In keeping with his emphasis on epistemology, he opens the part of his chapter that deals with this topic as follows:

> A more specific epistemological query than the mode of explanation is the unit of analysis. Any analytical explanation will involve one or more units of analysis, so that the phenomena to be explained are explained in terms of the unit of analysis.

McFarling's central contention at this point is that mainstream economics employs a fixed unit of analysis. This he describes as "selection from alternatives, followed by performance". By this McFarling is presumably focusing on the mainstream frequent concern with (typically rational) decision theory, with actions resulting from selection (optimising) over a range of options. McFarling adds that authors as far apart in time as Thorstein Veblen (1898) and Richard Posner (1995) have identified this unit of analysis. From this insight, McFarling concludes that "even if much of the theory of the mainstream project is in a state of flux, this unit of analysis clearly exhibits greater longevity".

McFarling makes several uses of this assessment.

First, he employs it as a criticism of the mainstream, arguing that various real world phenomena, such as culture, cannot be explained by "selection from alternatives, followed by performance".

Second, McFarling seems to think that the identified unit of analysis is universal in mainstream practice, and thus suggests that we focus on this, rather than formalistic modelling, when characterising the mainstream. For he supposes it is this (rather than formalistic modelling) that explains how mainstream economics is reproduced.

Third, McFarling suggests that a mainstream economist committed to the identified unit of analysis will react to the criticism that his or her ontology is wrong by merely interpreting the critic's proposed alternative ontological features in terms of the same fixed unit of analysis.

## Units of analysis and ontology

Now it is not entirely clear, but I am assuming that McFarling runs through all this because he thinks that making a critique based on what he identifies as the mainstream unit of analysis is somehow more telling or relevant than one based on (philosophical) ontology. My response is to contend that there is a place for both critiques, where they are relevant. That said, though, I do believe, contra McFarling, that the ontological critique is the more fundamental. Let me briefly indicate why.

First, I am sure that McFarling is right to suggest that culture cannot be properly captured by an explanatory method that has "selection from alternatives, followed by performance" as its unit of analysis. McFarling sets this up as a particular explanatory failing. But I think the same, and a more general point, can be made, drawing on ontology. For the latter shows most features of social reality to be emergent from human interaction, and though continually reproduced and transformed through human practice, are so in largely unacknowledged, unintended and often ill-understood ways, and bear causal powers of their own, synchronically irreducible to human acts. In other words, the social world is of a nature that not everything is a result of (and so explicable in terms of) "selection from alternatives, followed by performance". Culture is but an example.

In fact, we can go much further and argue on the basis of ontological analysis that social reality is of a nature such that any reductionist analysis claiming to identify fixed units of analysis is suspect. Indeed, I do argue as much in *Reorienting Economics*.[3] I cannot help but think that theorising in terms of given units of analysis is always bound to mislead (so that to substitute an alternative basic unit of analysis in place of any mainstream one – as for example some institutionalists have sometimes sought to do, proposing the *institution* as the unit – is to commit the same sort of error). McFarling's specific criticism, then, is a special case of the ontological argument.

McFarling's second claim is that focusing on the identified unit of analysis better enables us to understand the mainstream economist. McFarling seems to think that the given unit of analysis is universal. And he suggests focusing on it, rather than formalistic modelling, when characterising the mainstream, for it is the former rather than the latter that explains how mainstream economists are reproduced.

I am sure this claim is in part correct. There has to be substantive content to the formal models. And if some claims are very pervasive, this presumably will tell us something about the thought processes in which economists are moulded as academics.

But I think McFarling overstates his case. It is only the emphasis on mathematical-deductive reasoning that is found to be universal in mainstream economics, and it is this, with its presuppositions that the social world is everywhere closed and atomistic, which drives the theorising, including units of analysis. Indeed, the analytical unit that McFarling identifies, if often adopted, is certainly not always so.

In fact, mainstream theorising need not even be couched in terms of individuals; but the formalism remains compulsory. As the mainstream theorist Alan Kirman argues, because of the explanatory shortfalls of the mainstream project, its proponents should give less attention to theorising in terms of independent individuals, and more to endeavours concerned to "theorise in terms of groups who have collectively coherent behaviour" (Kirman, 1989, p. 138). However, if Kirman is prepared to abandon the individualistic unit of analysis, he is more reluctant to give up on the formalism:

> The argument that the root of the problem … [is] that we are confined by a mathematical strait jacket which allows us no escape, does not seem very persuasive. That the mathematical frameworks that we have used made the task of changing or at least modifying our paradigm hard, is undeniable but it is difficult to believe that had a clear well-formulated new approach been suggested then we would not have adopted the appropriate mathematical tools.
>
> (Kirman, 1989, p. 137)

McFarling's third contention is that a mainstream economist committed to the unit of analysis he identifies will react to criticism that his or her ontology is inadequate by interpreting the alternative ontological features in terms of the preferred unit of analysis.

But this is quite wrong. If McFarling believes it is difficult to express culture in terms of "selection from alternatives, followed by performance", I suggest he considers how even more difficult it would be to

accommodate features like emergence, openness, process, internal relationality and so forth. In any case, the mainstream challenge is to interpret such features in terms of, or within the context of employing, their
mathematical-deductivist models. Given that the ontological presuppositions of the latter are at best rather rare special cases of the ontological
properties just listed, whatever substantive theories or units of analysis
are selected, the ontological critique clearly stands.

In fact, in *Reorienting Economics* and elsewhere I note how mainstream
economists have found it all too easy to construct closed-system substi-
tutes of heterodox claims or emphases, once it is admitted that heterodox
economists have made a point. Thus, post Keynesian uncertainty is
mapped on to risk; institutionalist evolutionary concepts are shorn of
their Darwinianism and reinterpreted in terms of the requirements of
non-linear, or game theory, modelling; and feminist conceptions of care
for others become transformed into variables in utility functions and so
on.

The fact that heterodox economists resist the mainstream reformula-
tions of their concepts of uncertainty, evolutionary developments, care,
institutions and history, etc., reveals that these heterodox groups are
committed not just to the latter categories per se but to their possessing
the ontological properties of openness, processuality and internal relationality, etc. that I defend (see *Reorienting Economics*, Chapter 2). Once
the heterodox groups make their attachment to this ontology explicit the
mainstream's transformative manoeuvres are pre-empted. The heterodox challenge becomes at once more powerful and less easily bypassed
or accommodated. As I say, I believe the ontological critique still stands.

## The role of ontological elaboration in advancing an epistemological framework

McFarling's third and final central theme or contention, as I understand
it, is that when I do advance an alternative explanatory approach to that
of the mainstream, ontology barely figures. This alternative explanatory
approach is said to constitute my critical pragmatism.

McFarling's argument is as follows. Noting that I contend that social
reality is open, McFarling first criticises me for entirely ruling out
methods that presuppose event regularities (which of course I do not, as
I have often pointed out – see for example my replies to Downward and
Mearman, and to Hodgson in this volume). His main point, though, is
that merely emphasising that social reality is open does not get us far. In
consequence, McFarling seeks, and finds, a more "positive" account in
*Reorienting Economics*. This turns on the transformational model of social
activity. However, the manner in which I make use of this ontological
theory seems to leave McFarling feeling uncomfortable. In any case, he
finds my analysis here to be somewhat controversial:

Thus in trying for a positive statement, Lawson must elaborate on what kind of open system he means. That elaboration appears to be whatever kind of open system is compatible with social ontology and his realist transformational model of social activity. And it is here that the argument appears to become controversial. As Vromen (2004) points out, there is a substantial inconsistency between the qualifications with which Lawson wraps this model, and the ultimate authority that Lawson grants it as a final arbiter between properly and improperly oriented economic theory.

McFarling is explicit that my qualifications to which he refers are that the ontological results I achieve are "practically conditioned, historical and fallible". Thus the apparent "substantial inconsistency" he finds in my writing is that I both emphasise these qualifications and yet simultaneously make some further analytical and critical use of the (practically conditioned, historical and fallible) ontological results achieved (here we return to the concern also raised by Davidsen and Vromen in the current volume).

But there really is no inconsistency here or, in fact, any cause for concern at all. All understanding is to some extent practically conditioned, historical and fallible. I emphasise the matter in the context of ontology just because critics of ontology frequently assert (or anyway suppose) that those engaged in ontological elaboration claim otherwise. But to take results or insights regarded as fallible, etc., and to apply them, is no more than we all do in our everyday lives, as well as throughout science. No matter how much (or how little) our action takes for granted the understanding on which it rests, *the latter is always practically conditioned and fallible*. To suggest that to act on the basis of ontological results regarded as fallible is somehow inconsistent with a recognition of the fallibility of these results would be to dismiss all forms of practical action as similarly problematic.

Of course, McFarling, following others, loads his case by suggesting that I grant to the social ontology I defend, particularly the transformational model, the role of "final arbiter between properly and improperly oriented economic theory". But do I?

Let me acknowledge, and indeed emphasise, that although I heavily qualify the conception of social ontology I defend, I do nevertheless regard it as the most sustainable account of which I am aware. Indeed, I regard it as well grounded. Consider the transformational model, the aspect on which McFarling, like Vromen in this volume, focuses most. It states that social structures that endure to any extent are neither created anew every second, nor somehow fixed and out of time, but continually reproduced and/or transformed through ongoing practice. We do not, for example, (re)create the English language every second. Nor is the English language fixed and unchangeable. And just as our (English) speech acts depend on the English language, so the latter in turn depends on these practices (in total).

As far as I can see, we can make sense of these observations *only by way of the transformational model*. According to it, social structures (e.g. language) are (typically unacknowledged) conditions of our practices (e.g. speech acts) as well as the (typically unintentional) reproduced (or transformed) outcomes of those same practices. This, it seems to me is the mode of being of all (enduring) social structure. I think it is the best account available, and perhaps the only coherent one, even though I remain fully aware that it is fallible, etc. (for a further defence of this conception see my response to Vromen in the current volume).

But I do not thereby assign it (or anything else) the role of "final arbiter between properly and improperly oriented economic theory". Indeed, how could there reasonably be an arbiter or anything similar that is final? My claim about ontological results serving to provide theoretical guidance (that apparently so worries Davidsen, Vromen and McFarling) is merely the following. If the transformational model turns out to be a feature of our best grounded, most sustainable ontology, and if according to the latter, the transformational model expresses a characteristic of all relatively enduring social structures, it makes sense, and seems entirely reasonable, to investigate whether or how a conjectured novel form of social structure fits with this conception.

This is particularly so in a situation where there is debate and confusion over whether a specific form of structured process that holds in a non-social realm has an equivalence or analogy in the social domain. In such circumstances, it seems to me not at all unreasonable, and indeed quite sensible, to enquire whether or how such a process might be rendered consistent with the transformational model.

Furthermore, in the absence of any competing ontological conceptions it equally does not seem arbitrary, dogmatic or otherwise unreasonable, to go further and suggest that conceptions that do conform to this ontology are in this way at least *advantaged* over conceptions that do not (for example, over those that presuppose that social reality is everywhere closed and atomistic).

To follow this strategy is no more like treating the ontological conception as a "final" arbiter than, say, physicists or astronomers are invoking a final "arbiter" in checking out how some newly posited entities fit with their best understandings of thermodynamics or whatever. Or perhaps closer to home, it is no different from the way in which anthropologists or sociologists or even some economists act when seeking to interpret behavioural patterns of unfamiliar communities in terms of a conformity to rules or customs or at least routines. In each such case, the feature in question is not being treated as some "final arbiter" but merely serving as one way of seeing that, or how, novel features fit with what we already (think we) know. Where there is a clash, it is, of course, in principle feasible that either may give way; although given the ontological conception is grounded, then where the conjectured novel structure does not, this will presumably be brought into consideration.

In the passages of *Reorienting Economic* with which Vromen and McFarling are concerned I consider the borrowing of "models" of evolutionary theorising from (evolutionary) biology. And I suggest that in the absence of better grounded or more explanatorily adequate ontological theories, we might check if and/or how a conception of a social evolutionary process can be rendered consistent with the transformational model, and *ceteris paribus* take seriously any conception that is found to be consistent with it. But that is all. I in no way suggest that this is the only ground on which we go about selecting a social evolutionary conception. Even less do I suggest that there be some final or ultimate criterion (even though I give reasons for supposing that the ontological conception I defend be taken seriously and for the time being, at least, be used to inform the abductive process).

It seems to me that at points McFarling wants it all ways. For if the ontological conception I defend is described as fallible, he goes on to conclude, "this is a weak basis for launching a revolution". But to the extent that the ontological conception might be considered correct nevertheless, he raises the possibility that the manner of discovering it is then likely more important than the discovery:

> This is the crux of the question of whether ontology or epistemology should have the starring role in this play. If we have the "right" ontology, how did we discover that it is the right ontology? And if we have a way of discovering the right ontology, which is more fruitful to convey: the method of discovery or the ontology itself as received wisdom?

My response to the former conclusion is to suggest that there could be no infallible basis for launching a revolution or anything else.

And my response to the question posed in the preceding passage is to ask why there must be one or other feature that must typically be the "more fruitful to convey"? It all depends on context.

Remember, in any case, that ontology is the *study* of the nature or structure of (a domain of) being, not the results obtained. In arguing for a reorientation of social theory that includes ontology as a central component, my emphasis is on *this type of study*. And if this is my concern, the method of study, as well as the results of any seemingly appropriate and insightful study, are clearly both of central relevance. To single out either one as the more fruitful to convey whatever the topic of discussion seems unwarranted and likely to serve only as an unhelpful distraction.

## Explanatory advance

McFarling's additional contention at this stage is that a critical pragmatist position can be found in *Reorienting Economics*. In making his case, McFarling argues that my central contribution is "the epistemology" that I am said to work out as a side effect of bridging a gap between my ontological conception and a potentially scientific practice of economics. My position is seemingly described as a form of pragmatism because I advance (as a feature of this epistemology) "a pragmatic criterion" for assessing the "epistemological fitness of a mode of explanation and ... units of analysis". In truth, I am not fully sure how to assess this pragmatist interpretation of my position.

McFarling motivates his interpretation of my position as a critical pragmatism with the question: "Yet how are we to discriminate between different explanations, once we have reoriented ourselves to open systems?" The answer that he contends is found in *Reorienting Economics* runs as follows:

> Lawson describes a method of forming hypotheses in terms of relative contrasts that are to be expected if a hypothesis is correct. He then argues that "The hypothesis that performs best in terms of empirical adequacy in this sense over the widest range of relevant conditions can, with reason, be accepted as better grounded" (2003: 97).
>
> What we have here, of course, is a pragmatic criterion for judging the epistemological fitness of a mode of explanation and unit of analysis – or units of analysis, since the criterion accepts successful eclecticism as readily as successful and rigorous modes of explanation. Note that this is a basis for a pluralism that extends beyond those approaches that we agree with....
>
> This, then, is Lawson's critical pragmatism.... Its core is the epistemology that Lawson works out as a side effect of bridging the gap between his critical realism and a potentially scientific practice of economics.

Now I confess that I am a bit unsure as to whether McFarling really means a *mode* of explanation here. This is the term that McFarling uses throughout his chapter to describe, for example, the deductivism of mainstream economics. It seems to express a type of explanation rather than any specific substantive explanatory hypothesis. Presumably, then, the approach to explanation that I sometimes defend, namely contrast explanation (or the method of explaining critical contrasts), is an example.

But if so, I am not convinced that the criterion mentioned by McFarling in the preceding passage ("The hypothesis that performs best in terms of empirical adequacy in this sense [of explaining empirical contrasts] over the widest range of relevant conditions can, with reason, be accepted as better grounded") is one for judging the epistemological fitness of a *mode* of explanation at all. Rather this is a criterion appropriate for assessing specific substantive (causal) explanations or hypotheses.[4]

Any criterion for evaluating the causal *mode* of explanation (inherent in the form of contrast explanation being discussed) is going to be in part at least ontological (see chapters 1–4 of *Economics and Reality*). The argumentation for anticipating that it is empirical contrasts that constitute the sort of phenomena most likely to ground explanatory inference (to theories of causal factors) is also mostly ontological (see chapter 4 of *Reorienting Economics*).

It seems likely, then, that McFarling just means that I provide a pragmatic criterion for judging the epistemological fitness of particular substantive explanatory hypotheses. If so, it is important to recall that my references to "empirical adequacy" in the extracts of my contributions that McFarling notes, are not given in isolation. In my books, I defend a structured ontology and a causal approach to explanation. Contrast explanation, or, more informatively, the *method of explaining critical contrasts* (see Lawson, 1997, 2003), as well as being causalist is also a dialectical approach. Specific endeavours conforming to this explanatory mode are initiated by, and oriented to, explaining differences, and specifically differences that are considered surprising, noteworthy, inconsistent, disturbing or in some other way interesting from the standpoint of current understandings.

Feelings of surprise, doubt, wonder, disagreement or being disturbed, induced by a surprising contrast are only possible if, prior to their occurrence, there is an initial achieved stage of understanding bearing on the matters in question. The surprising or unexpected contrast is the second, dialectical, stage, contradicting, but presupposing, the first level of understanding.[5] The third stage is a resolution of the initial understanding and surprising findings, in a manner that can account for both. The result may be achieved by transforming the initial understanding, or adding to it, or revising the observations that surprised us, etc. It depends on context.

The point is that knowledge progresses as a totality; it does so by way of dialectically absenting some kind of inadequacy in the achieved understanding; it is not an especially eclectic process. It is with this conception of dialectical causal explanation taken for granted (i.e. already defended), and a certain sort of contrast explanatory endeavour under discussion, that, at the relevant point in *Reorienting Economics*, I argue that, in an open social world, the sorts of empirical phenomena likely to prove most appropriate to gauging the empirical adequacy of causal hypotheses are empirical contrasts.

I should stress, too, that critical contrasts that initiate, or are otherwise utilised within, contrastive explanatory endeavours cannot all be said to be empirical. Actually, before elaborating this point, it warrants emphasis that, in any case, phenomena designated empirical are *always* interpreted (and so in some part "theoretical") and, in the social domain especially, open to contestation. Thus in the sorts of illustrations discussed elsewhere in this book (for example in explaining the unexpected discrepancies between prices of relatively new second-hand cars with prior expectations of those prices as focused upon by George Ackerlof [1970] – see my response to Bruce Caldwell in this volume) the critical contrast initiating the explanatory research is between an expectation conditioned upon a prior theory, or understanding, of a causal process (over some contrast space) and an a posteriori theory or interpretation of what has actually turned out to be the case (the empirical observation). As already noted, in any particular investigation, either the initial understanding or the a posteriori "observation" or both may be found wanting on examination, and so warrant revision in the dialectical process of adjustment.

But critical contrasts that initiate the explanatory endeavour might not be interpreted as empirical anyway. For example, critical contrasts can also be found in a situation where two individuals or groups of individuals address the same phenomenon, but provide surprisingly contrasting or inconsistent interpretations. Here, too, there is a *prima facie* case for supposing that a reason for the discrepancy can be uncovered, particularly where both claim to be sharing values, or to be similarly situated, or informed by a similar initial background understanding. Of course, it may simply be that one explanation is straightforwardly more adequate in some relevant way than the other. But equally, it may be that by adjusting the conceptual frameworks accepted by each of the disputing parties the competing accounts can be shown to be two aspects of the same explanation or conception. (This latter scenario is found, for example, in my account of the nature of gender, initiated by seeking to overcome seemingly irresolvable tensions in existing accounts focusing on the analysis of gender – see Lawson, 2007, and also my response to Davidsen in this volume.)

Equally, though, the different, and sometimes competing, accounts to emerge may be provided neither by a specific individual's *prior* theory/expectation and a posteriori interpretation of some given situation, nor by the competing accounts of different individuals or groups, of the same outcome, but instead by a single individual who is observed to speak in "different voices" about a given situation. That is, there may be a voice of the unconscious, inconsistent with the voice of reflected upon thought, but bound up with it, and in need of disentangling from it;[6] and so on.

I run through such possibilities merely to indicate that my account of how explanation can proceed in an open system is rather more complex, if seemingly less eclectic, than McFarling contends, perhaps thereby rendering my position to be not a critical pragmatism at all.

Still I have not set out all this to claim I am not a critical pragmatist, because I confess to not being entirely sure what it means. Mostly I have in the last few paragraphs attempted to clarify where I do stand. I hope, though, that the above outline is sufficient to allow those that do have an understanding of critical pragmatism to evaluate McFarling's assessment. Certainly, if the position I defend does fit the bill of a critical pragmatism this is not because ontology does not play a major role. Indeed, I think it clearly plays a starring role, even if it ought not to be billed as the only star of this particular show.

## Concluding comments

The spirit of McFarling's position is very much one of encouraging trial and error experimentation with different explanatory methods, in the expectation that those methods that work will survive. On this vision, ontology can be more or less dispensed with. No doubt, this evolutionary vision captures a significant part of the story. But what counts as working is something that is environment or context dependent. Alternatively put, the specific trait within the population (of research practices) that is selected depends on the nature of the selecting environment. And for historical reasons (elaborated in chapter 10 of *Reorienting Economics*) the economics academy is currently characterised by an environment of selection that entails that conformity with formalistic modelling vastly improves chances of survival and flourishing in this context. For those committed to the view that ability-to-illuminate-social-reality ought to be the primary, certainly a dominant, criterion of selection, the goal will be to transform the environment of selection accordingly.

One route to changing dominant practices (of selection) is to influence the reasoning behind those practices. This is where ontology enters. The reasoning behind the modern academy's emphasis on formalism in economics is complex, but seemingly sustained by such ideas as: mathematical methods are essential to science or to all serious study; the use of formalism is neutral; there is no reason why the reliance on formalism should not lead to realistic social analysis eventually, and so forth. Ontology can be used to demonstrate the errors of all such preconceptions.

So, I retain the view that, at this point in time certainly, a turn to ontology is warranted, it being an especially effective aid to explanatory advance. But I would never want to suggest that ontology could ever be more than an aid or vital component of this endeavour; nor would I deny that ontological enquiry always requires a significant input from all the other various components of analysis. Indeed, like many other performers it seems to shine the more the stronger the support cast.

## Postscript – the pragmatist tradition

As a very short postscript, let me use the brief references to pragmatism in my response to McFarling, as an opportunity to add something about the American pragmatist tradition, and how I see my own approach relating to it. I do so not only because the above comments may be misread as my wanting to take a critical distance, but also because comments I previously made elsewhere have been interpreted as my being overly critical already.

At one point in *Economics and Reality* (Lawson, 1997), I considered the criteria whereby certain knowledge claims become accepted (as possibly true) and wrote:

> It can also be readily acknowledged that the criteria actually employed within (and outside of) science may not *all* be ontological/evidential, but will often turn on considerations of a pragmatist (persuasiveness, simplicity, standard of rhetoric, vested interests) or coherentist (consistency with existing general beliefs, or with those of some authority) sort. Of course, which pragmatic features are regarded as virtuous will depend significantly upon the prevailing social, historical, cultural and political context.
>
> (p. 242)

Now when I wrote these lines I systematised the criteria of persuasiveness and simplicity, etc., as pragmatist simply because (as well as this being a fairly common practice in European philosophy) the term pragmatist seemed to carry the appropriate connotations to cover the criteria in question. However, I did not wish to suggest thereby that I thought these criteria were prioritised in the writings of the particular tradition of American Pragmatism running through William James, Charles Saunders Peirce, John Dewey, George Herbert Mead and others (or indeed that the latter never adopted explicitly ontological orientations). This, though, has been the worry of some, and when interpreted in this way my statement has been rightly criticised (see e.g. James Webb, 2000).

Let me, then, take this opportunity to acknowledge that I actually think my own position, and those of say Peirce, Dewey and others, are in many ways very similar (though I recognise that there is significant variability within American Pragmatism). Thus, both the project to which I subscribe and many versions of American Pragmatism, most especially the *pragmaticism* associated with Peirce, can be described as self-consciously realist (all positions are implicitly realist in some ways of course), fallibilist, non-foundationalist, non-reductionist (especially non-individualist), anti-sceptical, promoting a structured and processual ontology and much more.

This is not to suggest that there are not some important differences, or that the two projects share the same motivations, or proceed using the same modes of argument. But similarities are clear.

The commonalities just emphasised are abstractly stated of course. But similarities can be found in numerous *details* of philosophical analyses too. An obvious case is the method of contrast explanation (or of explaining critical contrasts) referred to above and Peirce's method of enquiry.

The former, let me recall, starts with surprising or otherwise interesting contrasts causing the observer to question existing understandings, and so to seek out the cause of the surprising difference between what happened and what was expected. Peirce's account starts with determinate doubt[7] in (and so presupposing) current opinion/beliefs or "habits"[8] caused (according to one of the ways in which Peirce systematises doubt) by the occurrence of surprising outcomes,[9] the awareness of opposed views,[10] and so forth.

From this entry point, Peirce argues that scientific explanation moves next to a mode of inference, which he refers to as abduction[11] (an explanatory mode identical to retroduction as described in *Reorienting Economics*, chapter 4) in order to explain the factors stimulating the doubt. And so forth.

Clearly, a serious comparison of the realist/ontological project to which I have contributed and the writings of even one of the central contributors to the American Pragmatist tradition would likely warrant a book, certainly at least a full-length article. Whilst space is limited here, this topic is irrelevant to my response to McFarling anyway. So, I postpone further elaboration of these comments to another day (but note that the project of drawing comparisons in a serious fashion is already in progress – see Stephen Pratten, 2006).

I hope, though, that I have said enough to redress any impression I might earlier (or above) have imparted that I am overly dismissive, or especially critical. of the "American" or "classical" pragmatist tradition. To the contrary, I find very many aspects of the perspectives associated with James, Peirce, Dewey, Meade and others extremely appealing. I am grateful to McFarling for stimulating this introductory conversation. To explore our differences yet further, I suspect, would be a fruitful basis for dialectical (or is it pragmatic?) advance.

## Notes

1 And in chapter 2, the chapter that most concerns itself with ontological analysis, I qualify my efforts as follows:

> I have emphasised over and again (both above and elsewhere) that an ontological conception such as I defend, though practically conditioned, historical and fallible, always requires supplementing with rather more context-specific empirical claims before it can bear on substantive or concrete issues, whether concerning theory, method, politics or policy.

However, it should be equally clear that although critical realism stops short of licensing any specific empirical claims it does not follow that those who contribute to and/or defend this realist conception do, *or are even able to*, avoid invoking fairly context specific empirical claims continuously. Ontological theorising everywhere goes hand in hand with such empirical assessments.

It is easy to see how this is the case with the current book. Although my aim with it, particularly in the current chapter, is to make a case for an ontological turn in economics, the case made is in large part empirical in nature. It rests on the assessment that the state of modern economics is none too healthy, that a central feature of modern economics is a tendency to universalise certain (mathematical-deductivist) methods *a priori*, and that explicit ontological reasoning has, until very recently at least, been overly neglected in modern economics, and so on. All such assessments are, in some part at least, empirical in nature.

Irrespective of their validity I might have avoided making them. But only at the cost of leaving my discussion and advocacy of ontology at this time without motivation, point or context. Thus, I indicated above how the ontological conception sustained gives reason to be very cautious about universalising certain insights, or practices *a priori*. But to demonstrate just how relevant are the insights sustained for modern economics it was useful to remind the reader (i.e., to advance empirical assessments) of how widespread are existing practices of universalising highly particular conceptions of individuals, socio-economic systems, human practices and explanatory orientations.

The general point I am working towards here is that we each contribute always from within a context, being situated in particular ways, with very definite socio-cultural-political interests. In contributing we act on our situated interests, value assessments and perspectives. There is no escaping from any of this, or from the implication that there is always an empirical grounding of our particular pursuits, orientations, justifications and so on. Like everything else critical realism is a product of its place and time, as in particular are the motivations of those who contribute to it and the uses to which it is put.

(Lawson, 2003, pp. 61, 62)

2 Of course I do not at all wish to imply that ontology, even here, is the last word. This whole misguided orientation of the mainstream will itself have psychological determinants amongst others (see Vinca Bigo, 2007, and my response to Bernard Guerrien's piece in this volume).

3 Thus at one stage I conclude:

Ontological analysis such as sustained above, however, quickly reveals any such reductionist orientation to be significantly mistaken. Specifically, because of the fact of emergence (i.e., because social structure, though dependent on human agency, has powers that are irreducible to it) methodological individualism is seen to be false. For forms of social structure are as explanatory of (condition or facilitate) the things individuals do, as the actions of individuals in total, are explanatory of the reproductions and transformations of social structure.

More generally, because of the complicated ways in which social structure (in all its forms) and human agency depend upon, but remain irreducible to, each other, all methodological reductionist positions must be rejected. This applies not only to methodological individualism but also to methodological holism (social wholes are always the main unit of analysis) methodological institutionalism (institutions are always the main unit of analysis) methodological evolutionism (evolutionary processes are always the main unit of analysis) and much else.

(Lawson, 2003, p. 57)

4 McFarling seems to acknowledge as much when, as noted, he motivates the passage just reproduced with the question: "Yet how are we to discriminate between different explanations, once we have reoriented ourselves to open systems?"

5 At risk of seeming somewhat pedantic, we can thus see that the first sentence of the first paragraph of the passage reproduced from McFarling is somewhat misleading. Rather it should read that hypotheses are formed that are capable of explaining *unexpected* contrasts. The second sentence is correct so long as we understand it to be referring to the process of discriminating between hypotheses already formulated, these hypotheses having been constructed/ designed to explain some unexpected contrast.

6 To detect different voices we need especially to develop ways of listening (see for example Carol Gilligan, 1977, 1882). Watching, too, is an important supplement to listening. The hidden can reveal itself as much through the body as the words that arise against the ego's censorship. The free association of psychology can interrupt the surface story. The deeper account can be revealed not just in a slip of the tongue or computer keyboard, but in the play of fingers, the pose or "language" of the body, the speed and manner of walking or talking, signs of agitation, the movements of one's symptoms.

7 According to Peirce (1931–58):

> genuine doubt always has an external origin, usually from *surprise*; and that it is as impossible for a man to create in himself a genuine doubt by such an act of the will as would suffice to imagine the condition of a mathematical theorem, as it would be for him to give himself a genuine surprise by a simple act of the will.
>
> (CP 5.443)

8 Peirce writes: "There is every reason to suppose that belief came first, and the power of doubting long after. Doubt, usually, perhaps always, takes its rise from surprise, which supposes previous belief; and surprises come with novel environment" (CP 5.512).

9 He writes: "For belief, while it lasts, is a strong habit, and as such, forces the man to believe until some *surprise* breaks up the habit" (CP 5.524).

10 Peirce writes: "No matter how strong and well-rooted in habit any rational conviction of ours may be, we no sooner find that another equally well-informed person doubt it, than we begin to doubt it ourselves" (CP 5.168).

11 Abduction of course is distinct from both induction and deduction. Peirce writes:

> These three kinds of reasoning are Abduction, Induction, and Deduction. Deduction is the only necessary reasoning. It is the reasoning of mathematics. It starts from a hypothesis, the truth or falsity of which has nothing to do with the reasoning; and of course its conclusions are equally ideal. The ordinary use of the doctrine of chances is necessary reasoning, although it is reasoning concerning probabilities. Induction is the experimental testing of a theory.
>
> The justification of it is that, although the conclusion at any stage of the investigation may be more or less erroneous, yet the further application of the same method must correct the error. The only thing that induction accomplishes is to determine the value of a quantity. It sets out with a

theory and it measures the degree of concordance of that theory with fact. It never can originate any idea whatever. No more can deduction. All the ideas of science come to it by the way of abduction. Abduction consists in studying facts and devising a theory to explain them. Its only justification is that if we are ever to understand things at all, it must be in that way."

(*CP*, 5.145)

The logic of the abductive mode of inference is expressed by Peirce as follows: "The surprising fact, C, is observed. But if A were true, C would be a matter of course. Hence, there is reason to suspect that A is true" (CP 5.189). (Note that references to Peirce of the form "*CP* x.y" indicate his collected papers, volume x, paragraph y.)

# References

Akerlof, George A. (1970) "The Market for 'Lemons': Quality Uncertainty and the Market Mechanism", *Quarterly Journal of Economics*, 84(3), pp. 488–500.

Bigo, Vinca (2007) "Explaining Modern Economics as a Microcosm of Society", Mimeo: Jesus College, Cambridge.

Gilligan, Carol (1977) "In a Different Voice: Women's Conceptions of Self and Morality", *Harvard Educational Review*, 47(4), pp. 481–517.

Gilligan, Carol (1982) *In a Different Voice: Psychological Theory and Women's Development*. Cambridge, Ma: Harvard University Press.

Kirman, Alan (1989) "The Intrinsic Limits of Modern Economic Theory: The Emperor has no Clothes", *Economic Journal*, 99(395), pp. 126–139.

Lawson, Tony (1997) *Economics and Reality*, London and New York: Routledge.

Lawson, Tony (2003) *Reorienting Economics*. London and New York: Routledge.

Lawson, Tony (2007) "Gender and Social Change", in Jude Brown (ed.), *The Future of Gender*, Cambridge: Cambridge University Press, pp. 136–162.

McFarling, Bruce R. (2004) "The Clarence Ayres Memorial Lecture: An Institutionalist Reconstruction of Culture", *Journal of Economic Issues*, 38(2), June, pp. 339–352.

Peirce, Charles Sanders (1931–58) *The Collected Papers of Charles Sanders Peirce* (*CP*), edited by C. Hartshorne and P. Weiss (vols 1–6) and A.W. Burks (vols 7–8), Cambridge, MA: Harvard University Press.

Posner, Richard A. (1995) "The New Institutional Economics Meets Law and Economics" *Overcoming Law*. Cambridge, MA: Harvard University Press, pp. 426–443.

Pratten, Stephen (2006) "Domains of Reality and Ways of Being: Critical Realism and Peirce's Pragmaticism", Mimeo: Kings College London.

Veblen, Thorstein (1898) "Why is Economics Not an Evolutionary Science", *Quarterly Journal of Economic*, 12(4), July, pp. 373–397.

Vromen, Jack (2004) "Conjectural Revisionary Ontology", *post-autistic economics review*, Issue No. 29, article 4, 6 December (reprinted in this volume).

Webb, James L. (2000) "Warranted Assertibility: Economics and Reality and the Continuing Relevance of Dewey", Mimeo: University of Missouri-Kansas City, MD.

# 15 (Un)real criticism

*David F. Ruccio*

Reading the work of Tony Lawson and the growing literature on critical realism and economics, I am impressed by the power of this "underlaboring" philosophy both to shed light on the methodological problems that beset contemporary mainstream economics and to help create the theoretical space in which we, as heterodox economists, can imagine and develop alternatives to the mainstream. At the same time, I am troubled by the particular way Lawson and other critical realists are endeavoring to fill that space.

Let me put this a different way: Lawson and other critical realists raise a series of pertinent and probing questions concerning the ontological presuppositions of contemporary economic discourse. I am not, however, persuaded by the specific answers Lawson and others give to those questions.

I want to use this chapter, then, to explain why I think critical realism – at least Lawson's version of it, as spelled out in *Reorienting Economics* – deserves a great deal of credit for challenging mainstream economics and recognizing the value of heterodox economics, all in the name of "reality." In this, Lawson has established the ground for a new set of conversations in and about economics. He asks those of us who labor in the discipline of economics to become self-conscious about the conceptual schemes and methods we use when we take on the task of analyzing one or another aspect of reality and how those methods are inextricably related to issues of ontology, to how we understand the nature of being. Of particular significance to me, since I have never been much convinced by the ontological schemes presumed within mainstream (neoclassical and Keynesian) economics, Lawson's critical realism asks those of us who do heterodox economics to discuss and debate the general role that reality plays in our work and the particular conceptions of reality with which we conduct our work. How do we conceive of social reality and the relations between the various parts of that reality? What are the notions of subjectivity and identity we deploy in our analyses? What is the relationship between economic discourse and social reality? Instead of ignoring such questions, critical realism places them front and center, and in this has enlivened the conversations within and among the schools of thought that today make up heterodox economics.

I also want to argue that the specific conception of reality put forward by Lawson forecloses another set of conversations. In arguing that economic (and, more generally, social) analysis requires a specific ontology – an independent reality characterized by relations of depth between actual events, practices, and behaviors and underlying rules, codes, and structures, and much more – critical realism precludes a productive engagement with the constitutive effects of different economic discourses. It also leaves unexamined the existence of other – particularly, Marxian and postmodern – ontologies that have been developed and proven to be quite useful in recent years.

## Economic and social reality

While in much of this chapter I adopt a critical stance toward *Reorienting Economics*, I want to leave no doubt that I am quite sympathetic to a great deal of Lawson's work, and to critical realism more generally. And that's the case not only on strictly theoretical issues. In my view, credit should also be given to Lawson for the ways he has opened his Routledge book series to perspectives other than those of critical realism and the extent to which he has demonstrated, in contrast to many other economic methodologists these days, an interest in and a clear partisanship in favor of nonmainstream – feminist, Post Keynesian, institutionalist, and other – approaches to economic analysis.[1]

My interest in and support for Lawson's version of critical realism runs through a number of other themes and issues. For example, the extent to which the "ontological turn" brings discussions of social reality back into economics can only have a salutary effect. This is especially true since Lawson (as other critical realists) avoids the kind of naïve empiricism that still pervades much economic analysis, both mainstream and heterodox. (Generally but not always, an issue to which I return below.) The complexity and "messiness" of reality remind all of us that the theories we develop always leave something out; there is always a "remainder," which cannot simply be dismissed as unimportant or extraneous to our analyses of history and society. The "fullness" of material reality thus makes us suspicious of any attempt to derive a single order, whether a Subject or an Origin, that can be said to govern or give rise to – that can account for every dimension of – what we have before us. Invoking reality in this way allows us to raise questions about, and to pose alternatives to, both the theoretical models and policy prescriptions of our mainstream counterparts.[2]

There is another sense in which putting reality up front aids us in confronting mainstream economics and elaborating our own approaches to economic analysis and policy. If our conception of social reality is such that the economy is "open" with respect to other social spheres and practices – such that, for example, economic events and practices are affected by and spill over into culture, politics, and so on, and no strict lines can be drawn between these areas – then the kinds of theories and policies advocated by many mainstream economics, which presume a more or less isolated economy, can be challenged. Two particular examples might help to illustrate this point. Microeconomic analyses of decision making often presume that individuals will make rational decisions, unaffected by the "real" values (such as fairness and justice) or knowledges (including whether or not a decision is warranted or even possible) such agents hold. Similarly, if for a particular country a mainstream economist conducts a macroeconomic analysis, which uncovers an imbalance for which they propose a currency devaluation (or some such measure) as the solution, "reality" tells us that those with little or no power (women, workers, the unemployed, and so on) may be and often are adversely affected by such a policy. In such cases, reality can be used to complicate, undermine, and/or transform the usual pronouncements of mainstream economists.[3]

But, of course, Lawson claims more than that reality be brought to the forefront, that we confront head-on the twin challenges of making sense of and intervening to change contemporary social reality. He argues that the protocols of science require that reality be conceived in a particular fashion. In this arena, too, I find much to commend in his approach. A "social world structured by social rules or codes" that is "continuously reproduced or transformed"; social practices that are both "highly, and *systematically*, segmented or differentiated" and "constitutively other-oriented"; social reality as a "process" of becoming; social agents that have consciousness who, at the same time, are often engaged in "human doings that are carried out without being premeditated or reflected upon" – these and other attributes of the ontology elaborated by Lawson (in *Economics and Reality* as well as in *Reorienting Economics*) are exactly the kinds of things I emphasize in my research and teaching (both inside and outside the university), in contrast to many of the ways reality is depicted in and enforced by mainstream economics.

## Reality and science

If Lawson stopped there, then I would have not have cause to criticize his approach (except, perhaps, for quibbles around the edges). But then his discussion of ontology wouldn't carry the force of critical realism: because Lawson both wants to accord a particular status to this ontology and, following on that, to attribute to it a structure of "depth" or verticality. I (and I presume others) find both of these arguments problematic.

Lawson contends that ontology is important because science demands it – and the particular ontology he describes is said both to rule out the

formalist protocols of mainstream economics and to accord with his preferred "contrastive explanation" approach to economic and social
science. Once again, I find myself sympathetic with the questioning
(particularly of the fetishism of formal, including mathematical, models)
but not with the answer.[4] For the approach Lawson adopts is to develop
a particular definition of the goals and methods of science – to identify
"event regularities," to form causal hypotheses to explain such regularities, and to choose between competing hypotheses – and then to indicate
what reality must look like in order to follow the protocols of such a conception of science.

The result is that, instead of putting reality at the forefront, it is
science – and a specific understanding of science – that governs everything else. The ontological turn is, in the way I read it, actually a turn to
science. The emphasis on reality is further undermined by Lawson's frequent references to a kind of common sense as the warrant for his assertions about reality. *Reorienting Economics* (2003) is replete with such
phrases as "we all act on it" (p. 33), "highly generalized feature of
experience" (p. 38), "we all, it seems have" (p. 46), and "generalized fact
of experience" (pp. 51 and 85). Here, in an approach eerily reminiscent of
empiricism, the requirements of science (reality must be structured in a
specific way for science to work) are shunted aside in favor of the shared
observations of the scientists (who are presumed to agree that reality
looks such and such a way).[5]

My point is not to argue that Lawson is being inconsistent, either in
moving from reality to science or from the protocols of science to com-
monsensical empirical observations. But I do want to point out that
Lawson's moves are not the only ones available to us. For example, if we
want to place reality at the center of our work, then why must the protocols of science dictate the rules reality must follow? Why should reality
behave in a manner that fits a so-called scientific method? If reality looks
different – if it doesn't seem to match the particular model or concepts
we are using, if there is something left over or unaccounted for – then
why not change the science?

In the end, that's precisely the argument Lawson uses to rule out
mainstream economics and to embrace heterodox economics: the former
can't account for reality (at least as Lawson understands it) while the
latter can. Moreover, Lawson considers the different schools of thought
that make up heterodox economics to be merely different perspectives
on – different questions about, different ways of making sense of – a
common reality. But the only way this approach can work is if social
reality itself is taken to be both independent and singular: independent
of the way we think about it, and common to all forms of economic and
social analysis.

## Marxism and postmodernism

There are many alternatives to the way Lawson poses the problem of ontology. The two I have in mind, both of which question the independence and singularity of reality, are associated with Marxism and postmodernism (neither of which receives but brief mention in *Reorienting Economics*).

If Lawson's approach hinges on the idea that social reality is independent of the process of theorizing, the Marxian tradition emphasizes the dialectical, interdependent nature of that relationship. Without entering into unnecessary detail, what this means is, on the one hand, theory and social reality are seen to be mutually constitutive and, on the other hand, the conception of reality produced by the process of theorizing is considered to be distinct from reality itself. The mutual constitutivity of theory and reality is a way of focusing attention on the role that each plays in determining the other: changes in society lead to changes in theory, and vice versa. Thus, for example, social reality contains the conditions of existence of economics (both the discipline as well as individual schools of thought) and, in turn, the process of economic theorizing affects – constitutes, reproduces, changes – the society within which such theorizing takes place. This is not to say there is a simple, one-to-one correspondence between the two (as is often presumed in deterministic renditions of Marxism, according to which the emergence of capitalism leads to the birth of economics, or different stages of capitalism give rise to different economic theories). But it does place emphasis, in a way that Lawson does not, on how changes in one lead to changes in the other, in a never-ending pattern of interdependent influence and transformation.[6]

The contrast does not end there. Marxists also make a distinction between the thought-concrete and the concrete-real, between the conception of social reality produced in and by the process of theorizing and the social reality within which that process takes place.[7] The two are not the same. From a Marxian perspective, what social scientists (including economists) do is produce a conception of social reality in thought, and these thoughts are not to be conflated with the reality that exists outside of thought; they are literally the appropriations *within thought* of an external social reality. Thus, in a classical Marxian formulation, the "movement from the abstract to the concrete" is a process that takes place entirely within thought – the goal of which is to produce a more concrete analysis of society (or of some part thereof) than what one began with. It is more concrete in the sense that it includes more determinations; it takes into account more factors that are constitutive (and, of course, constituted by) the concepts under analysis. It makes no sense, then, to imagine or to specify a relationship of approximation or correspondence between the product of theorizing and the social reality that exists "out there," outside theory.

The postmodern way of handling this problem is to refer to the discursive construction of social reality.[8] Again, proceding at a relatively general level, postmodernism emphasizes both the way different social discourses produce different social realities and the idea that social reality itself comprises social agents and entities that use different discourses to construct the reality in which they exist. Thus, there are two, different but related, senses in which the economy can be said to be discursively constructed. First, different economic theories – mainstream and heterodox, from neoclassical to Marxian – produce different conceptions of economic and social reality. Economists literally see and analyze different economies, according to the discourses (or paradigms or theoretical frameworks) they use. And such "economic realities" may be and often are radically different and incommensurable, produced and elaborated according to different concepts and conceptual strategies. Thus, to choose but one example, neoclassical economists perceive an economic reality characterized by rational choices, factor payments, and equilibrium whereas Marxian economists see commodity fetishism, exploitation, and contradiction. And, from a postmodern perspective, there is no transdiscursive or nondiscursive standard whereby such different realities can be validated or adjudicated (although, of course, such judgments often do take place *within* particular discourses, leading to quite different conclusions).

The second sense in which postmodernists view the economy as being discursively constructed pertains to economic events and practices themselves. The idea here is that economic and social discourses – not just academic or scientific discourses but also "everyday" discourses, about the economy and much else – affect the way economic agents behave, institutions operate, and events occur. And, again, different discourses will have different effects on such behaviors, institutions, and events. The discourses I have in mind run the gamut from ways of making sense of desire and labor (particularly with respect to economic agents) through accounting conventions and notions of relevant stakeholders (in the case of economic entities such as corporations and international trade organizations) to the pronouncements of monetary authorities and corporate officials (which affect the movements of interest rates and prices of equity shares). The point is that the economy – specific parts or sectors as well as the economy as a whole – will be affected by which discourses are present, and it is important to analyze such discourses in order to understand economic reality.

Put the two together – call it postmodern Marxism – and ontology acquires a status quite different from the one outlined by Lawson. While a clear distinction is made between social reality and the discourses about that reality, that's just the beginning of the story. It then becomes important to recognize the complex ways social reality has an impact on social (including economic) discourses, on how those discourses affect social reality, and on how social reality itself is constituted by both academic and nonacademic discourses. What this means is not only are discourses about the economy influenced in important ways by the practices and discourses in the wider society; it also means that economic discourses are "performative," in the sense that economic agents and institutions are constituted – brought into being, reproduced, and changed – in and through the ideas produced within economics. Thus, for example, the "language of class" that characterizes Marxian economics serves both to highlight class processes and to offer a range of class identities and positions that can be inhabited by social agents.

## Critical ontologies

Not only do Marxism and postmodernism, alone and together, call into question the independence of theory and reality. They also offer ontologies that are quite different from the one Lawson articulates and expounds as the singular reality appropriate for economic science.

The ontologies associated with the Marxian and postmodern methodologies discussed in the previous part of the chapter are not based on the scheme of verticality or depth that characterizes Lawson's approach. For Lawson, all social systems are composed of "surface actualities" (actual events and states of affairs) and "underlying causes" (such as deeper structures, powers, mechanisms, and so on) – and the point of economic and social analysis is to show how the "deep" causes account for or explain the "surface" events. But what if reality is taken to be a surface, which comprises a wide variety of social agents, processes, and practices, wherein there is no relation of depth or verticality? Does such a horizontal array of elements make economic and social analysis impossible? The Marxian tradition has offered up one way of making sense of such a social reality: overdetermination.[9] Originally borrowed from Freud's interpretation of dreams, the concept of overdetermination is a way of producing an ontology wherein relations of depth (such as those between essence and appearance or base and superstructure) are discarded in favor of mutual relations of constitution and contradiction. Each problem or event that is under analysis is then seen as being constituted by myriad other aspects of social reality – to be the condensed effect of those other aspects or dimensions – no one of which is accorded causal priority over, or more ontological significance than, any other. It is the totality of such effects – the conditions of existence, in this language – that accounts for the contradictory constitution of any particular social actuality. Nothing behind, nothing underneath; no levels of ontological priority or causation. Just the constant movement and change that are occasioned by the overdetermined contradictions, the uneven pushes and pulls, that define each object.

What then of the rules of conduct, power, mechanisms, and so on that Lawson attributes to a deeper or transcendental level of reality? From a

Marxian perspective, they are present within the effects of the various processes and practices that make up social reality. Even stronger: they are nothing but the presence of those effects. Thus, for example, the rules of exploitation are contained within the practices whereby surplus labor is appropriated from the direct producers, practices that are themselves the overdetermined result of the other aspects of the social totality – economic, political, and cultural – within which that exploitation takes place. And it is that contradictory social reality that gives rise to practices of exploitation as they exist as well as to the emergence of other, non-exploitative class practices. It is in this sense that the flat, horizontal, surface ontology of Marxism provides the basis for a critical analysis of reality, including a project of emancipation.

Postmodernism also suggests alternatives to the vertically oriented ontologies of economic modernism.[10] Indeed, much postmodern critique has taken the form of a refusal or subversion of the idea that there are essences to be discovered and that appearances are to be probed for the truths hidden beneath the surface. Skeptical of all forms of determinism – whether of necessary cause-and-effect relations or, less strongly, probabilistic patterns that link particular events as causes with other events as effects – postmodernists are inclined toward ontologies characterized by "depthlessness," and emphasize the randomness of causation and effectivity of chance, the indeterminacy of events, the multiplicity of possible causes, the fluidity of the relationship between seeming causes and their effects, and the reversibility of positions between putative causes and effects. In the particular area of economics, postmodernists are critical of both the main forms of essentialism: theoretical humanism (according to which social reality can be reduced to and explained in terms of some underlying characteristics of human beings) and structuralism (in which underlying structures can account for and be used to explain social events). The alternative is a surface comprising heterogeneous elements – events, actualities, behaviors, flows, connections, and so on – that can be analyzed with alternative notions of causality – juxtaposition, simultaneity, textuality, decentering, and so forth. Based on its refusal of ontological hierarchy in favor of flatness, the goal of postmodern analysis is thus to read the "text" of social reality, to produce a "commentary" on the practices and subjectivities that define that reality.

Again, the conjunction of Marxism and postmodernism has produced alternatives both to mainstream economics and to critical realism – in this case, new ontologies and forms of social analysis. "Postmodern materialism" is one such example.[11] Originally inspired by Althusser's notion of the "aleatory," postmodern materialism was formulated in order to move beyond the systemic treatments associated with traditional Marxism the homogeneity and fixedness of social reality and the certainty of historical trajectory – and to bring to the fore the more antisystemic elements of the Marxian tradition – the heterogeneity and openness of social reality, the incompleteness of the bourgeois project, and the imagining of alternative economic and social realities. On this interpretation, many aspects of Marxian economic and social theory take on a new cast. The specificity of Marx's concept of value, to consider but one instance, instead of being an expression of an underlying "law" of the division of labor (which presumes an already constituted homogeneity of social subjects, of *homo faber*), is now seen to be a way of focusing on the cultural and political mechanisms whereby diverse communities are stripped of their identities and needs in order to be molded into the subjects of a single economic calculus. Thus, the "economy" would emerge not as a primitive foundation, an independent and singular underlying reality, but as the forced attempt to create a closed space whose principle of existence is based on a negation of social specificity, heterogeneity, and openness.

Similarly, "poststructuralist political economy" is an attempt to rescue the Marxian theory of class from the primacy of the "capitalist totality" – the capitalist system or mode of production, the global capitalist political economy, and so on – itself seen as the expression of an underlying cause (such as the "law of accumulation").[12] A poststructuralist approach suggests a reading of *Capital* that emphasizes class as the discursive entry point of political economy instead of being taken as a given of the social order. Once relinquished from the limitations imposed by a unified, centered ontology, an "accounting for class" suggests both a diverse and differentiated economic landscape – comprising both capitalist and noncapitalist practices and identities – and a field of theory and politics that is open and experimental. In other words, the ontology associated with poststructuralist political economy is characterized not by closure and certainty but by challenges and possibilities. It also clears the way for an active political role for theory in creating the terms in which the identities of subjects are constituted and through which they can create their futures. The result is to defamiliarize existing notions of social reality, to make that reality different from itself.

## Critical thought and realism

My aim in this brief chapter is not to elaborate or defend alternatives to critical realism in any detail. I merely want to indicate that alternatives to the ontology proposed by Tony Lawson, in *Reorienting Economics* and elsewhere, have been developed within heterodox economics, including Marxism and postmodernism. These alternative ontologies have led to projects of economic and social analysis that are not only critical of mainstream economics but quite productive in their own right.

And I certainly don't want to argue that the alternative conceptions of ontology I have mentioned are any more "real" than the one that can be found in Lawson's work. While I share with Lawson the idea that ontology is important, both for the critique of mainstream economics and for the flourishing of heterodox economics, I admit to being skeptical about the project of finding or producing a single ontology that will serve as the shared foundation of the various schools of thought that have come together in the post-autistic economics movement. In my view, we need to do everything within our grasp to keep critical approaches to economics alive by making reality as unreal as possible.

## Acknowledgment

I want to express my appreciation to Edward Fullbrook not only for the invitation to participate in this symposium (and his graciousness and patience in waiting for my contribution) but also for all the work he has done to keep the post-autistic economics movement alive. I also want to thank Antonio Callari for his comments on a previous draft.

## Notes

1 Disclosure: a volume I co-edited with Stephen Cullenberg and Jack Amariglio, *Postmodernism, Economics, and Knowledge* (2001), as well as another to which I contributed (Garnett 1999) were published, with Lawson's encouragement, in the Economics as Social Theory series.
2 I take this to be one of the main points raised by the students who initiated the post-autistic movement, in France, England, and the United States. See the statements and manifestos reprinted in Fullbrook (2003).
3 In the United States right now, there is a particular poignancy to siding with "reality-based" arguments against so-called "faith-based" ones. This is the case as much in the discipline of economics as in the wider society.
4 See, e.g., my critique of the use of mathematical models in Marxian economics (Ruccio 1988; Ruccio and Amariglio 2003, especially chapter 1).
5 Antonio Gramsci (1991) argued that common sense contains a "specific conception of the world" and that "in acquiring one's conception of the world one always belongs to a particular grouping which is that of all the social elements which share the same mode of thinking and acting" (324). Clifford Geertz (1983), for his part, reminds us that such common sense, a set of presumably shared observations about reality, "is not what the mind cleared of cant spontaneously apprehends" but rather "what the mind filled with [historical and cultural presuppositions] ... concludes" (84). It is, in other words, a historically and culturally specific knowledge – in this case, a local ontology.
6 To be clear, the Marxian tradition admits of many different interpretations. The one I develop here is often referred to as antiessentialist Marxism, associated with the journal *Rethinking Marxism* and the work of Stephen Resnick and Richard Wolff (1987).
7 The difference between the "concrete-in-thought" and the "concrete-real" was made prominent by Louis Althusser (1970, 1977) as a way of distinguishing the method of the "mature Marx" from that of Ludwig Feuerbach.
8 The postmodern approach briefly summarized in the text is developed at some length by Ruccio and Amariglio (2003). It is also more or less synony-

mous with poststructuralism (Amariglio 1998) and deconstruction (Ruccio 1998). See also the different interpretations of postmodernism with respect to economics in Cullenberg *et al.* (2001).

9  See, e.g., the pioneering contribution of Resnick and Wolff (1987).

10 Within social theory, postmodern ontologies have been developed perhaps most prominently within feminism, especially with respect to the gendered body. See, e.g., the work of Judith Butler (1990, 1993), Jane Flax (1990, 1993), and Elizabeth Grosz (1994). Gillian Hewitson (1999) and Suzanne Bergeron (2004), among others, have developed similar arguments with respect to economic discourse.

11 The concept of postmodern materialism and its effects on social analysis are elaborated by Ruccio and Callari (1996).

12 This view is developed at length in the essay by Gibson-Graham *et al.* (2001). On the theoretical and political problems created by an ontology defined solely in terms of capitalism – what one might refer to as capitalocentrism – see Gibson-Graham (1996) and Ruccio and Gibson-Graham (2001).

# References

Althusser, L. 1970. *Reading Capital.* Trans. B. Brewster. London: New Left Books.

——. 1977. *For Marx.* Trans. B. Brewster. London: New Left Books.

Amariglio, J. 1998. "Poststructuralism." In *The Handbook of Economic Methodology,* eds. J.B. Davis, D.W. Hands, and U. Mäki, 382–88. Cheltenham: Edward Elgar.

Bergeron, S. 2004. *Fragments of Development: Nation, Gender, and the Space of Modernity.* Ann Arbor, MI: University of Michigan Press.

Butler, J. 1990. *Gender Trouble: Feminism and the Subversion of Identity.* New York: Routledge.

Butler, J. 1993. *Bodies that Matter: On the Discursive Limit of Sex.* New York: Routledge.

Cullenberg, S., J. Amariglio, and D.F. Ruccio, eds. 2001. *Postmodernism, Economics, and Knowledge.* New York: Routledge.

Flax, J. 1990. *Thinking Fragments: Psychoanalysis, Feminism and Postmodernism in the Contemporary West.* Berkeley, CA: University of California Press.

——. 1993. *Disputed Subjects: Essays on Psychoanalysis, Politics and Philosophy.* New York: Routledge.

Fullbrook, E., ed. 2003. *The Crisis in Economics: The Post-Autistic Economics Movement.* New York: Routledge.

Garnett, R., Jr., ed. 1999. *What Do Economists Know? New Economics of Knowledge.* New York: Routledge.

Geertz, C. 1983. "Common Sense as a Cultural System." In *Local Knowledge: Further Essays in Interpretive Anthropology,* ed. C. Geertz, 73–93. New York: Basic Books.

Gibson-Graham, J.K. 1996. *The End of Capitalism (As We Knew It): A Feminist Critique of Political Economy.* Cambridge, MA: Blackwell.

Gibson-Graham, J.K., S. Resnick, and R. Wolff. 2001. "Toward a Poststructuralist Political Economy." In *Re/presenting Class: Essays in Postmodern Marxism,* eds. J.K. Gibson-Graham, S. Resnick, and R. Wolff, 1–22. Durham, NC: Duke University Press.

Gramsci, A. 1991. *Selections from the Prison Notebooks.* Eds. and trans. Q. Hoare and G.N. Smith. London: Lawrence & Wishart.

Grosz, E. 1994. *Volatile Bodies, Toward a Corporeal Feminism*. Bloomington, IN: University of Indiana Press.

Hewitson, G. 1999. *Feminist Economics, Interrogating the Masculinity of Rational Economic Man*. Aldershot: Edward Elgar.

Lawson, Tony, 1997. *Economics and Reality*. London and New York: Routledge.

——. 2003. *Reorienting Economics*. London and New York: Routledge.

Resnick, S.A. and R.D. Wolff. 1987. *Knowledge and Class: A Marxian Critique of Political Economy*. Chicago, IL: University of Chicago Press.

Ruccio, D.F. 1988. "The Merchant of Venice, or Marxism in the Mathematical Mode." *Rethinking Marxism* 1 (Winter): 18–46.

——. 1998. "Deconstruction." In *The Handbook of Economic Methodology*, eds. J.B. Davis, D.W. Hands, and U. Mäki, 89–93. Cheltenham: Edward Elgar.

Ruccio, D.F. and J. Amariglio. 2003. *Postmodern Moments in Modern Economics*. Princeton, NJ: Princeton University Press.

Ruccio, D.F. and A. Callari, eds. 1996. "Introduction: Postmodern Materialism and the Future of Marxist Theory." In *Postmodern Materialism and the Future of Marxist Theory Essays in the Althusserian Tradition*, eds. A. Callari and D.F. Ruccio, 1–48. Middletown, CT: Wesleyan University Press.

Ruccio, D.F. and J.K. Gibson-Graham. 2001. "'After' Development: Reimagining Economy and Class." In *Re/presenting Class: Essays in Postmodern Political Economy*, eds. J.K. Gibson-Graham, S. Resnick, and R. Wolff, 158–81. Durham, NC: Duke University Press.

# 16 Ontology and postmodernism
## Reply to Ruccio

*Tony Lawson*

It is a pleasure to converse with David Ruccio once more. A few years ago, I was fortunate to be invited to the US as the first holder of the Global Scholars Award. At the end of a week of lectures, I gave a final talk for which the two respondents were Robert Heilbronner and Ruccio himself. Following that interchange, Ruccio and I agreed to keep the debate going in the pages of *Rethinking Marxism* (which Ruccio now edits). Somehow, that plan did not work out, so I welcome this belated opportunity provided by the current forum to further our discussion.

In the first part of his commentary, Ruccio provides a summary of aspects of my position. I find his assessment to be not only accurate, but in many ways significantly more so than some interpretations provided by commentators who (unlike Ruccio) profess to adopting a (realist) philosophical position that is similar to my own on a wide range of issues.

I concentrate here, as usual, on areas of apparent disagreement. Although Ruccio highlights issues on which my contributions and Ruccio's alternatives seem to take quite fundamentally opposed stances, I believe the differences, in the end, are not as extensive as Ruccio suggests. I address the various concerns in the order that Ruccio introduces them. I will suggest that real disagreement between us increases as we advance down the list of topics, with those considered first, revealing hardly any differences at all.

Where there is a significant parting of the ways, I will give reasons for preferring my own conception over the alternatives brought to my attention by Ruccio. Ruccio mostly only *identifies* differences between us; he does not argue that the alternatives he considers are superior. But then I am not sure his position ultimately allows a relative evaluation; in any case, it seems sufficient for Ruccio merely to suggest alternatives. I believe, in contrast, that we can often, and typically should, go somewhat further.

## Ontology and the protocols of science

According to Ruccio my procedure is first of all to adopt a conception of the goals and methods or protocols of science, and then, second, to question what these objectives or methods presuppose about the nature of reality. Quite reasonably, Ruccio concludes that such an approach represents more of a turn to the asserted protocols of science (and its presuppositions) than to ontology per se. He thus asks why, if we are interested in ontology, should the protocols of science determine the way reality is or the way we conceptualise it.

My response is that I do not at all suggest that the protocols of science play the role suggested. This all relates to an important part of my argument. So, let me try and clarify my position on this.

In my efforts to do ontology, I certainly do not start by adopting a conception of the goals and methods or protocols of science. Rather if there is a first step it is to acknowledge my acceptance of (a stance that in *Reorienting Economics* I designate) the *intelligibility principle*. This is simply that reality is intelligible, and specifically that if something happened, there are conditions in virtue of which it was possible. Identifying the conditions of possibility of reasonably generalised phenomena is a part of the method I have adopted for doing ontology.

So, to repeat, the analytical starting point is the identification of certain actualised features of reality, typically those widely acknowledged as being highly generalised, and the goal is to identify their conditions of possibility.

I nowhere interpret these generalised features as matters of common sense as Ruccio at one point suggests. All claims of generalised features are obviously interpreted, often contested and always fallible. The aim is to choose those that seem as little contested as possible, and, where feasible, accepted not only by myself but also by opponents whose position I may be seeking to question.

These entry points do not have to be about science. They can be about everyday activities such as cooking or about playing games or travelling or whatever. The "starting points" I have employed (see *Reorienting Economics*, Chapter 2) are of the following sort: that we all follow numerous routines; that different groups systematically follow different routines; that many of the latter are other oriented, and so forth (interestingly Ruccio indicates his endorsement with many of these in his chapter). Or where science is indeed the focus, we can start from their agreed successes, their failures or any aspect we choose.

Where I have started from a conception of features relating to science, my entry point has *not* at all been any accepted protocols of science per se. Rather noting that my opponents accept that science seeks to elaborate event regularities, and noting (the generalised feature of experience) that such event regularities mostly occur under very specific conditions, namely those of experimental control, I have pursued the question as to why these regularities are restricted to such contexts.

So, my entry point is not the methods or goals of science, but the observation that event regularities are mostly restricted to experimental contexts. By seeking to account for the fact that event regularities occur in these conditions and not (many) others, it is possible to come up with a conception of the way the world is, as opposed to an account of the presuppositions of certain scientists. It is thus an exercise in ontology.

Of course, the question arises as to why, if it is not necessary, I bother so often to look at the conditions of scientific successes (or failures) at all. The answer is simply that it is strategic to do so. Unlike deductivists and perhaps some postmodernists, I hold that science is more about uncovering causal mechanisms than identifying event regularities. Opponents of this view, though, stress the necessity of uncovering event regularities, and in doing so frequently point to the experimental situation as exemplary of the scientific process of uncovering such regularities. For it is in the experimental laboratory, almost all are agreed, that most event regularities of interest to science are to be found.

As I say, we can seek to explain relative confinement of event regularities to these experimental conditions. And the only compelling explanation of which I am aware is that the experimental laboratory allows intrinsically stable causal mechanisms to be insulated from countervailing mechanisms and thereby empirically identified. The event regularity that is experimentally produced correlates the triggering of a mechanism of interest with its unimpeded effects.

The point, then, is that even experimental work is found to be concerned to identify causal mechanisms rather than seeking out event regularities per se. In other words, even in the conditions most favourable to certain of my opponents, it is shown that causal analysis is primary.

In any case, my response to Ruccio is hopefully apparent. If we were to begin the analysis with methods or goals or protocols, then we would, as Ruccio suggests, learn not about the features of reality being studied but about the scientists' presuppositions concerning the nature of that reality. We would indeed be prioritising science. If instead, though, we start from features of reality found to be highly generalised (for example, human practices are often highly routinised, segmented and other-oriented; event regularities are mostly confined to situations of experimental control), we can hope to uncover those further aspects of reality that constitute the conditions of possibility of these features. This has been an element of my approach. It constitutes a turn not to science (and its presuppositions), but to (philosophical) ontology.

## Theory and reality

Ruccio next raises two issues that he treats as related, issues that he rightly recognises as being fundamental to any conception of social ontology sustained. The first is the matter of whether reality is one/singular or many. The second is the nature of the relationship between theorising and the object of theorising (i.e. with what it is that theorising is intended to be about).

According to Ruccio's assessment, I necessarily assume a social reality that is, first, unique or singular and, second, independent of the way we think about it. This assessment seems to be inferred from my arguing that the various heterodox traditions are best viewed as divisions of labour in one overall project, and my subsequently emphasising advantages of programmes of linked or co-development between the various heterodox traditions. In any case, Ruccio writes:

> Lawson considers the different schools of thought that make up heterodox economics to be merely different perspectives on – different questions about, different ways of making sense of – a common reality. But the only way this approach can work is if social reality itself is taken to be both independent and singular: independent of the way we think about it, and common to all forms of economic and social analysis.

In fact, Ruccio situates Marxism and postmodernism as united in their opposition to the position he associates with me: "There are many alternatives to the way Lawson poses the problem of ontology. The two I have in mind, both of which question the independence and singularity of reality, are associated with Marxism and postmodernism." Let me state very clearly that although I do indeed assume a singular or common reality, albeit, of course, one that is highly differentiated and constantly evolving, my position on the relation between theory and its object of study is a little more complicated than the version with which I am credited by Ruccio. But these are important issues. So let me go into some detail on what I do believe and why, starting with the relation of social theory, to what it is about.

## The relation between theory and the objects of study

I have consistently taken the social realm to be that domain of phenomena whose existence depends in part on us. Thus, it depends on our practices. The latter in turn are affected by our understandings and motivations (conscious and unconscious). So, by theorising the nature of aspects of social reality we may come to transform our practices, and often those of lay agents appropriating the insights of social theorising, developments which in turn may eventually, and do often, impact on those aspects of social reality we have been theorising. So, theory can affect what it is about (see e.g. Lawson, 1997, p. 197).[1] Because we ourselves, our embodied personalities, as well as all forms of social structure, are reproduced and transformed, moulded or shaped through practice, then clearly theory or discourse (whether correct or otherwise), by affecting our practices, tends to have a profound impact also on society at large.

Equally, the object of analysis lays the conditions for its analysis (this is part of the argument for ontology) and so affects how it can be known. Thus, the features of reality make a difference to, that is, causally affect, how we come to know it.

As Ruccio rightly points out, there can be no question of correspondence between theory and what it is about (see e.g. Lawson, 1997, pp. 58–9).[2] Theory and its object are typically very different types of thing. But they do, to repeat, causally impact on each other; they are anything but independent. So on all this Ruccio and I actually agree.

Does any of this undermine my argument that heterodox economists are effectively involved in the same overall project, one that can likely benefit from further linked or co-development? Not as far as I can see. This would follow only if the recognition that social theory and its object are causally interdependent is thought somehow to undermine the possibility of successful social theorising; if it is thought that the processual, ever changing, nature of social reality and our making a difference to it through our research undermines our possibility of coming to know it.

Perhaps this is Ruccio's view. But in any case, I believe it is not correct. The significant issue here is that everything takes place sequentially, in time. At the precise moment we come to study an aspect of contemporary social reality, it exists in a particular form. As such, it constitutes a proper object of study. The fact that our study may (eventually) lead to it being transformed is a different issue, something that may (or may not) happen in the future.

We may want an extended study of a relevant feature of reality at a particular moment that is now past. But this need not be a problem. After all, palaeontologists successfully study the developing history of life on earth, of ancient plants and animals based on the fossil record, evidence of their existence being preserved in rocks. The fact that the objects of study are no longer with us does not prevent their being studied.

If we want to study social reality as an ongoing contemporary process then we have to accept that we are part of our own field of study. Our theories and the theories of others feed into social reality in many ways. Lay agents interpret social reality, and we interpret lay agents interpreting social reality. This is the so-called double hermeneutic. Indeed there are often multiple-level hermeneutics going on, as, for example, X interprets Y interpreting Z interpreting A, etc.

In fact, at this very moment I am interpreting Ruccio interpreting me interpreting the nature of social reality in abstract form. But as this last example demonstrates, time matters. I first wrote *Reorienting Economics*, then Ruccio reviewed it, then (now) I am responding to Ruccio's review (if anyone is reading these lines they are taking the process one step further, and so on).

Ruccio and I may well be affecting each other's thought processes, and practices, and in turn other features of reality. But it does not all happen simultaneously. So, in short, although the study of a feature of reality can lead to the transformation of that feature, this realisation itself does not in itself prevent that object serving as an object of study. So, as I say, on these issues at least it seems that Ruccio and I largely agree, though without, I believe, my assessment of the possibility of heterodox cooperation being compromised.

## Reality as one or many

If the interdependence of theory and those features of reality being studied does not undermine my assessment of the possibilities for heterodox cooperation, it is likely that the latter would be undermined by the existence of multiple realities, with different groups confined to different domains. It is my view, though, that there is only one (albeit differentiated and ever-changing) reality. Here, at face value, Ruccio and I seem to have a genuine point of disagreement. So why do I maintain my conception over Ruccio's?

Actually, on examining Ruccio's argument I cannot help but conclude that the difference between us here is mainly one of terminology. Even so, this does not prevent Ruccio drawing different conclusions for my own, or anyway from interpreting himself as saying something quite different. So terminology matters. But I do believe that in this case Ruccio's terminology serves mostly to mislead. And it (mis)leads Ruccio himself to suppose that, in certain significant respects, the status of ontology in his postmodern Marxism is quite different from that of the conception I outline, whereas we shall find, I think, that this is not the case at all. Let me briefly elaborate.

Central to the issue before us is the way the term "reality" is used, and I suspect some increased consistency might be helpful. When discussing the Marxian tradition with which he associates himself, Ruccio writes:

> on the one hand, theory and social reality are seen to be mutually constitutive and, on the other hand, the conception of reality produced by the process of theorizing is considered to be distinct from reality itself. The mutual constitutivity of theory and reality is a way of focusing attention on the role that each plays in determining the other.

As this passage is formulated Ruccio does give the impression of supposing that our conceptions or theories are not part of reality. I reject this interpretation and I doubt this is Ruccio's intended meaning (it is certainly out of keeping with many post structuralist contentions, and nor is it consistent with Marx). But if Ruccio is suggesting that our conceptions or theories of certain aspects of reality are (mostly) distinct from, and do not stand in correspondence to, those aspects of reality that they are intended to be about, then I agree entirely; in this case the passage is unexceptional.

I reproduce it, because the terminology employed seems at variance with Ruccio's formulations when he next turns to consider the post-modernist case for multiple realities. Here he writes:

> The postmodern way ... is to refer to the discursive construction of social reality. Again ... postmodernism emphasizes both the way different social discourses produce different social realities and the idea that social reality itself comprises social agents and entities that use different discourses to construct the reality in which they exist. Thus, there are two, different but related, senses in which the economy can be said to be discursively constructed. First, different economic theories – mainstream and heterodox, from neoclassical to Marxian – produce different conceptions of economic and social reality. Economists literally see and analyze different economies, according to the discourses (or paradigms or theoretical frameworks) they use. And such "economic realities" may be and often are radically different and incommensurable, produced and elaborated according to different concepts and conceptual strategies. Thus, to choose but one example, neoclassical economists perceive an economic reality characterized by rational choices, factor payments, and equilibrium whereas Marxian economists see commodity fetishism, exploitation, and contradiction. And, from a postmodern perspective, there is no transdiscursive or nondiscursive standard whereby such different realities can be validated or adjudicated (although, of course, such judgments often do take place *within* particular discourses, leading to quite different conclusions).

The most striking contrast between the two extracts is that whereas in the former one, theories are considered distinct from reality, in the second, reality and indeed realities are discursive constructions. In particular, "Economists literally see and analyze different economies, according to the discourses (or paradigms or theoretical frameworks) they use".

I believe this postmodernist way of putting things is somewhat misleading. Consider the following formulation (the second sentence of the preceding passage): "Again ... postmodernism emphasizes both the way different social discourses produce different social realities and the idea that social reality itself comprises social agents and entities that use different discourses to construct the reality in which they exist." In the first part of this sentence we have social discourses producing different social realities, but in the latter half we have a conception of a single social reality, a reference to "social reality itself", where the latter is said to comprise social agents and entities that use different discourses. Of course, right at the end we revert to the idea that discourses construct particular realities.

This switching between different (multiple) realities and a single reality is at best misleading, and I think unnecessarily so. All we need to acknowledge is that different social discourses produce different (even competing) conceptions or theories or understandings (of features of social reality) all of which may (and often do) impact upon and contribute to the (ongoing) transformation of (those and other features of) social reality. There is nothing here that requires, or benefits, from talk of multiple realities, and I believe there is a clear gain in consistency, coherence and clarity if we desist from so doing.

If we avoid Ruccio's preferred postmodernist terminology, we can indeed accept with Ruccio "that different economic theories – mainstream and heterodox, from neoclassical to Marxian – produce different conceptions of economic and social reality", but not equate this to the claim that "Economists literally see and analyze different economies, according to the discourses (or paradigms or theoretical frameworks) they use."

Each tradition, through its own discourse (or paradigm or theoretical framework), may affect those aspects of reality or economy that are being studied but economists do not literally see and analyse different economies. At least if different economies are being studied, they are differentiated by space–time location, they are not brought into being by the varying conceptions of economic traditions, even if the conceptions of the latter do (subsequently) impact back on what they are about. Different economists see and analyse different (their own) theories perhaps, but the competing theories can nevertheless be of a given set of features of our one reality, and to the extent that the varying conceptions are relevant at all, each will be about the one (ever changing processual) reality.

Furthermore, when Ruccio suggests that " 'economic realities' may be and often are radically different and incommensurable, produced and elaborated according to different concepts and conceptual strategies", I take it that the scare quotes are employed as an implicit acknowledgement that the entities thought to be incommensurable are theories and other cognitive structures rather than what it is that the theories are thought to be about.

Of course, Ruccio can choose to use these categories as he wishes. He can indeed refer to an economic discourse as a separate reality. But if consistency matters at all then all discourses should be so interpreted (as "separate realities") as should discourses about those discourses etc. I believe that it is less misleading to talk of one (ever changing) reality that encompasses both discourses as well as (but distinguished from) what they are or might be about, and as well as discourses on discourses. But even if Ruccio persists in his current practice, and sticks to it consistently, it is hopefully clear that our differences remain merely terminological. As far as I can see, we are not saying different things or defending different positions; we are (so far) merely saying the same things differently.

As a consequence I believe there is nothing in the matters so far considered that necessarily threaten my assessment that the heterodox groups of contemporary economics can reasonably be regarded as compatible divisions of labour in one overall project, with likely benefits resulting from linked or co-development. At least there is nothing problematic per se arising from the fact that Ruccio adopts the practice of talking of separate realities, whereas I talk of one reality and alternative conceptions or discourses. With this terminological difference out of the way, however, we can turn to the seemingly real problem that Ruccio, I suspect, is getting at, the possibility that the different conceptions or discourses might not be comparable.[3]

In other words, once, or if, we recognise that Ruccio and I are saying the same things, albeit in different ways, we can see that the difficulty to which Ruccio is pointing is *not* incompatible realities but incommensurable theories of the one (always differentiated and changing) reality. Ruccio really acknowledges as much himself when, in the last of his passages reproduced above, he not only puts *economic realities* in scare quotes, but suggests that these (conceptions or theories in my terminology) may be "incommensurable". This is because they are "produced and elaborated according to different concepts and conceptual strategies".

## Incommensurability

So, are the various conceptions or discourses of the different groups in modern economics incommensurable? I notice that unlike many others inclined to postmodernism, Ruccio does *not insist* that incommensurability of competing theories is inevitable; he merely points out that such is possible. However, Ruccio clearly thinks incommensurability is a frequent occurrence, and he suggests that this characterises the various theoretical conceptions of modern economics.

I am not convinced of this; so there may be a real difference between us here. I do agree with Ruccio's postmodernism that "there is no transdiscursive or nondiscursive standard whereby such different realities [I would say theories or conceptions] can be validated or adjudicated". But I think we can nevertheless often adjudicate *within* discourse.

As an example of incommensurate discourses, Ruccio notes that "neoclassical economists perceive an economic reality characterized by rational choices, factor payments, and equilibrium whereas Marxian economists see commodity fetishism, exploitation, and contradiction". Let me explore this a little.

Now, the way in which Ruccio frames his contention is that where different sets of categories are used throughout it is difficult to *validate* either one or *adjudicate* between them.

A first point to make is that the contrast between any two heterodox projects can be expected to be less stark (or more obviously commensurable) than between a heterodox tradition such as Marxism and the mainstream. For as I argue at length in *Reorienting Economics* and elsewhere (see e.g. Lawson, 2006 a, and my response to Davis in the current volume), not only do the heterodox groups implicitly accept a similar ontology to each other, one at odds with mainstream atomistic presuppositions, but a significant number of individuals seem to circulate around all (or many) of the separate heterodox meetings, and even publish in several of the separate heterodox outlets. Nor is it clear that each distinct heterodox group uses unique categories. So even if Marxian theory and mainstream or "neoclassical" theory were to prove to be incommensurable, Ruccio would need to do more work to establish that the different heterodox conceptions are equally so. Indeed, the evidence is not only that the heterodox groups can, but that they already do, interact and debate and (to a limited degree) engage in joint research. So I am not convinced that Ruccio really points to practical problems here.

But that said, I do not even think that the mainstream and Marxian economics are incomparable in the sense of our being able to evaluate the relative worth of their contributions. Let me briefly indicate why.

## Mainstream versus Marxian economics

The first thing to note is that Ruccio draws our attention to the conceptions or perceptions of two competing groups of economists. This is familiar. Those who emphasise incommensurability rarely make claims like Einsteinium theory and vegetables are incommensurate. The examples are always of things that most of us accept as being comparable at some level and warranting comparison where it is feasible. And this presupposes that commonalities or commensurable features are at some level already perceived by all concerned. This insight is important; for as long as there is some accepted commonality, I think it will very often turn out that relative evaluations of theories can be made after all.

Now Marxian theory and the mainstream project both at least strive to provide insight into social reality. Yes their categories are different, but each might first of all be judged in terms of its performance in terms of its own chosen criteria, whether they be explanatory, predictive or whatever.

It is plain to me that Marxian theory, on its own terms, is vastly superior to mainstream contributions, on their own terms. Indeed, the former, on its own terms, is very successful. It is explanatorily powerful in accounting for aspects of reality as it perceives them, and the theory progresses dialectically in line with its own conception of progress. Mainstream economics, in comparison, is in a state of intellectual disarray. It neither explains nor predicts satisfactorily (Ariel Rubinstein, 1995, p. 12); it is marked by theory/practice inconsistencies (Edward Leamer, 1978, p. vi; David Hendry *et al.*, 1990, pp. 178–9); and it flits though fads and fashions (Stephen Turnovsky, 1992, p. 143), sometimes dressing up the latter changes as a commitment to pluralism, desperately seeking outcomes that it can present as successes on its own terms. It is also full of anomalies that range over its various sub-programmes (Richard Lipsey, 2001, p. 173).[4]

The latter set of assessments, it can be seen, is clearly not (just) my own made from outside the mainstream; these are the conclusions of mainstream economists themselves, as I have often noted.[5] All in all, as I say, the mainstream project is in a state of intellectual confusion.

But perhaps an extreme incommensuralist may still argue that I am not making an appropriate comparative evaluation. Mainstream economists pride themselves on being scientists in the fashion of natural science. This explains their focus on mathematical-deductivist methods (and willingness often to tolerate claims recognised as unrealistic). In consequence the appropriate (internalist) criterion of mainstream achievement, it might be argued, is *not* whether mainstream economists have yet achieved empirical (explanatory or predictive) successes or some such, but whether they are succeeding in following proper scientific protocols. In other words, some defenders of the mainstream may suggest that the criteria implicit in the mainstream self-criticisms noted above and elsewhere are not the most important; what matters is that the protocols of (natural) science are followed.

But it is even possible to show that the mainstream fares poorly on this criterion as well. Applied mainstream economists everywhere seek out event regularities or correlations of the sort required for the employment of their mathematical-deductivist methods. For science, according to these "deductivists", advances through the accumulation of such event regularities. As I have already noted, these would-be natural scientists readily admit that most of the event regularities regarded as significant in natural science are largely restricted to conditions of experimental control. But without considering why this should be so, our mainstream (would be) naturalists optimistically go about seeking such regularities in all locations imaginable.

Now in the midst of all this is a commonality: we can, I suspect, all agree with these deductivists that the event regularities of significance to natural science are (to repeat one more time) mostly located in conditions of experimental control. We can, though, once more pose the question that these deductivists fail to pose: why are these event regularities systematically restricted to conditions of experimental control? And the answer, as we have already seen, is that under such conditions stable causal mechanisms can be insulated from countervailing causal forces, and thereby empirically identified. Event regularities, to repeat, precisely correlate the triggering of such mechanisms and their unimpeded effects (for a detailed argument and analysis see Lawson, 1997, chapters 1–5; 2003, chapter 1).

The point, of course, is that by focusing on premises accepted by mainstream opponents, it is possible to show that the latter group presuppose an account of science – the search for causal mechanisms – that is contrary to the account they give. In other words, the mainstream fails even by its own criterion of following the practices of natural science. For natural science is found to be only contingently concerned with correlating events (a practice mostly restricted to situations of experimental control, which anyway are mostly unavailable to social science) but fundamentally concerned with identifying causal forces.

As it happens, although Marxian economists do not strive especially to be like natural scientists, and focus more on dialectical advance (in which they are often successful), it is easy enough to show that the causalist account of natural science just defended, fits with the dialectical account of knowledge advance accepted in traditional Marxism.[6]

In short, Marxian analysis not only advances dialectically according to its own notion of progress, but is actually more consistent with science in the sense of natural science than is the mainstream project, whilst the latter bases its practices on a misconstruel of the latter.

## Newton versus Einstein again

Parenthetically, an argument of the sort I have just sketched (which is an example of determinate negation) is not the only means of making comparative evaluations in unpromising circumstances. Typically, incommensuralists pick on theories such as those of Newton and Einstein that seem to theorise more or less every category differently, *where it is held that no commonalities are apparent*. Of course there are commonalities at some level. For here, once more, of course, we are not comparing a theory with a vegetable or whatever. In making reference to Newtonian and Einsteinian theory, a good deal of commonality in the nature of the orientations at least of their respective projects is being presupposed.

But even if determinate negations seem unlikely, a noteworthy observation is that scientists do *not* hold back from making comparative evaluations. In terms of an account of the way the world is (as distinct from its practical use in everyday earthly affairs), Einstein's conception is everywhere held to be the better or truer account. Why? Because, in its own framework, on its own terms, it can account for all the things the Newtonian conception can explain (on its own Newtonian terms) *and more*. For example, Einsteinian theory accounts (on its own terms) for Mercury's perihelion and Newtonian theory does not. About ten test situations of this sort now reveal Einsteinian theory to be the most explanatorily superior.

Here, though, I no doubt stray too far from social analysis. The question that prompted all this is effectively whether the various heterodox traditions are able to cooperate in their research. I see nothing in the discussion or the prevailing situation to suppose otherwise. Yes different traditions draw on different frameworks from analyses (a common) social reality, but there is every reason to expect that there is enough common ground for dialectical advance to be possible. Indeed, we can see it happening in practice.

The differences between he and I that Ruccio emphasises seem mostly to stem from ambiguities in the use of terms like reality. As long as we maintain a distinction between our conceptions and those features of reality being studied, these sorts of unhelpful ambiguities need not arise. For sure, social reality is complex. Yes, it is being continuously transformed, in part through the multiplicity of conceptions of it constructed by the numerous theorists of it including (but not only) academics.[7] But this is the nature of the beast. As I say, social theory and philosophy are part of their own field of study. However strange this may seem to someone more familiar with natural science, it in no way prevents social reality being studied (scientifically) and nor does it constitute a necessary barrier to projects of linked or co-development between sub-disciplines or traditional (heterodox) projects within any sub-discipline.[8]

## Depth ontology or a world of surface flux?

I turn now to an issue on which disagreement between us does finally seem to be firm and significant. In the concluding part of his chapter, Ruccio raises the idea that social reality might be just a surface, a world that is depthless or "flat", and he correctly points out that this is quite different from the "scheme of verticality or depth that characterises [my] approach". Ruccio does not seek to defend his alternative conception; he mostly raises it as a possibility, merely asking "Does such a horizontal array of elements make economic and social analysis impossible?" However, it clearly constitutes an ontological conception towards which he feels well disposed.

Now the quick answer to the question of whether "such a horizontal array of elements make[s] economic and social analysis impossible" is that, if by the latter we mean successful explanatory analysis and not merely deconstructive critique, then yes: such a horizontal array of elements would make economic and social analysis more or less impossible, certainly difficult.

If social (or indeed any form of) analysis is to be possible, some continuity and/or generality must be exhibited by its subject matter. This is why Humeans (seemingly with a not overly dissimilar ontology from that to which Ruccio draws our attention) emphasise the importance of event regularities (constituting Human causal laws). These are regularities that connect events that lie in historical sequence. For if there is no structure or depth to real phenomena, they are merely (and entirely) surface actualities, then the only feasible generalities are regularities connecting them. Of course, without depth, and so (any basis for) natural necessity, there is no guarantee that any patterns observed in the past will repeat themselves, whatever the context in which they are observed. This problem is compounded, of course, by the observation that in the social realm, few regularities of this sort are ever observed. So yes, on this conception social analysis would be difficult. This is a clear advantage of my position over those pointed to by Ruccio.

Why is Ruccio so positively disposed to a flat ontology? Suggesting that the Freudian notion of overdetermination can make sense of such a surface ontology, he associates the latter ontology with various properties that are clearly of a sort with which Ruccio feels most comfortable. They include openness and a rejection of naive forms of essentialism as well as of all forms of determinism, especially conceptions that interpret reality as fixed or the trajectory of history as certain. It is an ontology "characterised not by closure and certainty but by challenges and possibilities".

Our differences here could be debated at length, and perhaps should be. But because of space limitations, I restrain myself to making and defending one basic point. This is that neither the notion of overdetermination nor the sorts of properties that Ruccio finds appealing are inconsistent with the sort of depth ontology I defend. To the contrary, they are aspects of it.

### Depth, overdetermination and openness

Let me consider first the notion of overdetermination. According to Freud, this simply expresses the idea that a single observed effect or outcome can be determined by multiple causes simultaneously, any one of which might alone be enough to account for the effect.

This, of course, is closely related to the notion of an open system in my own project. In open systems, strict event regularities do not occur. The path of each autumn leaf is unique. And the reason for the lack of such regularities is that any particular outcome may be the result of a multiplicity of changing causes. Obviously, such a scenario includes the possibility that, in some cases at least, a subset of causes may be working in the same direction so that any one of them may have been sufficient to bring about that actual outcome that emerged.

It should be clear, then, that *if* overdetermination in the Freudian sense is consistent with a flat ontology, it does not require it. A world of structure, with underlying causal mechanisms bearing on actual outcomes is just as consistent. Freud and Marx were themselves quite convinced that reality is structured, of course. The unconscious is as good an example of an underlying cause as any, as indeed are labour power or value.

Nor does the avoidance of naive forms of determinism or essentialism, an outcome that is clearly important to Ruccio, require a flat ontology. Think again of the path of the autumn leaf. According to the conception I defend, this may be subject to a host of underlying causal forces, including gravitational, aerodynamic, thermal, tendencies, etc. The result is that the actual path will typically be entirely unpredictable, contextually dependent on which factors are in play, with countervailing forces likely operating as well as others possibly pulling in the same way/direction. So understood, natural reality is seen to be open (potentially), overdetermined and non-deterministic (other than in the sense that outcomes do have causes). Further, there are no necessary grounds for considering certain causal factors as (more) essential (than any other).

Social reality is easily shown to bear the same properties. Of course, there are those social theorists who accept the depth ontology I defend but who also adopt naive deterministic or essentialist positions on some matters, and perhaps on more or less everything. Ruccio points to versions of "Marxist theory" in this regard. But my point here is to note that it is not necessary to abandon depth to avoid this orientation.

It does seem to be a common postmodernist strategy to adopt certain positions wholly on grounds that they intrinsically *disallow* certain orientations considered undesirable (see also my response to Irene Staveren later in this volume). But in such cases, no matter how commendable the motivation for doing so, we should recognise that positions are being taken on strategic considerations only, not because they are regarded as explanatorily grounded or defensible in some more constructive fashion. The problem, I fear, is that such strategies can typically be shown to be not only unnecessary (as here – albeit constituting easy ways of avoiding unwanted conclusions) but also costly in terms of lost opportunities, such as explanatory power.

## Overdetermination, depth and contrast explanation

Now having argued that the approach I take does not typically single out particular causes as more significant or essential than others, let me provide a qualification to that argument, which will hopefully avoid some misunderstanding.

The explanatory approach I often defend is a dialectical procedure that I have systematised under the head of *contrast explanation*. The point of contrast explanation is to explain *not* why some outcome y came about, but *why some outcome y occurred rather than some other outcome x in a situation where we had reason to expect x.*

A typical scenario is one in which our understanding leads us to suppose that over a particular region (which I designate the contrast space), a set of relevant outcomes have the same causal history, and so will be roughly the same in some way. The explanatory process starts when we discern that one or more outcomes is not as expected. In such a situation, it remains possible that we can identify the cause *that makes the difference*.

For example when cows in the UK in the late 1980s started wobbling their heads and falling over (with the onset of "mad cow disease") it proved possible to track down and isolate a cause (the prion) *that made the difference*. There is no claim, or attempt, to identify all the numerous factors bearing on the behaviour of cows at any one point. Rather by taking a contrastive perspective, by noting a surprising aspect of the behaviour of a certain subset of cows that seems to distinguish them from all other cows, it has proven possible to gain an insight to what made or makes the difference.

In the experimental example sketched earlier, the potentially "surprising", or anyway epistemologically significant, contrast was that in an open, and we can now include overdetermined, world, event regularities are nevertheless found systematically to occur in (to be confined to) some locations. The fact that (in the manner outlined above) we need a depth ontology to make sense of this, reveals of course, that in our actual world *overdetermination itself fits more comfortably with a depth rather than a flat ontology*.

What if different causes seem capable of producing the same effect? The answer depends on context of course. Imagine the situation that I have previously discussed (e.g. *Reorienting Economics*, chapter 4) where crop yield is systematically higher at one end of the field than elsewhere. An examination of the scene might lead us to hypothesise that the explanation (of the difference) could be the passing river, or it could be shade from the trees; both being situated at the end of the field where the yield is higher. Can we discriminate? Possibly. If in the next field, conditions seem similar except that the river passes across the middle of the field, whilst the edge of the field remains shaded, we can check whether the higher yield follows the river or the shade. If it follows just one of them we can conclude that it is the cause of the higher yield.

What if the increased yield follows both? This, I guess, is a case of strict (Freudian) overdetermination. But even here, we cannot say we have learnt nothing. We have found that both the shade and the stream separately increase the yield of the crop in question, even if it is the case (and this is a further insight) that when they act together the crop yield is still increased in the same way.

## Significant or essential causes?

So, this explanatory approach does not seem inconsistent with openness or with overdetermination. The reason I run through all this is to note that, despite what I earlier said, this approach on occasion may allow (and even encourage) us to talk of causes that are significant or essential. However, this is so only relative to some *contrast* that is chosen for explanation. Any outcome is multiply determined. However, by contrasting it to some other outcome we in effect highlight a single aspect of it, and this aspect is something that sometimes we might hope successfully to account for, and in a not overly partial fashion.

In other words, if we are talking of any single multiply determined event or outcome not only can we *not* expect to identify all the relevant causes, but equally there are unlikely any grounds for supposing that any one is more significant than others.

But where, instead, by contrasting two events or outcomes, we are able to focus on a single aspect of one of them (for example instead of looking at the whole range of behaviours of cows we focus on the fact that these cows are wobbling their heads and falling over, but those cows over there are not) there is reason to suppose that we can give a fuller account of this particular (now far more partial) phenomenon.[9] We may even be able to identify its most immediate cause(s).

All this is to say that if we take an interest in a particular aspect of some multiply determined outcome, we may often be able to identify causes that are more fundamental to it. But this is but a minor qualification to the more general thesis that, adopting a depth ontology, there is no reason out of context to suppose that there must be one cause more essential than the others.

## Final comments

Ruccio provides a lively commentary, and I find that our intuitions on what makes for good and bad methodology are rather similar. I fear, though, that in order to guarantee that certain features regarded as undesirable are avoided, Ruccio is prepared to cede too much. Most significantly, Ruccio seems prepared to give up on depth in order to avoid the excesses of determinism and essentialism. I have indicated that this move is unnecessary for avoiding the noted excesses. It is also undesirable. For there is a cost to it as well, which is the foregoing of explanatory insight.

Although I have not addressed here the issue of emancipatory practice, I also think that such a strategy as followed by Ruccio undermines its possibility (see Lawson, 2003, chapter 9, also Lawson, 2007). In one passage in his chapter, Ruccio asserts otherwise, but without explanatory elaboration. Perhaps this, then, is a topic for further debate on a future occasion.

## Notes

1 Where I write for example that:

> economic enquiry can lead to a transformation in any social object that becomes the focus of study. Lay agents may in principle appropriate useful insights of social science and incorporate them in their activities, a response which may well constitute, or result in, a transformation of the object of study. [...] Indeed, the very *objective* of this current study is to help facilitate a rapid transformation in orthodox economists. Yet there can be no denying that, whatever its longevity, orthodox economics is a project that is currently real and highly efficacious. If strands of that project are only remotely concerned with achieving an empirically adequate expression of reality they are nevertheless currently an aspect of this reality (thus qualifying the way the term *"and"* should be read in one possible interpretation of the title of the current book).
>
> (Lawson, 1997, p. 197)

2 Where I write that:

> such knowledge as we actually possess cannot be identified, or be said to be in correspondence, with such objects; it is not reducible or equivalent to them. Knowledge, rather, exists in a historically specific, symbolically mediated and expressed, practice-dependent, form.
>
> (Lawson, 1997, pp. 58–9; see also pp. 238–40, and response to Geoffrey Hodgson in this volume)

3 Parenthetically, how does this all this fit with my frequently made observation that the mainstream is often irrelevant just because its substantive theorising is forced to be consistent with the ontology of atomism, encouraged in turn by its insistence on employing only mathematical-deductivist methods? Is it not the case that mainstream economists study merely the properties of its models and so merely study their own realities?

First let me stress that I believe that mainstream economists wish to be as realistic as the rest of us, but are merely constrained from being so by their methods. Clearly, the latter make a huge difference, and often result in fictions, or "non-descriptive claims". But in my experience the mainstream do endeavour to incorporate claims that seem plausible, wherever possible, to provide accounts that the formulators usually consider are approximations to reality, or, at worse, temporary stand-ins.

Nevertheless assumptions are frequently made that are acknowledged as being fictitious. What do we make of an assessment like that of Frank Hahn who declares a goal other than being realistic, as in the following statement?

> The great virtue of mathematical reasoning in economics is that by its precise account of assumptions it becomes crystal clear that applications to the "real" world could at best be provisional. When a mathematical economist assumes that there is a three good economy lasting two periods, or that agents are infinitely lived (perhaps because they value the utility of their descendants which they know!), everyone can see that we are not dealing with any actual economy. The assumptions are there to enable certain results to emerge and not because they are to be taken descriptively.
>
> (Hahn, 1994, p. 246)

Hahn is here dealing almost solely with properties of models, so perhaps could in this particular case (or cases like this) talk of a world quite different from our own (a "separate reality") that, if it were to come about, would render Hahn's claims realistic. But in a sense, this is the exception that proves the rule. For contributions of those, like Hahn, who acknowledge that their claims are unrealistic or not about the real world, do not raise problems of communication – and it is possible problems of communication that drive Ruccio's discussion on separate realities – just because we can all agree with Hahn that he (and other mainstream economists making the same sorts of assumptions) is knowingly and (unlike most heterodox economists) not dealing with any actual economy.

4   Lipsey notes that:

> anomalies, particularly those that cut across the sub-disciplines and that can be studied with various technical levels of sophistication, are tolerated on a scale that would be impossible in most natural sciences – and would be regarded as a scandal if they were.
>
> (Lipsey, 2001, p. 173)

5   Thus for example, Ariel Rubinstein (1995, p. 12) notes that as practised, "Economic theory lacks a consensus as to its purpose and interpretation". He adds that "Again and again, we find ourselves asking the question 'where does it lead?'" Nobel Memorial prize winner Wassily Leontief observes that "Page after page of professional economic journals are filled with mathematical formulas leading the reader from sets of more or less plausible but entirely arbitrary assumptions to precisely stated but irrelevant theoretical conclusions" (Leontief 1982, p. 104). Milton Friedman, a second prize winner, concludes that "economics has become increasingly an arcane branch of mathematics rather than dealing with real economic problems" (Friedman, 1999, p. 137). A yet further Nobel Memorial prize winner, Ronald Coase writes that "Existing economics is a theoretical system which floats in the air and which bears little relation to what happens in the real world" (Coase, 1999, p. 2) and so on (for more assessments and a lengthy discussion see Lawson, 2003, chapter 1).

Notice, too, the problem is not just that the results of the project lack explanatory and predictive power and are widely regarded as irrelevant. In addition it is recognised that its theory and practice are highly inconsistent. For example econometricians put huge resources into elaborating the methods they take to be appropriate and justified, yet their practices diverge wildly from their own methodological strictures. As a result Edward Leamer finds that "The opinion that econometric theory is largely irrelevant is held by an embarrassingly large share of the economics profession."

If a summary statement were required I could do no better than repeat (as I often have before) one provided by Mark Blaug, a methodologically oriented economist, once of the mainstream, and who has spent considerable resources throughout his career attempting to shore up the mainstream tradition. His current assessment runs as follows:

> Modern economics is sick. Economics has increasingly become an intellectual game played for its own sake and not for its practical consequences for understanding the economic world. Economists have converted the subject into a sort of social mathematics in which analytical rigour is everything and practical relevance is nothing.
>
> (Blaug, 1997, p. 3)

6   Though apparently not in Ruccio's postmodernist Marxism, see below.
7   It follows, of course, as I have already stressed, that the ideas produced by economists and everyone else, whether they are realistic in their claims or otherwise, always carry the potential to shape human beings, and social

structures at large. On this, in my view there never was any significant disagreement between Ruccio and me, except in the manner we present things.

8 Parenthetically, the misleading use of the categories of reality and realities
finds a parallel confusion in the way categories of truth and truths are often
employed. Foucault is an example of someone who likes to talk of us each
possessing our own truth. The implication of course, is that once more comparative evaluation is impossible.

The confusion is quickly dissolved by a change in terminology. We do not
possess our own truths. A proposition is true or false (or contains [a certain
degree of] truth etc.) in virtue of the way the world is, independently of
how we think the world to be. If I say "I left my house keys in my car" the
truth or falsity of that statement (once we agree on the meaning of the
terms) depends on the way the world is. If the statement is true, it is so not
because I believe it to be, but because of the way reality is. Truth can come
in degrees; some propositions may contain more truth than others. But,
unlike belief, the truth of a proposition is not ours, yours or mine. It
depends on the way the world is.

9 Ruccio does not talk much about explanations being complete or exhaustive.
However, he references the influence on him of the "pioneering" work of
Stephen Resnick and Richard Wolff. And these authors do seem to be explicit
in using such terms.

Indeed, accepting that the notion of overdetermination, as they interpret
it, bears the consequence that it is "quite impossible to produce complete or
exhaustive explanations of anything" (p. 125), Resnick and Wolff (1992)
suggest that there are three ways to handle what they see as "an epistemological as well as a practical problem" (p. 125):

i    to give up in frustration and proclaim "the effort at explanation to be
     hopelessly misguided, and prefer meditations on undecidability, the futil-
     ity of partisanship in politics or much else, and so forth";

ii   to produce explanations "by (1) presuming that some conditions of exist-
     ence (causes or determinants) are more important than others, (2) identi-
     fying these essential conditions, and then (3) building explanations
     around them";

iii  to produce partial explanations on the understanding that:

     a   no theorists "can ever know which one or several of an always infinite
         set of explanatory causes or elements are 'the most important or
         influential'",

     b   "no essences or essential causes exist",

     c   the "inevitably partial explanations" constructed can never be inter-
         preted as "more or less adequate, better or worse in any general or
         absolute sense",

     d   the basic orientation is to see that "explanations are *different* in accord-
         ance with (1) which factors we select to emphasize and (2) whether or
         not we claim that the factors we select are the essential causes of what
         is to be explained".

Resnick and Wolff support option (iii) as presumably does Ruccio. And
Resnick and Wolff are quite explicit in playing down any insight that explanation can give into the nature of causal processes. Indeed, these authors are
just as concerned with the political impact on society of the explanatory constructions themselves. Academic and other debates and arguments about
alternative theories and explanations matter because they both reflect, and in
turn shape, those impacts on society. Thus Resnick and Wolff write:

In the explanations we construct, no claim is made that we have figured out the essential cause of anything. Explanations are valued no more for the very partial insights they achieve than for how their different particular visions illuminate and shape society. Explanations are socially significant products of human activity because of their impacts on the world. Debate and argument among alternative theories and explanations matter because they both reflect and in turn shape those impacts.[...]

What matters about alternative explanations is not some absolute truth to be attached to this or that among them, but rather the different causes and social consequences of the partialities they embody. A commitment to overdetermination requires that we confront each inevitably partial explanation with questions about the origins and consequences of the particular causes or elements it stresses and how it stresses them.

(Resnick and Wolff, 1992, pp. 125–6)

My point here, though, is merely to suggest that options (ii) and (iii) are not absolute alternatives. If the object of focus is some total outcome, option (iii) is the legitimate response. However, unless every phenomenon of reality is overdetermined in the sense that had any one cause been absent the outcome would have been the same (for example the symptoms of mad cows disease would have occurred without the prion), then by employing contrast explanation we can pursue partial explanations in the manner of option (ii). That is, we can sometimes hope to obtain explanations of essential or significant causes where the phenomenon being accounted for is (via a contrastive approach) rendered itself extremely partial.

# References

Blaug, Mark (1997) "Ugly Currents in Modern Economics", *Options Politiques*, 18(17), September, pp. 3–8.

Coase, Ronald (1999) "Interview with Ronald Coase", *Newsletter of the International Society for New Institutional Economics*, 2(1), spring, pp. 3–10.

Friedman, Milton (1999) "Conversation with Milton Friedman", in B. Snowdon and H. Vane (ed.), *Conversations with Leading Economists: Interpreting Modern Macroeconomics*, Cheltenham: Edward Elgar, pp. 124–44.

Hahn, Frank H. (1994) "An Intellectual Retrospect", *Banca Nazionale del Lavoro Quarterly Review*, XLVIII(190), pp. 245–58.

Hendry, D.F., E.E. Leamer and D.J. Poirier (1990) "The ET Dialogue: A Conversation on Econometric Methodology", *Econometric Theory*, 6, pp. 171–261.

Lawson, Tony (1997) *Economics and Reality*, London and New York: Routledge.

Lawson, Tony (2003) *Reorienting Economics*, London and New York: Routledge.

Lawson, Tony (2006) "The Nature of Heterodox Economics", *Cambridge Journal of Economics*, 30(2), July, pp. 483–507.

Lawson, Tony (2007) "Gender and Social Change", in Jude Brown (ed.), *The Future of Gender*, Cambridge: Cambridge University Press.

Leamer, Edward E. (1978) *Specification Searches: Ad Hoc Inferences with Non-Experimental Data*, New York: John Wiley and Sons.

Leontief, Wassily (1982) Letter, in *Science*, 217(4555), pp. 104–7.

Lipsey, Richard G. (2001) "Successes and Failures in the Transformation of Economics", *Journal of Economic Methodology*, 8(2), June, pp. 169–202.

Resnick, S.A. and R.D. Wolff (1992) "Everythingism, or Better Still, Overdetermination", *New Left Review*, I(195), September–October, pp. 124–6.

Rubinstein, Ariel (1995) "John Nash: The Master of Economic Modelling", *Scandinavian Journal of Economics*, 97(1), pp. 9–13.

Turnovsky, Stephen J. (1992) "The Next Hundred Years", in Hey, John. D. (ed.) *The Future of Economics*, Oxford: Blackwell.

# 17 Feminism and realism

## A contested relationship

*Irene van Staveren*

## Introduction

This chapter engages with chapter 9 of Tony Lawson's (2003a) *Reorienting Economics*, "Feminism, Realism, and Universalism". The chapter appeared as a journal article in *Feminist Economics*, in 1999 (Lawson, 1999a). That publication provoked a remarkable set of comments by feminist economists – some of these highly critical – which were published in the same journal as a dialogue, in 2003, including two responses by Lawson. Earlier (in 1999), as well as in the set of comments in 2003, feminist philosopher Sandra Harding gave her response to Lawson's views. In my discussion of the chapter/article on feminism and realism, I will regularly refer to this dialogue. But before doing so, let me first briefly give some indication of Lawson's position towards feminist economics as a discipline.

Although I could not find his name in the two latest membership directories of IAFFE, the International Association For Feminist Economics, he can certainly be characterised as a supporter of feminist economics. In his book series with Routledge, Economics as Social Theory, he has published several books by feminist economists (Nancy Folbre, 1994; Julie Nelson, 1996; Irene van Staveren, 2001; Drucilla Barker and Edith Kuiper, 2003). He is member of the editorial board of *Feminist Economics*, the associations' journal, and he has participated in several annual IAFFE conferences over the past ten years. Lawson, together with some other male economists involved in IAFFE and/or *Feminist Economics*, can undoubtedly be characterised as a supporter of feminist economics as a sub-discipline within economics. Acknowledging his clear support for the feminist cause in economics, this chapter will now focus on the ideas of critical realism that he brings to feminist economics: what are these, how are these connected to feminist economic research, and how are these evaluated by feminist economists?

The objective of his chapter on feminism is "to argue that ... there are possible advantages to feminist explanatory and emancipatory projects from engaging (or engaging more fully) in the sort of explicit ontological analysis associated with modern versions (at least) of scientific realism" (Lawson, 2003a: 219). In his view, feminists too often reject universalism wholesale (rather than only reject a priori universalism as expressed in values, experiences, objectives and interpretations of dominant groups), which would "be debilitating for the feminist project" (ibid.). In order to clarify his point, he illustrates his argument with three examples, on formalistic modelling, epistemology, and emancipation. The responses to his article agree unanimously with his critique on formalistic modelling, whereas they disagree almost unanimously (except Julie Nelson, who, however, has a related disagreement) with Lawson's universalism underlying his arguments on epistemology and emancipation.

In this contribution, I will first discuss the strong disagreement of the feminist economists participating in the dialogue with the universalism they detect behind his critical realism. In doing so, I will not only rely on the dialogue following Lawson's article in *Feminist Economics*, but also draw from a recent book (published in the book series under his editorship) that provides a state-of-the-art overview of feminist economic philosophy (Barker and Kuiper, 2003). Second, I will critically question the apparent agreement between Lawson and the participants in the dialogue on formalistic modelling as unhelpful for both ontological economic analysis and feminist economics. For this part of my contribution, I will partly make use of a paper on feminist econometrics by Brigitte Bechtold (1999), who instead argues for a feminist approach to modelling. I will end with a conclusion, arguing for a more explicit two-way relationship between realism and feminism.

## Feminist opposition to universalism

In his original contribution "Feminism, Realism, and Universalism", to which I will refer to as chapter 9 of his book (Lawson, 2003a, with page numbers referring to the book version), Lawson rejects a priori universalising, that is, the mere assumption or assertion of a widespread validity or relevance of a particular position. But he warns feminists for the opposite danger he signals in feminist work, namely that "all approaches or stances are as legitimate as each other" (Lawson, 2003a: 218). Now, what does realism offer to feminism? First and foremost, Lawson claims, realism enables feminists to study gender as an ontological category, that is, as a real kind of entity rather than (only) as a representation of certain beliefs. Since gender, and its derived concepts such as gender relations, gender inequality, and gender roles, is at the heart of feminist research, including feminist economics, the potential contribution of realism to feminist research is not trivial. Indeed, as Drucilla Barker and Edith Kuiper (2003: 2) state in the introduction to their valuable volume on feminist economic philosophy, "Gender analysis remains integral to feminist scholarship." Lawson hastens to emphasise that an ontological understanding of gender does in no way imply essentialism:

> there is nothing essential to scientific or ontological realism that supposes or requires that objects of knowledge are naturalistic or other than transient, that knowledge obtained is other than fallible, partial and itself transient, or that scientists or researchers are other than positioned, biased, interested, and practically, culturally, and socially conditioned.
>
> (Lawson, 2003a: 220)

The participants in the dialogue, however, are not convinced, as they notice a strong universalist claim in his defence of realism. This disagreement underlies much of the dialogue. Lawson perceives an understanding of realism among feminists that reduces this philosophy to a simple, naive version of realism, from which he distances himself. The feminists in the dialogue, however, perceive a strong version of universalism to his position, that is, essentialism, a claim about the nature of human beings, a claim against which the whole project of feminism is set up, in particular post structuralist feminism. So, the dialogue centres round the opposition between essentialism on the one hand and relativism on the other hand.

Now, do feminists, and in particular feminist economists, reject or downplay realism as Lawson assumes? Does critical realism indeed have the balanced position that feminists favour between universalism and relativism, as Lawson claims in his assertion that realism is not essentialist? In order to shed light on these questions, let me now review the most important comments and replies from the dialogue on the opposition between essentialism and relativism.

On naive realism, Sandra Harding (1999) agrees with Lawson that this version does not do justice to realism. At the same time, however, she explains that strategically, feminists have found it more helpful to argue from an epistemological perspective, in order to be heard in the scientific debate (and get research funding, for example), than from a realist perspective, in which they often remain marginalised. She argues that feminists have experienced that ontologies are embedded in moral and political projects, and are in no way disinterested. Therefore, she claims, "it requires a great deal more than just 'clear thinking' to dislodge such ontologies from their status as obvious" (Harding, 1999: 130). Indeed, feminist economists have analysed the economic importance of unpaid labour and caring, the discriminatory part of the gender wage gap, negative impacts of structural adjustment policies for women in developing countries, to mention only a few feminist economic concerns. But these studies have been largely ignored by the mainstream, as is visible in the selection of articles in the discipline's top-ranking journals and chapters in economic textbooks. That is why, Harding states, feminists have found it more useful to rely more often on an epistemological strategy, focusing on how standards are set for what should count as knowledge, good method, objectivity, or rationality. This is precisely why feminist economists have also spent time and effort in challenging mainstream notions of economic rationality, efficiency, and work, among others, as well as their underlying gender dichotomies of fact/value, reason/emotion, and efficiency/equity. Lawson agrees with this point. The volume on feminist philosophy of economics by Barker and Kuiper provides several examples of such studies.[1] To quote just one author in their rich volume, arguing strongly against an essentialist notion of gender, urging feminist economists to hold "no presumption that gender underlies economic processes except in culturally specific, path-dependent ways" (Eiman Zein-Elabdin, 2003: 333).

But there is more than strategy to the feminist preference for epistemology and standpoint theory, expressing the situatedness of knowledge. Fabienne Peter (2003) draws the attention to Lawson's assumption of a common human nature, referring to a genetic constitution and species-wide needs and capacities, which could be studied in analogy to the study of physical objects in the natural sciences. This assumption, Peter points out, denies the problematic character of science itself, and the still largely positivist science practices in economics. She argues that Lawson appears to suffer from this bias himself, with his notion of "judgemental rationality" that seems to stem from a positivist conception of objective scientific explanation. Feminist economists, instead, tend to follow Harding's position of "strong objectivity", as a recognition of the situatedness of the scientist (see, for example, Harding, 1995), acknowledging that the ideal of objectivity is untenable and rather than denying its problems, one would better recognise them explicitly. Referring to Lawson's example on the emancipatory project of feminist economics, Peter (2003: 99) makes clear that in the face of oppression, "accommodating the potential contestedness of needs is more important than issuing universalizing statements". Drucilla Barker (2003) elaborates this point by questioning the grounds of the presumably shared interests, needs, and motives of human beings – between women and men, but also between women or any other group. Referring to Donna Haraway (1988), Barker (2003: 107) clarifies that "collective subject positions are always socially constructed and partial". A good illustration of this point can be found in a recent article in *Feminist Economics* on the different perceptions of labour standards by some Western feminists and other activists on the one hand, and women workers in exporting industries in Bangladesh on the other hand. In that article, Naila Kabeer (2004) points out why a different perspective is needed, precisely for the sake of emancipation, rather than a unified image of human interests, needs, and motives. Zein-Elabdin (2003: 333) therefore proposes a feminist economic philosophy of hybrid subalternity, which she defines "as subordination deriving from heterogeneous sources rather than a single axis such as gender or colonial subjectivity". She explains that such a philosophy should be non-modernist and grounded in a self-critical approach and ethical sensitivity to subaltern difference:

> This framework remains feminist to the extent that it is partially anchored in a concern for women's welfare; however, it is paradigmatically guided by the multiformity and instability of difference, and is deeply aware of its own complicity in the cultural hegemony of economic discourse.
>
> (ibid.)

Lawson's reply on the critique of his essentialism is that he rather pleas for seeking commonality with recognition of differences, and not a priori assuming this, which, however, makes one question what is left of the ontology of human beings' needs and interests. Since he argues that "despite our interrelatedness and differences, indeed as a result of appreciating these features, I believe that, at an abstract level, we can give a formulation of the sort of society that is desirable" (Lawson, 2003b: 125). But the abstract level does not allow for interrelatedness and differences. Feminists instead tend to discuss what is desirable in a society at the level of the concrete. Feminist economists Barker and Kuiper are therefore explicit on their epistemological and methodological stance for economics, a discipline they see as an integral part of culture, power relations, and change:

> Economics is not an abstract notion; it does not exist without people. Rather, it is a state of affairs, always implicated in global politics, regional interests, and local alliances. As economists, we are part of the picture – we study, write, and teach from interested positions. Such interests are affected by intellectual pleasure, ethnical sensibilities, as well as by prestige, uncertainty, and a variety of other institutional constraints. Explicitly recognising our location ties us concretely to the world and enables us to envision effective strategies for change and new perspectives on economic issues.
>
> (Barker and Kuiper, 2003: 3)

They add, on page 15, that they adhere to the idea of a desirable society, just like Lawson, but recognise that "what constitutes the 'social good' can no longer be taken for granted". Lawson appears more convincing in his reply to Barker who labelled his universalism as humanist. He agrees, but explains that his humanism is minimalist as it concerns the recognition of human capacities to flourish in human society, as distinct from the capacities of non-human beings. This conception of humanism is very close to Amartya Sen's and perhaps even closer to Martha Nussbaum's theories of capabilities and human development – a perspective with which feminist economists have engaged to quite an extent – largely supportive as well as, to some extent, critical.

Julie Nelson (2003: 110) shifts the attention to another bias she perceives in critical realism, namely its "privileging reason, abstraction, and precision over emotion, particularity, and what is vaguely known". She argues that this bias against emotion will not help feminist economists to get the economic analysis of caring out of the margin. My example on modelling care in the next part of the chapter will illustrate this point. Although agreeing with the general ideas offered by scientific realism, Nelson does not find the particular branch of realism very helpful for this type of feminist research. As an alternative, she points at the work of Alfred North Whitehead on process ontology, which she finds a more organic and interconnected version of realism than Lawson's. "By emphasizing experience, including human bodily experience, as the fundamental unifying reality, he removes the mind-vs.-matter conundrum" (Nelson, 2003: 113). In his reply to Nelson, Lawson feels misinterpreted, and argues, extensively quoting from Whitehead, that his critical realism is much closer to Whitehead's than Nelson claims. That may be so, but his three examples that aimed to show the usefulness of critical realism for feminist economics do not make this explicit – an example on core feminist concerns such as the economic analysis of childcare, or care as a motivation for certain types of unpaid and paid labour might have been a better choice to bring this point across.

In his reply to the comments, Lawson (2003b: 128) restates the objective of his chapter, as "to encourage consideration of an ontological turn in feminist theorizing". But the dialogue that followed on his initial contribution signals that this objective, modest as it may seem, has a problematic undertone. What about a feminist turn in realist theorising? In other words, what about a discourse in which both feminism and realism are open to mutual influencing? This seems even more desirable in the light of what Harding recognises as an oversight in Lawson's assumption of a feminist neglect of major messages of realism. She argues that much of Lawson's advice on ontology to feminists is ill-informed about what feminist theorists already do, and for quite some time have developed thoughtfully within feminist discourses of philosophy. She refers to work by feminist theorists from the mid-1970s onwards that have "largely already made the claims Lawson 'proposes'" (Harding, 1999: 131). Indeed, she argues, his suggestions on acknowledging situated knowledge "are the main points of standpoint theories" (ibid.), but she finds them argued stronger in standpoint theory than in critical realism. She finds Lawson's arguments helpful additions in the continuous defence that standpoint theory is required to do against common misunderstandings. However, the point she makes, referring to others as

Feminism and realism 303

well, is that science is embedded in networks of beliefs, a point which she summarises in a question to Lawson: "Shouldn't we expect critical realism, too, to be a network of ontological, epistemological, moral, political, etc. beliefs, even though it focuses only on ontological issues?" (Harding, 2003: 154).

## Formalistic models in feminist economics

In his chapter 9, Lawson uses the example of formalistic modelling to illustrate why realism/ontology matters. He argues that the method of formalistic modelling is not at all well equipped for illuminating the social realm and he notices that feminist economists have also criticised it as masculinist, with which he concurs. He convincingly argues that the basic assumption for phenomena to be appropriately analysed with the method of formalistic modelling is that they occur in closed systems, while the social realm, of which the economy is part, is characterised by openness, as well as by structure and dynamics. Moreover, his critique extends beyond the particular type of models that are formalistic (relying on mathematical proofs) to also include econometrics (relying on statistical tests). He claims that both types of models – theoretical as well as econometric – have been rather unsuccessful. Feminist economists have, however, used modelling as one among a variety of methods, although the type of models used are far more often econometric than formalistic (except for some household bargaining models). Lawson rejects both types of modelling for feminist economic analysis: formalistic as well as econometric approaches. "I think that feminists may have been too cautious in their criticisms of formalistic modelling" (Lawson, 2003a: 228). On econometric models, he continues: "there are grounds for supposing that those empirically-oriented feminists in economics insistent upon applying standard econometric methods in all contexts are proceeding wholly in the wrong direction" (ibid.).

Now, how did the feminist economists participating in the dialogue react to this assertion? Surprisingly, perhaps, they agreed. Peter (2003: 94) agrees with Harding's endorsement of Lawson's critique, finding "Lawson's article [...] strongest in its critique of formalistic modelling." Barker (2003: 104) states: "I think that many feminists will find this argument familiar and persuasive." But she adds that his ontological critique misses the sociological fact that it is precisely formal modelling that provides mainstream economists with their status as scientists. Finally, Nelson (2003: 111) asserts that the critical realist approaches shares with the feminist approach a wish "to develop a more adequate investigatory practice, not hidebound by allegiance to formal modelling". These three confirmative responses to Lawson's critique on the use of formalistic modelling in general, and within feminist economics in particular, require, however, a bit more detailed discussion than they received in the dialogue. There is not enough space in this chapter to do that, nor would I be best positioned to do this, as predominantly employing qualitative rather than quantitative methods in my own work. But I do think the matter deserves somewhat more attention than it received in the dialogue. Therefore, I will try to point out briefly how feminist economists tend to make use of modelling, and to what extent the outcomes of this method contributes to the understanding of the economic behaviour of women and men and how economic processes influence differently on the economic lives of women and men.

It seems fruitful to start with the example of the disappointing results of modelling the gender wage gap in an illuminative entry on econometrics by Julie Nelson in the *Elgar Companion to Feminist Economics*. In that chapter, Nelson (1999) points out that econometrics has not been able to settle the dispute on the (extent of) discrimination underlying the pay difference between women and men.

> Consider regression results suggesting that a wage gap still exists between men and women, even when they have the same observable skills, experience, and so on. Those who do not believe discrimination exists commonly argue that such results could be explained by the omission of important – perhaps unobservable – variables (for example, greater ambition on the part of men). On the other hand, those who believe that the impact of discrimination is actually understated by such studies will argue that some of the included variables (for example, seniority) themselves reflect labour market discrimination.
>
> (155)

She explains the different positions on this as resulting from different underlying beliefs, arguing that econometric testing therefore will never be able to settle the argument. This shows again the importance of epistemology for feminist economists, and the need to challenge masculine beliefs reflected in econometrics.

The ways in which feminists address these biased beliefs is partly through employing a broader set of quantitative tools for empirical investigation, including more refined data sets, the use of survey data, and creative technical specifications of models, as well as triangulation with qualitative methods. At the annual conference of feminist economics held in Oxford, in August of 2004, a roundtable on the relationships between feminist economics and Post Keynesian economics, Lawson restated his view on the uselessness of models for feminist purposes, while various of the feminist economists present in the session pointed out that this would throw the baby out with the bath water. Feminists have done valuable econometric work in a different way from that commonly done by the mainstream: not axiomatic but explorative, not claiming explanation but complementing found correlations with theoretical analysis relating to gendered norms, institutions, and power. An example of technical specifications that point to gender inequalities in explanatory variables are power parameters in household production models, that reflect male control over household resources such as labour time, land, or income. Such parameters do more justice to the underlying gender mechanisms than including only a few separate variables for men and women, such as male and female labour time. Moreover, feminist econometricians tend to be quite cautious about the explanatory power of models, often being aware that more is needed than just regressions with observable variables in order to explain gender differences.

In a recent article (van Staveren, 2005), I have reviewed modelling work on unpaid labour and the care economy. Of course, modelling is not an end in itself or a substitute for theory (although for some economists there is hardly any difference between model and theory). But given the high status that modelling has in the discipline, as Barker has pointed out, it seems strategically wise not to shy completely away from it, not even in the case of analysing caring, a highly under-measured economic activity. Various feminist economists therefore have expressed a need for experimentation with the modelling of care (Frances Woolley, 1993; Martha MacDonald, 1995; Irene van Staveren, 1999; Sue Himmelweit, 2003) – despite the acknowledged limitations. In a comparison I did of two models, each including a variable for unpaid labour (childcare or a broader variable including domestic work), the feminist model appeared to do more justice to the gendered structure of labour markets and the gender division of labour in the household than the non-feminist model. That is because the non-feminist model assumed high substitution elasticities between paid and unpaid work as well as between male and female labour time. Hence, the only way that model could account for observed inflexibilities and rigidities was by including extra constraints for one or both genders. It did opt for a maximum value for female paid working time of 20 hours a week and a minimum value of 20 hours of female time spent on childcare at home, for women with children. For men, no such limits were set. Such choices by modellers severely limit the explanatory power of the model, as it assumes what needs to be explained and thereby does not allow for changes towards a more gender equal distribution of labour between men and women. In the words of Lawson's example on the emancipatory project of feminist economics, the model excluded such a project from the beginning. The other model, however limited in other aspects, did allow for changing gender relations to some extent, as it modelled low substitution elasticities, reflecting job segregation in the labour market as well as norms and institutions supporting the status quo of the unequal division of paid and unpaid labour between women and men. Admittedly, these needed to be explained outside the model, but at least the choice of low substitution rates made such additional explanation possible, whereas the non-feminist model foreclosed the possibility of emancipation altogether.

My conclusion of the discussion of the models referred to above and several other models of care that I have reviewed is that they may be useful to clarify the *structural* dimensions of economic relationships, including gendered structures. Choices between exogenous and endogenous variables appeared to matter, as well as inclusion of care receivers next to care givers; including care in the savings function (as a substitute for purchased services) that appeared to enable one model to show a counter-cyclical trend in women's unpaid labour time; and, finally, the modelling experiences indicated that the care economy can be understood as much richer than only in terms of labour time, by including variables such as caring goods, caring productivity, and substitutability with market goods. Such empirical models remain important in order to bring marginalised topics (such as unpaid labour) and differentiated economic processes (such as the gender wage gap) to the attention of the discipline. Moreover, such models on the structure of gender in the economy often serve to refute commonly held beliefs on the benign effects of markets for all economic agents. To give just one example, the carefully developed regressions with additional institutional analysis, by Stephanie Seguino (2000) on the gender wage gap in the Asian tiger economies has shown that wage discrimination is an important factor behind the export success and economic growth of these countries. Such empirical studies are necessary in the discourse on globalisation, especially in the light of unsubstantiated views held by well-known trade economists such as Jagdish Bhagwati (2004, in particular in his chapter on women), on a presumed equalising impact of global trade.

But models appear to be very limited, in line with Lawson's claims, when we are interested in learning about the *causation, dynamics, and meaning of these relationships* in the economy, which relate to motivation, reasons, beliefs, and interaction effects of economic agents. But perhaps we should rather give up the ideal of (full) explanation and use models pragmatically to explore possible relationships between gendered variables, than dismissing models wholesale.

Finally, let me say a few words on the possibility of feminist econometrics as suggested by Brigitte Bechtold (1999). She starts by listing ten practices in econometrics that she labels as non-feminist, including the violation of random sampling for gender differences (as well as class and other differences), the emphasis on monetary variables, and the use of dummy variables as a way to accommodate gender differences. She argues that some types of modelling do better than others, while she deems time-series analysis as particularly problematic. But, she does not imply that we should discard econometrics, but rather use it more carefully and with more attention to data gathering.

While bulky and seemingly detailed simultaneous equation macro-models as well as VAR [vector autoregression, IvS] models have major shortcomings in terms of inclusiveness, and the basic classical regression model is lacking in stochastic qualities required to apply limiting theorems, all is not lost.

(49–50)

Instead, she recommends eight "feminist econometric habits": look for higher t-values; use limited dependent variable methods; avoid technical corrections for serial correlation (they may hide misspecification); avoid dummy variables; use survey and experimental methods; link to findings obtained in other disciplines; avoid re-affirming the status quo; and replace deductive hypothesis testing with inductive methods of analysis. Interestingly, this last recommendation comes close to Lawson's recommendation of contrastive explanation as an alternative to formalistic modelling – apparently, modelling and inductive methods are not necessarily mutually exclusive. Bechtold even suggests that deduction can be done through formalistic models, applying mathematical proofs.[2]

## Conclusion: from realism to feminism … and back?

Lawson's chapter 9 has triggered an important debate among feminist economists, a feminist philosopher, and Tony Lawson, on the importance of realism versus epistemology, the balance between universalism and relativism, and strategic choices for the emancipatory project of feminist economics. Various issues were resolved, as they appeared merely misunderstandings or partial interpretations – for example the role of culture in knowledge construction (not only a hindrance but also productive) and the role of humanism (about human capabilities rather than common interests, needs, and motivations) in realism. Also, the dialogue has shown that much of what Lawson had proposed to feminist economists is already wide-shared practice among many feminist economists. Other issues, however, remain unresolved, in particular because feminist economists reject, more strongly than Lawson does, universalist conceptions of human beings and human agency.

On modelling, the participants in the dialogue largely agreed with Lawson's realist/ontological critique, but the point was also raised that modelling has high status in the discipline as is driven partly by modellers' beliefs. Therefore, it remains necessary, next to critiquing modelling as a masculinist practice with limited explanatory power, to engage in theoretical and empirical modelling and the discourses that surround these two forms of modelling. Several suggestions were made how this can be approached in a gender aware, and generally more inclusive way.

Finally, a note on the tone of the dialogue and the various misinterpretations that contributed to the somewhat tense tone. It seems to me that part of the critical tone of the dialogue may be arising from a, at least seemingly, one-way interest by Lawson in linking realism and feminism: from realism to feminism, and not also the other way around. Feminist theorists, and particularly feminist philosophers like Sandra Harding, appear to have something valuable to say on realism with implications for realism. In particular in issues of epistemology. Moreover, feminist economists working on the philosophy of economics, may also have something to contribute to Lawson's critical realism project in economics, for example in the area of identity and agency, as well as from their analysis of caring in economics. Lawson's message in his chapter on feminism is clearly one of urging feminist economists to learn from realism, and not about what realism may learn from feminism. This one-way approach of his critical realism project towards feminism does not stand alone, as he has published similar articles on the relationship from realism to Post Keynesianism (Lawson, 1999b) as well as to institutional economics (Lawson, 2001). This is not to say, of course, that such urging of heterodox traditions in economics to consider more explicitly a certain philosophy of science would not be relevant or legitimate – we have probably seen too little engagement with philosophy in economics over the past decades. But there appears to be an implicit request for a stronger commitment to mutual learning in the dialogue on Lawson's chapter 9 that should not be ignored, in particular if both strands of thought – realism and feminism – are to benefit from future dialogues.

## Notes

1 The volume includes, among other things, a review of work on consumer theory by an early twentieth-century economist; a literary analysis of the notion of efficiency; a political-economy study of wage setting; a critical reading of Adam Smith, revealing the construction of masculine identity; a demonstration of cultural biases in social statistics; two studies of the identity gap in rational economic man; four chapters analysing caring and unpaid labour as economic activities; and various chapters focusing partly or completely on the importance of a postcolonial or subaltern perspective for feminist theorising in economics.

2
>  A mathematical proof using induction uses three steps: (a) prove the proposition at hand for the first element, (b) prove it for consecutive representative elements 'k' and 'k + 1,' and (c) draw the conclusion that it holds in the sample or population under consideration.
>
> (Bechtold, 1999: 51)

## References

Barker, Drucilla (2003) "Emancipatory for Whom?", *Feminist Economics* 9 (1), pp. 103–8.
Barker, Drucilla and Kuiper, Edith (2003) "Introduction. Sketching the Contours

of a Feminist Philosophy of Economics", in Drucilla Barker and Edith Kuiper (eds) *Toward a Feminist Philosophy of Economics*. London: Routledge, pp. 1–18.

Bechtold, Brigitte (1999) "The Practice of Econometrics: a Feminist Critique", *Review of Radical Political Economics* 31 (3), pp. 40–52.

Bhagwati, Jagdish (2004) *In Defense of Globalization*. Oxford: Oxford University Press.

Folbre, Nancy (1994) *Who Pays for the Kids? Gender and the Structures of Constraint*. London: Routledge.

Haraway, Donna (1988) "Situated Knowledges: The Science Question in Feminism and the Privilege of Partial Perspective", *Feminist Studies* 14 (3), pp. 579–99.

Harding, Sandra (1995) "Can Feminist Thought Make Economics More Objective?", *Feminist Economics* 1 (1), pp. 7–32.

—— (1999) "The Case for Strategic Realism: A Response to Lawson", *Feminist Economics* 5 (3), pp. 127–33.

—— (2003) "Representing Reality: The Critical Realism Project", *Feminist Economics* 9 (1), pp. 151–9.

Himmelweit, Susan (2003) "An Evolutionary Approach to Feminist Economics", in Drucilla Barker and Edith Kuiper (eds) *Toward a Feminist Philosophy of Economics*. London: Routledge, pp. 247–65.

Kabeer, Naila (2004) "Globalization, Labour Standards, and Women's Rights: Dilemmas of Collective (In)action in an Interdependent World", *Feminist Economics* 10 (1), pp. 3–35.

Lawson, Tony (1999a) "Feminism, Realism, and Universalism", *Feminist Economics* 5 (2), pp. 25–59.

—— (1999b) "Connections and Distinctions: Post Keynesianism and Critical Realism", *Journal of Post Keynesian Economics* 22 (1), pp. 3–14.

—— (2001) "Why Should Economists, Including (Old) Institutionalists, be Interested in Critical Realism?", in Yuji Aruka (ed.) *Evolutionary Controversies in Economics. A New Transdisciplinary Approach*. Tokyo: Springer, pp. 227–42.

—— (2003a) *Reorienting Economics*. London and New York: Routledge.

—— (2003b) "Ontology and Feminist Theorizing", *Feminist Economics* 9 (1), pp. 110–50.

MacDonald, Martha (1995) "The Empirical Challenges of Feminist Economics", in Edith Kuiper and Jolande Sap (eds) *Out of the Margin. Feminist Perspectives on Economics*, London: Routledge, pp. 175–97.

Nelson, Julie (1996) *Feminism, Objectivity and Economics*. London: Routledge.

—— (1999) "Econometrics", in Janice Peterson and Margaret Lewis (eds) *The Elgar Companion to Feminist Economics*. Cheltenham: Edward Elgar, pp. 154–7.

—— (2003) "Once More, with Feeling: Feminist Economics and the Ontological Question", *Feminist Economics* 9 (1), pp. 109–18.

Peter, Fabienne (2003) "Critical Realism, Feminist Epistemology, and the Emancipatory Potential of Science", *Feminist Economics* 9 (1), pp. 93–101.

Seguino, Stephanie (2000) "Accounting for Gender in Asian Economic Growth", *Feminist Economics* 6 (3), pp. 27–58.

Staveren, Irene van (1999) "Chaos Theory and Institutional Economics: Metaphor or Model?", *Journal of Economic Issues* 1 (33): 141–67.

—— (2001) *The Values of Economics. An Aristotelian Perspective*. London: Routledge.

—— (2005) "Modelling care", *Review of Social Economy* 63 (4), pp. 567–86.

Woolley, Frances (1993) "The Feminist Challenge to Neoclassical Economics", *Cambridge Journal of Economics* 17 (4): 485–500.
Zein-Elabdin, Eiman (2003) "The difficulty of a Feminist Economics", in Drucilla Barker and Edith Kuiper (eds) *Toward a Feminist Philosophy of Economics*. London: Routledge, pp. 321–38.

# 18 Feminism, realism and essentialism
## Reply to van Staveren

*Tony Lawson*

Do realism and/or essentialism constitute positions from which feminists ought to distance themselves? These are the more fundamental questions raised by Irene van Staveren's comments. Her thoughtful contribution contains two basic parts. In the first, she critically reviews a debate or dialogue in *Feminist Economics* between myself and various feminist economists and philosophers over the relevance of an ontological orientation to feminist theorising. In this part of Staveren's chapter, the topics of realism and especially essentialism come to the fore. In the second part, Staveren offers support for a feminist approach to econometrics. In each part, Staveren takes a position somewhat different from my own on the issues raised. In my response, I address the topics both of realism and essentialism and of feminist econometrics, starting with the latter.

## Feminist econometrics

I shall deal only briefly with the issue of a feminist approach to econometrics. For econometrics is a topic on which I have had much to say before (and to which have relatively little to add), and I want to focus here on other relevant matters on which hitherto I have elaborated rather less.

Reading through Staveren's comments on feminism and econometrics it is clear that Staveren is worried that other participants in the *Feminist Economics* dialogue to which she refers have been too quick, or insufficiently critical, in accepting my critique.

Her point is that many feminists have approached econometric modelling in a manner different from the way in which most mainstream economists have gone about their endeavours. Providing various illustrations of feminist econometric contributions that she takes to be insightful, Staveren emphasises, for example, feminist practices of "employing a broader set of quantitative tools for empirical investigation, including more refined data sets, the use of survey data, and creative technical specifications of models, as well as triangulation with qualitative methods". Staveren stresses that feminist econometric work, unlike that of the mainstream, is often "not axiomatic but explorative, not claiming explanation but complementing found correlations with theoretical analysis relating to gendered norms, institutions, and power". Staveren suggests, too, that "feminist econometricians tend to be quite cautious about the explanatory power of models, often being aware that more is needed than just regressions with observable variables in order to explain gender differences", and so on.

After discussing such cases Staveren is quick to emphasise that we should not expect too much from econometrics, that we should be careful and cautious in the way we use it, and such like, but she insists that we should not give up on the enterprise altogether.

I cannot but agree. I am not suggesting that we necessarily give up on anything. My starting point has been the widely recognised and continuing failures of the econometrics project (and in indeed the unfortunate performance of the mathematical-deductivist modelling endeavour that constitutes the mainstream project of modern economics more generally) and I have offered an ontological explanation. Specifically, I have argued that social reality is basically open and complexly structured and processual, whilst standard methods of econometrics presuppose that it (or any domain of reality to which they are applied) is closed (in the sense of comprising systems of event regularities or stochastic near equivalents) and its elements atomistic. My criticism has been directed chiefly at the mainstream *insistence* that these standard methods be everywhere used. This is an unnecessarily dogmatic stance, and it seems especially unhelpful in the face of continuing econometric failure.

But ontological argument (even if correct – and like everything else it is fallible) cannot establish that localised closures may not occur here and there. So not only do I not criticise explorative endeavour, I do not rule out the idea that the use of standard econometric methods may occasionally prove useful either (see *Reorienting Economics*, chapter 1); and I am especially interested in the sorts of non-standard approaches that Staveren mentions.

I believe an especially valuable aspect of the endeavour that Staveren seeks to defend is the attitude or orientation underpinning it. The dogmatic insistence of mainstream economists that only formalistic methods be used tends to work against applied work being carried out in a manner that allows sensitivity to both context and limitations of method. Once we accept that the use of any method is not neutral, but warrants discussion and justification, that exploration, or trial and error experimentation, is a potentially valuable component of any explanatory endeavour, then the whole research process advances in a more self-critical and honest manner. The result, I believe, can only be the more insightful for it. Such an orientation is to be welcomed from whatever quarter it emanates; and if this is Staveren's impression of much of modern feminist output in economics, I certainly do not wish to oppose it.

Having said that I suspect I remain rather more pessimistic than Staveren about how much headway can actually made through the use of formal econometrics, no matter how carefully applied, and even with all the qualifications or distinctions that Staveren attributes to feminist contributions. But this is mostly an empirical matter; it does follow directly from ontological argument, and, in any case, I acknowledge once more that all assessments, including deconstructive ontological ones, are fallible.

I should perhaps mention, though, that I am not persuaded by all of Staveren's reasons for persevering with economic modelling. In particular, I wonder at her urging that: "given the high status that modelling has in the discipline ... it seems strategically wise not to shy completely away from it".

It seems to me that feminists are one group that need not be overly constrained by something just because it has high status conferred upon it by a clearly male dominated and highly narrow and unreflective mainstream community. Indeed the question of hierarchies of all kinds, including of research practices, are constructions that feminists in many disciplines have very usefully deconstructed.

But still as I say, there are other reasons to experiment with research methods, econometric ones included, and I repeat that I am never suggesting that we should abandon any set of methods entirely.

## Realism and essentialism

The major part of Staveren's contribution is a critical assessment of points arising from the earlier *Feminist Economics* dialogue that relate to broadly philosophical positions. Staveren does a very good job reviewing aspects of this dialogue and I see no point in my covering all of the same ground here. Rather I focus on points where Staveren seems most critical.

In the course of this review, Staveren acknowledges that, in defending an explicit realist orientation, I distance myself from any naive realist position. However, she suggests, in effect, that the position I set out is not only realist but essentialist too; it is essentialist in that I am prepared to make certain universal claims about human beings. And essentialism is clearly regarded as a problem. Thus she writes:

> The participants in the dialogue, however, are not convinced, as they notice a strong universalist claim in his defence of realism. This disagreement underlies much of the dialogue. Lawson perceives an understanding of realism among feminists that reduces this philosophy to a simple, naive version of realism, from which he distances

himself. The feminists in the dialogue, however, perceive a strong version of universalism to his position, that is, essentialism, a claim about the nature of human beings, a claim against which the whole project of feminism is set up, in particular post-structuralist feminism. So, the dialogue centres round the opposition between essentialism on the one hand and relativism on the other hand.

Although I never actually mention essentialism in my original essay, it is clearly relevant to issues raised by the dialogue that ensued. So let me state my position on it, which in any case bears resemblances to my position on realism.

It seems to me that with each of the categories before us there are two polar extremes being set up as though they are exhaustive options. That is, we are, in effect, presented with the following dichotomies:

- naive realism versus anti-realism;
- naive essentialism versus anti-essentialism.

My response, in each case, is to refuse the choice; I reject the presumption that these oppositions are exhaustive.

Of course, I doubt many contributors actually attach the qualifier "naive" to their position(s). But I do so here to signal that there is more than one way in which one can be either a realist or an essentialist; where some of these ways are less defensible than others. The worry I have is that in making various (quite appropriate) critiques of specific claims that seemingly presuppose certain realist and essentialist positions, feminists are in effect (mis)universalising the claims in question as characteristic of (indeed as essential to) realism and essentialism respectively. Once this step is taken, it is but a small second one to a rejection of realism and essentialism *tout court*, as if the anti-realist and anti-essentialist positions are the only alternatives available. My contention is that this move is as unnecessary as it is undesirable. Let me briefly elaborate.

## Realism

I have already covered the question of realism in the earlier dialogue; so let me be very brief. My primary emphasis in my original contribution was to encourage an ontological turn within feminist theorising (or at least a more explicit and systematic concern with ontology). I saw this being resisted behind an often explicit distancing from scientific realism. My assessment of the feminist accounts I surveyed was that the category of realism was being used to reference only particular naive versions. This I argued was illegitimate.

The sort of realism of central concern here is scientific realism. Now if there is any feature that is fundamental to the latter, it is an acceptance that the objects of (scientific) analysis exist, at least in part, or in some way, independently of us, or, in the social realm, prior to their analysis (see my response to Ruccio in this volume). I take it, too, that realism more broadly (or philosophical realism) is the thesis that there is a real world that, in part at least, exists independently of us, but with at least some features that can come to be known by us (in some ways and under some descriptions).

Now there are clearly social realists who argue something more than this. For example, some argue as though the objects of the social domain exist independently of us in precisely the same ways that natural objects do. Others seem to suppose that various claims, especially those presented as observation reports or "data", can be treated as directly reflecting their objects, as infallibly capturing the world precisely as it is. Further still, there are those who suppose that reality can be revealed only using methods and orientations that are thought to be somehow neutral, objective, proper, intrinsically scientific, of ubiquitous relevance, value-free and so on. Feminists have rightly deconstructed such positions.

But if the contributions in question are usually presented in such a way that an adherence to realism is clear, the additional sorts of features just noted (and rightly criticised by feminists) are additional to, and in no way tied to, an adherence to realist presuppositions.[1]

In my earlier piece, I was thus suggesting that if the goal was to distance the feminist project from perspectives that failed to recognise the practically conditioned, partial, fallible and situated nature of knowledge it was *not* necessary to distance the project from realism. To the contrary, the assessments of the material conditions of the researcher that figure in these critiques clearly presuppose a realist orientation. And just as clearly, any acceptance of fallibilism presupposes a (in part) mind independent reality, or at least objects that are irreducible to their scientific study, about which it is possible to be right or wrong. Indeed to criticise (or accept) anything (whether text, beliefs, patriarchy, forms of practice), is to presuppose the existence of that which is being criticised.

In truth, realism, not least scientific realism, is inexorable; it is not really an option. However, acting as though it is avoidable, or seeking to distance oneself from it, does, I suggest, have undesirable consequences.

One obvious such consequence on which I have previously focused is that an explicitly ontological orientation is discouraged. For ontology is the study of the nature of a domain of reality, and it is clearly difficult to sustain or justify such an orientation if, or whilst, distancing oneself from realism *tout court*. The benefits of adopting an ontological orientation are numerous, and detailed elsewhere. But counted amongst them is that ontological insight can be used profitably to guide (though of course never determine) emancipatory and epistemological projects (see e.g.

Lawson, 2003a, 2003b, 2007), which, I am presuming, are projects that many feminists wish to sustain.

So in short, my overall argument in the early dialogue was that realism was actually something feminists ought not to seek to reject. Indeed, I continue to maintain that feminist theorising and the contributions of those who adopt a realist framework are capable of being reciprocally enriching. Incidentally, I do mean the benefits are bound to be reciprocal. Although I am here attempting to persuade feminists that forms of realism can be advantageous, I am, of course, more than aware of the huge contribution of feminist scholarship to social understanding and much else, a contribution that benefits scientific realists and indeed all of us. *Indeed this is something I have continually acknowledged.*[2]

## Essentialism

It is with an acceptance of the conception of realism laid out that I now turn to the vexed topic of essentialism. If realism is studiously avoided in much feminist theorising, essentialism gets an explicitly bad press. In fact, essentialism tends to be rejected throughout much of modern social theory, not least amongst radical and progressive thinkers. This is quite a turn around from the state of affairs of about forty years ago.

Essentialism, as I understand it, is a philosophical term that mostly denotes the (ontological) doctrine that certain entities, things or substances, etc., possess a set of essential or necessary properties or causal conditions that make them one kind of "thing" or entity rather than another.[3]

Notice that, so specified, there is nothing in this doctrine that stipulates that entities cannot possess other contingent (or extrinsic) properties, alongside any essential (or intrinsic) properties or conditions.

For example, we might say that having an atomic weight of 63.5 is an essential feature of (any piece of) copper, whereas the fact that a portion of copper before us serves as a lead from an amplifier to a set of speakers in a music system is an accidental or contingent feature. The latter is contingent because if the portion of copper were used for some other purpose it would remain copper. If the substance had a different atomic weight it would however no longer be copper.

Similarly, the molecular and atomic structure of water is an essential feature of (any portion of) it. Whether or not a portion of it sits in a glass or a kettle is a contingent feature, not an essential or intrinsic one.

But essential properties or essences can also come in two sorts: nominal and real. The nominal essence consists of those properties that allow the thing or substance to be correctly identified as one of a certain type. The real essence is that (causal) structure or constitution or causal condition in virtue of which the thing or substance (necessarily) tends to behave the way it does, including the manifesting of those properties that constitute its nominal essence.

The nominal essence of copper might consist in its being of a reddish colour, malleable and a good conductor of electricity, etc. If there is a real essence to copper it is most likely its atomic (electronic) structure.

Similarly, a nominal essence of water might be its tendency to boil when heated to a certain level, depending on conditions, whereas the explanation of this tendency, the molecular and atomic structure of water, might be said to be its real essence.

Is essentialism so conceived a doctrine that necessarily warrants rejection? If the presumption is that essentialists necessarily claim that essences are always transparent; or that theories of essences are not fallible and open to revision; or that things, substances, entities, including people, are completely determined by their essences or natures; or that all members of a kind are identical in every respect; or that things of any particular kind cannot change in any way over time; or that essences themselves cannot change; or that social phenomena are not in a sense socially constructed; or that complex objects cannot have multiple necessary features; or that essences cannot be relational; or that any commonalities in a class of objects necessarily constitutes an essence; or that essential properties are always more important or significant than are contingent ones; then we would seem to have reason to be anti-essentialist. And anti-essentialists do (paradoxically) often attribute one or more of such features to essentialism. But it should be clear that none of these claims are necessarily related to the basic essentialist position.

The term naive essentialism is employed to denote any essentialist doctrine that additionally insists on one or more of these latter claims. As such, it should be clear that essentialism need not reduce to any of these naive varieties.

Sometimes essentialists seem to take the position (or anyway are portrayed as taking the position) that *everything* has an essence. But it is not clear to me that this either is an essential feature of essentialism. Just as realists do not have to be committed to the existence of every posited entity (I am a realist about economic theories but not about all the entities posited in those theories [equilibria, utilities, representative agents]) so, it seems to me, essentialists do not have to commit to the thesis that everything has an essence.

It seems reasonable, and is not unusual, to use the label *strong essentialism* for the thesis that everything has an essence. As I say, it is clearly logically feasible to be an essentialist in the sense of maintaining that some things have essences without subscribing to strong essentialism.

It is not obvious, then, that feminists need to oppose essentialism per se. Indeed, so long as we do not reduce essentialism to a naive or the strong form, it is not clear that opposing it is appropriate at all. In other words, it is not clear that there is anything wrong or distasteful about the idea that at least some parts of reality possess a set of essential or necessary properties that make them one kind of "thing" rather than another.

In fact, isn't such a position quite *vital* for feminist thinking? How can we give support for various projects (emancipation, feminism, flourishing) or voice opposition to others (patriarchy, oppression, abuse, discrimination) if we are not able or prepared to say what they are? Of course, we must be sensitive to differences of cultural context, time and place, etc., and to the processual nature of everything. But still collectivism criticism of specific forms of practice requires that we are able to identify what they are.

Is it even *possible* to avoid essentialism of some form? Is it not the case that anti-essentialism itself inevitably assumes an immovable if usually undesirable essence to essentialism? If not, then on what basis is an explicit oppositional orientation adopted? Certainly any claim by any party that essentialism is inherently reductionist or determinist or reactionary in some way seems to commit itself to a moderate essentialism at least.

Of course, even if a moderate form of essentialism seems sustainable, it does not yet follow, if Staveren is right in describing some of my arguments as essentialist, that I am adopting a non-naive version, or that, even if I am, I am attributing essences appropriately (a concern of course that can only make sense from a realist perspective).

To recall, Staveren writes:

> The feminists in the dialogue, however, perceive a strong version of universalism to his position, that is, essentialism, a claim about the nature of human beings, a claim against which the whole project of feminism is set up, in particular post-structuralist feminism.

Here, then, my essentialism is being tied into my account of human being; it is suggested that I am prepared to make universal claims about human nature.

I can certainly understand the caution with which feminists react to any humanist position, i.e. to claims that all humans, or perhaps certain identified subgroups, have things in common. Both in academic writing and in our daily lives we frequently find (universal) claims of the form that human beings are distinguished by being $P$ where $P$ is little more than a practice or way of behaving favoured/adopted by some locally dominant group ($P$ might be "competitive" or "aggressive" or "selfish" for example). Similarly, we find (universal) claims of some taking the form of derogatory assertions about various "others"; it is not uncommon to hear or read statements of "others" taking the form "all women are X", "all blacks are Y", "all immigrants are Z", etc., where "X", "Y" and "Z" typically involve descriptions of behaviour regarded as inferior or wanting in some way by the formulators of the propositions.

Yet it is easy to see that we can usually reject any such universal claims as these as invalid without rejecting essentialism per se. However, it is not yet clear to me that we must reject every version of humanism; which is the issue facing us here.

Many, though, have argued that all we can say about human beings is that we are all different. This (universal) claim, where accepted, certainly defeats the possibility of (consistently) making derogatory generalisations of others. This no doubt in part explains its popularity. But it is not necessary to go so far in order to escape the overly narrow or unfounded discriminatory claims of certain essentialists. Nor do I think such a move is even helpful in the long run, at least not for those feminists concerned with emancipatory projects. Let me briefly elaborate.

I think there is little doubt that we each have our own unique pathways and experiences and, at a concrete level, are each unique or different. But it is easy enough to demonstrate that there is more to social reality and to each of us than this. This is where ontology comes in.

First, although our experiences are unique this is not inconsistent with the assessment that we can be similarly situated to (some) others and facing (for example) the same discriminatory relations and mechanisms.

Elsewhere (e.g. Lawson, 2003a, 2003b) I argue (in opposition to an ontology of mere differences) that social reality is structured. Specifically, it consists in part of relatively wide-ranging and enduring (albeit of course always space–time and culturally restricted) deeper structures, including social rules, relations and institutions, etc., many, if not most, of which are gendered in a discriminatory way, affecting all who come within their range and which warrant (collective) opposition (from those concerned with emancipation).

Notice that such a position is not at all in tension with a recognition that our experiences and pathways are unique – any more than the continuing relatively uniform impact of gravity across the earth's surface is at odds with, or somehow undermines, the possibility that the path of each autumn leaf is unique. In other words I am suggesting that the enduring social structures and forces act at a different ontological level to the events and other phenomena of experience.

Second, although our experiences and pathways are unique this does not negate the possibility that human beings too are structured, and that commonalities exist at a deeper level. Now it is at this point that I become a humanist in Staveren's eyes. If she is correct it is important to be clear as to how.

I (of course) reject any naive essentialist views that we are biologically determined, or somehow fully formed in nature after the first few years of our lives, and so forth. Equally, though, I reject the idea that we are totally pliable, mere cultural products, perfectly mirroring our ever-changing contexts.

In place of these two extremes, I adopt a minimal humanism. Of course, our experiences etc. are unique to ourselves. But in arguing that we are structured, that we possess by capacities as well as exhibit behaviours, I am open to the idea we have certain capacities in common. That is, I take the view that we do share at least some commonalities as human beings rooted in our species being, not least (if perhaps not much more than) a capacity to enter social (as well as natural) being. This includes a competence for acquiring complex languages and for engaging in modes of discourse. Of course, how we develop our capacities, acquire competences and exercise and maintain them are highly context dependent affairs, and likely unique. Human beings are themselves processes of continuous transformation (itself a further humanist statement). But I see no reason not to allow both that human individuals are continually reshaped overtime and that there is always a degree of durability and substantiality in our being.

In short, I reject both the polar conceptions of naive essentialism and anti-essentialism. I believe that it is a mistake of much social theorising to suppose that to reject either one is necessarily to accept the other.

Capacities such as those to enter social being are, I think, conceivable as our nominal essences.[4] In suggesting that they apply to all human beings I am making a particular, if cautious, universal claim. The nature of our real essences I am less certain about. It may include aspects of our genetic makeup or something like morphogenetic fields. But I admit to being unsure.

In any case, I hope it is at least clear that in adopting a particular realist and essentialist stance on the issues in question, and in tentatively advancing some specific generalising claims, I am not being overly reductionist, determinist, fixist or hierarchical, or adopting any other questionable features that feminists and others have (erroneously) associated with these positions, and (rightly) rallied against.

## Gender

As already emphasised, my conception of essentialism is not dependent on my take on humanism. But if many feminists look upon humanism with suspicion, formulations of essentialist positions on gender seem to be regarded as even more problematic.

At risk of causing more consternation, however, I wonder if this position too is warranted; I wonder if it is not possible to make use of the sorts of arguments drawn on above to defend a qualified essentialist position on gender too. In fact, I think such a position was at least implicit in the earlier dialogue.

Of course, it is not just feminist critics of essentialism that so conclude. For example, in an earlier comment on Staveren's piece, Andrew Sayer defends a position that is very similar to my own; but he too pulls back from suggesting that gender has an essence. Indeed, he writes:

> Anti-essentialism has been dominant in feminism, and not surprisingly, for gender surely has no essence. Gender does not have a

stable, uniform fixed set of characteristics; rather the term refers to common bundles of associations and contrasts and axes of domination that are contestable and shift continually across space and time. However it simply does not follow that because gender has no essence, nothing has any essence.

(2004)

But I am concerned that even Sayer might be conceding too much. That is, in focusing upon "common bundles of associations and contrasts and axes of domination that are contestable and shift continually across space and time" I wonder if he too is not being overly influenced by the postmodernist concern with surface phenomena. In any case I have elsewhere suggested a conception that might be regarded as essentialist and might yet be sustainable (Lawson, 2007).

According to it, gender is a system of identification and differentiation, one that typically serves to privilege some over others. Essential to such a system are the following two components:

1  A distinction repeatedly drawn between individuals who are regularly/mostly observed or imagined to have certain bodily features presumed to be evidence of a female's biological role in reproduction and others who are regularly/mostly observed or imagined to have certain bodily features presumed to be evidence of a male's biological role in reproduction.
2  A set of mechanisms or processes that work in any given society or locality to legitimise/motivate the notion that individuals regarded as female and those regarded as male ought to be allocated to, or to have allocated to them, systematically differentiated kinds of social positions (with associated rules, obligations and practices etc.) where the nature of the allocations encouraged need not, and typically does not, reflect any commonalities or differences located at the biological level.[5]

For sure this conception is pitched at a high level of abstraction. But (despite Staveren's dismissive comment to the contrary) this in itself is not problematic. Currently, of course, at least in most societies, the positions characterised as women's roles (i.e. those to which it is held that individuals regarded as female ought to be allocated [whether or not they always are]) are in fact mostly subordinate in some ways, whilst those viewed as men's roles are typically privileged.

I am suggesting, then, that gender is a social totality, a social system. It is a system of processes and products (of processes in product and products in process). The processes in question (which are always context specific) are precisely those that work to legitimise/motivate the notion that individuals regarded as female and those regarded as male ought to be allocated to, or to have allocated to them, systematically differentiated kinds of (relationally defined) social positions. The products are the (equally transitory and spatially/culturally limited) outcomes of these processes. If the processes serve *to gender*, i.e. are gendering processes (or processes of genderation), the products (aspects of social relations, positions [with associated rights and norms], practices, identities) must be regarded as *gendered*.

*Where* precisely is the gender system? So conceived I do not think the gender system can be isolated from the rest of social reality; rather it is the whole of social reality considered under a particular (albeit only one)[6] aspect. That is, the gender system comprises all social processes/products viewed under the aspects of gendering/being rendered gendered. In all our practices, we draw upon the structures of society as we (momentarily) find them, including their gendered aspects. And through our acting, these structures – whether bearing on issues of material distribution, status, power or whatever – are, wittingly or not, continually reproduced and/or transformed. This transformational activity is the mode of being of all social processes. And all structures and their processes of reproduction seemingly have gendered aspects.

I make no presumption that any aspects of social structure, including its gendered features, are other than intrinsically dynamic, or are everywhere the same. It is evident that gender relations in most places (still) serve to facilitate (localised) practices in which men can dominate/oppress women, or appear in some way advantaged. But the extent of commonality/difference across time and space is something to be determined a posteriori.

## Final comments

The specific positions on humanism and gender that I have touched upon here may well be shown to have difficulties. This matters less, I think, than my contention that we ought not to shy away from seeking to develop the *sorts* of positions defended.

In the original dialogue published in *Feminist Economics*, I used a specific ontological conception I defend to suggest how ontology per se might make a difference to feminist theorising, and seemingly in constructive ways. My main argument was that ontology is being neglected in feminist economics for reasons that are not wholly sustainable or desirable; I was not suggesting that the conception I defend is the only possible alternative worth considering (see Lawson, 2003a, p. 244).

Here, I am arguing in a similar fashion that the idea that at least some things possess certain properties or conditions that (help) make them one sort of thing rather than another, should not be rejected out of hand, *just because* certain forms of essentialising exercises are easily seen to be untenable and even abusive, or used to "justify" undesirably discriminating practice.

As it happens, I do currently stand by the conceptions of human beings and gender I have elaborated above. But I hope it is clear that even if they are easily shown to be inadequate, this per se would be insufficient to undermine the broader conceptions of realism and essentialism that I have above sketched and partly defended. My goal all along has been not just to advance specific ontological conceptions, but as much to suggest that certain potentially useful modes of reasoning are being pushed aside on the basis of questionable reasoning.

## Notes

1 Specifically, if realism is as stated above then, if I may reproduce my earlier statement that Staveren also notes above:

> there is nothing essential to scientific or ontological realism that supposes or requires that objects of knowledge are naturalistic or other than transient, that knowledge obtained is other than fallible, partial and itself transient, or that scientists or researchers are other than positioned, biased, interested, and practically, culturally, and socially conditioned.
>
> (Lawson, 2003a, p. 220)

2 I do mean to emphasise these last remarks. Towards the conclusion of her piece Staveren suggests that, when I have previously argued that feminists should not be too quick in rejecting realism, I was imagining only a one way input: from realism to feminist theorising. But I am not sure this is fair. The truth is that I myself am very aware of my enormous debt to feminist theory, and have made no secret of this. If I failed to signal this sufficiently in the earlier dialogue then this is a significant oversight. But in truth even in the earlier exchanges I made various observations along the following lines:

> I view such projects [as feminist theorising and social realism] as mutually supportive and capable of reciprocal illumination. I am aware, in particular, that my own project has gained much from the results and manner of feminist theorising, as I indicated in the earlier *Feminist Economics* paper and as I acknowledge again below.
>
> (Lawson, 2003b, p. 234)

3 The term "essence" derives from the *ousia*, the Greek word for "being". *Ousia* is clearly still echoed in the English word "is".

4 In suggesting this position, I am clearly taking a view in which the evolution of both human being and society are interrelated.

5 I hope it is clear that, in advancing this conception, I neither assume fixity, nor deny variability (if within limits), at the biological level, and nor do I suppose that any biological sex form, or for that matter form of sexuality, is more natural than any other (nor, of course, do I endorse any such differences as there are, or perceptions of them, being used to legitimate social inequalities). I do hold that if biological differences/commonalities, as they are perceived, affect emergent social structure, then equally the (emergent) social structure can act back on the biological. However, the two domains, the biological and the socio-structural, remain ontologically distinct, though causally interacting; neither is reducible to, or explicable completely in terms of, the other. It will be clear, then, that whatever the manner in which I suggest we conceptualise gender as an aspect of social structure (see below), I am accepting the reality (and the explanatory significance), of maintaining the sex/gender distinction.

6   In viewing gender as everything considered under only *one* aspect (but without wishing to detract from the emphasis on *everything*) I concur with Nancy Fraser (2007) in viewing "gender struggles as one strand among others in a broader political project aimed at institutionalizing democratic justice across multiple axes of social differentiation".

## References

Fraser, Nancy (2007) "Feminist Politics in an Age of Recognition: A Two Dimensional Approach to Gender Justice", *The Future of Gender*, Cambridge: Cambridge University Press, pp. 17–34.

Lawson, Tony (2003a) *Reorienting Economics*, London and New York: Routledge.

Lawson, Tony (2003b) "Ontology and Feminist Theorising", *Feminist Economics*, 9(1), March, pp. 119–150. Reprinted in John B. Davis (ed.) (2006) *Recent Developments in Economic Methodology*, Cheltenham: Edward Elgar.

Lawson, Tony (2007) "Gender and Social Change", in Jude Brown (ed.) *The Future of Gender*, Cambridge: Cambridge University Press, pp. 136–162.

Sayer, Andrew (2004) "Feminism, Critical Realism and Economics: A Response to Van Staveren", *post-autistic economics review*, Issue No. 29, article 5, 6 December. Online, available at: www.paecon.net/PAEReview/issue29/ Sayer29.htm (accessed August 2006).

# 19 Conjectural revisionary ontology[1]

*Jack Vromen*

## Mainstream economists also aim at identifying underlying mechanisms

Tony Lawson (1997, 2003) has both been cherished and chastised for his characterization of mainstream economics as being positivist in methodological orientation, as dealing with closed instead of open systems, as aiming to represent event regularities (of the form "whenever event x then event y") instead of underlying causal structures and mechanisms and as exemplifying a mathematical-deductivist style of theorizing and modelling.[2] Lately, in a reply to Reiss (2004), however, Lawson states that he never held that mainstream economists are only interested in event regularities. Nor did he ever assert that neoclassical economists ignore or deny the existence of underlying causal mechanisms. Lawson asserts that he never questioned that mainstream economists entertain broader visions of economic reality consistent with the causalist ontology that he himself accepts. What he rather always held, Lawson argues, is that their preferred mathematical-deductivist style of theorizing cannot possibly do justice to such broader visions: "the prior attachment to certain sorts of mathematical methods imposes an (often unnoticed) ontology mostly inconsistent with those visions" (Lawson 2004, 337).

What I like about this argument is that it gets a possible misunderstanding that mainstream economics denies the existence of underlying causal mechanisms out of the way. What I disagree with, however, is the presumption that adherence to a mathematical-deductivist style of modelling imposes a "flat", non-layered empiricist ontology. I think this presumption is simply wrong. Of course, if one accepts Lawson's understanding of deductivism as a type of explanation in which regularities of the form "whenever event x then event y" are a necessary condition (Lawson 2003, 5), the rightness of the presumption follows by definition. But if by "deductivism" is meant (as I think it often is) a strong preference for a particular type of inferences from axioms and assumptions, then the presumption seems unwarranted. One can insist that a theory should be axiomatized, that axioms (or postulates, or first principles) should be at the basis of any theory and that all of its hypotheses should be deducible from them, for example, and yet maintain that what the axioms and theorems are (or should be) about are underlying causal mechanisms rather than observable regularities.

As far as I can see there is nothing in the Bourbaki-type, set-theoretic *ethos* that long dominated economics that prevents theorists from trying to represent underlying causal mechanisms and from exploring their consequences. What is more, many mainstream economists arguably aimed at doing precisely this. A case can even be made that Friedman, taken by many to be the spokesman of a non-realist orientation in economics *par excellence*, professed his belief in a layered ontology:

> A fundamental hypothesis of science is that appearances are deceptive and that there is a way of looking at or interpreting or organizing the evidence that will reveal superficially disconnected and diverse phenomena to be manifestations of a more fundamental and relatively simple structure.
>
> (Friedman 1953, 33)

Elsewhere Friedman argues that economic theory should concentrate on such an underlying fundamental structure, on "common and crucial elements", and abstract from other elements and factors in "explaining" phenomena (ibid., 14). Precisely because economists in their theories abstract from non-common and non-crucial, but nonetheless actually occurring disturbing factors should the regularities or tendencies that their theories predict not be expected to be empirically observable event regularities. Yet if the elements that their theories do concentrate on are really crucial, the regularities predicted should somehow be discernable in observed empirical data.[3] This depiction of Friedman of what economic theory does and does not do and what it can and cannot aspire to is not some credo of "Official Methodology" that is alien to what practising mainstream economists actually do. It seems that in his own contributions to economic theory Friedman set out to do exactly this: to identify and specify crucial underlying structures and mechanisms.

This is not to say that *what* underlying structures and mechanisms economists believe to be actually working in "the real world" can be readily read off from their theories and models. Sometimes the structures and mechanisms that they believe in are explicitly theorized and modelled. But at other times their assumptions and hypotheses do not reveal their ontological beliefs. Again Friedman (1953) is exemplary. Friedman famously argued that assumptions of economic theory should not be taken too literally. In particular, economic theory is not committed to the belief that economic agents actually go through the deliberations and calculations that economic theory's behavioural assumptions seem to ascribe to them. Economic theory is only committed to the belief that economic agents behave *as if* they actually went through these deliberations and calculations. For example, business men need not actually base their decisions on a comparison of marginal costs and revenues, as is assumed in neoclassical theory of the firm. As long as their actual behaviour is consistent with this assumption, is the theory applicable. At this juncture one might rightly wonder what then are the actually operating underlying mechanisms that make economic agents behave the way they do, if they are not the deliberations and calculations ascribed to them that make them do so. At some point in his essay Friedman suggests that it is something like "natural selection" in competitive markets that leads businessmen to behave *as if* they increase production until the point where marginal costs equal marginal revenues (see Vromen 1995 for a more detailed discussion).

What this shows, to repeat, is that the particular beliefs that economists entertain about underlying mechanisms in the real world need not be readily discernible from the assumptions and hypotheses in their theories. Even theorists such as Friedman who argue that the actual determinants of behaviour are irrelevant (as long as the behaviour actually displayed is consistent with the assumptions made) happen to entertain particular beliefs about underlying mechanisms in the real world. This raises the question why such economists do not see a need to model their beliefs explicitly. Why does Friedman not model competitive "market selection", for example, if he believes that that provides the key to understanding industry behaviour? As I take it, here we come across one of the main differences between how mainstream economists and how Lawson think how a multilayered real world should be tackled theoretically. The real difference is not that their adherence to mathematical-deductivism forecloses mainstream economics to focus on underlying mechanisms, whereas Lawson insists that focusing on underlying mechanisms is exactly what a satisfactory economic theory should do. Both camps hold that a satisfactory economic theory should identify underlying mechanisms. A real difference is rather that Lawson urges economists to model real underlying mechanisms explicitly, whereas many mainstream economists seem to think that this is not necessary.

The reason why these mainstream economists do not think this is necessary, I submit, is that they weigh various theoretical virtues that a theory might have differently from how Lawson weighs them. If some assumption is not believed to identify and specify an actually working underlying mechanism in the real world, then Lawson most probably would reject such an assumption as being deficient. By contrast, as we have just seen, at least some economists do not see a need to reject it. Following the dictum "If it ain't broke, don't fix it", they apparently do not believe the assumption to be deficient. Why not? It seems that one of the reasons that they cling to this assumption is that it allows them to retain models that they cherish for their elegance, simplicity, parsimony, tractability, unifying power and the like. It seems that Lawson wants to assign greater weight to other theoretical virtues such as truth, realism (or realisticness), credibility and plausibility. Elegance, simplicity, parsimony and the like cannot compensate for the deficiency of theories lacking in these respects. Theories and models that have greater plausibility in identifying real and important underlying mechanisms should be preferred over theories and models having less credibility in this respect, even if that would go at the expense of parsimony and tractability. Lawson's plea to bring about an ontological turn, to bring in ontology, can thus be understood as an attempt to redress the balance in theoretical virtues in economics.

A second significant and more straightforward difference between mainstream economics' and Lawson's preferred take on underlying mechanisms is that each camp has a different view on what are the important underlying causal mechanisms. Lawson presents his own theory of social ontology that self-consciously differs from the mostly implicit social ontology that mainstream economists have in the back of their minds. In Lawson's theory of ontology, social structure is an emergent property that has an existence and that has causal powers of its own (i.e. that irreducible to the individuals involved in its emergence and persistence), for example. Social rules and social positions are allotted a prominent place in Lawson's ontology. In mainstream economics' social ontology all this is denied. That is to say, many mainstream economists subscribe to some sort of ontological individualism, according to which only individuals and their properties really exist. Social phenomena are seen as intended or unintended consequences of actions and interactions of individuals. As it is denied that social phenomena have an existence of their own, they cannot causally affect properties and behaviour of individuals.

## Ontology as a final arbiter in assessing economic theories

Taken together, the two significant differences between mainstream economics and Lawson's plea to reorient economics identified here seem to suggest that the thing to do next for Lawson is to work out his own social ontology in a fully-fledged alternative economic theory. Such an alternative economic theory should not necessarily be as elegant, simple, parsimonious and the like as mainstream economic theory. Losses in these theoretical virtues would be more than compensated for by the alleged gain in terms of truth, realism and the like. I would be all in favour of this. But this is not the direction in which Lawson takes his social ontology. Lawson puts his social ontology and his realist transformational model of social activity to a different task. These he uses to assess the merits and demerits of economic theories and models put forward by others. Lawson adds all kinds of qualifications and disclaimers to his realist transformational model of social activity. He argues that his own social ontology is "practically conditioned, historical and fallible" (Lawson 2003, 61). But this does not prevent him from endowing it with quite some authority in assessments of economic theories and models. It is his transformational model of social activity that he uses as some sort of template to accuse mainstream economics of misplaced universalising. It is on the basis of his transformational model that Lawson argues that whereas mainstream economics pretends to provide a universally applicable theory, it is applicable to special cases only. Similarly, although Lawson is much more sympathetic to evolutionary economics, evolutionary economics is also argued to cover only some of the possible sources of economic change. It is his own transformational model that is said to offer a fuller story (ibid., 131). Evolutionary psychology and memetics are criticised on the same basis (ibid., 134). Lawson argues that memetics entails the proposal to reduce economic and social study to evolutionary psychology and/or biology (ibid., 139). Lawson objects to this on the ground that such attempts ignore emergent properties at levels of organisation higher than that of biology and psychology. In sum, what we see here is that Lawson's own social ontology, the transformational model of social activity, serves as a benchmark for assessing whether or not some particular economic theory suffers from attempts at misplaced universalising or reductionism.

Unlike Lawson I think that "borrowing from evolutionary biology", in the sense of assuming that the abstract structure of evolutionary theory in biology is a useful starting point for studying ongoing processes of economic evolution, does neither entail a denial of agency nor a commitment to reductionism. But arguing for this position is not my concern here (for an argument, see Vromen 2004). For now I want to examine more closely what makes Lawson so confident that any economic theory that is inconsistent with his social ontology cannot possibly be on the right track. This examination is meant to temper overdrawn hopes fostered by Lawson as to what ontology in general (not just Lawson's own ontology) can do for us. What grounds does Lawson have for believing that his ontology provides some sort of impeccable neutral ground for assessing whether there is for example misplaced universalisation or misplaced reductionism going on in specific economic theories? The issue at stake here can be unpacked into the following two questions. First, where does Lawson get his own specific ontology from (and how does he derive it)? Second, to what does Lawson's ontology owe its authority in matters of assessing the merits and demerits of specific economic theories?

Lawson claims that his transformational model of social activity is a social ontology that is derived a posteriori (Lawson 2003, 34, 42, 132–133), in a transcendental deduction (or inference), from some uncontested generalised observations about social reality. Given this claim, one would expect that Lawson explicitly states the bases of his transcendental deductions, the alleged uncontested observations about social reality, and that Lawson shows us how the transcendental deductions from them proceed. Unfortunately, neither is the case. Only now and then does Lawson report an uncontested observation about social reality from which he proceeds. And transcendental deductions are rarely if ever carried out (or presented) in any detail. Most of the time, only the (alleged) results of the (alleged) deductions are presented. Lawson ends up presenting a vast list of elements or items that together are supposed to make for the transformational model of social activity.

So the route via which Lawson arrives at his social ontology is far from transparent. This is a serious omission, I think, for it is questionable that there are many uncontested generalised observations about social reality. One such (alleged) observation is that people tend to be successful in their actions and in their attempts to find their ways in a complex society (35–36). It remains to be seen whether this is something everyone would readily agree on. It seems that among other things this depends on what criteria of "being successful" and "getting along quite well" we invoke. On sufficiently demanding (and perhaps even conventional) criteria we could perhaps as well agree that many people are not successful (and many firms go bankrupt, for example), that there are many "outcasts" in society and that contemporary societies are plagued by social conflicts, coordination failures and mutual misunderstandings. Why not take these observations as the appropriate basis for our quest for a suitable social ontology? Without further arguments why we should start with Lawson's own generalised observations about social reality, Lawson's observations, which are the basis for his transcendental deductions, appear to be somewhat arbitrary.

What is more, the status and exact workings of transcendental deductions are not uncontested either. Sometimes it seems that Lawson follows Kant in a search for conditions without which the alleged general facts observed could not possibly exist (44–45). Thus understood the social ontology uncovered consists of necessary conditions for the (alleged) existence of general patterns in social reality. The idea is that the nature of social reality must be as identified in Lawson's social ontology. For otherwise the general patterns that we observe in social reality could not have existed. The problem is that attempts at making transcendental deductions in this sense are either trivial or questionable. As an example of the former possibility, consider: "We walk, talk, read, write, sing, interact, imitate, etc. In order to do these things we must possess the capacities to do these things" (45). Well, in order to write this chapter I must have the capacity to do so. This is certainly and trivially true. But in and by itself this is not very informative. For the transcendental deduction to deliver substantive results more is required. What does the capacity consist of, what exactly is the capacity, what is the quality of the behaviour if the capacity is exercised, when does exercising the capacity yield good results, are among the things we might want to know about the capacity. It is highly questionable, however, and here I come at the latter possibility, that any answer to one of the questions could possibly be the result of a transcendental deduction. For note what an argument backing up the claim that a transcendental deduction could produce such a substantive answer would imply. It would imply the claim that the social activities or phenomena observed could not possibly have been produced otherwise. It is impossible, it seems, to live up to the burden of proof that this claim implies.

Thus it seems that transcendental deductions either border on vacuity or on invalidity.[4] Either they do not produce interesting new insights, but merely paraphrase what is assumed. Or the transcendental deductions do not stand up to serious scrutiny. If capacities are not understood in such a way that they are presupposed by definition, then it is hard if not impossible to demonstrate that without certain capacities in place, social reality could not possibly have existed. The situation here with Lawson's social ontology is similar to that with Searle's social ontology (Searle 1995). Searle argues that collective intentionality is a necessary precondition for social reality. He furthermore argues that a pre-intentional sense of us (or of community) is in turn a necessary precondition for collective intentionality. Now it is possible to understand "social reality", "collective intentionality" and "a pre-intentional sense of us" in a way that makes "a pre-intentional sense of us" a necessary precondition for collective intentionality and collective intentionality in turn a necessary precondition for social reality by definition. But on such a reading Searle's claims are not very interesting. If on the other hand "social reality", "collective intentionality" and "a pre-intentional sense of us" are defined independently of each other, Searle's claims seem to be untenable. There clearly seem to be parts of social reality for which collective intentionality is not required. And there seem to be avenues leading to collective intentionality that do not involve a "pre-intentional sense of us" (see Vromen 2003 for a more elaborate argument).

Given all the obscurities and problems that surround Lawson's transcendental deduction of his social ontology, I conclude that it cannot play the adjudicating role that Lawson imputes to it. One of the reasons for Lawson to argue for the primacy of ontology is that "all methods, frameworks and points of view carry ontological presuppositions". This arguably is true. But what follows from it? Lawson seems to infer from this that in assessing existing theories and in constructing new ones we'd better start with ontology, rather than with methodology and epistemology, for example. But with what ontology should we start then? What ontology has sufficient credentials to play this role? Lawson's assertion that all methods, frameworks and points of view have ontological presuppositions can also be turned upside down here. Any attempt to formulate an appropriate ontology presupposes a point of view and has epistemic presuppositions. Where do we get an appropriate ontology from? How credible is a proposal for an appropriate ontology? What evidence and support can the proposal draw on? It is hard to avoid the impression that Lawson's social ontology is a renewed attempt at *prima philosophia*. It is an attempt to identify the basic and essential building blocks of social reality without taking recourse to, and even without being informed by empirical science and empirical research. Apparently, Lawson believes that his attempt succeeded. But what reasons or evidence does he give those who do not already have the same persuasion to come to share this belief? Not many, I submit. To put it bluntly, why would or should we believe that Lawson's social ontology is more credible than the specific economic theories that he assesses on the basis of it?

## An alternative: conjectural revisionary ontology

History is replete with examples of situations in which new insights and new findings in science proved firmly held ontological convictions about the nature and constituents of reality wrong. This raises questions not just about the credibility and reliability of Lawson's ontological convictions, but also, more generally, about the proper role of ontological views in scientific theorizing. The lesson to be learnt from the historical examples is not, I think, that ontological views can only stand in the way of the breakthrough of new scientific insights that threaten to undermine those ontological views. New, revisionary ontological views can also inspire and guide the development of new scientific insights. And this, I submit, is the role that Lawson's realist transformational model of social activity in principle and ideally could play. Rather than acting as some supposedly self-evidently correct template of the totality of social reality (which, I argued, it in fact isn't) for the unmasking of existing theories and models as being non-universal and reductionist, as it now does in Lawson's work, the realist transformational model of social activity could serve more constructively as a first sketch or outline of a yet to be worked out new theory. Lawson's realist transformational model of social activity could act as a *conjectural revisionary economic ontology* (Vromen 2004). It would be revisionary in that it is different from the ontological views that mainstream economists entertain and it would be conjectural in that it does not and cannot pretend to be more than a first guess about how social reality in fact is constituted. The merits of this first guess can only be ascertained after it has been worked out into a new fully fledged theory and after this new theory is assessed properly. The standards or criteria to be invoked in this assessment are fairly standard ones, I think. As Kincaid (1996) argues, they fall within three broad categories: evidential, explanatory and formal. The theory should be supported by empirical and theoretical evidence, it should display explanatory power and it should meet certain formal requirements such as parsimony, internal consistency and tractability.

Unlike in mainstream economics, formal standards (or theoretical virtues) should not outweigh evidential and explanatory ones. Considerations pertaining to elegance, parsimony, tractability and the like should not be called upon to defend a theory, for example, that is obviously at odds with available theoretical evidence. Such considerations should not be abused in particular to ignore relevant findings and insights obtained in other disciplines. Of the other standards critical realists such as Lawson are likely to find that of empirical adequacy most suspicious. After all, one of the key insights of critical realists is that we should not expect the functioning of underlying mechanisms to result in event regularities. This seems to disqualify empirical adequacy as an appropriate standard. But one does not need to be a fan of Friedman to appreciate that if some allegedly crucial or essential mechanism really is crucial or essential, it must be possible to somehow trace its workings and its effects in empirical data.

To sum up, I think that Lawson's plea to bring in considerations of an ontological kind in attempts to reorient economics is to be welcomed. Such considerations deserve more attention and deserve to carry more weight in economics than they currently have. In particular, if specific beliefs about real underlying mechanisms are strongly held, then this should result in attempts to theorize and model these mechanisms explicitly, even if this would go at the expense of parsimony, simplicity, theoretical elegance, tractability and the like. But such ontological considerations should not and cannot play the "final arbiter" kind of role, adjudicating once and for all the shortcomings of existing economic theories and models, that Lawson attributes to them. Instead of playing this negative and critical role, ontological considerations such as the ones that went into Lawson's realist transformational model of social activity should rather play a more constructive role. They should function as heuristic principles, guiding the development of a new economic theory (or of new economic theories). Only after such a new theory is developed and assessed in a fairly standard way can the fruitfulness of Lawson's realist transformational model of social activity for economic theorizing be evaluated.

## Notes

1 This is an extended and revised version of section 2 of Vromen (2004).
2 For the sake of convenience I comply with Lawson's practice to refer to mainstream or modern economics (as if it were a monolithic bloc), but only reluctantly, because I believe that it is increasingly difficult to identify a distinguishing set of features that widely accepted or respected economic theories have in common with each other.
3 If this is a fair representation of a typical mainstream economist's position,

then mainstream economics does not believe that the real world is a closed system. What's more, mainstream economics then does not display a preference for closed system theorizing either. If closed systems really are systems in which event regularities occur, as Lawson argues, then on my representation theories in mainstream economics do not present closed systems.

4 For a more elaborate discussion of Lawson's use of transcendental deductions, see Guala (2003). Guala tries to do more justice to Lawson's assertion that his transcendental deductions are fallible. But in the end he reaches a conclusion that is similar to mine: transcendental arguments cannot possibly deliver the kind of substantive non-trivial insights that Lawson wants to derive from them.

## References

Friedman, Milton (1953), *Essays in Positive Economics*, Chicago, IL: University of Chicago Press.

Guala, Francesco (2003), Talking about structures: the "transcendental" argument (revised version of paper presented at INEM Conference, Stirling, September 2002).

Kincaid, Harold (1996), *Philosophical Foundations of the Social Sciences: Analyzing Controversies in Social Research*, Cambridge: Cambridge University Press.

Lawson, Tony (1997), *Economics and Reality*, London and New York: Routledge.

—— (2003), *Reorienting Economics*, London and New York: Routledge.

—— (2004), Reorienting economics: On heterodox economics, themata and the use of mathematics in economics, *Journal of Economic Methodology* 11 (3), 329–340.

Reiss, Julian (2004), Critical realism and the mainstream, *Journal of Economic Methodology*, 11 (3), 321–327.

Searle, John R. (1995), *The Construction of Social Reality*, New York: Free Press.

Vromen, Jack (1995), *Economic Evolution: An Enquiry into the Foundations of New Institutional Economics*, London: Routledge.

—— (2003), Collective intentionality, social reality and evolutionary biology, *Philosophical Explorations* VI (3), 251–264.

—— (2004), Conjectural revisionary economic ontology: Outline of an ambitious research agenda for evolutionary economics, *Journal of Economic Methodology* 11 (2), 213–247.

# 20 Provisionally grounded critical ontology
## Reply to Vromen

*Tony Lawson*

Jack Vromen advances an interesting critique of the way I make use of ontology to criticise aspects of mainstream (and other) practices. He holds, in particular, that my portrayal of the mainstream is inaccurate and my use of ontology unjustified. His critique takes the form of a set of interrelated steps. Let me consider each of these in their turn.

### Mainstream deductivist modelling

Vromen starts out acknowledging that I accept that mainstream economists, like the rest of us, undoubtedly adhere to a causal ontology as part of their broader visions or presuppositions.

Vromen also notes my contention that the mainstream emphasis on "mathematical-deductivist style of theorizing cannot possibly do justice to such broader visions". My concern, indeed, is that this emphasis almost inevitably leads these economists to distort their substantive conceptions of social reality, so much so that their professional contributions become, to a very significant extent, irrelevant.

Vromen, though, takes issue with me here. As he puts it, I am simply wrong to suppose "a mathematical-deductivist style of modelling imposes a 'flat', non-layered empiricist ontology". Vromen accepts I would be right if mainstream deductivism meant or entailed "a type of explanation in which regularities of the form 'whenever event x then event y' are a necessary condition". However, reasons Vromen, mainstream economists often just make "inferences from axioms and assumptions", and one can "maintain that what the axioms and theorems are (or should be) about are underlying causal mechanisms rather than observable regularities".

Vromen acknowledges, that in forming hypotheses about these underlying mechanisms, mainstream economists do predict exact event regularities. However, in his view these should not be "expected to be empirically observable event regularities" just because of the real world interference of "non-common and non-crucial, but nonetheless actually occurring disturbing factors". Even so, Vromen continues, if mainstream economists correctly abstract the underlying structures then "the regularities predicted should somehow be discernable in observed empirical data".

Vromen adds, "there is nothing in the Bourbaki-type, set-theoretic *ethos* that long dominated economics that prevents theorists from trying to represent underlying causal mechanisms and from exploring their consequences".

## Atomism not empiricism

Vromen, though, is slightly misconstruing me in all this. My contention is not that the emphasis on mathematical-deductivist methods forces the mainstream to accept a "flat", non-layered empiricist ontology. It is rather that this emphasis restricts the mainstream to theorising in terms of closed worlds of isolated atoms. By atoms, I do not mean something small of course. I mean, rather, stable entities that (if triggered) have their own separate and invariable effects whatever the context. If such an atomistic ontology were not imposed then deductive inferences would not be feasible, we would not expect mechanisms to be manifest as event regularities distorted merely by the odd disturbing factor, and nor in particular would theorems to which Vromen refers be possible.

I nowhere suggest that this necessity to theorise in terms of an atomistic ontology prevents mainstream practitioners from surrounding their models with a rhetoric of underlying structures or potentials. It does not even prevent them from making sets of underlying structures or potentials a feature of the analysis (see *Reorienting Economics*, chapter 1); the latter can indeed be specified in axioms and assumptions, or whatever. The mainstream deductivist orientation does though entail that any such set of structures be conceptualised as cohering as a stable entity that, when triggered or stimulated, always has the same effect. Thus individuals always optimise, firms always maximise profits, or whatever.

Furthermore, if, as I argue, social reality is not closed and atomistic, but open and complex (being, for example, processual and highly internally related) and characterised by emergent properties, then mainstream theorising, with its inevitable atomistic constructions, will frequently be so divorced from the real world that its various claims will very often not have any empirical, or even any real world, counterparts (even after allowing for "actually occurring disturbing factors"). So, I nowhere characterise the mainstream ontology as empiricist.

What is relevant here is *the structure of mainstream explanation*. Deductivism posits claims of the *form*: "whenever event or state of affairs x then event or state of affairs y", even if the events and states of affairs are totally implausible, quite impossible fictions or counterfactuals. And this is the structure imposed whether or not (or whichever) causal factors are stipulated in the axioms. If deductive inference is to proceed, and

Vromen seems to recognise that this is a mainstream requirement, this structure of explanation is always presupposed. The result, in effect, is a set of theories always taking the form: "under conditions x then (given the typically optimising framework expressed in the decision structure of the theory [a structure that may reference numerous causal mechanisms, etc]) outcome(s) y will follow". Or, "whenever x then y". This ontological scenario is in no way disturbed if, like Vromen, we add that these event regularities will be manifest not exactly, but subject to merely contingent and non-systematic disturbing factors.

Vromen's reference to Bourbaki thinking only reinforces this interpretation. For the defining feature of the Bourbaki school is that theorems, etc., can be developed in purely abstract terms, that interpretations are irrelevant, variable and, if required, something to be tagged on after the mathematical processes have been completed (see e.g. Debreu's comments discussed in *Reorienting Economics*). The feature that is regarded as essential in Bourbaki thinking is not the content of the axioms, whether couched in terms of causal factors or whatever, but the *structure* of the reasoning. And the manner in which formalistic reasoning has been employed in economics is inherently deductivist, presupposing chains of reasoning of the event regularity *form*. Once, or if, substantive content is also implicated, and in economics it always is, the ontology is necessarily of closed worlds of isolated atoms.

So in short, I do not claim that mainstream deductivist modelling necessitates "a 'flat', non-layered empiricist ontology". Certainly, the posited actual outcomes need have no empirical aspect or counterpart. And theories can reference underlying or deep structures, so long as they are collectively constrained to cohere as entities of a form that, when triggered, act atomistically.

Of course, given that any theorised powers and structures must be so constrained, and given too that the modelling emphasis additionally requires that capacities *are always actualised* in behaviour, we can nevertheless with reason talk of reality being somewhat flattened. If, say, due to the needs of the modelling exercise, any theorised capacities for rationality must in the end be treated as always reflected in (rational) *behaviour* (so that the issue of whether or not to be rational is not under the control of the agent) then there is a sense in which reference to powers becomes to a degree superfluous and, in this sense, the ontology is flattened.

But my central claim about the mainstream reliance upon certain sorts of mathematical-deductive systems is that this practice necessarily results in sets of theories couched ultimately in terms of closed systems of isolated atoms (whatever may be the form of any associated but inevitably inconsequential rhetoric).

## Merely "as if" theorising

Having argued (as if against me) that mainstream economists can theorise in terms of causal mechanisms, Vromen next suggests that the causal mechanisms actually specified by the mainstream may not be the causal mechanisms believed actually to be operative. This, Vromen contends, is because mainstream economists follow Milton Friedman (1953) and frequently argue that it is *only as if* any mechanism explicitly specified within the theory applies:

> For example, businessmen need not actually base their decisions on a comparison of marginal costs and revenues, as is assumed in neoclassical theory of the firm. As long as their actual behaviour is consistent with this assumption, is the theory applicable.

Why should we expect actual behaviour to be (or even imagine that it could be) consistent with a theory that does not describe it? Social reality, according to Friedman is an evolutionary process, effectively selecting those who act in the most rational or optimal way, so that, for survivors, it will be *as if* they optimised.

Now the reason that Vromen runs through all this is seemingly to emphasise that particular beliefs about underlying mechanisms cannot be read off from the accounts that mainstream theorists explicitly formulate. And this claim feeds into Vromen's contention about the (first) real difference between the mainstream and me. This is that although I believe that causal mechanisms actually responsible for phenomena of interest should be explicitly theorised, the mainstream regards this as unnecessary:

> The real difference is not that their adherence to mathematical-deductivism forecloses mainstream economics to focus on underlying mechanisms, whereas Lawson insists that focusing on underlying mechanisms is exactly what a satisfactory economic theory should do. Both camps hold that a satisfactory economic theory should identify underlying mechanisms. A real difference is rather that Lawson urges economists to model real underlying mechanisms explicitly, whereas many mainstream economists seem to think that this is not necessary.

Now even if it were the case that mainstream practitioners, with their recourse to "as if" reasoning, do not need to elaborate real causal mechanisms, they might still choose to do so. Why, though, does Vromen suppose that they mostly seem to prefer not to?

The answer is that these mainstream economists believe that their "merely as if" modelling practices are adequate as they stand, and so ("[f]ollowing the dictum 'If it ain't broke, don't fix it'") decide instead to prioritise other criteria over realisticness of causal hypothesis. In other words, the mainstream, according to Vromen, stick to causal claims known to be false where the latter are of a sort that "allows them to retain models that they cherish for their elegance, simplicity, parsimony, tractability, unifying power and the like".

Vromen rightly portrays me as not being too impressed by such reasoning, pointing out that I prioritise realisticness "even if that would go at the expense of parsimony and tractability". However, Vromen thereby concludes that my urging of an ontological turn in *Reorienting Economics* is best viewed as my merely preferring a reordering of what he calls the "theoretical virtues in economics" with realisticness (or search for truth) taking the top slot.[1]

## The state of the mainstream

The feature that most surprises me about Vromen's exposition and analysis in this part of the chapter is how uncritical he remains of the mainstream, and of Friedman's arguments in particular. Though he does not quite say it, he encourages the idea that there is nothing inherently wrong with mainstream practice. He merely observes that it is different from my own, and specifically that it reflects a preference for alternative "theoretical virtues". The latter may result in theoretical fictions, but these are regarded as entirely satisfactory because (or where) they are legitimated by Friedman's "as if" form of theorising. So indeed, if it ain't broke, why fix it?

But of course it is "broke". Mainstream economists themselves testify to this often enough (see e.g. Coase, 1999; Kay, 1995; Rubinstein, 1995). Friedman himself concludes that "economics has become increasingly an arcane branch of mathematics rather than dealing with real economic problems" (Friedman, 1999, p. 137).

Let us be clear. When Friedman (1953) introduced his methodological paper arguing the benefits of "as if" theorising, he claimed that this approach is adequate because event prediction is essentially all that economists require. This contention was criticised by very many methodologists at the time, mostly arguing that prediction is not sufficient for analysis. None, though, seemed to disturb Friedman's conclusions. The reason for this is that these methodologists, implicitly taking it for granted that event regularities are everywhere to be had, accepted that ubiquitous (conditional) event prediction is (if not sufficient) both possible and necessary (see Lawson, 1997, pp. 309, 310).

But any presumption that prediction is necessary or even typically possible is also false. It is not necessary just because, in a structured reality, the uncovering of deeper causal structures and mechanisms gives us most of what we need to understand and capably transform (aspects of) social reality. And conditional event prediction is rarely possible just because it presupposes event-regularities of a certain sort that are found rarely to occur in the social realm. And we can understand why. For the presumption of ubiquity of event regularities, in turn presupposes (if they are to be guaranteed), an ontology of closed systems of isolated atoms. This ontology, it is easily shown, is not at all like the nature of the social world in which we actually live. No wonder, then, that so many mainstream economists themselves report that their project fails by its own standards, and in particular, as we see even Friedman acknowledges, is not very good at dealing with real economic problems.

It makes little difference here whether or not, in their broader reflections, the mainstream think beyond the narrow constructions of their explicit formal modelling, or whether the latter takes the form of "as if" theorising. The reliance on formalistic models forces the mainstream on to the path of irrelevance in the sense of constructing substantive content for a closed and atomistic world, and anyone who claims that the project ain't broke can really only be expressing a matter of hope and faith and ignoring widespread experience of academic economic endeavour.

Vromen is right, though, when he suggests that I want to prioritise the criterion of being realistic or the pursuit of truth. But, as I say, I do so *not* in a context where the mainstream project is getting along fine by way of prioritising tractability, etc. And my stance here is not an alternative to calling for an ontological turn. For not only do ontological considerations help explain the enduring explanatory and predictive failings of the mainstream, but the mainstream stance is "justified" typically by the suggestion that the emphasis on formalism is consistent with proper science. As I have demonstrated often enough, ontological analysis can easily reveal that this conception of scientificity is untenable. So in various ways, my call for an ontological turn, and my prioritising of seeking realistic theories are connected.

## Emergence and individualism

To complete the first stage of his argument Vromen elaborates what he describes as a "second significant and more straightforward difference" between the mainstream and me. This is that whilst I defend an emergent, non-reductionist, social ontology, the ontology supported by the mainstream is individualist.

In truth, however, this takes the form of an additional (second) difference in Vromen's exegesis just because, to this point, he misconstrues me as imputing an empiricist ontology to the mainstream. Once we acknowledge that in reality I criticise the mainstream *not* as empiricist but as insisting on (mathematical-deductivist) methods that presuppose an (unsustainable) atomistic ontology, then this supposed "second difference" can be seen to be more of the same, and in effect a special case.

For ontological individualism of the sort that Vromen finds in modern mainstream economics is precisely a particular version of such an ontological atomism. Individualism does not exhaust the mainstream project just because the latter has occasional recourse to other sorts of atomistic entities such as (of course naive and implausible) conceptions of firms and even versions of collectivities (see e.g. Alan Kirman, 1989, p. 138, and the discussion in response to Bruce McFarling earlier in this volume).

## Conjectural revisionary ontology?

In any case, Vromen identifies what he supposes are the two main and valid differences between myself and the mainstream, and proceeds to make use of them as the second basic stage of his argument. The first such difference is that I prioritise realisticness, or the search for truth, in substantive work, while the mainstream is more concerned with tractability, elegance, simplicity and the like. The second difference is that I defend an emergentist ontology while the mainstream adheres to an individualist (really an atomistic) one.

According to Vromen the existence of these two differences makes it sensible that I seek to develop fully fledged substantive economic theories that are both (1) consistent with the emergentist ontology I defend and (2) evaluated in terms of their realisticness or explanatory power (rather than in terms of their elegance, simplicity, parsimony, tractability, unifying power and the like).

Vromen, though, is disappointed to find that I seem to proceed in a quite different way and use my ontological conception solely to criticise various approaches of others.

Vromen's worry is that my ontology is not up to this task. For first, or so Vromen asserts, I do not justify my ontological conception at all adequately. In particular, I am said to resort to transcendental arguments that are not up to the job.

In consequence, reasons Vromen, my project might best be interpreted as one in *conjectural revisionary ontology*.

> It would be revisionary in that it is different from the ontological views that mainstream economists entertain and it would be conjectural in that it does not and cannot pretend to be more than a first guess about how social reality in fact is constituted

(a charge, as we have seen, that was picked up and reasserted by Davidsen elsewhere in this volume).

## Underlabouring with ontology

Now I do acknowledge that Vromen correctly identifies certain differences between myself and the mainstream, even if Vromen's process of identifying them is, as we have also seen, strewn with claims and arguments that in themselves are often not correct.

But the assertion that I nowhere justify my ontological conception is perplexing (see e.g. chapter 2 of *Reorienting Economics*). Still Vromen's worry does provide an opportunity for me to run through some of it again.

Before I do so though let me clarify a feature of my practice that Vromen is criticising. For at times, Vromen runs together different sorts of claims, some of which are correct, but some of which are not.

At times Vromen makes claims or poses questions like the following:

> Lawson puts his social ontology and his realist transformational model of social activity to a different task. These he uses to assess the merits and demerits of economic theories and models put forward by others.

> But this does not prevent [Lawson] from endowing [his social ontology] with quite some authority in assessments of economic theories and models.

> In sum, what we see here is that Lawson's own social ontology, the transformational model of social activity, serves as a benchmark for assessing whether or not some particular economic theory suffers from attempts at misplaced universalising or reductionism.

> Second, to what does Lawson's ontology owe its authority in matters of assessing the merits and demerits of specific economic theories?

> To put it bluntly, why would or should we believe that Lawson's social ontology is more credible than the specific economic theories that he assesses on the basis of it?

At other times Vromen argues as follows:

> It is his transformational model of social activity that he uses as some sort of template to accuse mainstream economics of misplaced universalising. It is on the basis of his transformational model that Lawson argues that whereas mainstream economics pretends to provide a universally applicable theory, it is applicable to special cases only. Similarly, although Lawson is much more sympathetic to evolutionary economics, evolutionary economics is also argued to

cover only some of the possible sources of economic change. It is his own transformational model that is said to offer a fuller story ... Lawson argues that memetics entails the proposal to reduce economic and social study to evolutionary psychology and/or biology (ibid., 139). Lawson objects to this on the ground that such attempts ignore emergent properties at levels of organisation higher than that of biology and psychology.

Now the latter longer passage I more or less fully endorse, but not the former shorter statements (the latter claims appearing, in Vromen's text, on either side of the longer passage or in his conclusion). The difference between these two sets of passages is that each of the former group of shorter statements portrays me as supposing that the sort of (philosophical) ontological conception I defend can be (and has been) brought to bear on the critique of individual substantive theories; the latter longer passage portrays me as underlabouring in a rather more general sense. It is only the latter assessment that describes my practices and intentions. Let me briefly elaborate.

For the moment I will take it for granted that, contra Vromen, the ontology I defend is grounded (a matter to which I turn below). This is not the issue before us at the current point; my concern is with how such an ontology, if (thought to be) grounded, is, and/or could be, used.

Let me first turn to the second, longer passage by Vromen. It is indeed the case that I believe the ontology I defend, for example the transformational model, is (if correct at all) highly generalised (though this is not to claim that it is in any sense neutral). Social phenomena are those whose existence depends at least in part on us. And the contention being advanced is that where social phenomena, not least social structures, are found to endure it is because they are reproduced and/or transformed through human practice (rather than say somehow fixed, or recreated anew every split second). I also argue that social structures are everywhere internally related to practices on which they depend and to other structures (for example all positions and identities are constitutionally other-oriented).

Now, in acknowledging the generality of claims such as these, I do suggest that the ontological conception I defend as a whole situates, as special cases, both the implicit ontology of mainstream economics, as well as the quite different ontology of evolutionary thinking that builds on the natural selection metaphor. Indeed, I spend a good deal of time arguing that this is so, and pointing out how, as a result, we might interpret the ontologies presupposed by mathematical-deductive and natural-selection evolutionary thinking from the perspective on the ontology I defend.

But I do not suggest that either mathematical modelling or social evolution of the natural selection sort cannot be relevant. In fact, in

*Reorienting Economics* I indicate the sorts of restrictions on the ontological conception I defend that would have to occur for either approach to be applicable.

Because there are indeed conditions that must be satisfied if mathematical modelling or evolutionary theorising of the natural selection sort are to be guaranteed success, I do caution against universalising these approaches in advance of investigation. And in the light of our experience of (the reductionist practices of) the mainstream so frequently failing to provide insight, we can offer an explanation of this failure. As regards to the evolutionary approach, I have done little more than caution against universalising it a priori.[2]

I turn, then, to the former listed set of (smaller) statements by Vromen that refer to specific theories and models. Now, I have always insisted that (philosophical) ontology cannot do the work either of (wholly) constructing, or of deconstructing, any *specific* substantive theory or model. The first part of this contention holds just because so many empirical claims must be introduced in order to get from the ontological conception I defend to any particular substantive theory or model. As a result, numerous competing (successful and unsuccessful) theories can all claim to have been derived in a manner consistent with the ontology in question.

Further, turning to the second part of the qualificatory contention, the ontological conception I defend is insufficient for undermining any particular substantive theory, in part because false substantive claims may yet be consistent with this ontology, but for other reasons too. Specifically, although it is possible, from the perspective of philosophical ontology, to be critical of generalist approaches like mainstream deductivism, it is impossible to rule out the possibility of their having individual successes. That is, it is at least possible in principle that the specific empirical conditions uncovered in substantive work occasionally act to constrain a domain of reality in such a fashion as to render it locally and temporally close to, say, a closed atomistic world such as presupposed by mainstream deductivist modelling, or some such (see *Reorienting Economics*, chapter 1).

This does not apply for most interesting cases of scientific ontology (see my response to Davidsen in this volume), for example studying the nature of capitalism, technology, money and so forth. Here, given the predominance of the features typically focused upon, the ontological conception I defend (if reasonably correct) can be expected to be more clearly and predominantly manifest. But very specific local processes (for example driving in a busy town centre in the UK in the rush hour) may produce temporary behaviour of the event-regularity sort. So, I repeat once more, that although I certainly caution against the universalisation of conceptions of closed atomistic scenarios and other unlikely and very special cases, I do not assert that they cannot, or have not, come about.

Determining whether or not they occur is a task for substantive social science, not philosophical ontology.[3]

This issue of the relation between ontology and substantive theory also connects to Vromen's discussion at the end of his chapter where he introduces his notion of "conjectural revisionary ontology". I am, of course, going to argue that the conception I defend is sufficiently grounded that it is misleading to view it as merely conjectural. But even if this were not so, it would not follow, as Vromen seems to suppose, that the ontological conception could be assessed according to the empirical adequacy of *specific* substantive theories guided by it. I say this, not because I am opposed to empirical work as Vromen seems to imply (indeed I certainly am not), but for the reasons given above. I repeat again, that to move from the ontological conception I defend to substantive work requires the addition of numerous empirical claims. A large number of theories (of some phenomenon of interest) could be generated all consistent with the ontological conception I defend. As such, the explanatory success or failure of any one of them would have little direct bearing on the adequacy of the ontological conception in question.

I elaborate at length on this issue in my reply to Davidsen, so I will not say more here. But it is worth bearing in mind that if my conception were as conjectural as Vromen suggests, we would need methods for, or ways of, assessing it that are quite different from those that Vromen suggests, and actually along the lines I have been working anyway.

## Grounding ontology

With these preliminaries out of the way, let me turn to Vromen's central contention: that the ontological conception I defend is not sufficiently grounded for the use I make of it. Indeed, Vromen, as just noted, thinks it is little more than an unsupported conjecture.

Unfortunately, Vromen's discussion at this point is mostly assertive. He notes that I have sometimes resorted to transcendental arguments to ground the conception I defend. For this I require premises about generalised features of experience to initiate the analysis, and then I need to make an explanatory move (the transcendental deduction or inference) to elaborate a conception of a feature of social reality such that, if the conception were correct, the conditions identified in the premises would be accounted for.

Clearly, the process seems firmer if the initiating premises are relatively uncontested (perhaps even accepted by opponents of my position). It will be firmer still if it is feasible to come up with only one social ontological conception that can straightforwardly render the content of our initiating premises intelligible.

I think the arguments made in supporting the conception I favour do work. However Vromen writes:

Lawson claims that his transformational model of social activity is a social ontology that is derived *a posteriori* (Lawson 2003a, 34, 42, 132–133), in a transcendental deduction (or inference), from some uncontested generalised observations about social reality. Given this claim, one would expect that Lawson explicitly states the bases of his transcendental deductions, the alleged uncontested observations about social reality, and that Lawson shows us how the transcendental deductions from them proceed. Unfortunately, neither is the case.

I am not sure why Vromen asserts that I do not explicitly state the generalised features of experience from which I start, features chosen because they seem likely to be not too contentious. In *Reorienting Economics*, for example, I am explicit that, in making transcendental arguments, I use as initiating premises: "the experience that routinised behaviour is pervasive" (p. 36); the "fact that practices governed by rules are not always, or on average, in conformity with our formulations of these rules" (p. 37); the further "fact that rules are often (or even sometimes) so much, and possibly systematically, out of phase with the practices they condition" (p. 37); the observation that "the practices people follow, including routines (which may or may not become habitual), are highly, and *systematically*, segmented or differentiated" (p. 38); the "yet further generalised observation, that practices which can be followed in any context [...] are often independent of the particular individuals carrying them out at any point in time" (p. 38); "the further generalised feature of experience that our practices are not only differentiated but typically systematically and constitutively other-oriented (p. 39)"; the "significant observation here is that there is an a posteriori degree of *continuity* in our everyday affairs" despite an absence of the sorts of event regularities that deductivist modellers seek (p. 40); "a further and related generalised feature of experience [is] that where these (strict or partial) empirical patterns are more abstract, the greater, very often, is their space–time reach or stretch" (p. 42); "the further generalised feature of experience that we regularly act in many habitual ways simultaneously" (p. 45); and so on.[4]

Showing how the transcendental deductions proceed (as opposed to stating the conceptions arrived at) is less easy. Transcendental reasoning is of course a special case of retroductive reasoning, the move from some phenomenon to its (causal) conditions, or conditions of possibility. There is no algorithm for this; though it will often be governed by a logic of analogy or metaphor. But how we make the move is often difficult to say, or even remember. It is typically a speculative move. The important matter is that certain conceptions, however arrived at, do the job in the sense that they are such that, if true, they would (be able to) explain the content of the initiating premises.

Perhaps Alfred North Whitehead captures the process well. In *Process and Reality*, Whitehead is concerned, in particular, with speculative philosophy, the central feature of which he understands to be "the endeavor to frame a … system of general ideas in terms of which every element of our experience can be interpreted" (Whitehead, 1978 [1929], p. 3). He is explicit that in "metaphysics" and "whenever we seek the larger generalities", the relevant method must include "the play of free imagination" (p. 5). He continues:

> The true method of discovery is like the flight of an airplane. It starts from the ground of particular observation; it makes a flight in the thin air of imaginative generalization; and it again lands for renewed observation rendered acute by rational interpretation. The reason for the success of this method of imaginative rationalization is that, when the method of difference fails, factors which are constantly present may yet be observed under the influence of imaginative thought. Such thought supplies the differences which the direct observation lacks. It can even play with inconsistency; and can thus throw light on the consistent, and persistent, elements in experience by comparison with what in imagination is inconsistent with them. The negative judgment is the peak of mentality.
>
> (p. 5)

Consider the example that seems to be Vromen's main concern, the transformational model of social activity. A first initiating observation is that everything in the social realm depends on us; indeed this is precisely my conception of the social. So, if there are social structures that are ontologically distinct from our practices (a result established earlier in my text by transcendental reasoning – see Lawson, 2003a, pp. 36, 37), these structures do depend on our practices. But a further relevant generalised feature of experience is that most examples of enduring social structure – think of language, culture, social institutions – are not created every moment anew by us; we find them already in place and draw on them in our practices. An additional generalised feature is that social structures such as these enable and constrain our practices but do not determine them. The English language system, for example, does not determine what I say. So social structure and human agency each depend on, but neither creates nor determines, the other.

How do we make sense of all this? The thesis I defend here is that all relatively enduring social structure is reproduced or transformed through practice. How is this thesis derived? I suppose, in part, by running though all imaginable alternatives (though it is difficult to say what limits the scope of imagination). Certainly, the idea that structure is fixed independently of us is difficult to sustain. Who fixes it? How? It is equally difficult to sustain the notion that social structure such as language is recreated anew every split second. We would not even know how to recreate existing social structure, even if it were practically conceivable, which given the continuous nature of human interaction and complexities of intentional human coordination, it clearly is not.

It makes sense, though, to see all social structure (again we might think of language), as a typically unacknowledged condition of our (speech) acts, and to recognise its continued reproduction and/or transformation as an unintended consequence. This, indeed, is the only conception that I can come up with that can at all make sense of the generalised facts of experience before us.

I fear it may not always be possible to give more detail than this of how conceptions are derived. But what matters, I submit, is that, however derived, if a conception is to be retained, it should be seen to possess the required explanatory power. And the transformational model just described is not only clearly demonstrated to do so, but also, as far as I can see at least, is the most explanatorily powerful contender currently on offer.

## An arbitrary point of entry

Vromen's next line of attack is to suggest that the premises, the generalised features of experience I fix upon, are arbitrary. That is right. This is surely a strength of the argument. The premises could be almost anything. My claim is that more or less any sustainable claim concerning a generalised feature of experience can serve as a premise, and we would still find the same (philosophical) ontological conception to be a condition of its possibility. As I make clear in my response to Davidsen in this volume, when I am addressing particular debates on specific literatures, I focus on generalisations relative to those debates. In the examples above, I have chosen factors that merely seem relatively non-contentious.

If the goal is to convince others, and it often is, then by far the most satisfactory scenario is for the opponent to supply her or his own premises. For then charges of somehow choosing overly convenient observations and suchlike can also be avoided. Fortunately, Vromen does provide some alternative premises himself. So let us take a closer look.

One observation I make is that individuals everywhere seem rather successful at negotiating the usually complex social localities in which they are (over a lengthy period) located. Vromen responds as follows:

> One such (alleged) observation [noted by Lawson] is that people tend to be successful in their actions and in their attempts to find their ways in a complex society (35–36). It remains to be seen whether this is something everyone would readily agree on. It seems that among other things this depends on what criteria of "being successful" and "getting along quite well" we invoke. On sufficiently

demanding (and perhaps even conventional) criteria we could perhaps as well agree that many people are not successful (and many firms go bankrupt, for example), that there are many "outcasts" in society and that contemporary societies are plagued by social conflicts, coordination failures and mutual misunderstandings. Why not take these observations as the appropriate basis for our quest for a suitable social ontology? Without further arguments why we should start with Lawson's own generalised observations about social reality, Lawson's observations, which are the basis for his transcendental deductions, appear to be somewhat arbitrary.

So, let me indeed take Vromen's observations as an appropriate basis or entry point for our quest for a suitable social ontology. What is a condition of possibility of a firm going bankrupt or of someone being an outcast in society? Clearly, each is inconceivable, and even without clear meaning, without a widely accepted, understood and sanctioned system of (relatively enduring) social rules, internal relations, positions, routinised practices and so forth. If bankruptcy is a specific outcome, it presupposes the condition of not being bankrupt which in turn suggests that firms can be successful in our complex society. This in turn seems to presuppose (reproduced and relatively enduring) shared rule systems and the rest of it. The notion of outcast also presupposes both community as well as those that are "included" within it, again presupposing rules of inclusion (and rules for the included, and perhaps for the excluded too), constituting, and/or presupposing, a variety of (internal) relationships, positions and so forth. And what does Vromen mean when he observes "contemporary societies are plagued by social conflicts, coordination failures and mutual misunderstandings"? Presumably by the terms "societies" and "social" and "conflicts" etc., he refers not to individuals debating the role of ontology or whatever (though even that could not be done without shared understanding of rule systems concerning language and modes of interaction), but to religious, ethnic, class and/or other forms of intercommunity agreements over ownership rights, legitimates forms of practices and so forth. Clearly, we cannot even begin to make sense of the latter without shared (if less than universally acknowledged) conceptions of relatively enduring yet transformable social rule systems, positions, power relations and so forth.

Of course, this all needs fleshing out. But even this brief sketch is surely sufficient to indicate that the conception I defend (or something very similar) is required to render intelligible (and so is effectively presupposed by) Vromen's observations.[5]

So, in short, I remain of the view that there is no good reason to avoid assigning to the ontological conception in question the critical tasks that Vromen has noted. This is not to deny that other purposes (frequently viewed as more constructive, if sometimes perhaps erroneously so – see my response to Davidsen in this volume) can also be, *and indeed are regularly*, served. Indeed much of Chapters 2 and 4 of *Reorienting Economics* is devoted to the range of conceivable endeavour. But whether primarily deconstructive or (critically) facilitative in its impact, I think it is clear that philosophical underlabouring of the sort I defend is justified, and even constitutes a rather urgent undertaking.

## Final comments

Vromen closes his chapter expressing a positive orientation to ontology. And I believe his various contentions about the possibilities for, and limits of ontology, are in large part accurate. Where we mostly disagree is over whether, or the extent to which, the particular ontological conception I defend is justified.

Vromen's concerns are important ones, and I acknowledge there is more work to be done to ground further the conception in question. But I believe I have given enough reason to reject the idea that the status of this conception in question is one of mere conjecture. Rather I regard the social ontology elaborated as relatively grounded, albeit, of course, always provisional. And it is a conception capable of being wielded not just in deconstructive exercises but at least as much in (critically) constructive endeavour. Indeed, in place of Vromen's conjectural and revisionary imagery for the nature, status and uses made of the conception achieved, I would suggest that a more reasonable description is provisionally grounded critical ontology.

## Notes

1   Thus Vromen writes:

> The reason why these mainstream economists do not think this is necessary [to portray actual causal mechanisms realistically], I submit, is that they weigh various theoretical virtues that a theory might have differently from how Lawson weighs them. If some assumption is not believed to identify and specify an actually working underlying mechanism in the real world, then Lawson most probably would reject such an assumption as being deficient. By contrast, as we have just seen, at least some economists do not see a need to reject it. Following the dictum "If it ain't broke, don't fix it", they apparently do not believe the assumption to be deficient. Why not? It seems that one of the reasons that they cling to this assumption is that it allows them to retain models that they cherish for their elegance, simplicity, parsimony, tractability, unifying power and the like. It seems that Lawson wants to assign greater weight to other theoretical virtues such as truth, realism (or realisticness), credibility and plausibility. Elegance, simplicity, parsimony and the like cannot compensate for the deficiency of theories lacking in these respects. Theories and models that have greater plausibility in identifying real and important underlying mechanisms should be preferred over theories and models having less credibility in this respect, even if that would go at the expense of parsi-

mony and tractability. Lawson's plea to bring about an ontological turn, to bring in ontology, can thus be understood as an attempt to redress the balance in theoretical virtues in economics.

2   Alternatively put, I do caution against a range of methodological reductionist positions including "methodological institutionalism (institutions are always the main unit of analysis), methodological evolutionism (evolutionary processes are always the main unit of analysis) and much else" (Lawson, 2003a, p. 57).

So I think it is misleading for Vromen to assert, as he does, that I claim that "borrowing from evolutionary biology" necessarily involves a "commitment to reductionism". Rather my contention, repeatedly stated in *Reorienting Economics*, is as follows:

> my thesis is simply that the social world is such that certain social phenomena *can* result from evolutionary processes of this sort, specifically from processes that manifest evolutionary natural selection aspects. Where this is so, an evolutionary explanation of the type in question, in part at least, is clearly called for. But this particular socio-evolutionary model ought not to be universalised *a priori*.
>
> (Lawson, 2003a, p. 112)

3   It will be possible to deconstruct a specific contribution if the substantive claim is explicitly accompanied by additional ontological contentions such as a denial of openness, emergence, structure or whatever. But then in such a case the focus is rather more than a substantive claim anyway.

4   Of course, here I just summarise the initiating premises. Very often they are elaborated in detail. For example:

> A further widely observed fact of experience is that the practices people follow, including routines (which may or may not become habitual), are highly, and *systematically*, segmented or differentiated. It seems we are not in all cases all empowered to do the same sorts of things as each other. Teachers follow routines and other recognisable practices, which are different to those, followed by students. Similarly there are differences between the regular practices of employers and those of employees, between those of land ladies/lords and those of tenants, and so forth.
>
> (Lawson, 2003a, p. 38)

Or again:

> Notice, too, as a yet further generalised observation, that practices which can be followed in any context, and so the rules governing the obligations and prerogatives in play, are often independent of the particular individuals carrying them out at any point in time. Each year, for example, I am, as a university lecturer, faced by an array of students who are expected to attend lectures, write essays and sit exams (just as I am expected to give the lectures, etc.). But equally, each year the set of individuals facing me as students is found to be different from that of the previous year. The practices are continued but the individuals enacting them frequently change.
>
> (ibid., p. 38)

And again:

> For example we can take note of (and seek to explain) the further generalised feature of experience that our practices are not only differentiated but typically systematically and constitutively other-oriented. The defining

practices of any one group are usually oriented to the practices of others, which, if often to a degree similar to the first set of practices, are typically quite distinct. Thus, the practices of students are oriented towards (though mostly different from) those of teachers, and vice versa. In similar fashion this feature of being other-oriented characterises the practices of employers and employees, land ladies/lords and tenants, parents and children, preachers and congregations, performers and audiences, etc.

(ibid., p. 39)

5   Vromen makes some additional critical asides, but mostly small points, none of which I believe withstand critical scrutiny.

For example, he questions the process of transcendental deduction itself. But, on examination, it seems that he is mostly unhappy either because this form of reasoning does not deliver substantive insight (which was never its role; this is the task of retroduction more generally [transcendental reasoning is but a special case oriented to ontology – see for example Lawson, 1997, p. 212]) or else because it produces results that are inevitably practically conditioned, fallible and open to contestation.

But why should the latter be a problem? Such is the nature of all beliefs, even those we consider the most reliable. The relevant point here is that not only is the ontological conception I defend found to have some clear justification after all, but also there does not seem to be an alternative conception available that is anywhere near as (empirically) grounded or explanatory powerful.

Vromen points out that I argue that practices presuppose the capacities for those practices, and suggests that this is no insight until I elaborate the nature of those capacities. But this is not the work of philosophical ontology. My point at the time was to indicate that human beings too are structured. That a point is easy to establish makes it no less insightful or relevant. Even the old Institutionalist tradition has sometimes lost sight of the structured nature of human beings (see Lawson, 2003b).

Vromen also asserts that I argue for the primacy of ontology, that we must always start with ontology and that the ontological conception I defend is determined without recourse to empirical work or science. None of these claims withstand scrutiny though. The former two are dealt with in my reply to McFarling, whilst hopefully the above outline (as well as my response to Davidsen) will dispel the last concern.

Vromen makes a strange closing comment that because I think event regularities are rare then I will be suspicious of any contention that theories of mechanisms should be assessed by their empirical power. But this is just not so as my discussion of contrast explanation should make clear (on this see my responses to Caldwell, McFarling and Ruccio).

# References

Coase, Ronald (1999) "Interview with Ronald Coase", *Newsletter of the International Society for New Institutional Economics*, 2(1), spring.

Friedman, Milton (1953) *Essays in Positive Economics*, Chicago, IL: University of Chicago Press.

Friedman, Milton (1999) "Conversation with Milton Friedman", in B. Snowdon and H Vane. (eds), *Conversations with Leading Economists: Interpreting Modern Macroeconomics*, Cheltenham: Edward Elgar, pp. 124–44.

Kay, John (1995) "Cracks in the Crystal Ball", *Financial Times*, 29 September.

Kirman, Alan (1989) "The Intrinsic Limits of Modern Economic Theory: The Emperor has no Clothes", *Economic Journal*, 99(395), pp. 126–39.

Lawson, Tony (1997) *Economics and Reality*, London and New York: Routledge.

Lawson, Tony (2003a) *Reorienting Economics*, London and New York: Routledge.

Lawson, Tony (2003b) "Institutionalism: On the Need to Firm up Notions of Social Structure and the Human Subject", *Journal of Economic Issues*, XXXVII(1), pp. 175–201.

Rubinstein, Ariel (1995) "John Nash: The Master of Economic Modelling", *Scandinavian Journal of Economics*, 97(1), pp. 9–13.

Whitehead, Alfred North (1978 [1929]) *Process and Reality* (corrected edition – edited by David Ray Griffin and Donald W. Sherbourne), New York: Free Press.

# Author index

# Subject index

Lightning Source UK Ltd.
Milton Keynes UK

175923UK00003B/27/P

9 780415 546492